The British Expeditionary Fo

C000066702

The British Expeditionary Force, 1939–40

Edward Smalley
University of Kent, UK

© Edward Smalley 2015

Softcover reprint of the hardcover 1st edition 2015 978-1-137-49419-1

First published 2015 by
PALGRAVE MACMILLAN

Palgrave Macmillan in the UK is an imprint of Macmillan Publishers Limited, registered in England, company number 785998, of Houndmills, Basingstoke, Hampshire RG21 6XS.

Palgrave Macmillan in the US is a division of St Martin's Press LLC, 175 Fifth Avenue, New York, NY 10010.

Palgrave Macmillan is the global academic imprint of the above companies and has companies and representatives throughout the world.

Palgrave® and Macmillan® are registered trademarks in the United States, the United Kingdom, Europe and other countries.

ISBN 978-1-349-50478-7   ISBN 978-1-137-49420-7 (eBook)
DOI 10.1057/9781137494207

This book is printed on paper suitable for recycling and made from fully managed and sustained forest sources. Logging, pulping and manufacturing processes are expected to conform to the environmental regulations of the country of origin.

A catalogue record for this book is available from the British Library.

Library of Congress Cataloging-in-Publication Data
Smalley, Edward, 1985–
The British Expeditionary Force, 1939–40 / Edward Smalley,
University of Kent, UK.
pages cm
Includes bibliographical references.

1. Great Britain. Army. British Expeditionary Force—History—World War, 1939–1945.   2. Dunkirk, Battle of, Dunkerque, France, 1940.   3. World War, 1939–1945—Campaigns—France.   I. Title.
D756.5.D8S48   2015
940.54'21428—dc23   2015002667

Typeset by MPS Limited, Chennai, India.

In memory of my grandfather Horace Cook

Contents

Acknowledgements

This book is the fulfilment of a lifetime's ambition; however, it could not have been achieved without considerable support. Professor Mark Connelly and Dr Timothy Bowman selflessly provided continual encouragement during my time at the University of Kent. Their patient guidance will forever be appreciated. My thanks also go to Dr Niall Barr and Dr Peter Donaldson for offering constructive comments, in terms of content and the process of creating a book suitable for publication. I alone am responsible for any errors of fact or interpretation. For assisting my research, I would like to thank the staff of the British Library, the Imperial War Museum, the Liddell Hart Centre for Military Archives, the National Archive and the National Army Museum. Extracts from LHCMA material is reproduced with the permission of the Trustees of the Liddell Hart Centre for Military Archives. Crown copyright material in the National Archive and elsewhere is reproduced under the Open Government Licence. Palgrave Macmillan's willingness to guide and support a first-time author is greatly appreciated. This book is testament to the power of the NHS which has frequently preserved the quality of my life and, on occasions, life itself; many individuals are worthy of inclusion within these acknowledgements, but Dr K.S. Hills deserves special mention for her exceptional care, kindness and wisdom. My grandparents have provided ceaseless encouragement throughout my life, but my grandfather, Horace Cook, sparked my interest in this subject thanks to his recollections of service with the BEF, and his subsequent time as a prisoner of war. Most important of all has been the love, time and advice of my parents Robert and Patricia, and also my sister Catherine; without them this book could never have been started, let alone finished.

List of Abbreviations

A	Administrative Branch of Headquarters
AA	Anti-Aircraft
AASF	Advanced Air Striking Force
AC	Army Council
ACIGS	Assistant Chief of the Imperial General Staff
AEC	Army Education Corps
AFV	Armoured Fighting Vehicle
AG	Adjutant General
AMPC	Auxiliary Military Pioneer Corps
AOC	Air-Officer-Commanding
APM	Assistant Provost Marshal
ATM	Army Training Memorandum
BAFF	British Air Force in France
BBC	British Broadcasting Corporation
Bde	Brigade
BEF	British Expeditionary Force
BGS	Brigadier General Staff
BL	British Library
BP	Battle Post
C3	Command, Control and Communication
C3I	Command, Control, Communication and Intelligence
C-in-C	Commander-in-Chief
CAS	close air support
CCRA	Corps Commander Royal Artillery
CGS	Chief of the General Staff
CIGS	Chief of the Imperial General Staff
CO	Commanding Officer
Coldm Gds	Coldstream Guards

CP	Command Post
CQMS	Company Quartermaster Sergeant
CRA	Commander Royal Artillery
CRASC	Commander Royal Army Service Corps
DAPM	Deputy Assistant Provost Marshal
DCGS	Deputy Chief of the General Staff
DCIGS	Deputy Chief of the Imperial General Staff
DF	direction finding
Div	Division
DMO	Director of Military Operations
DMT	Director of Military Training
DPM	Deputy Provost Marshal
DQMG	Deputy Quartermaster General
DR	Despatch Rider
DSD	Director of Staff Duties
DSO	Distinguished Service Order
Fd Coy	Field Company
Fd Regt	Field Regiment
FGCM	Field General Courts-Martial
FP	Field Punishment
FSPB	*Field Service Pocket Book*
FSR	*Field Service Regulations*
G	Operations Branch of Headquarters
GCM	General Courts-Martial
GHQ	General Headquarters
GHQ 2/Ech	General Headquarters 2nd Echelon
GOC	General-Officer-Commanding
GQG	Grand Quartier General
Gren Gds	Grenadier Guards
GSO	General Staff Officer
HQ	Headquarters
HRH	His Royal Highness

I	Intelligence Branch of Headquarters
IDC	Imperial Defence College
IGT	Inspector General of Training
IO	Intelligence Officer
IWM	Imperial War Museum
JAG	Judge Advocate General
L of C	Line of Communication
LHCMA	Liddell Hart Centre for Military Archives
MPSC	Military Provost Staff Corps
MT	Motor-Transport
MTP	Military Training Pamphlet
NAAFI	Navy, Army and Air Force Institute
NAM	National Army Museum
NCO	Non-Commissioned Officer
OCTU	Officer Cadet Training Unit
OFSTED	Office for Standards in Education, Children's Services and Skills
OR	other ranks
Pl	Platoon
PSC	passed Staff College
PTT	Postes, Télégraphes et Téléphones (French Post Office)
Q	Quartermaster General's Branch of Headquarters
RA	Royal Artillery
RAC	Royal Armoured Corps
RAF	Royal Air Force
RAOC	Royal Army Ordnance Corps
RAPC	Royal Army Pay Corps
RASC	Royal Army Service Corps
RE	Royal Engineers
RMA	Royal Military Academy Woolwich
RMC	Royal Military College Sandhurst
R/T	Radio Telephony

RTC	Royal Tank Corps
RTR	Royal Tank Regiment
RV	Rendezvous
SD & T	Staff Duties and Training Branch of Headquarters
SDT	Supply Directorate Transport
TA	Territorial Army
TEWT	Training Exercise Without Troops
TNA	The National Archive
VC	Victoria Cross
VCIGS	Vice Chief of the Imperial General Staff
WO	War Office
WOSB	War Office Selection Board
W/T	Wireless Telegraphy
WTO	Weapons Training Officer
WWI	World War One
WWII	World War Two
ZOAN	Zone des Opérations Aériennes du Nord
2i/c	Second-in-Command

Timeline

23 June 1938	War Office begins planning for overseas despatch of an expeditionary force.
22 February 1939	Cabinet orders ten divisions be equipped for European warfare; in effect, the formation of a British Expeditionary Force had been authorized.
15 March	German aggression continues with annexation of Czechoslovakia.
29 March	Territorial Army doubled in size.
27 April	Military Training Act introduces limited conscription.
1 September	Germany invades Poland.
3 September	Britain and France declare war on Germany. Lord Gort becomes Commander-in-Chief of the newly formed British Expeditionary Force.
4 September	Advance parties of the BEF begin arriving in France.
6 September	National Service (Armed Forces) Act introduces conscription of the physically fit aged 18–41.
9 November	Vincennes Conference – Supreme Commander Gamelin announces Dyle Plan.
18–20 November	Hore-Belisha visit sparks Pill-Box Affair.
30 November	Soviet Union invades Finland, delaying BEF build-up.
4 January 1940	Hore-Belisha resigns; replaced by Oliver Stanley.
10 January	Mechelen incident.
12 March	Soviet-Finnish Armistice.
9 April	Germany invades Norway and Denmark. Denmark surrenders.
14 April	British forces begin landing in Norway.
2 May	British forces begin evacuating from Norway.

9 May	Prime Minister Neville Chamberlain resigns.
10 May	Germany invades France and the Low Countries. Dyle Plan put into operation. Winston Churchill becomes Prime Minister.
12 May	Mons Conference – Belgian Army incorporated into the Allied order of battle; General Billotte appointed Allied Coordinator. Germans cross the Meuse River at Houx.
13 May	Germans cross Meuse at Sedan and Dinant.
14 May	Dutch surrender. BEF in contact with enemy along the Dyle.
15 May	Anglo-French forces in Belgium begin retreat to avoid encirclement.
19 May	General Weygand replaces General Gamelin as Allied Supreme Commander. GHQ warns War Office of possible evacuations.
20 May	Germans reach the Channel at Abbeville. Non-essential BEF personnel begin evacuating.
21 May	BEF counter-attack at Arras. Ypres Conference to coordinate Allied breakout from the northern pocket.
25 May	Gort abandons counter-attack south making evacuation inevitable.
26 May	Dunkirk evacuations begin (Operation Dynamo).
4 June	Dunkirk evacuations end with surrender of remaining troops.
5 June	Germans launch offensive south of the Somme River.
8 June	Remaining British troops in Norway evacuated.
10 June	Italy declares war on the Allies.
16 June	Offer of Anglo-French Union; Reynaud resigns; Petain becomes Premier; remaining BEF begin evacuating.
17 June	French government seeks armistice.
18 June	BEF operations in France officially end.
22 June	Signature of Franco-German armistice.

1
Introduction

For many people, the understanding of operations involving the British Expeditionary Force in France and Flanders can be summarized in the phrase, the fall of France, or even more succinctly in the single word Dunkirk. In reality this campaign retains considerable unrealized complexity. The BEF's campaign of operations from September 1939 to June 1940 did not occur in isolation, nor did its consequences end with the French armistice on 22 June 1940. The inter-war British Army had long prepared for future conflict, even against a first-class enemy, yet failed to accurately anticipate the characteristics of combat in 1939–40. The campaign had a lasting legacy in that it led to fundamental changes such as an increasingly scientific approach to discipline and the transformation of operational command to a brigade basis. Paradoxically, misinterpretation of events led to a continuation of flaws, such as retention of tempo-sapping written orders and discretionary training within units. As a result, the events of this campaign intrinsically influenced the development and performance of the British Army throughout the Second World War.

This book explores the downfall of the Allied forces in France in 1940 and, in particular, reveals how systemic weaknesses within the BEF hampered operations and culminated in defeat and evacuation. In a military force, courage and confidence alone are not enough. Training is vital for preparing personnel for the demands of the battlefield; communications inform units how to function effectively; discipline ensures the collective good is placed before the individual; and the decision-making of headquarters and staff enables the Army to act in a coordinated manner. When added to the men and material available these factors unite to produce combat capability and, if successful, victory; this book investigates not only how the BEF was defeated, but why that defeat was largely self-inflicted.

Examination of the command, control and communication systems of the BEF shows the British Army's total inability to identify and settle on a single effective approach within the critical areas of training, communications, discipline, headquarters and staff. Allowing unrestricted variation proved incompatible with consistent combat capability and detrimental to performance. The BEF deployed to France with no set training schedules, no standardized inspection mechanisms and no minimum capability requirements; these were considered internal matters and left to the discretion of each unit's commanding officer. Depending on their age, training and previous postings, military arms, units and even individuals would reveal unshakeable, sometimes illogical, preference for particular communication methods during the course of the campaign. Disciplinary regulations which determined the legality of action and the level of judicial response were interpreted inconsistently and creatively; subsequent sentencing could range from the inexplicably lenient to the exceptionally punitive. Leeway given to those involved in headquarter operations had a ripple effect within the BEF as, at each level, unit discretion allowed the accommodation of additional unique procedures and preferences; variably qualified and experienced officers further compounded this myriad of approaches. Elite officers theoretically benefited from the opportunity to operate free from inappropriate, inflexible regulations, but, in reality, the lack of standardization created a world of uncertainty within which even competent officers could underperform through ignorance, complacency or lethargy. The argument that a metric standard in any area of army life was impossible to achieve due to the multitude of terrains, threats and equipment with which the British Army interacted was not sufficiently challenged during the preparatory eight months of Phoney War, when the BEF gathered to fight as one formation, in one theatre, against a single enemy.

By focusing on essential military practicalities, original and substantive additions to the current historiography are possible, along with contextualization of other academic works. Military communications and staff work have been largely ignored due to apprehension about complex details and uncertain commercial viability. This book, alongside Simon Godfrey's recent work, has begun to correct this omission. Equally, original analysis in more familiar topics is possible through the historical equivalent of reverse engineering. Timothy Harrison Place and David French have identified continued training deficiencies throughout the 1940–45 period. These deficiencies did not suddenly materialize, but slowly developed from inter-war origins. Similarly, unease among senior officers about imperfect discipline within Britain's conscript army, as revealed by Jonathan Fennell and Christine Bielecki, was replicated in the volunteer pre-war army and BEF.[1] Discipline was dependent on officer supervision, deployment duration and proximity to temptation, rather than their unique volunteer make-up; ill-discipline occurred accordingly. More critically, the wilful concealment and unofficial resolution of ill-discipline helps explain why a scientifically designed and monitored system, beyond the traditional regimental approach, was considered unnecessary pre-war.

Only by analysing British pre-war activity, both at home and throughout the Empire, selectively from the Great War, but especially from 1936 onwards, can the BEF be revealed as a product of inter-war development. Furthermore, since the chain of command is of critical importance, evidence is drawn from the highest level to the lowest rank; to protect against excessive breadth or obsessive detail, closest attention is paid to the most influential levels of command, namely those between the War Office and the infantry battalion. Inter-service issues and operations are recognized, especially as the Army was the Cinderella service of the inter-war period, always behind the Royal Air Force and Royal Navy in spending priorities. The lifting of the financially restrictive ten-year rule in 1932 fired the starting gun for reformers and conservatives to seek ideological control of the Army and the debate delayed definitive preparations for a continental expeditionary force until early in 1939. Such was the belated change in mind-set that the modest rearmament requirements of four regular divisions and a mobile division in April 1938 became aspirations for 32 fully equipped divisions in March 1939.[2] Against this background the findings of this book are made.

The book covers the pre-war system used by the BEF until it was transformed beyond recognition. This varies from topic to topic and, accordingly, the following chapters replicate this diversity. In training, a completely new system was rapidly introduced, but too late to influence the BEF and its thought processes; the change is acknowledged, but not expanded on in this book. The traditional method of using Royal Military College Sandhurst and Royal Military Academy Woolwich to train and commission new officers was replaced almost immediately in autumn 1939 with more numerous, high-turnover Officer Cadet Training Units (OCTU). David French has shown that civilians with similar social backgrounds to the pre-war officer corps could access

OCTU and subsequently gain commissions into the new conscript army merely by making a positive impression on senior officers.[3] Similarly, Jeremy Crang has explored how OCTU trained personnel and, as a result, discovered that 'OCTU commanders were able to develop their own syllabus and so there was little uniformity of practice'.[4] This illustrates how individualism was perpetuated through the various army training systems of the war. In contrast, the headquarters and staff chapter reveals the equivalent change to the staff system did impact on the BEF and remained in operation for the duration. The January 1940 decision to reopen the Staff College with a shorter, wartime course removed long-serving officers from the Franco-Belgian border for training in divisional staff duties before reassignment to UK-based units; the BEF did not benefit. Subsequent modifications, especially those incorporated within an extended post-1945 syllabus, such as the internationalization of students and directing staff, are briefly reviewed to constructively demonstrate how this institution could have improved in the inter-war period.[5]

The complexity of operations is divided into four main themes – Training, Communications, Discipline, Headquarters and Staff. *Training* refers to what military capability the Army wanted to achieve, how it attempted to get there and whether it was successful. Training could range from a handful of low-ranking individuals participating in repetitive drill to basic tactical training with a battalion's vehicles and support weaponry to a complex and expensive operational manoeuvre at corps level. The bigger the exercise the less frequently it occurred and the more likely participants could be ignored or take unofficial shortcuts. Training could be prescriptive, with a defined objective, or a practical test of theoretical speculation. Only through experience could errors in procedure be discovered, capability installed and skills refined.

Communications are the two-way transfer of information, encompassing front-line to rear-echelon, the length of the chain of command and finally lateral conveyance within command levels. Methods range from technologically advanced wireless communications to technologically devoid human runners and carrier pigeons; they also vary in format from unequivocal type-written orders to unintentional rumours. Effective information distribution is linked to communication reliability, but poorly used communications can lead to information overload and a loss of tempo. Communication methods usually work within a portfolio of options, thereby providing system resilience; however, the failure of one method or unit can lead to cascade failure in others.

Discipline is far more complex than merely enforcing army regulations and sending rule-breakers to courts-martial. It involves the maintenance of proper subordination in the Army through self-control, obedience, orderliness and capacity for cooperation; all of which become unnatural characteristics under pressure and in combat. An individual's morale is integral to discipline because it enables orders to be obeyed and acted upon. Group mentality is equally critical because it allows both collective strength and collective weakness. The only difference between the best and the worst performers, in terms of ill-discipline, is the scale. Ill-discipline ranges from civil crimes, inevitable in any large group, to military specific technical infringements to unofficial offences unbecoming of service personnel. In addition to the military justice system with its numerous sentencing options, the British Army operated an unofficial in-house disciplinary system where NCOs, officers and regiments settled matters before involving the official system.

Headquarters and Staff deals with the personnel, procedures and headquarters that combined to form the Army's command capability. It examines how officers, both individually and collectively, learned and retained knowledge of how staffs functioned and how responsibilities were divided between the various headquarters. Through discussion of training manuals, Staff College teaching, regimental experience and imperial postings, this chapter explores how military problems were addressed and decision-makers assisted within the Army.

The sequence of chapters is designed to assist understanding of this complex campaign. The campaign overview provides a foundation of information on the BEF which enables comprehension of intricate arguments contained within the thematic chapters. Unlike the thematic chapters where the primacy of the argument overrides all other factors, in the overview the narrative is key, thereby allowing the inclusion of material which is helpful to understanding. *Training* is the first thematic chapter because of its fundamental importance to individual and collective performance. Ever-present themes of variation and complacency are perhaps strongest in the area of training, as is the impression that the BEF was the product of inter-war thinking and not a start-up army created from scratch without established views and experienced personnel.

The training chapter shows why the pre-war army rejected a standardized approach, highlights the process by which this policy was reversed and provides exploration of why both varied and substandard training remained. Obligated to perform the role of imperial policeman, the inter-war British Army avoided establishing a formal metric because of the varied terrain and tactics it confronted globally; hostile terrain occasionally required antiquated tactics, the Army lacked an OFSTED inspectorate to enforce standards and senior officers were considered sufficiently well versed in military principle to command independent of interference. However, a metric would have standardized rarely seen procedures, for example, air re-supply of ground forces was variously considered routine, impossible or unnecessary in different parts of the Empire. Despite UK-based units having different levels of manpower, instructors and equipment, most commanders, lacking a common training aim, independently concluded that a relatively undemanding combination of rank-and-file basic training, drill and cheap, objective-focused Training Exercise Without Troops (TEWTs) were the best way of maximizing theoretical capability with limited resources. This combination denied officers genuine experience of command in the field, hampered understanding of war's unpredictability and prevented practical procedural and equipment problems being identified. Furthermore, with limited expectations, innovation or pressure to achieve, enthusiasm for vigorous training drained from units, leaving a tick box culture which all ranks sought to get through as quickly and easily as possible; training quality and outcome were almost afterthoughts. Whilst Sandhurst prioritized excessive drill and regimental tradition, post-commission tactical training was carried out by unqualified, unsupervised, often disinterested officers liable to fall back on their own Great War training; the process varied and the outcome, inevitably, was inadequate. Staff College is largely covered in the *headquarters and staff* chapter, but is featured here to demonstrate how even elite institutions frequently bypassed tricky topics, for example the implications of air warfare.

As the War Office slowly realized the magnitude of training deficiencies, it endeavoured to overcome them through the dissemination of multiple documents and, in the process, gradually developed a British Army metric standard. Pre-war promotion of vague training principles transformed into critical language and prescriptive schedules for formations up to division strength. However, information was frequently misdirected and officers entrusted with new guidelines were the same complacent trainers who had both independently and collectively failed already. To confuse matters, GHQ was established outside of Army Council control, creating two competing centres of authority, neither in tune with the other. Metric enforcement was variously overseen by the Commander-in-Chief, War Office staff, the Staff Duties and Training branch of GHQ, and unit commanders. Individually and as a whole this system fundamentally failed; a deficiency in time, authority and willingness to interfere, or a combination of all three, undermined all metric enforcers. Variation occurred at all levels, with good commanders utilizing all available opportunities to make a difference and give their unit an edge over others who followed the easy option in training topic and intensity. Handicapped by commitments to flawed frontier defences, illusory war zones and political distractions, the BEF training effort paled in comparison to the practical, progressive, complex, tempo-sustaining training carried out in Phoney War Germany. British Army operating procedures were only truly standardized with the introduction of battle drills in 1942, by which time the unpredictability of commander-led training had left the Army craving minimum standards it could rely on in combat.

Communications are integral to the accumulation of information, the coordination of decision-making, the implementation of capability and ultimately, overall performance. The content of communications ranges from the legacy of the Great War, such as the continuing acceptance and reliance on cable-based communications, to the disintegration of BEF communications during the campaign's combat operations. Furthermore, the development of a portfolio of communication techniques during the technologically transient inter-war period, combined with the establishment of this portfolio in France over the prolonged Phoney War, was deemed worthy of a stand-alone starter chapter. Both communication chapters have been kept together to allow analysis to seamlessly continue into the events of May 1940, where so many of the seeds of catastrophe came to fruition. BEF communications facilitated the associated command and control system; foreknowledge of the collapse in communications aids the explanation of underperformance and failure in other areas of the BEF.

Communications examines how the British Army's evolutionary inter-war development of a system sufficient for Great War combat failed through under-resourcing and lethargy, leaving the BEF with communications unresponsive to its needs and insufficiently resilient to the dangers it faced. Half-hearted army aspirations to improve flexibility, diversity and the ability to operate on the move, combined with a deep-seated fear of unreliability, the determination to continue top-down control and passive acceptance of adequacy resulted in theoretical capability becoming increasingly out-of-kilter with practical reality. Whilst the inter-war High Command visualized battles fought exclusively with wireless, many combat units within the Empire were still using visual signalling, human runners and even carrier pigeons.

Differing equipment combined with the personal preference of the originating officer meant communication techniques and usages varied between theatres, arms, commanders and units. Whilst many pre-war communication hindrances were beyond the control of individual officers, the BEF compounded these with several self-inflicted and easily rectifiable system flaws. Fear of system misuse led to rigid BEF procedures involving excessive paperwork, the continued use of written orders and the restricted use of particular communication methods. Designed to protect the system, in reality these rules hampered efforts to introduce the use of abbreviations, disinclined units to diversify their communication pathways and, ultimately, failed to protect the system from being corrupted; common sense dictated message prioritization be left to the originator, but allowed unscrupulous officers seeking information or resources to leapfrog more worthy, rule-abiding competitors. Although the Phoney War system as a whole proved satisfactory, information transfer failures were commonplace and staff frequently sought face-to-face contact to bypass the system. When intense operations commenced, cascade failure of communications occurred much sooner than previously acknowledged and could not be recovered; unnecessary communications failure heavily contributed to the BEF's defeat in France in 1940.

The area of *Discipline* has received the most statistical analysis as courts-martial records offer a clear-cut method of comparing BEF units and arms, on an equal basis, without the intrusion of subjectivity. Whereas pre-war defects in training and communications largely continued into wartime, deployment to France saw a dramatic deterioration of military discipline as the temptations of Phoney War France and the pressures of a first-class conflict took their toll on the professional volunteers of the BEF.

There was a conscious decision within the British Army to under-record levels of ill-discipline in order to protect the reputation of individuals, units and the Army as a whole. Quantitative analysis of courts-martial records can identify officially recognized crimes and which units deviated from the norm, but only by combining this research with a quality assessment of memoirs and war diaries can a true picture of discipline within the British Army, especially the BEF, be revealed. All Field General Courts-Martial and the more serious General Courts-Martial relevant to the France campaign have been analysed and snapshot examples have been added to humanize any statistical conclusions. To echo the methodological approach of military law authority Gerry Rubin, this study will include some significant cases which demonstrate key characteristics of the disciplinary system.[6] With successful convictions as difficult to achieve in the military courts as they were in the civil courts, only the most serious, blatant or frequent offenders were officially prosecuted. The most prevalent specific crimes under this system were theft and drunkenness, but as detection was difficult and self-sufficient solutions tempting, official figures do not do justice to these endemic crimes. The ability of courts-martial statistics to at least represent trends in BEF discipline collapsed in May and June 1940, as battle conditions took precedence over investigating, prosecuting and recording the inevitable continuation of ill-discipline. In addition to statistically recordable crimes, analysis of subjective ill-discipline involving friendly fire, premature bridge demolitions and treatment of enemy combatants all indicate disciplinary failings beyond those officially recognized. Every individual has a breaking point and amidst the chaos at Dunkirk many found theirs, even those with previously immaculate disciplinary records. Poor discipline and morale were most widespread post-Dunkirk as self-preservation within the 150,000 BEF troops elsewhere in France took priority over determined resistance against German advances. Original analysis of previously ignored courts-martial figures is amplified by highlighting the flexibility and subtlety of the disciplinary system; sentencing was adapted to detention capacity, technically guilty men went relatively unpunished and the law-abiding could be admonished for breaking unwritten rules. The way individuals and procedures actively allowed ill-discipline to be under-recorded suggests this was an institutional problem that could not be addressed until it was illuminated in combat. The creation of procedures and institutions in 1941/42 to systematically reduce the likelihood of ill-discipline may have coincided with a series of British defeats, but impetus for their creation came from the realization that even volunteer, professional forces such as the BEF were capable of significant disciplinary problems; these problems were magnified in a larger, conscript army.

A chapter on headquarters and staff examines how, post-Dunkirk, the performance of BEF headquarters and the Commander-in-Chief were publicly endorsed as satisfactory by the political and military establishment, yet the British Army's operational framework was subsequently transformed and Lord Gort never served in the field again. The medium-term switch from division to brigade-based operations and the profound changes to Staff College that occurred during the campaign illustrates the BEF's considerable legacy. Statistical analysis of the Army List to demonstrate the inability to ensure all brigadiers had passed Staff

College before joining the small expeditionary force adds weight to the arguments, particularly about the self-inflicted lack of preparedness within the BEF.

The inter-war staff capability of the British Army was deeply flawed, but the magnitude and endemic nature of these failings were only truly illuminated during the Phoney War and combat in France. Their solutions were less obvious, leading to a prolonged period of trial and error before communications, experience and flexibility could develop sufficiently to provide competitive staff capability. Analysis of the Army List, in conjunction with official sources, war diaries and memoirs, demonstrates scarcity of best practice in BEF staff work; where it did occur, it remained dependent on defective training and operated within the straitjacket of peacetime procedures. The personnel, procedures and formations which confronted German aggression failed to comprehend the pressurized conditions of modern war because of the unsatisfactory formula of vague training guidelines, under-resourced exercises, unrepresentative overseas experience and educational establishments, for example Staff College, which were elite institutions in name only. The fundamentals of staff function and formation headquarter responsibilities remained largely unknown or unpractised because of the unwillingness of *Field Service Regulations* to be definitive, the scarcity of formation operations in inter-war Empire and the prioritization of combat manoeuvres over equally essential rear-echelon activities in pre-war TEWTs. Staff College entrance procedures persistently failed to sift the wheat from the chaff, leaving talented individuals, particularly within the Territorial Army, excluded from the opportunity to improve their own and the Army's staff capability. Those that did gain places qualified from Staff College almost regardless of their performance under pressure, their understanding of the excessively strategic syllabus or their preparedness for future roles. The consequence of the shortage of Staff College graduates was that many BEF staff positions were filled with the untested, old, unfit or unqualified, especially in backwater areas. Tested under wartime workloads for the first time, many headquarter procedures proved an immovable hindrance to diligent combat preparations, the dissemination of information and high-tempo operations. BEF staff personnel managed to tread water until the German advance forced them to accept their failings and delegate, even abdicate, their responsibilities in order to save the BEF.

The BEF has always been of considerable interest and, as a result, there is a wealth of popular history on the subject which has assisted in the entrenchment of Dunkirk mythology. Academic Mark Connelly has reflected on the way Dunkirk has epitomized British spirit and resourcefulness, yet also obscured the reality of key events affecting the campaign. The Belgian capitulation which exposed the British flank, the supposedly dominant role of the little ships and that the campaign ended after Dunkirk with the BEF unbeaten relate to events, but do not explain why the BEF performed poorly.[7] Only academic history is able to build upon anecdotal evidence and commercial sensitivity with statistical analysis, intensive archive work and detailed, coherent arguments. Crucial aspects of the campaign, such as training, communications, discipline, headquarters and staff have, at best, been superficially and sketchily studied by popular historians; academic history can significantly improve on this. Philip Warner's generalized criticisms of Phoney War training overlook the diverse range of capabilities which existed within BEF Territorials due to the varying degree of prioritization and attention provided by senior regular commanders. In the 2009 bestseller *Dunkirk: Retreat to Victory*, the absence of any discussion on how the entire communication portfolio developed and distributed its workload undermined Major General Julian Thompson's valid illustration of how Phoney War wireless silence negatively affected BEF training. Although the majority of popular historians dismissed British ill-discipline as a minority issue, Nicholas Harman has contentiously sought to puncture the angelic aura of the BEF by highlighting, without context, unpalatable incidents involving BEF personnel. Only a balanced argument, supported by overwhelming evidence, can demonstrate the presence of an unrecorded undercurrent of low-level ill-discipline within the BEF, albeit with variations from unit to unit. Superficial analysis of defensive, official histories and self-congratulatory memoirs can lead to popular historians being overly complimentary about headquarters and staff; for example, Julian Thompson has argued 'it is hard to fault much of the leadership of the BEF – some of it was outstanding'. In reality, belated recognition within the British Army of imperfections in pre-war staff training and the subsequent weak underlying performance of BEF headquarters compelled reorganization from a divisional to a brigade-based framework. Popular history is useful for capturing the public's imagination, but with the 75th anniversary of Dunkirk in 2015, an ideal opportunity dawns for academic studies to disseminate a more substantive and precise appreciation of this complex campaign.[8]

In the course of writing this book, a number of difficulties with source material have been discovered; efforts have been made to overcome these obstacles, but some have proved insurmountable and consequently shaped the findings of this study. Determining the exact nature of a unit's training was complicated by the succinct war diary summaries of activities undertaken; 4th Royal Tank Regiment made the effort to record 'Section & Company Training' on 23 separate occasions in February 1940 and 15 occasions in March, without ever recording what it was, why it was being done and what standards were being achieved.[9] The Army's training metric proved difficult to ascertain until it was realized it never existed in a single overarching document, rather it evolved gradually and was disseminated via a multitude of pamphlets and memoranda. With units reluctant to mention what training document they were using, possibly to avoid later criticism, this book had to concentrate on highlighting how units failed to achieve the metric standard, or had achieved the standard but remained vulnerable.

In their production of official documentation and personal memoirs, British Army personnel frequently treated communications either as a mysterious function that defied explanation or sufficiently routine to discourage description. The war diary of 2nd Cameronians Regiment records a signal exercise that took place over two hours on 8 March 1940, but participants, purpose and outcome are not mentioned.[10] Some sources did at least recognize that the communication system required more than magic to operate, for example, GHQ Petrol Section acknowledged the 'invariable kindness, patience and efficiency of Brassard [GHQ] Signals'; these sources were rare exceptions.[11] Historians have also treated the subject with contempt, for example, Brian Hall has commented 'there is a dearth of detailed information regarding the issue of communications in general. What little has been written on the subject has been limited in terms of its detail, focus and use of sources'.[12] This book aims to reverse this trend.

Using inter-war British Army annual reports, BEF discipline is contextualized by revealing pre-war courts-martial and conviction rates; this source material is available up to 31 December 1938 (published February 1939), before abruptly stopping due to the war. Faced with similar problems, Great War historians have been able to use *The General Annual Reports on the British Army (including the Territorial Force) for the period from 1 October 1913 to 30 September 1919*, which was belatedly published in 1921; no equivalent post-conflict documentation was produced to cover 1939–45 statistics, thereby hindering analysis of the BEF. It is possible to identify the best and worst disciplined infantry battalions in the BEF because court-martialled personnel are recorded alongside their regiment; ascertaining a breakdown of ill-discipline within a multi-unit Corps or Regiment is less straightforward, for example 256 court-martialled personnel are listed under the umbrella formation Royal Artillery, rather than their specific battery or unit. The names of court-martialled personnel could theoretically be cross-referenced with their individual service records and unit Field Returns, but the time required was adjudged to be disproportionate to the benefits. War diaries typically only acknowledge courts-martial in exceptional circumstances, resulting in a misleading impression of BEF discipline; the campaign average for courts-martial was 4.56 per infantry battalion, yet despite having 12 personnel court-martialled in March 1940 alone, the 2nd Cameronians Regiment War Diary makes no mention of ill-discipline. However, war diaries can often arouse suspicions by what they do include, for example, the sudden decision on 1 April 1940 to repatriate for UK duties Lieutenant Colonel D. Graham, 2nd Cameronians Regiment; only by combining quantitative and qualitative sources can an accurate picture of BEF discipline be achieved.[13]

Integral to any study of British staff is the Staff College, yet its internal workings have largely been concealed through unintentional obstruction and incompetence. Brian Holden Reid has complained that any research on the inter-war Staff College is handicapped by the failure 'to maintain any proper archive of papers. This lack cannot be made good very easily from private papers because graduates of the Staff College hardly ever keep their précis and notes. Veterans of war rarely think that the documents acquired in peacetime are of much use to historians'.[14] Consequently, reconstructing what was actually taught at a given date, and how it was taught, is a far from easy task. However, by casting a wide net for sources some of the scarce contemporary Camberley paperwork was located and, in combination with memoirs involving the Staff College and its syllabus, a compelling argument was formulated of its effects on the Army and, in particular, the BEF. These challenges and others mentioned in later chapters go some way towards explaining why many of these subjects were previously under-researched or ignored.

The inter-war British Army approached training from a predominantly imperial policeman outlook, functioned mainly on a Great War communication system, had a statistically negligible disciplinary problem and retained a long-standing organizational framework within which staff officers directed operations. As a result of the France campaign of 1939–40, the British Army promoted training standardization culminating in the 1942 introduction of battle drills, had renewed determination to develop and deploy a flexible, predominantly wireless-based communication system, adopted an increasingly scientific approach to combat ill-discipline, and began a fundamental reorganization, albeit temporary, to brigade-based operations. This book will examine the origins, actions and legacy of the BEF to highlight why this transformation occurred, how it occurred and the successes and failures. The real, often self-inflicted, causes of BEF underperformance have received scant recognition. This book seeks to redress that omission.

2
Campaign Overview

In response to the German invasion of Poland on 1 September 1939, Britain and France declared war on Germany on 3 September 1939, their armed forces mobilized and the British Expeditionary Force was prepared for imminent deployment to the continent. Although some decisions were made at the last minute, for example, the appointment of the BEF's Commander-in-Chief, the process of creating the BEF began months before, as both political and military leaders gradually accepted the increasing risk of war and the need for Britain to share the burden of conflict in France and Flanders. Although the BEF was formed almost exclusively of pre-war regulars and Territorials, its size and composition meant Allied strategy was controlled and directed by the numerically superior French, along with inescapable economic and political pressures. The failure of intensive hostilities to immediately materialize allowed the Allies to develop plans for confronting German aggression in Belgium and also diverted political and military attention towards alternative theatres of operations, such as Scandinavia. When German invasion occurred on 10 May, Allied war plans proved ill-judged, the French forces in the Ardennes region catastrophically collapsed and events spiralled out of the BEF's control. Facing destruction, decisions were taken to evacuate the remainder of the BEF, firstly through Dunkirk, and later, via more westerly Channel ports. This book examines the internal flaws which contributed to the BEF's downfall; as a way of introduction, this chapter outlines that downfall.

The BEF was created in an age of economic austerity and a political environment in which the Army always came last in the order of precedence. After the Great War, successive British governments assumed that there would be no major war for ten years and, as each year passed, the assumed decade of peace was moved forward with it. The three services were drastically reduced in the inter-war period and for 13 years (1918–32) deficiencies in equipment were allowed to accumulate. In March 1932, the ten year rule was officially abandoned and the need for rearmament gradually rose up the political agenda. Even when rearmament was prioritized in the late 1930s in response to an increasingly militaristic and volatile world, the Army was side-lined in favour of the traditionally important Royal Navy and the deterrent offered by the Royal Air Force and its strategic bombers. In a continental war between France and Germany, many in the political establishment favoured restricting British involvement to naval and air forces in a policy known as limited liability; the Army would be reserved for home defence and the defence of the British Empire. However, under pressure from the French to share any burden of future conflict more equally, and in the forlorn hope of deterring German aggression, the British political establishment gradually accepted the need for a BEF.[1]

As a contingency against any European conflict, in June 1938, a new War Office branch called General Staff (Plans) was formed; led by Colonel L.A. Hawes, its remit was to overhaul and create plans for despatching an expeditionary force overseas. This was vital work as all pre-existing mobilization tables and deployment plans were 'for horse-drawn units'; these had no relevance to the needs of a newly mechanized British Army. In contrast, the Royal Navy Plans branch 'had plans ready docketed for every possible contingency' which were constantly 'kept up to date'.[2] With Germany threatening further European conquests after recent annexations of Austria and Sudetenland, Britain finally accepted the need for a military force capable of more than imperial policing. On 22 February 1939, the Cabinet ordered five regular infantry divisions, one mobile division and four Territorial divisions be equipped for European warfare; in effect, the formation of a BEF had been authorized. After Germany annexed Czechoslovakia on 15 March, the Territorial Army was doubled in size on 29 March and, in April, conscription was introduced. Finally, the Cabinet approved increases in industrial capacity and reserves of equipment to enable Britain to have 32 divisions in the field 12 months after the outbreak of war. Ironically, the arrival of these new recruits disrupted the summer training of experienced personnel and units who would form the majority of the BEF. Nevertheless, since the security of Britain depended on its French Ally, it was felt a contribution on land to the defence of France might be necessary for the defence of Britain, especially as German conquests had shifted the balance of power in Europe.[3]

On 1 September 1939, Germany invaded Poland and, in response, Britain ordered full mobilization of its armed forces including the BEF. Unwilling to accept another German conquest in Europe, Britain and France declared war on Germany on 3 September; advance parties of the BEF began arriving in France as early as 4 September.

The selection of a Commander-in-Chief for the BEF had been inexplicably left to the last minute, thereby preventing any future C-in-C directing training during summer 1939. Lieutenant General Sir John Dill had been a contender due to his strategic mind and his performance at Aldershot Command, the traditional home of the C-in-C designate of any British Army sent overseas. Another contender was General Sir Edmund Ironside, the Inspector General of Overseas Forces; his post had been briefly held by Sir John French prior to his appointment as BEF C-in-C in the Great War and Ironside had been led to believe this posting would be equally brief. In the end, Secretary of State for War Leslie Hore-Belisha appointed the Chief of the Imperial General Staff Lord Gort as the new BEF C-in-C. Lord Gort, who was 53 years old, was a highly decorated Grenadier Guardsman who had commanded at battalion and brigade level in the Great War. He had been wounded four times, mentioned in despatches on nine occasions and awarded the Military Cross, the Distinguished Service Order with two bars and the Victoria Cross.[4] Lord Gort's biographer, J.R. Colville, has claimed the French General staff had made several informal representations inferring Gort's suitability for the role. A more cynical view is that Hore-Belisha and Gort suffered from a personality clash and the new position of C-in-C created some distance between them. Leslie Hore-Belisha's own military assistant, Francis de Guingand, openly admitted the 'rough-shod riding' of his flamboyant boss caused tension amongst many senior officers.[5] Whatever the reason for his appointment, Lord Gort's lack of high command experience and obsession with detail made him ill-suited to the role. Lieutenant General A. Brooke, who served under Gort as GOC II Corps, felt Dill had been the superior candidate with 'twice the vision and ten times the ability'. Brooke concluded 'Gort's brain has lately been compared to that of a glorified boy scout! Perhaps unkind, but there is a great deal of truth in it'.[6] Major General Bernard Montgomery, who commanded the BEF's 3rd Division, also felt the appointment was a mistake; 'the job was above his ceiling'.[7] More recently, David French has correctly argued Gort had several admirable qualities that served the BEF well, including mental toughness, realism and decisiveness.[8] It is worth noting that whoever commanded the BEF, its small size and inadequate training makes it inconceivable that an alternative outcome to the campaign could have been achieved.

The last minute appointment of a C-in-C led to a flurry of changes at the War Office as key personnel were transferred to duties with the BEF. Director of Military Operations and Intelligence Major General H. Pownall was appointed Chief of the General Staff within the BEF whilst Director General of the Territorial Army Major General W. Brownrigg became the BEF's Adjutant General. The incoming CIGS, Sir Edmund Ironside, opposed these changes, particularly Pownall's appointment, and argued that to remove all those responsible for war planning would be a 'mistake' and leave the War Office 'mutilated'. Having already signalled the BEF's primacy by offering Gort 'carte blanche as to officers for the BEF', it is unsurprising Hore-Belisha dismissed Ironside's objections. The changes impacted upon the War Office as much as the BEF. Dubious about the new regime's prospects, Pownall recorded in his diary that Ironside had been begrudgingly appointed CIGS to engender good publicity and opinion amongst his political supporters, notably Winston Churchill; from a military viewpoint, Pownall concluded Ironside was 'unfitted to be C-in-C in the field or CIGS'. Strikingly, even Ironside reflected 'I am not suited in temperament to such a job as CIGS, nor have I prepared myself to be such'.[9]

Another last minute issue was the terms under which Lord Gort would conduct operations in France. Ordered to cooperate with the French in the fight against Germany, Gort and the BEF were placed under the command of General Alphonse Georges, C-in-C of French North-East Theatre of Operations. The importance of the chain of command was further reinforced: 'You will carry out loyally any instructions issued by him'. However, Gort was given 'liberty to appeal to the British Government' should any French order appear to 'imperil the British Field Force'. C-in-C Gort was also ordered to report regularly to the War Office, provide logistical support for the independent Advanced Air Striking Force (AASF) and, as far as possible, keep the BEF together as a unified fighting force; the only exceptions to this final clause were temporary detachments with specific purposes, for example, training.[10] Superficially comprehensive, these instructions included a number of grey areas and unforeseen complications. Although the BEF was instructed to take orders from General Georges, the Allied Supreme Commander was actually General Maurice Gamelin, whilst later in the campaign, the BEF was included within French First Army Group under General Gaston Billotte. No guide was given to the appropriate course of action should conflicting orders be received from these French superiors. Similarly, the instructions provided Gort with a right of appeal to the British government, but it was not specified whether this meant the Prime Minister, the Cabinet, the Secretary of State for War or the War Office. This ambiguity had been highlighted as early as 7 July 1939, when Hore-Belisha was questioned about who would consider the appeal; Hore-Belisha 'didn't know'.[11] It is understandable that this ambiguity crept into planning during the rush to war; it is scandalous that it was not dealt with when highlighted. A crisis is not the time to be deciding areas of jurisdiction, yet this is exactly what these vague instructions enabled. Even one of Gort's fiercest critics, Major General B. Montgomery, sympathized: 'One only has to read his instructions' provided by Hore-Belisha, 'to see what he was in for'; Montgomery concluded 'it would have taxed a much better brain than Gort's to deal with such a complicated problem'.[12] Thus, the BEF was already compounding long-term deficiencies with self-inflicted organizational defects.

British personnel began disembarking in France on 4 September 1939 and, proceeding rapidly, deployment reached 152,031 army personnel by 27 September. Commanded by Lieutenant General Sir J. Dill, I Corps (1st and 2nd Divisions) began taking over a sector of the frontier defences from French troops on 3 October; II Corps (3rd and 4th Divisions) commanded by Lieutenant General A. Brooke, moved into the line from its concentration area on 12 October. This fulfilled pre-war commitments to assemble two corps in France within 33 days of mobilization. During the relative lull before combat operations intensified in May 1940, further British units deployed at regular intervals. The regular 5th Division arrived in December 1939, followed in January 1940 by the Territorial 48th (South Midland) Division. In February 1940, the 50th (Northumbrian) and 51st (Highland) Divisions joined the BEF, and fighting strength was further added to in April with 42nd (East Lancashire) and 44th (Home Counties) Divisions; all of these were Territorial formations. These increases allowed the BEF to reorganize into three corps on 9 April; III Corps was commanded by Lieutenant General Sir Ronald Adam. In April, the deployment of three untrained, minimally equipped Territorial divisions also bolstered BEF manpower, albeit without significantly enhancing fighting strength; 12th (Eastern), 23rd (Northumbrian) and 46th (North Midland and West Riding) Divisions were assigned strictly non-combatant duties on the line of communications and were outside corps control. By May 1940, BEF strength had reached 394,165; of this total, 237,319 were in combat units and their related headquarters, whilst 156,846 were serving in rearward areas. Large numbers of these men were preparing bases, depots and infrastructure for an even larger expansion of the BEF to four corps in two armies; the German invasion of 10 May occurred before this could be achieved.[13]

With over 100 divisions, the French Army dwarfed the BEF throughout the campaign and, as a result, was allowed total control over Allied strategy in continental Europe. The primary objective of French strategy was the defence of French soil; literal interpretation of this policy had led to the pre-war construction of a vast, expensive chain of concrete fortifications, known as the Maginot Line, along the Franco-German border. It was believed a defensive strategy, in combination with an economic blockade, would weaken Germany whilst sufficient Allied resources for an offensive were built up; only then would the Allies actually try to win the war. The weak spot in the Allied front-line was the 250 mile flood-prone Franco-Belgian frontier which, due to a lack of pre-war finance, had minimal fortifications. Addressing this issue consumed BEF activity throughout the Phoney War and, according to Lord Gort's Despatches, far exceeded 'pre-war anticipations'.[14] Julian Jackson has stated the purpose of the Maginot Line 'was to free manpower for offensive operations elsewhere – especially important given France's demographic inferiority to Germany – and to protect the forces of manoeuvre'.[15] The purpose of the Phoney War defences constructed along the Franco-Belgian border was less clear cut because the Allies planned to move beyond them as soon as the Germans invaded.

Discounting the possibility of the main German thrust trying to breach the Maginot Line or the rugged terrain of the Ardennes region, Supreme Commander Gamelin concluded the most likely path of attack was across the plains of neutral Belgium. German forces had taken this path during the Great War; the scars of this conflict were seared into the French psyche and had influenced strategy ever since. Consequently, to further protect northern France from any fighting, Gamelin proposed to confront the German invader in neutral Belgium. On 9 November 1939, at a top-level military conference at Vincennes, Gamelin announced his intention to use the best troops in the Allied order of battle, including the BEF, to form a defensive line on the Dyle River, if and when the Germans invaded Belgium. The plan had several benefits; it provided a shorter front-line than the Franco-Belgian border, it would provide additional defensive positions (four rivers) between the German invasion force and France, and it would increase the likelihood of Belgium being kept in the war. There were, however, significant risks; it foolishly relied on strictly neutral Belgium to build defensive positions on the Dyle River, it risked an unpredictable encounter battle at an unknown location and it gambled that the Germans would repeat their Great War invasion plans. In his analysis of the Dyle Plan, Brian Bond has concluded at worst it was reckless and, at best, Gamelin allowed 'semi political considerations to outweigh practical operational factors'.[16] Any reservations Lord Gort had about this questionable plan were silenced by his predetermined position as a loyal subordinate and the perceived primacy of political direction, specifically to keep war away from France. The BEF did not object because, as Gort succinctly summarized, it was 'not for me to comment on it'. Gort's responsibility was restricted to ensuring any orders were within the BEF's capability and events proved that the physical process of reaching the Dyle was 'well within the capacity of the Force'.[17]

The final folly of Gamelin's Dyle plan was the March 1940 modification known as the Breda variant; Gamelin opted to strip the strategic reserve of some of its most mobile divisions in a superfluous effort to support the Netherlands (another neutral country threatened by Germany). The French Seventh Army included two motorized infantry and one light mechanized division; its seven divisions were ordered to advance on the extreme left flank of Allied forces to Breda on the Dutch frontier, seize control of the Scheldt estuary and bolster Dutch resistance. This plan was foolhardy for two main reasons. In spring 1940, the Dutch announced intentions to abandon their frontiers in the event of war, in favour of an eminently more defendable national redoubt in the vicinity of Amsterdam, Rotterdam and The Hague; in doing so, Seventh Army's mission became redundant. Secondly, and more importantly, by significantly reducing the numerical strength and mobility of the strategic reserve, Gamelin lessened his ability to respond to attacks elsewhere on the front. Gamelin remained unmoved even when General Georges warned against committing significant reserves to a peripheral objective before German intentions had been determined. Despite reaching Breda on 11 May, the Seventh Army found their mission impossible because of German airborne landings and the subsequent, previously announced, withdrawal by Dutch forces; with significant energy expended, Seventh Army was redeployed on 12 May.[18]

In the end, Gamelin's tunnel vision heavily contributed to the Allies' downfall, as the Germans had anticipated, and were ruthlessly prepared to exploit, the Allied advance into Belgium. After putting up a brave fight against unequal odds, Poland had been defeated by Germany by the end of September 1939. With Poland conquered, Germany transferred the bulk of its forces to its western borders and began planning for the invasion of France and Flanders. Initially wary about the step up in quality it faced, German planners prepared for a cautious advance through neutral Belgium and the Netherlands, with the relatively modest intention of forcing the Allies onto the back foot whilst simultaneously securing bases in Belgium for future operations against Britain. This envisaged the main attack coming from the right wing through central Belgium (Army Group B), whilst the more southerly left wing (Army Group A) would provide flank protection; the relatively small Army Group C would perform a diversionary role against the Maginot Line. These plans evolved during the course of the Phoney War with the biggest catalyst for change being the Mechelen incident. On 10 January 1940, a German aircraft carrying invasion plans made a forced landing in Mechelen, Belgium; the plans were captured before they could be destroyed and were subsequently distributed to the Allies. Ironically, the Allies actually doubted the plans' authenticity; Lieutenant General A. Brooke noted the consensus at BEF GHQ was that the plans were a 'plant', whilst Chief of the General Staff Pownall believed it was an elaborate attempt at providing a pretence for invasion, namely by forcing the Allies to enter Belgium prematurely.[19] The long-term effect on the Allies was limited as they had already anticipated an invasion of the Low Countries and had prepared their response accordingly. The critical point about the Mechelen incident was that it stirred the Germans into a total revision of their plans, and caused a far more ambitious approach to be taken. Army Group B would still advance into the Low Countries, but now its role was merely to lure the Allies northwards; its strength was reduced from 43 divisions to 29 divisions accordingly. The main thrust now came from Army Group A at the vulnerable hinge between the Maginot Line and the Allies entering Belgium; gambling that light resistance would enable the supposedly impenetrable terrain of the Ardennes region to be traversed, the 45 divisions of Army Group A would swing north-west and encircle the Allied forces in Belgium, away from their lines of resupply. It was a bold plan which balanced great risks with the chance of surprising and destroying the bulk of the Allied armies; it was made feasible by Gamelin's plan.[20]

The BEF faced many distractions during the course of the Phoney War, most notably the considerable number of visits by distinguished guests. Lord Gort's Despatches reveal how the BEF was toured by King George VI, the French President, Prime Minister Neville Chamberlain, members of the War Cabinet, ministers from the Dominions, many members of the Army Council and seven Field Marshals. While morale was improved, particularly by the visit of King George VI, the benefits were not always reciprocal; writing to his sisters in December 1939 after an extensive tour of the BEF, PM Chamberlain commented 'I understood very little' when key points were highlighted by accompanying senior officers.[21]

The visit with the most consequences, and therefore the most time-consuming from a BEF perspective, was the visit of Secretary of State for War Hore-Belisha from 18–20 November 1939. As has already been noted, Hore-Belisha's flamboyant personality and unorthodox working practices caused a great deal of irritation within the Army. Even his close friend and adviser Basil Liddell Hart was forced to admit when writing an extremely sympathetic entry in the Dictionary of National Biography 'Hore-Belisha could arouse strong feelings' in those he worked with.[22] Nevertheless, despite any built up resentment, the visit was relatively trouble-free; CGS Pownall remarked Hore-Belisha's behaviour was 'excellent'.[23] However, from this innocuous visit sprung the Pill Box Affair, a row amongst members of the political and military establishment about the state of defences on the BEF's front-line. Once back in London, Hore-Belisha tactlessly criticized BEF defences on the grounds of quantity, quality and speed of construction; in his defence this merely echoed comments from two Dominion ministers (R.G. Casey of Australia and Deneys Reitz of South Africa) who compared BEF positions unfavourably with the Maginot Line. Hore-Belisha's argument was compromised because he inadvertently used a section of British defences as an example of good practice, mistook French three-week construction schedules for three days, and misinterpreted the Dominion ministers' obvious contrast between the long established Franco-German frontier and more recent activities on the Franco-Belgian border. Hore-Belisha compounded his ill-judged criticism by unilaterally invoking the authority of the Prime Minister and the War Cabinet to strengthen his case, but surreptitiously conveyed his views via the BEF's Chief Engineer Major General R.P. Pakenham-Walsh.[24] Fuelled by a pre-existing ill-will, the backlash from within the BEF was ferocious and prolonged. On 29 November 1939, CGS Pownall described the criticism as 'A knife in the back of the man who should be free, above all others, to think of beating Germans. We [GHQ] are now here all facing *West*, to meet the more dangerous enemy there'.[25] Upon learning of the allegations on 30 November, Lieutenant General Brooke hoped the findings of an impartial inspection by CIGS Ironside would not only exonerate the BEF, but help 'make a liar' of Hore-Belisha.[26] Lord Gort's biographer, J. Colville, has summarized the reaction: 'Some resented the aspersions cast on their Commander-in-Chief; others were denigrated; all were united in finding an outlet for their anger' at Hore-Belisha.[27] What followed was a sustained, GHQ orchestrated campaign to have Hore-Belisha removed from government. Lord Hardinge (Private Secretary to King George VI), Sir Percy Griggs (Permanent Under-Secretary at the War Office), Sir Horace Wilson (Chief Industrial Adviser to PM Chamberlain) and Lord Hankey (War Cabinet) were utilized by GHQ. All helped a campaign to undermine the confidence of the establishment in Hore-Belisha. The campaign prompted the morale-raising, fact-finding visits of the King and the Prime Minister; these distinguished visits required even more preparation and parades, all of which distracted from training for combat. The campaign was dedicated to a single goal; for example, on 30 November CGS Pownall recorded: 'I pray heaven this may be the last of him. I am doing my best to make it so'.[28] With attempts at reconciliation unsuccessful, Hore-Belisha's position gradually became untenable and on 4 January 1940 he was forced to resign. PM Chamberlain explained 'there existed a strong prejudice against him for which I could not hold him altogether blameless'.[29] Post-resignation, Hore-Belisha was remarkably loyal to both the government and the war effort, but the perception that the issue could linger proved more powerful. Senior officers, such as CGS Pownall and Lieutenant General Brooke, continued to be distracted from their duties by the conviction that Hore-Belisha would pursue a vendetta against the BEF. Furthermore, Pownall noted his C-in-C's worrying temperament meant 'he [Gort] has been turning the thing over in his mind until he is really in quite a jumpy condition'.[30] The press furore about Hore-Belisha's removal lasted until the end of January; the PM's Private Secretary J. Colville recorded how only then did the issue end as a distraction for both government and the BEF.[31]

For the BEF, a complacent political and military establishment was more dangerous than any single visitor, because it enabled sideshows and gimmicks to leach away precious military resources. The commitments of Empire continued in wartime; for example, during the Phoney War, British and French commanders in the Middle East sought reinforcements to guard against local rebellions.[32] However, overshadowing all decisions about resources was a desire to safely engage Germany without destabilizing the Western front; this resulted in operations in strategically convenient but geographically peripheral Scandinavia. The Soviet Union's invasion of Finland in November 1939 and the German invasion of Norway on 9 April 1940 twice offered the Allies (as guardians of neutrals) pretext for intervention; on both occasions, the military planners' main target was war materials, especially iron ore, exported to Germany. Whilst Allied military operations finally occurred after the Norwegian invasion, both events had a damaging legacy for the

BEF. With considerable understatement, the official campaign history recorded 'operations in Norway made rival claims on our naval, military and air forces and equipment'.[33] Brian Bond has more accurately argued 'from January to April inclusive the Allies were more concerned, one might fairly say obsessed, with extending the war to Scandinavia'.[34] The scale of the Scandinavian distraction is best illustrated by the exponential expansion of the proposed intervention. The release of 150 RAF aircraft for Finnish use in late 1939 became, by spring 1940, ambitious plans for operations across Norway, Sweden and Finland involving 100,000 British and 50,000 French Army personnel.[35]

The reason increasingly unrealistic schemes gained momentum was that foreboding about German invasion had been replaced by a complacent belief amongst key individuals that the threat had been contained and prepared for. Deluded about Allied preparedness, CIGS Ironside recorded in February 1940, 'if France is secure – and I think she is – we could not possibly create a better diversion' than intervening in Scandinavia.[36] Similarly, on a visit to France, Secretary of State for War Oliver Stanley informed Lieutenant General A. Brooke that he was 'very doubtful whether the Germans would attack' the Western front in 1940; Brooke's protestations to the contrary fell on deaf ears. It is worth noting the monotonous nature of Phoney War duties warped the priorities of BEF personnel; within Brooke's II Corps 'Everyone's spirits rose at the prospect that something might happen at last' after Germany's invasion of Norway and Denmark on 9 April 1940.[37]

The impact of these distractions on the BEF was stark in terms of men, material and morale. Credible planning became impossible after the British government deemed it 'necessary' to postpone the deployment of III Corps along with anti-aircraft, administrative and labour units, in case of unexpected developments in Scandinavia. Repeatedly issued threats to recall 5th Division from France restricted its integration into the BEF although, in the end, only 15th Brigade was forfeited to the Norway campaign. Whilst Lord Gort's Despatches diplomatically suggest these actions delayed BEF expansion, in private, the Commander-in-Chief robustly informed the War Office that reductions in strength would impair BEF capability, leadership, morale and training.[38] The material impact on the BEF was equally damaging; for example, Lord Gort informed Oliver Stanley on 23 March 1940, 279 vehicles were immobilized awaiting spare parts from England, and a multitude of ordnance and equipment was in short supply or simply absent. CGS Pownall subsequently concluded two months of BEF preparations had been lost and that 'the tide is setting away from us, which is very depressing'; Lieutenant General Brooke felt government interference had cost the BEF 'six good weeks', but the general consensus was BEF development had been irrevocably harmed by the Scandinavian side-show.[39] The eventual arrival of III Corps in mid-April made it physically impossible for its undertrained Territorials to complete even the briefest of GHQ training schedules before the German invasion in May; further-more, IV Corps was delayed until July 1940 and, consequently, missed the campaign altogether. This, in turn, postponed the reorganization of the BEF into two separate armies (each of two corps) and, also, the separation of the position of army commander from commander-in-chief; measures which may have bolstered the resilience of BEF com-mand, control and communication systems when they were eventually confronted by invasion. It is worth noting the BEF was not alone in its disdain for the distractions of Scandinavia; Brigadier General Staff L.A. Hawes, Eastern Command, despaired when his attempt to brief a high-ranking Joint Intelligence Committee on the deficiencies in home defence was forced to compete on the agenda with 'The pronunciation of place names in Norway'.[40]

Ironically, the biggest repercussions of the Scandinavian distraction were political in nature. The Allied failure to aid Finland against Soviet Union aggression in winter 1939–40 forced the replacement of French Prime Minister Edouard Daladier with Paul Reynaud; Daladier had staked his premiership on the issue and, as a result, lost the confidence of the French parliament. This loss of parliamentary confidence was repeated in Westminster in May 1940; the catastrophic operations of British land forces in Norway led to PM Neville Chamberlain resigning after an unconvincing performance in a vote of no confidence and, subsequently, the appointment of Winston Churchill. Finally, on 9 May, French PM Paul Reynaud tendered his government's resignation after a similarly poor performance by French forces in Norway and, also, inter-nal divisions about government policy. On 10 May, French President Lebrun refused on the grounds that a divided government was better than no government on the day of the German invasion. Consequently, both Britain and France were in political turmoil when confronted by an intensification of hostilities on 10 May 1940.[41]

The German invasion of the Low Countries on 10 May took these neutral countries by surprise. Whilst German land forces flooded across the border, parachutists and dive bombers targeted critical positions, bridges and aerodromes. In the Netherlands, 9th Panzer Division successfully prevented Allied support reaching the Dutch and, as a result, the neutral's small armed forces were isolated and overwhelmed.

On 14 May, the devastating bombing of Rotterdam further emphasized the mismatch in forces and the Dutch surrendered the same day. In Belgium, the fighting began equally badly with the immediate undermining of the primary defence line along the Albert Canal and the Meuse River. Expected to hold out for several days, the Belgian fortress of Eben Emael was the line's defensive linchpin, in that it denied the advancing Germans use of vital bridges in the vicinity of Maastricht; in the early hours of 10 May, an elite German glider force landed on the fort's roof and neutralized its heavy artillery and, therefore, its garrison. Having breached this formidable natural barrier the Germans were now free to advance deep into Belgium; thus, with the entire defence line 'gravely prejudiced', the Belgian Army was forced into an immediate and unexpected fighting withdrawal.[42]

For the Allies, the invasion's timing was also a surprise and several hours elapsed before the ill-fated Dyle plan was implemented. The BEF's advance into Belgium began at 1300hrs and proceeded relatively smoothly with minimal interference from the Luftwaffe. CGS Pownall described 10 May as a 'surprisingly light day' in terms of enemy interference and casualties, whilst Lieutenant General Brooke summarized the advance as 'running like clockwork and with less interference from bombing than I anticipated'.[43] The first BEF troops reached the Dyle River by late evening 10 May and, by 11 May, forward infantry divisions had established defensive positions. Paradoxically, the apparent ease of the Allied advance was already troubling some individuals. Major General H. Alexander, 1st Division, felt 'highly suspicious' of the Germans' willingness to tolerate the BEF's forward movement; he later realized 'they must have welcomed it – by drawing us forward they could hope to encircle our southern flank'. Similarly, Edward Spears MP 'felt slightly uncomfortable. Were our forces by any chance doing what the Germans had expected them to do'. The Germans had not only anticipated the actions of Allied forces, but were fully prepared to exploit them.[44]

With the Allies rushing to the Dyle and the bait of Army Group B, the 45 divisions of Army Group A, with its larger proportion of armour, poured through the weakly defended Ardennes forest at the critical juncture of France, Belgium and Luxembourg. General H. Guderian, whose XIX Panzer Corps provided the vanguard of the Ardennes attack, recalled 'our knowledge of the enemy's order of battle and of his predictable reaction at the beginning of the German advance' heavily contributed to victory in France.[45] The French dismissed the undulating, forested terrain of the Ardennes as unsuitable for mechanized operations and, if the Germans were foolish enough to attack here, their progress would be sufficiently slow to allow French reserves to be concentrated. Consequently, the steep, wooded banks and concrete fortifications of the Meuse River, the principal line of resistance in this sector, was thinly held by elderly, ill-equipped personnel of Second and Ninth French Armies. As illustration, the nine divisions of General A. Corap's Ninth Army had an 80 kilometre front to defend. This would have been challenging for the best units, but Julian Jackson has shown personnel within two Ninth Army divisions were at least 35 years old, had performed their military service up to 20 years earlier and came bottom in the pecking order for new equipment. Worse still, the official history reveals French troops in the Ardennes sector were not only weak, but in disarray, because of 'bad liaison, an embryonic state of organization on the ground and defective subordination of command'.[46] In the face of such disorganized resistance the Germans reached the Meuse rapidly, the first troops made an unopposed crossing at Houx late on 12 May and, by 13 May, multiple bridgeheads had been established at Sedan and Dinant. Massive air-support from 310 bombers, 200 dive bombers and 200 fighters brushed aside resistance and enabled assault engineers to build pontoon bridges and unleash the panzers of Army Group A into the open countryside beyond. Once achieved, early on 14 May, a cohesive defensive line could not be maintained, German units made extraordinary advances each day and Ninth Army was systematically rolled up from its right flank. On 15 May, XLI Corps faced little opposition for 60 kilometres as it advanced from Montherme to Montcornet, whilst on 16/17 May 7th Panzer Division travelled 110 kilometres into France. In contrast to the cautious, methodical approach of French military doctrine, the German strategy of concentrating force and aggressively exploiting success enabled Army Group A, in the words of General H. Guderian, to 'drive a wedge so deep and wide that we need not worry about our flanks'.[47] An immediate Allied counter-attack may have restored the situation, but French spirits had been broken as much as French lines; on 15 May, PM Reynaud informed PM Churchill: 'We are defeated – We have lost the battle'.[48]

On 12 May, at a conference in Mons, it was decided to incorporate the Belgian Army into the Allied order of battle and for coordination of the Allied response to the German invasion to be delegated to General G. Billotte, French First Army Group. This extremely challenging role required the coordinator to inspire confidence in his subordinates, issue practical orders and, most importantly, appreciate the diverse positions of three national contingents divided into six separate armies

(The Belgian Army, the BEF and First, Second, Seventh and Ninth French armies). With Supreme Commander Gamelin basing his headquarters at Vincennes near Paris and General Georges, C-in-C North-East Front in nearby La Ferte-sous-Jouarre, it was felt that an officer in closer proximity to the front, such as Billotte and his Douai headquarters, was necessary to coordinate events. This proved illogical, however, because the personnel of French First Army Group lacked the confidence and the capability to fulfil this immense role; Julian Jackson has noted General Billotte burst into tears when informed of the sudden increase in his responsibility. As illustration of how proximity to the front did not automatically equate to greater comprehension, on 12 May, General Georges recommended Second Army at Sedan be the main priority for air-support; the newly empowered Billotte was more concerned about central Belgium and continued to dedicate two thirds of available air power to the less embattled First Army. Once events in the Ardennes did become clear, Billotte's main impact on the campaign, and in particular the BEF, was to order the retreat from the Dyle.[49]

As the calamity of the Meuse breakthrough befell the French, the BEF continued to consolidate its position on the Dyle River in blissful ignorance. On 13 May, BEF cavalry units stationed beyond the Dyle made contact with the vanguard of Army Group B and, by 14 May, BEF infantry formations all along the Dyle were in contact with the enemy. On 15 May, significant pressure was exerted on the BEF for the first time, particularly on 3rd Division at Louvain; however, there was growing recognition that events beyond the BEF's control were undermining its position. On the BEF's right flank, French First Army felt compelled to abandon the Dyle line after its own right flank was exposed by the routing of Ninth Army and, equally significant, it began to lose positions to German forces advancing through Belgium. The BEF and Belgian Army were forced into similar manoeuvres to prevent their own flanks being exposed in turn. Whilst Lieutenant General Brooke, II Corps, recorded 'A day filled with depressing news as to the fate which is befalling the French in the south', CGS Pownall despaired: 'I hope to God the French have some means of stopping them and closing the gap or we are bust'.[50] In a considered assessment, Lord Gort's Despatches declared prolonged defence of the Dyle 'impracticable' from 16 May onwards, and that, with a 20 mile gap created in Allied lines, the overall military situation was 'grave'.[51]

With French First Army already falling back and no orders forthcoming from any of the BEF's superiors, early on 16 May, Major General T.R. Eastwood was despatched by GHQ to prise orders from General

Billotte for coordinated Allied withdrawal. The belatedly agreed schedule involved consecutive overnight withdrawals between Belgium's many rivers; from the Dyle to the Senne on 16/17 May, from the Senne to the Dendre on 17/18 May and finally from the Dendre to the Escaut on 18/19 May. It is worth noting a car accident involving a key liaison officer was sufficient to significantly delay Belgian awareness and preparations for this manoeuvre, such was the perilous state of Allied communication systems. With German forces rapidly approaching the Channel ports, Brian Bond has argued a rapid withdrawal to the Franco-Belgian frontier was vital to avoid encirclement and, secondly, to prepare a counter-offensive to interrupt the German advance. The inability of anyone in the Allied chain of command to give such a drastic order led to the more leisurely withdrawal schedule and, ultimately, contributed to Allied defeat. As illustration of French indecision, on 18 May, the BEF received conflicting orders to both stay and depart the Dendre position; having rearranged once, Lord Gort refused to countenance further changes and unilaterally remained until 19 May. Already, the ability of the Allied armies to act in harmony was collapsing.[52]

In an effort to re-energize his country's failing defence, PM Reynaud made two desperate and, ultimately, futile decisions on 19 May. His patience weakened by setbacks in Norway and developments on the Meuse, Reynaud finally dismissed Gamelin after the latter's admission at a Supreme Council meeting that no reserves or coherent strategy existed to counter the German breakthrough. Gamelin's replacement was 73-year-old General Maxime Weygand, the recently recalled C-in-C of French forces in the Middle East. Weygand had been chief of staff to the legendary Great War commander General Foch and it was hoped his experience could help rectify the military situation. This was a forlorn hope considering Weygand was Gamelin's immediate predecessor and was, therefore, partially to blame for French military failings. Similarly, in a last-ditch effort to bolster French morale, Marshal Philippe Petain, the hero of Verdun in the Great War, returned to government as Vice-President of the Council; he was 84 and increasingly blighted by a pessimistic turn of mind. Petain's return had minimal combat implications, but Weygand's arrival, and subsequent desire to personally assess the situation, actually hindered plans for a counter-attack in the short term. Whilst the French dallied, the campaign continued to develop apace. On 19 May, CGS Pownall rang the War Office and warned for the first time of the increasing likelihood that the BEF would require evacuation from the Channel ports. 2nd Panzer Division reached the Channel at Noyelles near Abbeville on 20 May, cutting Allied lines of communication and completing the encirclement of First Army Group, including the BEF; only immediate action could now prevent the need for evacuation.[53]

On 21 May, an Allied attack was made southwards from Arras to test the level of German resistance to a break out by First Army Group. An attack which on paper consisted of two British infantry divisions and the BEF's 1st Army Tank Brigade, supported by a French light armoured division, in reality, involved a main strike-force of 74 mechanically worn-out British tanks and two infantry battalions (6th and 8th Durham Light Infantry). Brian Bond has highlighted how the operation's limited aim meant Lord Gort's orders contained no mention of a counter-attack or territorial objective. The Allied force had minimal experience of operating together, limited artillery support, no air-support and no comprehension of the multitude of German formations operating south of Arras. The advance was initially successful; for example, General Erwin Rommel, whose 7th Panzer Division sustained the brunt of the attack, recalled the chaos and confusion amongst his troops who were left in an extremely tight spot. The official history of 7th Panzer Division states that losses on this day were 89 killed, 116 wounded and 173 missing; that was four times the loss suffered during the breakthrough into France. The small Allied force involved inevitably meant the attack stalled, made no territorial gains and merely reinforced the considerable difficulty in achieving an Allied breakout.[54] Nevertheless, its impact on the German High Command was very marked and out of all proportion to material results; for example, General Guderian, XIX Panzer Corps, noted the attack made 'a considerable impression on the staff of Panzer Group von Kleist [the superior formation], which suddenly became remarkably nervous'.[55] This caution spread as far as General von Rundstedt, Army Group A Commander, who issued an order on 23 May, endorsed by Supreme Commander Adolf Hitler the following day, to halt any advance on the BEF's southern flank from Lens to Gravelines; this caution continued until 26 May, allowed the BEF to stabilize the front and contributed to successful evacuations at Dunkirk.[56]

Also on 21 May, Supreme Commander Weygand attempted to hold a high-level conference in Ypres, Belgium to discuss the military situation and coordinate a counter-attack by Allied forces in the north and south. The conference was badly disrupted by nearby fighting, failing communications, early departures and late arrivals; as a result, the key players from France, Belgium and the BEF never occupied a room together. Furthermore, the only person of authority to attend all the meetings was Allied coordinator General Billotte who, upon leaving the conference, was fatally injured in a car crash. Billotte had been ineffective, but the failure to appoint a replacement for three days (General Blanchard, French First Army) allowed the mind-sets of the various Allied contingents to diverge further. The conference ended with tenuous agreement for coordinated counter-offensive involving Allied forces in the northern pocket and French forces south of the Somme River. No agreement was reached on where the heaviest burden of responsibility for closing the gap between Allied forces lay. In reality, any significant attack on the rapidly hardening German flank was already implausible; for example, Lord Gort's Despatches make clear the BEF would have been obliged to disengage seven divisions in contact with the enemy, fight a rear-guard action, simultaneously attack south-westwards to break through significant German forces, all whilst absorbing irreplaceable losses in men and material. As illustration of the increasing constraints within the northern pocket, on 23 May, the BEF was placed on half rations to conserve supplies. Despite Weygand's confidence about the possible contribution of French forces on the Somme, the reformed Seventh Army was similarly ill-suited to offensive operations, containing just six divisions spread over a 105 kilometre front. The mission to reunite the Allied armies was made even more difficult on the night of 23/24 May, when military prudence compelled Lord Gort to withdraw the Arras Garrison 25 kilometres to avoid its loss in an increasingly vulnerable salient. Many French officers, including Weygand, seized on this action as an act of betrayal, a symbol of 'Perfidious Albion' and the reason for their inevitable defeat; most disingenuously, Gort's withdrawal parallel to the coast was talked about as a 40 kilometre retreat towards the ports.[57] However, the official history is clear on this issue: 'the evacuation of the Arras salient is not open to criticism'.[58]

Despite the withdrawal from Arras, preparations continued, in accordance with the Weygand conference, for an Allied counter-attack southwards. Early on 25 May, plans were completed for an attack the following day involving the BEF's III Corps (5th and 50th Divisions) and three divisions from V Corps French Army. However, a combination of crumbling Belgian resistance to the north and hardening German resistance to the south convinced Lord Gort of the futility of the operation and, more importantly, the urgent need to preserve the BEF's escape route to Dunkirk, the last remaining Channel port capable of evacuating troops in the northern pocket. At 1800hrs 25 May, without consulting French superiors or the War Office, Gort ordered 5th and 50th Divisions to abandon preparations for the attack southwards and, instead, immediately fill the threatening gap between the British and Belgian forces near Ypres. Lord Gort's actions saved the BEF because the Belgian Army safeguarding Dunkirk had already expended all its reserves, its ability to resist was disintegrating and, even with British reinforcements, it was forced to capitulate at midnight 27/28 May. Although this action left evacuation as the only viable option, the situation was sufficiently desperate that there was considerable anxiety regarding the BEF's fate within the British High Command. Privately estimating that only 30,000 men could be saved, on 26 May, CIGS Ironside noted 'it will be a matter of getting as many men out as possible with very little equipment'.[59] Similarly, Lieutenant General Brooke envisaged a very hazardous enterprise in which 'we shall be lucky if we save 25% of the BEF'.[60] CGS Pownall summarized the situation: 'How many of us survive is on the knees of the Gods. But it's the only thing to be done'.[61]

As early as 20 May, once the Allied armies in the north had been encircled, informal evacuations began of casualties and non-combat personnel deemed useless mouths; 26,402 British and 1534 Allied personnel were repatriated before official evacuations commenced. The official evacuation from Dunkirk (codenamed Operation Dynamo) was planned, organized and conducted by Vice Admiral (Dover) Bertram Ramsay; it began on 26 May. From this point, Allied forces began withdrawing into a defensive perimeter around Dunkirk and its beaches, from where Royal Navy personnel organized arriving units and oversaw their evacuation. With Dunkirk's docks destroyed, personnel were lifted directly off the beach by inshore boats and the famous little ships before being transferred to larger offshore vessels. From 28 May, more numerous evacuations were achieved from the East Mole (harbour sea defence), alongside which destroyers and large civilian ships could berth and embark personnel directly. Frequently Luftwaffe attacks hampered embarkation throughout the evacuation with 228 ships lost and 45 badly damaged before the evacuation ended on 4 June 1940; a considerable number of smaller boats were also lost. Furthermore, the evacuation did not run smoothly because of French reluctance to evacuate combat units; 58,583 British personnel had been evacuated before Supreme Commander Weygand finally authorized the general evacuation of French troops on 28 May. To facilitate trust between the Allied nations and in accordance with British government orders, the Royal Navy ensured embarkation facilities were shared equally from 28 May onwards; to their credit, both the BEF and Allied forces each evacuated a further 139,000 men. In total, 338,226 Allied personnel including 198,315 British troops were evacuated during Operation Dynamo; of these, approximately 100,000 men were lifted from the beaches and the remainder were embarked via the East Mole. As the encircled BEF dwindled in size, senior officers handed over to subordinates and returned home. On 29/30 May, overnight evacuees included CGS Pownall and Corps Commanders Lieutenant Generals Brooke and Adam; Lord Gort was evacuated alongside II Corps overnight on 31 May/1 June, leaving only I Corps commanded by Major General H. Alexander. Both Alexander and Senior Naval Officer ashore Captain W. Tennant ensured they were amongst the last British personnel evacuated at 0300hrs 3 June. Despite the encircled BEF's repatriation, the evacuation continued until dawn 4 June in order to save as many French personnel as possible; with the enemy closing in on every side, the remaining French, numbering approximately 40,000, surrendered at 0900hrs 4 June.[62] It is worth noting that Dunkirk was only a successful operation in terms of men evacuated; all the transport and heavy weapons of the units evacuated had to be left behind.

The battle of France continued for another fortnight after Dunkirk, but the end result was now inevitable. Reorganized and refreshed, the German Army deployed 104 divisions between the sea and the Meuse River, with five panzer corps providing the spearheads, each of two panzer divisions and one motorized infantry division. Facing them along a 225 mile front were 43 French infantry divisions (25 of which had been extracted from the Maginot Line), three weakened armoured divisions and three understrength light cavalry divisions. Skeleton forces remained in the largely redundant Maginot Line and along the eastern borders with Switzerland and Italy. Despite the Dunkirk evacuation, a considerable body of British Army manpower remained in France, based largely on the BEF's lines of communication and numbering almost 150,000. These units had been cut off from GHQ on 20 May and included 51st (Highland) Division, the bulk of 1st Armoured Division and an ad hoc force of ill-equipped line of communication troops known as the Beauman Division. A great deal of confusion and overlapping command jurisdictions meant these unfortunate formations received conflicting orders, sometimes simultaneously, from Supreme Commander Weygand, French army and corps commanders, and regional BEF commanders; combat operations suffered as a result. With Dunkirk finally secured, the German forces broke south; between Amiens and the coast on 5 June and, later, further east on the Aisne River on 9 June. General Weygand's only strategy was to hold a line of heavily defended villages and woods along the length of the Somme River valley and hope for the best. Some Allied units fought tenaciously, but with the Germans benefiting from overwhelming numerical and aerial superiority, overall resistance crumbled and the front broke. Armoured spearheads soon began fanning out along the coast, into the French interior, behind the Maginot Line and towards the Swiss border. To compound French misery, on 10 June, Italy had declared war on the Allies in an attempt to share the victor's spoils and the French government was forced to abandon Paris and declare it an open (undefended) city to spare its destruction.[63]

In Britain there remained a forlorn hope that the BEF could be reformed, albeit on a smaller scale, and that somehow this token of loyal support would bolster French morale and ensure continued resistance in France. Accordingly, 52nd Division was despatched in early June, further formations were prepared for deployment and, on 13 June, Lieutenant General A. Brooke returned to France to take command of all British troops, both new and old. However, by now France was militarily and politically exhausted and nothing could save it. On 14 June, Supreme Commander Weygand informed Brooke that the French Army was unable to 'offer organized resistance and was disintegrating into disconnected groups'; no amount of British reinforcements could change this.[64] Similarly, on 16 June, in a last desperate attempt to prevent the French seeking an armistice, PM Churchill made an extraordinary offer of an indissoluble union between the two Allies. The proposed declaration stated 'France and Great Britain shall no longer be two nations, but one Franco-British union', thereby legalizing the continuation of French military action, from overseas if needed. Preferring the consequences of an armistice with Germany, a majority of French Cabinet rejected the proposal, believing it rendered them a British dominion. PM Reynaud resigned on 16 June in protest at this decision, leaving his deputy, Marshal Petain, free to seek an armistice on 17 June; the armistice was signed on 22 June 1940.[65]

With the fate of France now beyond doubt, the remaining BEF personnel had little option but to evacuate. Non-combat personnel had begun evacuating in early June and this process had been intensified by Lieutenant General Brooke who was fully aware of the futility of further BEF operations in France. Between 16 and 25 June the overwhelming majority of British personnel left in France, including recently arrived fighting units, were evacuated from any available channel port. BEF operations in France were officially ended on 18 June, but Royal Navy evacuations persisted on behalf of British stragglers and Allied troops willing to continue the fight from Britain. Incredibly, amidst the country's post-armistice break-up into German occupied territories and Vichy-controlled France, evacuations of some Allied troops and British consular staff continued from Mediterranean ports up to 14 August. Overall, the Royal Navy brought away from the area south of the Somme 191,870 Allied troops including 144,171 BEF personnel.[66]

This chapter has reviewed the France campaign's main participants, units, strategies and events. It has shown how the BEF was created in response to events in Europe, at a time of economic and political pressure. The BEF's activities were guided not only by GHQ, but by the French military and Allied governments. A battle for receiving and retaining resources was waged long before the intensification of hostilities in May 1940. The German invasion exploited inadequacies in Allied war plans and military capabilities; inadequacies that because of its small size, the BEF was unable to rectify alone. However, these factors and the subsequent fall of France do not absolve the BEF from criticism about its own performance. The following chapters will reveal how many of the debilitating flaws in British operating procedure were long-standing, foreseeable and self-inflicted. Only then can a substantive and precise appreciation of this complex campaign be reached.

3
Training

The absence of an acceptable training metric which could be worked towards or maintained was a consistent and debilitating flaw of the British Army throughout the inter-war and Phoney War period. Variation of terrain and opponent during imperial policing duties prevented the overseas units establishing standard procedures for the Army as a whole. Undermined by inadequate manpower, equipment and facilities, UK-based units struggled to move beyond theoretical procedures and skeleton exercises. Whilst pre-war training material was vague, tolerant of flexibility and errors, Phoney War training material was misdirected, too focused on platoon tactics and surprisingly critical of commanding officers' pre-war efforts. Restricted by overlapping jurisdictions, oversight procedures lacked authority and resources to intervene in failing units and can be summarized as flimsy. Officer training at Sandhurst, post-commissioning and at Staff College undervalued initiative and overly relied on imagination. Generally, the Army placed viability and hassle-free training before effectiveness and productivity. To compound pre-war flaws, the opportunity to prepare more thoroughly for a specific threat during the unexpected lull after the declaration of war was wasted with endless distractions, both local and political, the construction of useless defences and misleading assignments to illusory war zones.

Raymond Callaghan has argued: 'Training is a very dull subject ... for that reason, military historians, professional and amateur, official and academic alike, get past it as quickly as they can' despite training being 'as powerful as technology and institutional structure, perhaps as potent as societal and cultural factors' in determining how an army fights.[1] Nevertheless, several historians have identified training as a key determinant in the performance of the British Army. Timothy Harrison

Place has demonstrated how deficiencies in experience, realism and operating procedures overshadowed Army training throughout the war due to external distractions and a lack of self-assessment.[2] With particular reference to the Far East, Timothy Moreman has highlighted dramatic changes to fighting methods, tactical doctrine and training, which occurred because 'no real thought had been paid' to the combat environment.[3] David French has succinctly argued: 'British training did improve as the war continued', perhaps most dramatically with the introduction of battle drills in 1942. However, some defects, such as the absence of a universal interpretation of doctrine in practice, or of a single guiding executive to enforce it, remained throughout the war.[4] These three studies make clear that training was a constant problem for the Army throughout the war, and despite various efforts was never overcome. This chapter aims to explain why training problems occurred in the inter-war period and were retained once war began – in particular, why the Army struggled to identify correct training procedures, achieve uniform acceptance and carry out effective oversight and enforcement. Before France, faith in fundamental principles allowed the Army to indulge in variation in training and procedure; conflict with Germany transformed this self-confident world of possibility into an insecure world of uncertainty. This was why the Army sought the security of a standardized skills-set, particularly with the introduction of battle drills in 1942.

During the inter-war years, the main focus of training was procedure relating to the Army's traditional role of imperial policeman. This was encouraged by successive governments; for example, in 1933, Financial Secretary to the War Office Duff Cooper stated: 'The British Army ... is not designed for Continental wars. The purpose of the British Army is to maintain order in the British Empire only'. The obligations of Empire consumed the majority of the Army's manpower and limited resources, preventing significant training for alternative roles. The military consequences were acknowledged by contemporaries such as General Ironside, who complained on 29 December 1937: 'Imperial commitments absorb the Regular Army surprisingly quickly – with 30,000 men and 2000 officers short – and there is no reserve'.[5] On 1 January 1938, out of 138 infantry battalions, 74 were overseas guarding the British Empire.[6] Typically, after six months basic training, only two of H. Atkins' training platoon were posted to 2nd Queen's Royal Regiment based on the Isle of Wight; the remaining 23 reinforced 1st Queen's Royal Regiment in India.[7] This ratio of distribution was not ideal in terms of training; full-strength units based overseas often had to squeeze training into a shortened working day, for example, 0830hrs to 1230hrs in India, whilst in the UK, the longer working day of under-strength units was swamped with the routine duties and fatigues of a home-based battalion. Private L. Arlington's pre-war career within 2nd Middlesex Regiment 'consisted of spit and polish parades and square-bashing' reminiscent of a 'Crimean display'.[8]

Guided by financial limitations, the Army adapted its organizational structure and equipment almost exclusively to the most favourable combination of fire-power and mobility for imperial policing. In 1938, the War Office reorganized 'establishments so as to reduce the size of existing divisions and provide a large number of more compact forma-tions, in which firepower and mobility will be primary considerations'. Leslie Hore-Belisha, Secretary of State for War, argued in a 1938 Cabinet Paper, small divisions would be easier to manage, move, supply and ship, and in principle allow deployment of 'the men available with an increasing ratio of effect'.[9] During this process, mobility was given undue precedence over fire-power to ensure compatibility with the imperial policeman role, leading to the introduction of weapons of limited calibre and range, such as the 2-inch mortar.

Despite the obvious importance of imperial policing, the Army still considered it a distraction from preparing for a first-class war. The official report on the 1936 Arab Rebellion complained that operations in Palestine were handicapped by restrictions on the use of force, 'which deprived the services of making proper use of the weapons with which they were equipped and the methods of war to which they had been trained'. The two British divisions involved in suppressing the Rebellion from April to October 1936 could neither train for a first-class war, nor experience the fullest use of their weapons whilst acting in aid of a civil power with all the consequential restrictions.[10] Had this report been written post-1945, it could be accused of providing retrospective justification for the Army's poor performance in World War Two. However, as it was published in February 1938, the concern appears genuine. The Official History of Operations on the North-West Frontier of India 1936–37 is equally critical of the Army being used for imperial policing, but, having been published in 1943, its motives are more open to debate.[11]

The diverse characteristics of combat throughout the Empire help explain why the Army struggled to establish a universal operating procedure. The Arab Rebellion was symbolized by sniping, bombings and acts of terrorism against infantry on defensive duties in an urban environment. The campaign history believed sustained combat was difficult to achieve because 'The Palestinian Arab is not a fighting man'. Enemy combatants frequently demonstrated 'carelessness, lack of enterprise, and a wholesome regard for their own skin'.[12] As rebels regularly withdrew under cover of darkness, troops rigorously trained in techniques for maintaining contact throughout the night and renewing battle in the morning. In contrast, Afghan tribesmen were respected for their fanatical bravery, particularly during sustained combat against British forces equipped with superior firepower and supported by air power. The Afghans were capable of inflicting heavy casualties against ill-disciplined or unwary troops, forcing British night operations to be much more limited in scope, closely controlled and carried out in force. However, in both campaigns inhospitable terrain and lack of infrastructure restricted Royal Artillery participation; fire-support was largely carried out by mountain artillery in Waziristan and infantry mortars in Palestine. Similarly, in both campaigns, horsed cavalry were preferred to mechanized units. In an assessment decades out of date for a European battlefield, the 1943 report on NW India Operations 1936–37 cited a successful cavalry charge in November 1936, arguing: 'Occasions will always arise when a mounted attack, boldly delivered, will enable the infantry to get on when they have been held up'.[13] Conflict involving occasionally intensive fighting, without armour or artillery, provided minimal comparable experience for an army that would soon confront a first-class, multi-armed enemy.

The British Army neither established nor sought a uniform training metric in the pre-war period. In December 1937, War Secretary Hore-Belisha stated his desire for 'reducing the authority of the War Office and increasing that of the Generals' outside', further emphasizing the rejection of a standardized training metric.[14] This example is evidence of Hore-Belisha's prioritization of visible policies, such as new buildings and uniforms, over subjective and mundane training for war. This merely endorsed the 1932 Kirke Report which argued for the relaxation of 'standardization and rigid control from above', and that officers should be judged on the results of their independently devised 'methods of command and training'.[15] Training Regulations 1934 authorized Home Command Generals to independently supplement any Directorate of Military Training Memoranda, or perhaps more dangerously, reinterpret it 'to emphasize points important for their command'.[16] This policy was retained during active operations; for example, to counter rebellion in 1936, Palestine was divided into military areas, troops allotted to each area, and commanders given 'as free a hand as possible within their boundaries'.[17] Ironically for commanders who cherished their independence, there was concern in the pre-war period at the lack of training metric. In December 1937, General Ironside (Eastern Command) impressed upon Chief of the Imperial General Staff Gort the need for 'homogeneity' which, without official lead, independently trained Commands would find impossible to achieve.[18] Although political interference is generally counter-productive, on this occasion insisting on a training metric would have better co-ordinated war preparations and facilitated more fluid interchange of units.

Had the War Office chosen to impose a strict training metric, it would have required self-assessment, for the Army had no department capable of visiting, scrutinizing and advising units on a national basis. The Army's previous attempt to establish a metric was in June 1918, when Lieutenant General Ivor Maxse was appointed Inspector General of Training and instructed to ensure, through a system of inspection and advisement, training was 'carried out in a methodical manner'. Although they differ on its impact, both Brian Bond and John Baynes argue the work of the Great War IGT had a positive effect on the British Army.[19] Realistically the IGT could achieve little in the few weeks before the war ended; its creation was more likely an attempt to sideline an out-of-favour general than a sudden desire to unify training procedures. Although themes such as effective time-management remained relevant to the Army, the IGT was abolished amidst inter-war cut-backs; the absence of an effective, methodical inspection system handicapped British pre-war preparations. In December 1937, General Ironside suggested the re-establishment of the Inspector-General position, independent of the Army Council and War Office, who could supervise training, establish a satisfactory metric and gain experience before becoming Commander-in-Chief of any expeditionary force; it should be noted Ironside had a vested interest in the creation of this position as he saw himself as the ideal candidate.[20] Once the decision to send a field force was made in spring 1939, not appointing a Commander-in-Chief meant subordinate commanders and staff could not train under their Chief's direction and develop a team spirit before the war.[21] However, the position was only worth re-establishing if it had the resources necessary to fulfil its objectives. When, on 6 May 1939, it was decided to make General Kirke, Inspector General of Home Forces, responsible for training below brigade level, and General Ironside, Inspector General Overseas Forces, responsible for higher training of troops allocated to an overseas expeditionary force, they were effectively artificial jobs for politically favoured generals; on 5 July 1939, Ironside complained his influence was limited as 'I still have no office, no staff, no clerks'.[22]

The Army's aversion to example-based training material further handicapped potential inspectors. Up-to-date thinking on army doctrine was provided by *Field Service Regulations 1935* and formulated around eight key principles: aim, concentration, cooperation, economy of force, security, offensive action, surprise and mobility. These principles provided the essence of correct procedure, both in training and combat. However, they were not a rigid metric, for example, *FSR 1935* stated the principles of war 'simply indicate a course of action that has been successful in the past and serves as a warning that disregard of them involves risk and has often brought failure'.[23] Directed mainly at senior officers within a battalion, specific examples or context were avoided for fear of infringing a commander's independence. Generalized approval of army/air cooperation and mechanization without specifying how much and what sort of training should occur left pre-war units deficient in guidance on preparing and commanding the rank-and-file.

Infantry training manuals produced by the Directorate of Military Training in the years between 1935 and 1939 also failed to provide detailed guidance on the vital subject of minor tactics training. *Right or Wrong? Elements of Training and Leadership Illustrated 1937* was more concerned that 'troops lay their kit and arms beside them systematically' than how they used them in battle.[24] Timothy Harrison Place has argued *Infantry Section Leading*, published in December 1938, concentrated on broad principles rather than detailed guidance on acceptable tactical standards; a situation not fully resolved until the introduction of battle drills in 1942. Harrison Place does not comment on how the manual dealt with 'the organization and armament of the infantry platoon, the training of its sections in peace and their leading in war' and yet distribution within units to non-commissioned personnel was discretionary.[25] NCOs were responsible for most section and platoon training, yet the War Office consciously chose not to guarantee NCOs access to the latest training or ensure uniform procedures in the Army's NCO-led units. The majority of COs distributed surplus copies to their subordinates, but they were not duty-bound to do so, and if the costs were too great, or the distances too far, for example, in a rural Territorial battalion, distribution could be scrapped. Also, with NCOs denied their own individual copy, COs could control how often *Infantry Section Leading* was referred to, what was referred to, and how it was interpreted; this further prevented the establishment of a training metric.

The 1932 Kirke Report argued a standard metric of training throughout the British Army was unachievable whilst Territorials were restricted to home service. Regular soldiers serving throughout the Empire gained wider peace-time experience of unexpected conditions and problems, which could not be replicated in Britain; 'It would be a sad commentary on our long service training if this were not so'.[26] However, double standards in the distribution of training material prevented a level playing field between regulars and Territorials, thereby further hampering the establishment of a metric. As with many inter-war training manuals, for no other reason than cost, Army Training Memorandum No. 20A was issued in June 1938 to all ranks down to Commanding Officer amongst regulars, but only down to Brigadier level in the TA.[27]

The War Office did provide COs with some general training instructions which, if enforced, could be construed as a metric. In April 1938, Military Training Pamphlet No. 3 demanded every recruit 'receive a sound basic instruction in the rifle', be highly trained in the light machine-gun and 'be capable of killing an enemy presenting a good target'.[28] Subsequently, whilst isolated on the Isle of Wight in 1938, it was easier for officers of the 2nd Queen's Royal Regiment to justify continuous musketry on the Island's only training facility, the Newtown Ranges, than it was to organize the use of mainland facilities. This guaranteed accurate marksmen, but Private H. Atkins despondently noted 2nd Queen's Royal Regiment field-craft skills did not improve, because 'very little can be done in the way of field training'.[29] Relying solely on COs to enforce training instructions led to varying outcomes; for example, despite supposedly training since spring 1939, on the eve of combat operations, 'of the 2000 men in 70 Brigade, 1400 had not yet fired a Bren gun and 400 had not completed the war course with a rifle'.[30] Clearly publication of a War Office document did not equate to uniform acceptance and enforcement throughout the British Army. In July 1939, another training diktat demanded all personnel eligible for deployment on operations should participate in daily physical training, except 'when units are undergoing prolonged physical effort'.[31] This merely reinforced an existing trend in Army training, for example, in 1938, Private S. Beard's first training camp on Salisbury Plain, with 8th Worcestershire Regiment, was demoralizingly dominated by endless route marches because they were easy to organize and favoured by General Staff.[32] In units where marching was not prioritized, the sudden intensification of physical activity came as a shock. In August 1939, after a long day's training, the decision to march C Company, 2nd Middlesex Regiment five miles back to Gosport Barracks led to a virtual mutiny, during which the Company Commander and Company Sergeant Major nearly came to blows.[33] The training that benefited personnel most was varied, had obvious practical applications and sparked the interest of those involved. In 1932 Kirke Committee member J. Kennedy warned his colleagues, 'training is inclined to be rigid', which allowed officers 'to follow a set programme year by year'.[34] In effect a tick box culture was developing, where training was considered a burden to be overcome with minimal organizational effort and little regard for actual combat capability.

As Aldershot Command had the best facilities, most resources and largest proportion of regulars, the subordinate units of I Corps were seen as an unofficial example of best standards in Britain. In 1934, when Aldershot, Eastern and Southern Commands attempted to purchase simultaneously additional training areas in Aldershot, Colchester and Salisbury respectively, it was the prestigious reputation of Aldershot which led to it being prioritized over competing Commands. However, Aldershot Command was handicapped as much as the rest of the Army. Held up by fierce criticism by Lieutenant General Sir Harry Knox (Adjutant General 1935–37) who prioritized ceremony and drill, the request by the GOC Aldershot Command to convert a waterlogged, undulating parade ground (known as Laffan's Plain) into an infantry training facility for hedgerow fighting, was not approved by the War Office until January 1936, and not completed until January 1938.[35]

I Corps was held in such regard that units were obligated to perform in the annual Aldershot Tattoo to help promote Army recruitment, amenities and charities. Predominantly based in Aldershot during the 1930s, 1st Duke of Wellington's Regiment complained the time spent in rehearsal and performance every year substantially eroded opportunity for large formation training.[36] Similarly, between 1935 and 1938, 1st Worcestershire Regiment despaired: 'From June to August the Tattoo took precedence over all considerations', limiting much needed brigade training during its allotted months.[37] Nevertheless, on 28 July 1939, Inspector General Ironside argued: 'The only Corps which is functioning is the Aldershot one and we must take the training of that as the basis of the rest of the Army'. However, I Corps was far from battle ready; for example, having observed a 2nd Brigade night operation, Ironside complained 'there is still made the simplest of mistakes by young officers'.[38] The inadequacies of I Corps were more systemic than a few inexperienced junior officers; there remained within senior officers a fundamental lack of understanding about the realities of modern warfare. As illustration, on 1 September 1939, 3rd Brigade ordered that during mobilization 'no bugles were to be blown in case the sound should give away our position to enemy aircraft'.[39] This clearly demonstrates even units perceived to be the best in the Army experienced insufficient large formation, combined arms training. The strengths and limitations of air power were particularly liable to misconception.

Army/air exercises were inordinately expensive in manpower and resources and exceptionally difficult to umpire due to the speed of events, the difficulty in maintaining continuous control of aircraft and judging accurately the effect of ground-based fire. The variables in equipment, tactics, training and weather meant even with a large pool of army and air umpires, general restrictions had to be applied, so that anti-aircraft fire could only be 'considered effective against aircraft pursuing a straight course at constant height between 3,000 and 10,000 feet'. RAF umpires were exclusively responsible for assessing the accuracy of air attack against troops, and also for transmitting any assessment of aircraft casualties, further hindering the Army's practical exploration of ground/air interaction.[40] With practical experience scarce, the Army attempted to compensate with theoretical exercises at training establishments. However, within Staff College, the study of ground/air co-operation was frequently side-lined, even during second-year exercises involving the solitary RAF instructor. In January 1936, supervisors of a simulated major conflict between fictional countries warned senior students 'the opposing air forces are small and of approximately equal strength' and would have negligible impact on the conflict.[41]

When army/air exercises did occur they were often unrealistic, under-exploited and organized with obscure objectives. From 25–29 August 1936 Southern Command provided 1,655 personnel, in conjunction with RAF and naval forces, for a combined operations exercise involving an amphibious landing at Studland Bay, Dorset. The prestige and novelty of an exercise involving land, air and sea gave this exercise priority over alternatives more likely to benefit future operations. Although declared a success, the unrealistic absence of naval and aerial opposition was recognized, whilst the use of army co-operation aircraft in an artillery observation role was criticized as an improbable use of resources in combat. The legacy of the exercise was limited, as by April 1937 the WO informed the Air Ministry: 'We have decided that no good purpose could be served by writing to each other any more about it. (We all know what we thought of it)'. Perhaps greater attention should have been paid to the RAF conclusion: 'We have no policy on supply dropping' and 'we do not propose to enunciate one unless the War Office raise the matter'.[42] At the same time as the WO overlooked the Air Ministry's dismissal of the need for a policy on supply dropping, British forces suppressing the 1936 Arab Rebellion were frequently being denied requests for re-supply by air; later, the 1938 Campaign report implored: 'A RAF organization which can ensure supplies by air being delivered at short notice will be a most valuable adjunct'.[43] The division of British policy is further highlighted on 12 December 1936, when the RAF routinely dropped over a ton of supplies in bad weather to British forces at Jaler Camp, Waziristan, in response to requests for re-supply.[44] The confusion in policy in 1936 is clear from the WO and Air Ministry believing re-supply by air unnecessary, yet it was considered impossible in Palestine, and accepted as routine in Waziristan, India.

Without a centralized metric, the integrity and effectiveness of training was vulnerable to complacency. The desire for hassle-free training, where the risk of embarrassing failure was reduced to negligible proportions, heavily influenced many officers who not only organized exercises, but participated in them. Before collective training could occur, an inter-war battalion's Adjutant had to put in some hard work surveying the area, allotting sub-areas to companies, and preparing materials that befitted the principles being taught. Complacently, many officers sought to reduce their workload by copying what had been approved in previous years with only minor alterations to ensure a façade of originality. During the 1930s, the relentless use of Windmill Hill on Salisbury Plain for the annual camp of 8th Worcestershire Regiment meant that by 1937, battalion personnel had become 'over-familiar with the topography', and officers required only good memories, rather than a good grasp of military principles. Despite this, the battalion continued to use Windmill Hill for two more years, further undermining their readiness for war. In contrast, the topography was kept fresh and challenging by the 4th Royal Berkshire Regiment who, in 1935, occupied an undulating site near Weymouth for a fortnight; in 1936 they went to the open spaces on Salisbury Plain around Windmill Hill; in 1937 they settled into the sand dunes of Porthcawl in Wales; and in 1938, training camp was held in Bulford Fields. However, without new weapons, new ideas or the presence of other service arms, the benefits of such varied terrain was tempered.[45] Senior officers were often complicit in allowing complacency to result in monotony. Kirke Committee member J. Kennedy personally confessed: 'All of us who are "second class" find it easier to use our memory than our brains'. Explaining how peacetime training encouraged shortcuts, Kennedy informed colleagues:

> We look up what was done last year, quote the remarks made by some star turn we have served under, or slightly alter one of his schemes, but we daren't give our brains a run, it is too risky, we might crash. That is something in the nature of a personal confession but is it only me – I wonder?.[46]

In reality, many Army officers consciously failed to productively utilize training opportunities despite the growing threat of war.

The locality of TA units greatly impacted on their training. In August 1938, the Committee on TA Finance and Organization acknowledged the costs of maintaining rifle ranges bore heavily 'upon some Associations and very lightly upon others'. Many urban units, including every London Territorial Association, escaped maintenance costs by renting nearby regular army facilities at such an advantageous rate that each recruit was allocated 100 rounds. Until a more generous establishment grant was proposed by the Committee, the cost of owning and maintaining their own ranges meant many rural Territorial units were unable to guarantee the statutory 50 rounds each infantryman was required to fire on an annual basis.[47]

Realism should have been crucial in peacetime, but inadequate exercises, equipment, manpower, training techniques and limited numbers of instructors all severely restricted effective training. *The Official History of Training 1939–45* emphasized: 'The more practically and realistically troops are taught when they are not fighting the better they will perform when they are, and the impact of battle will be less strange to them'.[48] Nevertheless, inter-war exercises misled personnel about their readiness for war. In 1935, King's Somborne, Hampshire hosted over four days the only corps exercise between 1925 and 1939; no significant new theories, tactics or weapons were tested. Although many participants were happy just to be involved, a more critical assessment of the exercise's impact came when the observing German Attaché enquired 'when the *real* practices of war took place'.[49] Umpires were responsible for improving realism, but prevented sides intermingling to avoid confusion and allow easier oversight, thereby reducing some exercises to fantasy. At 1937 divisional exercises in Saffron Walden, anti-tank tactics umpire Colonel L. Hawes oversaw an assault on an established defensive position by infantry in combination with supporting infantry tanks. The attackers consisted of a Sergeant armed with a rattle, an infantry section armed with rifles and a wooden bren, and six three-tonne lorries with T painted on them. After a couple of fire-crackers and a few waves of the rattle, the two overseeing 'umpires met to decide how many tanks would have been knocked out'. An observing American colonel complained the exercise was 'turrible' [*sic*] and inconsistent with the narratives, situation reports and marked maps being issued to assembled military attaches on a daily basis.[50]

In contrast, on 26 September 1937, the largest German exercises of the year culminated in an attack on defensive positions by 800 tanks and 400 aircraft, lasting over an hour. Amongst the numerous foreign dignitaries and military attaches who witnessed the attack, General Ironside was struck by the noise and intensity of the explosions, before acknowledging it showed 'what a force Germany had created in such a short time'. The acquisition of practical experience through realistic training was considered sufficiently worthy that the Commander of the German Armed Forces (Field Marshal von Blomberg), his Second-in-Command and the Army's Commander-in-Chief all actively participated in this exercise.[51] No senior British commander gained this kind of experience between 1936 and 1939; further training was considered unnecessary for generals well versed in the Army's fundamental principles. This accounts for the lack of advice on full-scale or skeleton exercises for corps formations in 1934 Training Regulations.[52]

Witnessing German manoeuvres in 1937 could and should have assisted British preparations for war, but there was no urgency or even desire to disseminate the information learnt. In mid-October 1937, Ironside complained in his diary: 'I sent in a report on what I had seen at the German manoeuvres. I understand that Belisha has read neither CIGS Deverell's report nor mine'.[53] Throughout the 1930s, British military attaches and access to Allied equivalents yielded little of value. 1936 Anglo-French information exchanges were abandoned after they were discovered to be of no value. The vague responses of French military attaches on infrastructure capability, never mind German tactics and strengths, also hampered 1938 conversations.[54] Uncertain of their own facilities, effective analysis of German capability proved beyond the French. Meanwhile British attaches, instead of seeking knowledge on German forces, were distracted by domestic issues; for example, in September 1937 Hore-Belisha asked the Military Attaché in Paris, Colonel F. Beaumont-Nesbitt, his opinion of CIGS Deverell whom he was considering replacing.[55] The failure to effectively utilize the military attaché system allowed the development of an inaccurate picture of German forces. In 1937, a Staff College continental war exercise woefully forecast German Army strength in 1940 as six armoured, one cavalry and 36 infantry divisions plus 13 army tank battalions.[56] During the France campaign the BEF actually faced 136 divisions, including ten Panzer divisions; this reality gap could have been reduced with more effective use of military attaches, which in turn would have encouraged greater realism in British pre-war training. Despite war looming, realism improved only slightly; for example, in 1938 brigade exercises 1st Royal Berkshire Regiment twice attacked with supporting tanks, 'although all, except one "Matilda" were of an age that raised smiles on the faces of the foreign military attaches who attended'.[57]

Although a lack of modern equipment frequently hampered training, volatile equipment demands did not help matters. Requirements escalated on four occasions between April 1938 and March 1939, from equipment for four regular infantry and one mobile division to equipment for 32 infantry divisions. Although the availability of 60 infantry tanks in August 1939, despite requirements for 1646, may be an extreme example, there can be little surprise the final pre-war progress report from the WO noted shortages across the board caused by inadequate production capacity.[58] A bad situation was compounded by a catastrophic reorganization of procurement procedures when, in early 1939, Hore-Belisha abolished the position of Master General of Ordnance, and its influential Army Council seat, but failed to establish a replacement, until the eve of hostilities. Once formed, the Ministry of Supply became exclusively responsible for weapon design, manufacture and procurement, with the Army restricted to stating how many divisions they wished to equip. The new system was so strict, the CIGS could only correspond with the Ministry of Supply through the War Office (a third party); a situation Hore-Belisha refused to overturn despite complaints. The Army's urgent request for 600,000 rounds of medium artillery ammunition in April 1939 was finally approved by the Treasury two weeks after war was declared, wasting a summer of potential training.[59]

With shortages prevalent throughout the Army, official historian J. Gibb has argued best practice involved the use of mock-ups in training because 'it was preferable to have symbolic tanks rather than none at all'. However, mock-ups can unwittingly legitimize incorrect tactics; for example, 1st Queen's Own Royal West Kent Regiment stretcher-bearer Ken Clarke recalled being taught in May 1939 to fire at wooden tanks with his Lee-Enfield rifle. Futile and dangerous, this misled future BEF participants about the vulnerability of armour and the effectiveness of rifle fire. The official history of training defines military training as 'the process of giving instruction or imparting military knowledge'. By using mock-ups the British Army exposed recruits to incorrect instruction and ineffective military knowledge; this self-inflicted error cost BEF personnel dearly in France 1940.[60]

Insufficient manpower was another factor which dramatically reduced realism in pre-war training. In September 1937, the War Office Committee on the Supply of Officers acknowledged the shortage of manpower and equipment meant 'training acquires a disconcerting atmosphere of unreality and "make-believe"'.[61] Inter-war commanders had little control over this perpetual deficiency. Reviewing Eastern Command in May 1937, General Ironside argued 'our training is going

to be just as poor this year as last', before later stating 'too much imagination was needed in training owing to a lack of manpower'. Army
regulations stated if a skeleton force replicated the dispersal and speed
of the force it represented, a company could represent a battalion without excessive unreality. However, constructive criticism from senior
officers became virtually impossible even before this level of manpower
deficiency. Although battalion strength in 1938 was supposed to be 28
officers and 763 men, several battalions in 4th Division had a strength
of only five officers and 300 men. In these circumstances the supervising area commander General Ironside conceded: 'With no artillery and
insufficient men to make up one brigade of infantry I simply haven't
the heart to push these people too hard'.[62] In 1937, manpower within
1st Royal Berkshire Regiment (4th Division) was so poor, numbers failed
to justify a training camp: 'Composite battalion and brigade exercises
were carried out from barracks'.[63] Large formation training was difficult
enough for inexperienced personnel, but when flags represented whole
units or pieces of equipment, it became virtually impossible for any
soldier to understand the practical complexities of combat such as communications, logistics or camouflage.

After the Munich crisis in September 1938, the Government allowed
TA units to recruit up to 30 per cent over establishment, causing a
massive influx of untrained personnel. This placed an unrealistic burden on the permanent training staff of TA units, particularly those
dispersed over considerable areas. A TA unit usually had a regular CO
or Adjutant assisted by a few sergeants, including a senior NCO, who
acted as instructors. However, rather than preserving a unit's combat
readiness, their peacetime role focused on everyday management of the
battalions' social clubs, maintaining men's interest and keeping the unit
alive. Inadequate facilities, equipment and, above all, instruction forced
the War Office in 1938 to circulate a critical memorandum submitted by
disgruntled anti-aircraft battery personnel in an effort to boost instruc-
tional standards.[64] By 1939, demand for instructors within Territorial
units was increasing exponentially, due to the introduction of new
equipment, ideas, recruits and the decision to send an expeditionary
force to France. However, in 1939, Brigadier R. Cherry, Commander
Royal Artillery 55th Division, acknowledged the 'small cadre of regular
personnel is hardly enough to train instructors for the first line units,
let alone those of the second line'. Cherry publicly appealed for further
investment in a pool of regular instructors 'for all Territorial Army units
so that sufficient NCOs and specialists may be trained for all eventuali-
ties'.[65] It is understandable that in a time of economic hardship in the

1930s the Government did not want to maintain wartime establishments. It is lamentable the Government failed to maintain sufficient
instructor capacity in order to restore, when required, highly trained
units to wartime establishment strength.

Training Exercises Without Troops (TEWTs) were used to minimize
manpower problems and maximize the impact of instructor-led training
through the collective analysis of military problems. Timothy Harrison
Place has argued TEWTs was flawed because participants remained
unable to train rank-and-file subordinates in peace or efficiently command them in combat.[66] Although accurate, this insufficiently empha-
sizes the practical benefits of training with troops, namely the ability to
identify mundane, yet essential, deficiencies overlooked by theoretical
assessment. In the 1936 Palestine campaign, it was only discovered after
sustained use of the infantry mortar that 'night-firing equipment was
found to be needed, and the spare parts bag proved to be inadequate'.
Furthermore, a unit's proficiency in crucial skills, such as camouflage
and night operations, was dependent on universal competence. Only
post-deployment to Palestine was it discovered that 'few battalions had
ever seen a mortar before', leading to emergency training.[67] The accessibility of TEWTs meant they were thought of favourably by British
Army commanders. Within his 1932 contribution to the Kirke Report,
Director of Military Training McNamara argued the prevalence of TEWTs
was correct, reports from WO TEWTs were of great value and that 'as
regards our actual curriculum of training in command there seems little
to improve on'.[68] However, given the choice, commanders invariably
chose the realism of training with troops over low-cost simulations. In
the semi-active service conditions of Waziristan, the commanders of
the Razmak, Bannu, Wana, and Mir Ali garrisons all independently concluded infrequent mobile training columns, rather than TEWTs, were
the best way to maintain regular troops' readiness for hostilities. Only
the Quetta Garrison in nearby Baluchistan favoured TEWTs, possibly
due to the presence of instructors and umpires at Staff College.[69]

British TEWTs over-generously allowed an hour's thinking time, their
German equivalents only a few minutes. Training designed to minimize
cost, time and facilities left British units, particularly the TA, uncompetitive compared to their German counterparts.[70] With large-scale,
combined arms exercises involving full-strength units an option seldom
even available to regulars overseas, it is difficult to identify unilateral
action other than TEWTs, which was open to Territorial battalions
restricted to UK service. Owing to difficulty procuring suitable countryside for exercises, many Territorial units devoted their officers' and

NCOs' entire allocation of four summer training weekends to TEWTs; a skeleton staff occupied rank-and-file with uncomplicated tasks, for example, musketry.[71] The failure of inter-war Territorials to experience practical exercises compelled Brigadier R. Cherry to complain in a 1939 article: 'Very few of the section and platoon leaders' in urban units 'have had the opportunity of acquiring an eye for country or learning to connect map and ground'. Although officers and occasionally NCOs developed problem-solving skills and an eye for country from participation in TEWTs, on the modern battlefield all ranks required these skills. The over-use of TEWTs throughout the Army caused a systemic disconnect between officers and rank-and-file. To counter this, some officers favoured weekend training which prioritized company skeleton exercises involving 'personnel down to section leaders on a simple scheme that includes movement on foot across unfamiliar country'.[72] However, the absence of a metric meant this advice went largely unheeded. British Commander Central Norwegian Expeditionary Force, Major General Carton de Wiart, highlighted the inevitable consequence; once combat operations began 'it was soon evident that the officers had little experience in handling men'.[73]

Individuals joining the Army as officer cadets soon learnt the duties of platoon commander were of secondary importance to the Army's determination to instil obedience, create the perfect private soldier and, once commissioned, imbue regimental tradition. Training Regulations 1934 made clear Cadet College training 'despite strong military bias, is primarily one of general education', within which only broad military principles were studied.[74] In 1938, Sandhurst Cadet W. Blaxland complained: 'We thus knew all about the follies of generals, while having only the vaguest notion of problems likely to confront the subaltern'.[75] David French has argued that RMC Sandhurst and RMA Woolwich, dealing almost exclusively with young men new to service life, produced young officers who were physically fit, who could perform polished drill, and who felt themselves to be members of an elite. Drill dominated the Sandhurst course in order to ensure future discipline and instinctive obedience to orders: 'Out of a total of 1,350 training hours, no less than 515 hours were spent "producing the private soldier cadet"'.[76] Operating in an educational bubble, with war looming ever closer, Sandhurst continued to consider discussions on tactics a superfluous distraction from intellectual lectures, foreign language courses and equitation. This was strictly enforced, for example, Cadet Blaxland noted: 'Platoon and section tactics appeared to be banned subjects, almost as if they were obscene'.[77]

The production of seemingly incomplete officers was not seen as a failing because the British operated a system of post-commission training in which commanders tailored recruits' tactical knowledge in accordance with their unit's requirements. Training Regulations 1934 explicitly stated: 'The young officer receives his military training after he had received his commission'.[78] Perfectly drilled and obedient Sandhurst graduates were incorrectly adjudged best suited to absorbing this information. This was compounded by new subalterns' military education being left to officers untrained in teaching others and untested on the newly mechanized army's procedures. With this inherently flawed system the establishment of any uniform metric became an impossibility as decentralized training led to uncoordinated variation, both in types of training and in timescale. Pre-war, Second Lieutenant C. Barker recalled how Sandhurst graduates were carefully briefed to keep a low profile and warned that for the first few months no other officer would talk to them in the mess during their acclimatization.[79] Having joined 2nd Buffs Regiment in July 1939, along with four other newly-commissioned officers, Second Lieutenant Blaxland discovered Lieutenant Colonel G. Hamilton 'did not believe in patronising young officers, and it was some time before he showed any sign of being aware of our existence'.[80] With war imminent, battalion commanders should not have squandered limited training time on institutional traditions. In complete contrast, three newly-commissioned subalterns at a battalion within 2nd Division were welcomed with a motivational speech from the CO. The importance of post-commission training was further enforced when, within one week of posting, one officer participated in a supplementary training course devised by the regiment with the sole purpose of 'training us to do things in the regimental style and not merely as we had been taught to do them at Sandhurst'.[81] The belief that the perfect private soldier could most easily absorb the lessons of further training was shown to be faulty when the officer failed the course examination, much to his CO's displeasure and potential risk to his subordinates.

Regulations stressed: 'It is essential that the military training of the young officer, particularly infantry officer, on joining his unit should be carefully organized'.[82] However, post-commission training programmes assumed extra importance because training of officer cadets was reduced to meet the requirements of the expanding Army. Second-year cadets should have been commissioned in mid-July and granted six weeks' leave before joining their regiment. Written exams were cancelled, leave was reduced to a fortnight and commissions dated

1 July 1939. Cadets who had completed one year (intermediates) were commissioned on 3 July 1939. Regardless of course duration, the pre-war syllabus at Sandhurst was incapable of producing a fully-trained officer. The wartime replacement Officer Cadet Training Units further reduced courses to as little as four months, but post-commission training remained critically important. Pre-war deficiencies continued; for example, despite 30 weeks at 170th MG OCTU, newly-commissioned Second Lieutenant E. Brown was still expected to learn battle tactics, the layout of a defensive position and the complexities of the Vickers machine-gun only after being posted to 2nd Middlesex Regiment in September 1941.[83] This illustrates how some training system flaws were deeply entrenched and persisted beyond the France campaign.

It was considered the duty of senior battalion officers to assist subordinates in the interpretation of *FSR* principles, military history and procedural points highlighted by training memoranda.[84] New subalterns were therefore at the mercy of their superiors' training whims, be they ceremonial, based on the Great War or incomprehensible. Despite looming war clouds in mid-July 1939, 2nd Buffs Regiment fully expected to be deployed to Jamaica for an overseas tour, and accordingly, concentrated subaltern training on the important task of colonial duty, of which the keystone was ceremonial.[85] In contrast, Second Lieutenant C. Barker was not passed fit for duty within 1st Gordon Highlanders until he had completed an intensive training programme, lasting several weeks, on the requirements of a Highland officer. This included the need to be correctly presented in the appropriate uniform, to be proficient in Highland dancing and to be well versed in the intricacies of piping and drumming, for many routine calls and orders were played on the pipes.[86] Once passed fit for duty, without approving his tactical knowledge, Barker was appointed a platoon commander.

Whenever uncertain what to teach new subalterns, senior officers fell back on their own training which invariably was not up-to-date. The junior officers of 2nd Buffs Regiment were trained for a conflict similar to World War I by long-serving officers and NCOs. Training in the recognition of toxic gases came from a WWI Gas Sergeant, who was also Provost Sergeant, whilst tactical training provided by the battalion second-in-command concentrated on matters of routine and administration in trench warfare.[87] In 1939, senior officers within 1st Gordon Highlanders based battalion training schedules 'on their experiences of the 1914–1918 war' during which 'an officer went to war with an ash walking stick and a .38 revolver'. Only after Dunkirk did many BEF veterans realize how dated were their training procedures and understanding of an officer's responsibilities; Second Lieutenant Barker reminisced 'we thought we were ready – how wrong we were'.[88]

During training, the organizing officer risked getting asked difficult questions and, consequently, their reputations; this deterred originality and risk-taking. Second Lieutenant Blaxland felt a pre-war TEWT on preparing a company position in defence was undermined by instructions to ignore the local topography since 'no proper war would ever be fought amid the banks that littered the Pembrokeshire countryside'.[89] Yet within weeks MTP No. 23 emphasized an 'eye for ground' as an essential attribute for all military commanders involved in tactical operations and one which 'can be acquired only by constant practice'.[90] Junior officers nevertheless were expected to imagine not only their troops and the terrain, but also the role of the Bren gun Carrier Platoon as a mobile rearguard, flank protection and a reconnaissance force, was never explained to them.[91]

Variation in British training contrasted with the German Army's more centralized approach. German officer cadets were already fully-trained private soldiers before attending cadet colleges; this allowed instructors to concentrate on tactical training and ensure cadets 'learned everything an infantry battalion commander had to know in any kind of pre-combat or combat situation'. Centralized tactical training guaranteed German junior officers were capable of fulfilling their obligations, were theoretically capable of replacing their superiors in battle and, perhaps most importantly, that the officer corps acted in unison to the same tactical doctrine.[92] Only after war was declared did the British begin to adopt a similar approach.

The geographic dispersal forced on infantry personnel by the destructive firepower of modern warfare meant junior officers required initiative to function effectively. David French has argued the 1932 Kirke Report clearly affirmed the British Army's need for autocratic control systems and the sacrosanct nature of senior officers' intentions; subordinate initiative was of minor importance.[93] Accordingly, failure to further develop the initiative of newly-commissioned officers was a minor defect of the training system, because in combat they were expected to obediently follow orders, not act independently. However, the Kirke Report was not as clear-cut as French suggests. With a preconceived idea that training and regimental duties were failing to develop the necessary skills within junior officers, Kirke urged the development of greater 'self-reliance and initiative' through training, before warning of dire consequences if this was not acted upon.[94] Using this interpretation, the failure of battalion commanders to develop the initiative of their subalterns was a much greater dereliction of duty than previously thought. The exposure of an absence of initiative amongst BEF junior officers in 1940, despite the Kirke Report's previous warnings, suggests a fundamental flaw in pre-war training.

The Army's default role of imperial policeman disadvantaged the future BEF by overly influencing formation size, organization, weaponry, dispersal and education of officers; preparation for continental conflict was a low priority. A metric standard was impossible because of the negligible input from *Field Service Regulations* and the War Office, the absence of input from the Inspector General of Training and the unique input of individual commanders. Without effective oversight, complacency insidiously undermined the planning, vigour and realism of training. Insufficient manpower, instructors and equipment were acknowledged weaknesses, but never overcome. TEWTs were worthwhile, cheap, focused training on achievable objectives, and ensured theoretical capability. However, the rank-and-file did not benefit directly, officers subsequently lacked practical experience of command and inaccurate views were inadvertently indoctrinated on the reliability of communications, speed and clarity in war. No one element of training gave officers the skills they needed to command effectively in combat. Sandhurst produced perfectly drilled private soldiers rather than capable junior officers. Post-commission training was variable, undervalued, and failed to develop initiative within newly-commissioned subalterns. Staff College was more concerned with creating future generals than disseminating skills necessary for a modern battlefield. The failure to reinvigorate unrealistic, piecemeal, varied training in the pre-war period meant these problems continued in the BEF.

The BEF which deployed to France in September 1939 was the embodiment of pre-war training policy; it has attracted the attention of historians ever since. The official campaign history, written by L.F. Ellis, has argued the BEF extensively trained during the Phoney War and vastly improved its capability. Ellis argued 'training was vigorously pursued in so far as time could be spared from front-line duties and work on defences'. Furthermore, many BEF units supposedly gained valuable experience in the Maginot Line, whilst Territorials participated in 'a balanced programme of training'. Ellis concluded that by May 1940, the BEF 'was in good health and ready for the coming fight, fitter and better trained than it had been when it landed in France'.[95] Modern historians have questioned this assessment of the campaign and recognized that the BEF collapse was partially self-inflicted by their Phoney War training methods, or lack of them. According to David French, the 'BEF failed to take advantage of the lull in operations in the winter of 1939–40 to train for the campaign they actually fought'.[96] French argued a failure to overcome practical difficulties, a complacent lack of realism in training and an insufficient number of large formation exercises left the BEF severely under-prepared. Furthermore, those most in need of development, the Territorial units, were the most likely to be diverted to other duties. Hugh Sebag-Montefiore has argued that the BEF under-utilized eight relatively quiet months because of the numerous distractions of Phoney War, many of which proved attractive to young men on their first overseas trip. Consequently 'many British soldiers were more interested in making the most of the "facilities" offered by the French and improving their living conditions' than in correcting their lack of effective pre-war training.[97]

After Germany annexed Czechoslovakia in March 1939, war appeared imminent, compelling the Government to order the transformation of the Army from a force designed for imperial policing to a largely conscript army capable of modern warfare. With only the faintest understanding of the implications for training, the TA doubled, reservists were recalled and conscripts enlisted; British Army strength increased from 645,000 men in April 1939 to 1,065,000 on 3 September 1939, yet very few of these new recruits would serve in the BEF.[98] Brian Bond has argued the General Staff accepted the Government's measures philosophically: 'True, in the short term these measures would actually reduce the army's efficiency but at least the most chaotic period might be muddled through before the outbreak of war'.[99] This fails to recognize that the expansion of the Army, which was a necessary evil, was badly handled, disrupted training, diluted fighting capability and wasted months of preparatory time.

The training literature of the British Army was also transformed in the late summer and early autumn of 1939, as the War Office gradually imposed a standard system of training which was more rigorous and regimented than the individual efforts of senior officers. The process was complicated by the multiple training documents within which the metric was disseminated, as well as the slow formulation of WO expectations. Training standards considered acceptable as late as July 1939 were considered unacceptable as early as September 1939.

The 1935 edition of *Field Service Regulations* was still in force in summer 1939 and was the foundation upon which all subsequent training literature was built. It was designed around eight military principles, and contained no detailed examples of manoeuvres or when to enact them.[100] The importance of *FSR* as a training tool was reinforced in September 1939, when it was supplemented by the publication of Military Training Pamphlet No. 23, which contained the latest ideas on subjects dealt within *FSR*. Individual copies of MTP No. 23 were distributed to every officer and warrant officer, further emphasizing the importance of *FSR* and ensuring widespread dissemination of its principles of war. Half of the pamphlet was devoted to general principles, including simple explanations of why qualities such as leadership were needed in warfare. The second half of the pamphlet gave short descriptions of the fighting arms of the Army and their characteristics. On training specifically, it stated best practice would include the development of physical ability, mental initiative, skill capability and field-craft techniques necessary for survival on the battlefield; the pamphlet remained devoid of details throughout.[101] Written by WO staff in summer 1939 under the direction of CIGS Gort, it is impossible to believe the absence of detailed guidance was an oversight. Whilst it was important that the Army based its training on sound principles, it was not the duty of junior officers and NCOs to interpret guidance or even organize training according to generalized WO schedules. Another motive may have been CIGS Gort's desire not to infringe the right of the BEF Commander-in-Chief (ironically himself) to direct training as they saw fit.

The gradual realization that a training metric was necessary was most evident in the shift in tone and content between ATM No. 23 published in July 1939 and ATM No. 24 published in September 1939. ATM No. 23 laid out the training agenda for the 1939/40 period, in a pocket guide distributed to every officer in the British Army. The memorandum highlighted the War Office's belated recognition that in the event of war there would be no time for higher training of commanders and staffs of formations. Consequently, over the next 12 months, the WO planned to test the combat readiness of II Corps HQ and at least one other specially assembled Corps HQ, by holding an indoor headquarters exercise, including outdoor reconnaissance, at Camberley or Minley Manor. The WO hoped to practice 'the organization and movement of a Corps headquarters, particularly in the withdrawal', notably 'The control of the administrative and other units in the rear area of Corps and in the railhead area'. The WO also instructed the regional Commands of Aldershot, Eastern, Northern and Southern to similarly test divisional formations: 'These exercises will be repeated until all regular (except 1st and 2nd) and all original Territorial divisional commanders and staffs (the latter augmented as necessary) have been exercised in at least one such exercise'.[102]

Produced by the Army Council, ATM No. 23 was clearly written with an eye on long-term development of the Army rather than imminent hostilities. The clearest example is the prioritization of militia training over the TA, not only in training on 'the use of weapons and ground', but in the layout of the memorandum as well. The majority of militia would not participate in the France campaign, but as the Army needed expanding rapidly, their training was considered worthy of investment. ATM No. 23 urged units to prioritize movement by road exercises, junior officer training, map reading and physical training, but the tone was conciliatory and advisory; for example, 'it is not yet fully appreciated that this [physical] training should be contained throughout a soldier's service'.[103] Glaring omissions included a failure to prioritize night training, or complex combined arms exercises which would prove crucial once operations began.

Published in September 1939 by the Army Council and provided to all generals, ATM No. 24 contained a transformation in tone and training policy. It renewed the authority of generals by delegating responsibility for disseminating information on, and enforcing a new metric of, 18 topics for platoon, company and battalion training; these ranged from sentry duty to elementary infantry tactics.[104] This was in complete contrast to the May 1932 announcement by Director of Military Training McNamara that senior officers should restrict their involvement in training to TEWTs, because time should not be 'wasted on minor tactics which is the function of smaller people to deal with'.[105] It is questionable whether such fundamental training guidance should have been restricted to such a select group of senior officers, especially as they would not be organizing it and, more crucially, had failed to ensure the integrity of similar training in the pre-war period. However, the Army Council responded to the sudden realization that elements of training were falling short, with the determination that generals required much more prescriptive guidance, in order to control their Commands better. ATM No. 24 demanded improvement after criticizing excessive drill, increasing risk of sloppiness in turnout, inadequate camouflage skills and complacency over digging positions; for example, 'Troops in contact with the enemy or threatened by air attack must be taught to dig themselves in as soon as the tactical situation permits'.[106]

The first few months of hostilities saw a multitude of changes to training policy, as guidance became increasingly based on the short-term. In September 1939, the War Office instructed higher formation HQs to hold exercises once a week, varying from 'two hour exercises designed to make each member of the staff familiar with his war role, to more elaborate exercises which may last a whole day and in which signals will take part'. For divisions still based in England in October 1939, including the majority of Territorial formations which would join the BEF, the WO held two separate TEWTs for syndicates consisting of a divisional commander, part of his staff, and certain subordinate commanders. '*Withdrawal and Defence*' was held twice in the Cheltenham area during October, each time for five syndicates. '*Attack*' was held in the Winchester area, once in October for two syndicates, and twice during November, each time for four syndicates.[107]

Within the numerous sources of guidance there was surprisingly little practical advice to commanders about how to adapt to a wartime environment. ATM No. 24 offered common-sense advice on the increased dispersal of formation HQs: 'Corps, division and brigade headquarters will not be grouped in one building, but dispersed in the towns or areas where they are located'. Having failed to prioritize night training even in July 1939, there was a sudden realization that war did not occur during set hours. In response, the September 1939 ATM advised units, particularly urban units, they would not be capable of exploiting darkness 'without thorough and regular training in night work'.[108] This was reinforced when October guidance stated sleeping by day and working by night required several consecutive nights of training.[109] This common-sense guidance should have been in place long before war was declared.

A metric standard of training was finally established in October 1939, when ATM No. 25 was issued to every officer by the WO, with guidelines on collective training for brigade and division size formations. It listed 18 types of operation, each considered important for modern warfare, which a formation was expected to be capable of; these included an army/air exercise, 'a relief in trench warfare' and 'taping out a defensive position'.[110] With so many competing demands on manpower, and the order of training left to the CO's discretion, many formations were lulled into training for the easiest operation first. It is interesting to note that post-Dunkirk this training metric was retained; in June 1940, 2nd Queen's Royal Regiment, based in Palestine, was ordered to intensify their training for modern warfare using ATM No. 25 as guidance. The first exercise they carried out was to practise a trench relief.[111] Not until 1942 did the British Army attempt to create a minimum combat capability with the introduction of battle drills.

In addition to assimilating numerous sources of WO guidance into a single training programme, units also had to incorporate the competing guidance of Commander-in-Chief Gort, created entirely independently at GHQ. On their arrival in September 1939, all units received instructions from BEF Chief of General Staff Lieutenant General Pownall informing them of the need to remain in constant readiness to undertake active operations and to complete a programme of defence works. Beyond these immediate duties, the document highlighted the importance of using the delay in active operations to improve training: 'Subject to this, the Commander-in-Chief wishes every opportunity to be taken for training'. The scenarios the BEF was urged to train for throughout the winter were 'a defensive battle against a German attack supported by strong air forces and armoured and mobile formations' and, secondly, 'offensive operations against fortified positions and field defences'. Recognizing that a German invasion was more probable than Allied offensive operations, GHQ stated 'such training must not however be undertaken at the expense of training in mobile warfare'.[112] GHQ clearly understood the mobile nature of the threat and the need for additional training, yet this message weakened as it progressed down the chain of command, leading to a variety of outcomes.

Gort issued training guidance to the BEF, partly to explain his expectations and partly because he did not believe the Army Council had authority over him or his force. In peacetime, upon appointment by the War Secretary (acting on the advice of the Army Council), general ranking officers received their orders from the Army Council. In wartime, the C-in-C was appointed directly by the War Cabinet, and was therefore outside the jurisdiction of the Army Council and its orders. Hore-Belisha failed to resolve this procedural conundrum in the pre-war period, leading to an inevitable confrontation when interests diverged. In spring 1940, when the Army Council ordered Gort to prepare 5th Division for deployment to Scandinavia, Gort loyally complied with the order, but did so under protest. Although this was an unexpected and potentially grievous loss of manpower, Gort officially protested because 'he had been appointed by the War Cabinet and he could not recognize the authority of the Army Council to give him orders'.[113] If the C-in-C believed Army Council instructions did not apply to him, it demonstrates how the establishment of GHQ created two competing centres of authority, neither quite in tune with the other.

Oversight and enforcement of the training metric was carried out by C-in-C Gort, War Office staff, the Staff Duties and Training Branch of GHQ and unit commanders; in each case flawed oversight allowed variations and deficiencies in BEF training to continue. Oversight by Gort was hampered by his inability to move beyond his undoubted expertise in battlefield tactics, which undermined attempts to ensure the BEF in its entirety was ready to resist invasion. At a training conference on

29 October 1939, Lieutenant General Alan Brooke revealed to those in attendance 'the C-in-C was anxious that the dumping of rations and ammunition in blockhouses should be confined to the essential minimum. He suggested that 3 days rations would be adequate'.[114] Brooke noted in his diary on 22 November 1939: 'he [Gort] just fails to be able to see the big picture and is continually returning to those trivial details which counted a lot when commanding a battalion, but which should not be the main concern of a Commander-in-Chief'.[115] As an example, on 25 November Gort, CGS Pownall and various staff officers visited 8th Brigade HQ, where 'Gort gave a short dissertation on Fighting Patrols' in which he discussed how they should be 'armed'; only after this was Gort 'taken to see a waterlogged trench' and its consequences on construction and training, which had been the declared purpose of his visit.[116]

The ability of the CIGS (as first military member of the AC) to oversee BEF training was hampered by organizational, procedural and political issues. Pre-war, the Directorate of Military Operations and Intelligence, the Directorate of Staff Duties and the Directorate of Military Training all reported directly to the CIGS. Once war commenced, the increasing workload led to the three directorates being split into six departments, reporting in turn to three new ACIGS who in turn reported to the new VCIGS. Although it was impossible for one CIGS to oversee in detail all WO work once war started, the new links in the chain of command made the CIGS more detached from the details of military training. Furthermore, the combined SD & T Branch at GHQ had to report back to two different Directors and two separate ACIGS, further increasing the possibility of overlapping jurisdiction and subsequent indecision.[117]

During the Phoney War the CIGS, Lieutenant General Edmund Ironside, visited France over a dozen times, but they were nearly all for strategic conferences with the French High Command; if a visit to the BEF did occur, it almost always assumed the appearance of an end of visit distraction. On 20 November 1939, when Hore-Belisha was on his fateful pill-box tour of the BEF, Ironside was in Paris in conference with Finance Minister Paul Reynaud. Consequently, when the dispute between GHQ and Hore-Belisha (known as the Pill-Box Affair) began, PM Chamberlain judged Ironside to be sufficiently independent to be able to provide an impartial view of frontier defences; Ironside was so detached from the BEF, he informed Chamberlain he had 'only seen it once some weeks ago and I shall be able to see the difference'.[118] Ironside's ability to advise on BEF training during the Phoney War was reduced to instinctive judgments from snapshot visits.

Once the BEF deployed to France, the Staff Duties & Training branch of GHQ provided a two-way liaison service, returning data from unit inspections to the DMT for incorporation into training policy, and informing BEF formations of DMT advice. As SD & T had almost exclusive responsibility for inspecting BEF units, it was very rare that the DMT overruled them or acted unilaterally due to a lack of independent evidence. A rare example of this occurred in November 1939, after recently published photographs in the press showed BEF convoys with vehicles too closely and evenly spaced in violation of standard operating procedure. In one particularly provocative photograph, the WO despaired as 'fifteen heavy lorries on the move occupy road space of 250 yards, and this in broad daylight'.[119] The War Office unilaterally included within the November ATM a reminder of the need for convoy discipline, but as usual relied on SD & T and unit commanders to enforce it.

On the infrequent occasions when a representative of the DMT visited the BEF to discuss policy, they accompanied SD & T personnel on inspections. On 16 November 1939, Major Fitt (WO) and GSO3 (SD & T) visited 2nd Royal Warwickshire Regiment at Rumegies: 'CO showed officers complete layout of Bn, party visited a pillbox, breastworks, the anti-tank obstacles & saw the arrangements for billeting, feeding & bathing the troops'.[120] Despite the lack of training observed, SD & T were happy with the openness provided; in contrast, it was considered unworthy of recording in the 2nd Royal Warwickshire Regiment War Diary. Having already been inspected during November 1939 by C-in-C Gort, HRH Duke of Gloucester, Colonel of Regiment Tomes, Corps and Divisional Commanders, an inspection by a Major and a Captain held no fear, particularly as the 2nd Royal Warwickshire Regiment had been able to perfect a tour that showed it in the best light.[121]

Excluding the office administrator, a complement of one Lieutenant Colonel and two Captains within SD & T carried out OFSTED-style inspections throughout the BEF and were largely responsible for overseeing the implementation of training policy. BEF units ranging from battalions to corps were visited, but inspections were not systematic in their destination (unit) or objective (reason for visiting). With only three staff, visits rarely lasted more than a day and, in reality, daylight hours only. The size of the BEF meant a battalion might only get a few hours' inspection during the entire Phoney War. Nevertheless, training was supervised by observation and face-to-face discussion because as the SD & T War Diary makes clear, it was 'easier to clear up problems by visiting than by telephoning'. The overriding principle was to liaise and inform, rather than infringe the authority of a CO. This was reinforced by the woeful absence of authority within the inspecting team capable of enforcing training procedures. The senior GSO1 liaised with the WO, the Operation branch of GHQ and the RAF regarding training policy and replacements; the GSO2 was tasked with overseeing all training courses, schools and facilities, as well as liaising with all formations and technical fighting arms on training; the duties of the GSO3 included war establishments, equipment, replacements and liaison with GHQ A, Q and technical branches.[122] These duties would have proved impossible for any three individuals, but the relatively low ranks of these training experts meant they were continuously vulnerable to being ignored by senior officers who thought they knew better. The under-manned and under-ranked SD & T establishment implies the higher echelons of the British Army were in denial about the need to supervise the implementation of training by senior officers; the same officers who failed in the pre-war period.

The impact of SD & T could be significant and have a visible effect on BEF training guidelines. An example of this supervision occurred on 19 December 1939, when the GSO2 observed an army/air exercise in which the RAF simulated low-flying attacks on 6th Infantry Brigade convoys. I Corps Standing Orders for action in case of air attack during mechanical movement by road in 1939 stated: 'Troops will debus and all who can will also engage attacking aircraft with fire. No rifle fire, however, will be committed while still on the move'.[123] However, having observed separate attacks on the front, middle and rear of the 6th Infantry Brigade convoys, the GSO2 of SD & T reported: 'In each case the attack was over before the men got out of their trucks, and they had nothing to use their rifles on'; in some cases 'the attack was over before the last lorry had halted'. With the convoy travelling at 20 mph, with 15 vehicles to the mile, the GSO2 found the physical impossibility of the I Corps Standing Order was compounded by orders exclusive to 6th Infantry Brigade, which meant 'vehicles were not allowed to halt on their own; they had to wait for the signal from the commander. Rear lorries cannot see this; their only signal is to see the vehicles in front halt and the men jump out. This routine is not laid down by I Corps'. Although the GSO2 concluded the best way of avoiding low-flying attack was wide dispersion, the SD & T Branch advised formations that BEF training needed to change, in particular 'If an attack is made, drive on. There is not time to halt and take cover ... The fact applies even if each vehicle is allowed to halt on its own'; units were also informed their troops' best chance of finding the target was by firing from a moving vehicle.[124]

In complete contrast to the productive findings of SD & T, the participating Brigadier, N. Irwin, grumbled: 'The air attacks were not made in the anticipated way' and consequently 'it is suggested that the RAF have only learnt wrong lessons from the Exercise'; Irwin believed neither his men nor his procedures were at fault. Unknown to SD & T, Irwin unilaterally used the exercise to test the varied procedures of his subordinate battalions; 1st Royal Welch Fusiliers believed every soldier should debus and defend the convoy, whilst 2nd Durham Light Infantry believed only 25 per cent should take such action, the rest seeking cover. Despite Irwin being personally inclined towards the 2nd Durham Light Infantry method, the variation remained because the test had proved inconclusive and it was not worth infringing subordinate commanders' independence.[125] Clearly the BEF should have had one standard operating procedure, yet the variation between two battalions within the same brigade shows the impossibility of establishing a BEF-wide metric whilst accepting CO independence and restricting prescriptive guidelines to sub-battalion units.

The SD & T recommended changes to best practice when under aerial attack were sound, but Phoney War training failed to sufficiently inculcate these changes into the BEF, even within 2nd Division whose units participated in the decisive army/air exercise. On 14 May 1940, during the retreat from the Dyle, the War Diary of the 2nd Royal Norfolk Regiment, 2nd Division, noted: 'About midday contact with the enemy was made ... low-flying aircraft, which dropped a number of bombs'.[126] The War Diary makes no further comment about this incident; however, in an account of being bombed a short distance to the west of the Dyle, Captain R. Hastings, the second-in-command D Company, 2nd Royal Norfolk Regiment, revealed despite strict orders preventing trucks stopping and troops debussing: 'I was horrified to see that a large number of men were getting out of the trucks, and scattering to both sides of the road'.[127] Clearly some fault must lie with the battalion's officers whose failure to emphasize the importance of orders strongly enough led to incorrect procedures being followed and an increased risk to life. Fault also lies with GHQ who organized Phoney War training and failed to ensure flaws in training were irreversibly overcome. MTP No. 23 had stressed adequate training required a British soldier to 'be so practised that he will instinctively use his weapons to the best advantage'.[128] This required frequent practice, yet ATM No. 25 informed unit commanders, with regards to collective training: 'Arrangements must be made for troops to be attacked by low-flying aircraft on at least one occasion'.[129] One army/air exercise was insufficient in reversing pre-war neglect of collective training and denied inspectors the opportunity to assess units for improvement, leading to incidents such as that which occurred with 2nd Royal Norfolk Regiment.

BEF corps commanders retained significant responsibility for organizing training schedules, but instead of enforcing GHQ instructions, they used their authority to amend and even ignore them. GHQ intended all BEF infantry brigades and attached troops, and particularly newly arrived divisions, to be withdrawn in rotation to training areas in the rear to carry out continuous training, especially brigade exercises. For formations in forward areas, the allotment of time for construction of defensive positions and training depended on local conditions and remained at the discretion of corps commanders. GHQ was unsure how long the Phoney War would last, but hoped every unit would have completed progressive training programmes over a minimum of an 'eight weeks period' during which a minimum of 50 per cent of available time should be dedicated to training, and a maximum of 50 per cent dedicated to construction of defences.[130]

Almost immediately, BEF Corps diverged from GHQ's intended training regime, due to the obligation of assuming defensive positions along the Franco-Belgian border and the prioritization of the construction of frontier defences. At the II Corps training conference on 29 October 1939, the 'programme of allotment of training areas was agreed', but it was decided 'that Fd Coys RE should train in a RE Camp for a period of 14 days only per Fd Coy' rather than 21 days with the rest of II Corps. This was because at a previous Corps Commanders Conference the Chief Engineer of II Corps had stated that 'he doubted whether Fd Coys could be spared for as long as 3 weeks from the present work'.[131] The decision to allow only three weeks in training areas went against GHQ instructions, and the absence of any attached Royal Engineers went against ATM No. 25, which stated a false reality would be created during training unless all arms were involved.[132] Given his significant involvement with the WO until spring 1940, it is not surprising that Lieutenant General R. Adam's first training instruction to III Corps, once deployed in France, included the order 'Infantry Brigades must always be accompanied by proportion of other arms in all schemes and exercises'.[133] The training programme of II Corps was further restricted when, after organizing and sub-allotting training areas for an intensification of training in November 1939, the number of defensive positions

II Corps was obliged to create and man increased. The November War Diary for II Corps summarized 'the move of 4 Div into the line rendered impossible the original intention of sending each Div back for training in turn. The most that can now be done is to withdraw one Infantry Brigade at a time for a short exercise involving movement in MT'.[134] Despite a familiarity with WO instructions and an enthusiasm for training, the deployment of III Corps to France in March 1940 prevented former VCIGS Adam meeting GHQ expectations. The threat of imminent active operations severely hampered the training programme of III Corps during the Phoney War; for example, all subordinate units were put on at least six hours' notice between 11–22 April 1940, before III Corps allowed 'Normal activities including training to be resumed and all troops to return to their normal stations'.[135] Delays further compounded the impossibility of ensuring all BEF units completed a progressive training programme, as recommended by GHQ, before the Germans invaded on 10 May.

Despite their immense control over training, the oversight capability of Corps HQs was as flawed as other forms of inspection. During the period 1–9 May, 44th Division recorded how 131st Brigade and 132nd Brigade were involved in the preparation of defences along the Belgian frontier, whilst 133rd Brigade was based in the St Pol area for training purposes, 'including firing on Dannes ranges, sending down one bn at a time'.[136] III Corps supervised training by demanding weekly reports from divisional headquarters on the location, dates and nature of training exercises for units in rear areas. For units involved in work on defences on the front-line, III Corps requested 'a short report on the system of training being carried out in divisional areas as opportunity permits'.[137] However, despite the supervision of III Corps, and the exclusive use of training areas for 133rd Brigade, subordinate battalions did not fully utilize the training opportunities. According to Second Lieutenant P. Hadley, from 6–9 May 1940, 4th Royal Sussex Regiment carried out guard duty and pioneer work, from which the Battalion returned 'somewhat regretfully for I gathered that the work had not been exactly arduous'.[138] The loss of III Corps and 44th Division original war diaries for May makes it hard to ascertain whether the higher echelons of III Corps were aware of these training failures. However, it is clear there was a failure of oversight throughout the chain of command, but particularly at corps level, where it appears falsified reports were being accepted without question.

As their reputation depended most on the performance of their subordinate fighting units, corps commanders allowed the intensity of oversight to diminish as the distance to the front-line increased. In February 1940 the WO Committee on Repair in the Field

> found a general absence of 'control' in the sense in which that word is used in industry. None of the three corps concerned with repairs had within their own organization any clear and specialized means of controlling, coordinating, directing and reviewing in the interests of economy and efficiency, the activities of their several workshops and stores in combination.[139]

The BEF had no means of reviewing together, as a single repair organization, the resources of all three corps. To compound this, each corps commander had little interest in ensuring rear-echelon units were fulfilling their primary function effectively and no motivation to ensure they had sufficient combat training to defend themselves.

Divisional Headquarters had a role in directing training and overseeing the day-to-day organization of training. It was important that this was effective as divisions were the main fighting formation of the BEF and would manoeuvre together in combat. When senior members of GHQ, such as Lieutenant Colonel Bridgeman, identified Major General Montgomery as 'the best Div Commander' because he trained subordinates 'incessantly', they were not referring to some strange policy of training 24/7.[140] Instead they were highlighting Montgomery's determination to utilize any opportunity for training, his use of repetition to determine best practice, and the evacuation of 3rd Division via Dunkirk more intact than any other. David French has highlighted how the independence given to senior officers led to divisional variation in the 1939/40 winter, for example, 3rd Division held no fewer than four divisional exercises, each of which lasted for several days; 2nd Division conducted only two short movement exercises.[141] Analysis has shown this variation continued in the more routine training instructions within these divisions. In 2nd Division, the prioritization of constructing defences meant subordinate battalions in the front-line were obliged to provide training 'the equivalent of one day per week per man' only. Although 3rd Division had similar defensive commitments, it was considered important specialists such as Bren-gunners and signallers did 'not dig for more than half a day; the remainder of the day will be spent on specialist training'. Even in the front-line, this directive ensured 3rd Division specialists were guaranteed 2.5 days training a week, whereas 2nd Division suggested only a single day. Both divisions expected subordinate units posted to training areas to utilize the opportunity by ensuring a full eight hours training by all ranks each weekday. However, 2nd Division virtually prohibited complex training by ordering: 'Greatest economy will be exercised in the use of MT which will undergo thorough maintenance during the period out of the line'; instead it encouraged more basic, stationary and organizationally-easier training, such as 'grenade training, bayonet fighting and patrolling'.[142] In contrast, motor-transport was regularly available within 3rd Division, and its use was encouraged, allowing subordinate battalions such as 4th Royal Berkshire Regiment to carry out progressively more complex manoeuvres involving distances of 8, 30 and 60 miles over successive nights.[143] This repetition led to improvements in standard operating procedure; for example, the 3rd Division exercise from 6–8 March 1940 discovered moving at night using 'only underneath tail lights' prevented detection by enemy aircraft, but did not delay deployment.[144]

Divisions relied on superior formations for guidance on the characteristics of future operations in order to oversee training effectively. However, the failure of the BEF to fully appreciate how mechanization had transformed the speed and mobility possible in warfare, particularly with the use of concentrated armour and air power, forced Carton de Wiart, head of the British Mission to Poland, to conclude: 'We were still far from being alive to its full capabilities'.[145] Information was not always available, yet when divisions used their internal resources, for example, the investigations of 2nd Division's GSO3(I) into Belgian defences and infrastructure, I Corps reprimanded them for the improper and unauthorized use of resources. Further information gathering ended, but this did not prevent 2nd Division despairing: 'It is incredible how little useful information that is up-to-date and reliable GHQ and Corps have obtained'.[146] In contrast, with the encouragement of Lieutenant General Brooke, on 11 March 1940, Montgomery assembled all the officers of 3rd Division in a hall in Seclin for a two hour lecture on the impending campaign, and the result of recent exercises. Amongst the 1000 plus audience, many junior officers benefited from the exposition of the situation, a detailed forecast of how the battle would develop and an explanation of the final training programmes that would be undertaken by 3rd Division to meet envisaged contingencies.[147] Montgomery's predictions were not entirely accurate, but they served a purpose by giving training direction and reducing surprise. Generals who were less self-confident or merely less well-informed, having deployed to France in spring 1940, were less able to prepare their subordinates. Post-Dunkirk, Major General H. Curtis submitted a report on the operations of Polforce and 46th Division, which stated that the

Germans had won not merely because of the greater weight of their material, but because of 'surprise in the use of new tactical methods'.[148]

Both in regards to exercises and general training guidance, the willingness of brigadiers to intervene in subordinate affairs varied between divisions and even within divisions. Observing a wayward platoon circumventing the physical exertions of a route-march in full-kit on 8 March 1940, Brigadier C. Woolner, 8th Brigade personally intervened to rebuke the misguided platoon, explain the reasoning for the exercise and to ensure the exercise achieved its objective; this chance but critical oversight was followed up at battalion and company levels within the subordinate battalion.[149] In comparison, during a Phoney War exercise involving regulars of the 1st Queen's Own Royal West Kent Regiment, 10th Brigade, Brigadier E. Barker and his staff officers interviewed a rifle section of approximately nine men on their destination. According to stretcher-bearer Ken Clarke 1st Queen's Own Royal West Kent Regiment:

> We replied that we had no idea and the Brigadier then asked if we knew what the object of the exercise was. Again we all replied that we didn't and so he said 'as far as you are concerned you might just as well be marching in the opposite direction'. Our combined reply of 'Yes Sir' gave him cause for concern as he shrugged his shoulders and told us to carry on.[150]

Brigadier Barker may have noted the unit and reprimanded the commander at a later date or he may have considered it unworthy of action, but either way, these men never had the benefit of an explanation as to what went wrong, or how they could avoid a repetition in the future. For a rifle section not to know what they were doing, or why they were doing it, suggests a lack of guidance from their platoon commander and to some extent his superiors.

Within the more mundane areas of army life, brigade policy could vary on something as fundamental as routine on Sundays. 6th Brigade had a strict policy that 'Sunday and one half day per week will be regarded as non-working days' during which no training or alternative duties could take place, with 'the exception that maintenance of defences recognizes no holidays'.[151] Although 5th Brigade also recognized the need for a rest-day, on Sundays it was expected 'Companies will do 30 mins arms drill and 15 mins saluting drill', and it was encouraged that COs inspect positions and billets on this day, rather than divert companies from training during the week.[152] This approach may not have been more efficient, as troops may have been more tired during the week, but it highlights how each commander independently attempted to maximize training potential rather than follow standard guidelines. The absence of extensive training oversight by inspection systems could not always be compensated by brigade headquarters. In the untrained labour divisions, there was a sparsity of brigade staff; for example, 36th Brigade HQ consisted of two regular officers (an Acting Brigadier and a Major) and three newly-commissioned officers including Second Lieutenant C. Gilbert who, whilst attached from 6th Queen's Own Royal West Kent Regiment, had the acting rank of Captain. Such a small staff forced the two regular officers to carry out much of the reconnaissance for training areas, rather than concentrate on training oversight.[153]

At battalion level, E. Sixsmith has argued many COs were of a good standard, although there were still some, particularly Territorials, who had no ideas beyond the barrack square.[154] In fact, the monotonous and unrealistic nature of peacetime regimental service meant all home-based battalion commanders were in need of guidance and oversight as they adapted to wartime conditions. The response of noted machine-gunner Lieutenant Colonel Haydon to a forthcoming inspection was to double white-wash kerb-stones, intensify guard duty drill and have a large sign painted (Second Battalion, The Middlesex Regiment). On arrival at Roubaix barracks, the unidentified General gave Lieutenant Colonel Haydon a 'severe dressing down' and refused to continue the inspection of the battalion until the sign had been painted over.[155] Without encouragement battalion commanders were the command link least likely to be proactive in their actions; a laissez-faire attitude of Lieutenant Colonel Hamilton, which had previously manifested in ignoring new subalterns, and accepting without question ceaseless pioneer duties for his 2nd Buffs Regiment, on 10 May allowed him to read a novel in the orderly room, thus 'letting everyone get on with their jobs'.[156] With their view of training largely restricted to their own battalion, COs also were least likely to recognize the need for improvements. On 28 May 1940, when observing advancing German infantry making good use of terrain, Lieutenant Colonel Birch, 2nd Bedfordshire and Hertfordshire Regiment, noted only similarities with his own troops' procedures.[157] This symbolizes the misguided view held by many contemporaries that there was little to choose between BEF and German training. Regardless of their Commander's skills-set, battalions were extremely vulnerable to the fluctuating availability of assistance from superiors. Despite the best efforts of Lieutenant Colonel Fane de Salis only two companies of 1/8th Middlesex Regiment experienced, via brigade training, the role of a machine-gun battalion and 'the administrative difficulties connected with work in the field'.[158] Having been transferred from 50th Division to 5th Division and back again and trained alongside 15th, 17th and 150th brigades, the remainder of the battalion had been restricted to platoon and company training for the entire Phoney War.

Nevertheless, a CO could make a difference to his command through internally organized training, if he was sufficiently determined. On 26 January 1940, 7th Worcestershire Regiment '"A" and "B" Coys fired 5 [rounds] per man with rifle & one magazine per bren'; the remaining battalion personnel repeated this training programme on 30 and 31 January.[159] There was no shortage of small arms ammunition within the BEF, and to emphasize this, on 14 April 1940, 4th Royal Berkshire Regiment headquarters instructed its rifle companies: 'Practice will not be sacrificed for the lack of ammunition. If the present allotment is insufficient notice will be given to Bn HQ'.[160] Although Lieutenant Colonel Bull had been appointed in February 1940 to reinvigorate 4th Royal Berkshire Regiment, Lieutenant Colonel Parkes had assumed command of 7th Worcestershire Regiment in similar circumstances in September 1939, so vigour should not have been an issue. During the cold 1939/40 winter, musketry was an unpopular activity, and required the determined efforts of a CO to enthuse subordinates to utilize every opportunity rather than train for adequate proficiency. This was especially the case as generals were unlikely to oversee battalion musketry, despite ATM No. 24 delegating overall responsibility for some sub-battalion training to them.

Although the War Office acknowledged the Territorial Army faced numerous challenges during the pre-war period it did not accept these would undermine training of Territorials joining the BEF, or that capability would be significantly inferior to the standard of regular units. The War Office commented in July 1939: 'The duplication of the Territorial Army and the consequent lack of equipment available for training has made the task of unit commanders exceedingly difficult. Despite this the standard of training reached by all ranks has been satisfactory'.[161] Commander-in-Chief Gort was less contented with the combat capability of BEF Territorials, because pre-war training was often limited to drill and section work, rather than the complex formation training necessary for modern warfare. Consequently, in September 1939, GHQ issued instructions to all BEF units, stating: 'Certain formations have for various reasons been unable to complete part of their training prior to their arrival in France. The present period should offer good opportunities for concentrating on those items which were unavoidably left unfinished'.[162]

The flawed inspection systems of the War Office, GHQ and Staff Duties & Training all failed to enforce the prioritization of training of Territorial units already disadvantaged by inferior equipment, experience and training. As a result, I.F.W. Beckett has argued: 'Territorials had as much or as little training as the rest of the army but, of course, often beginning from a weaker position in terms of equipment'.[163] David French has highlighted, without investigating further, Gort's opinion in April 1940 that his Territorials were fit only for static operations.[164] These broad statements are inaccurate because they fail to recognize that Territorial training within the BEF was dependent on the view of each CO and therefore inherently variable. In order to overcome an inferiority in its standard preparedness the TA required additional guidance from training experts and the opportunity to witness and participate in best practice. The response of divisional commanders varied between the encouragement of 3rd Division, the indifference of 2nd Division and the absence of help from 44th Division. Major General Montgomery organized the temporary attachment of experts from regular battalions to 4th Royal Berkshire Regiment soon after their transfer to 3rd Division. In February 1940, Major Llewellyn 1st Grenadier Guards, assisted by two NCOs from 2nd East Yorkshire Regiment and two from 1st Suffolk Regiment, were attached to provide guidance on drill, tactical training and how to correctly reconnoitre a defensive position; in conjunction with this, Major Thomas 17th Field Company Royal Engineers provided several lectures on construction techniques for defensive positions. Ongoing assistance was provided throughout the Phoney War; for example, on 6 March 1940, a cadre course for 4th Royal Berkshire Regiment junior officers and NCOs commenced under the supervision of Captain Spencer, 2nd East Yorkshire Regiment. Experience within critical positions was increased by attaching 4th Royal Berkshire Regiment personnel to battalions with superior training. On 6 March 1940, 4th Royal Berkshire Regiment 'Intelligence Offr, MT Offr and Carrier Offr join 1 Gren Gds, 1 Coldm Gds and 2 Gren Gds respectively to accompany them on a Div scheme'; on their return a talk was arranged to share their experiences with all the battalion officers.[165]

In 2nd Division, the superiors of 7th Worcestershire Regiment took an alternative approach to raising TA standards, which involved no additional training and ensured formation exercises were not weighted so that the least experienced benefited the most. Although a I Corps exercise to simulate the occupation of a defensive line along the frontier started 0300hrs 1 April, when it ended on 3 April, only D Company and the mortar platoon of 7th Worcestershire Regiment (under command of 1st Queen's Own Cameron Highlanders on the left flank) had been involved in any simulated combat. Battalions on either flank were attacked, but during a three-day exercise 7th Worcestershire Regiment did little more than send out patrols who repeatedly reported 'situation quiet on our front'.[166] This was despite 7th Worcestershire Regiment being in greater need of training than their regular counterparts.

The arrival of III Corps in late spring 1940 meant 44th Division was able to provide only limited expertise or opportunity for additional training to raise standards. Nevertheless, 4th Royal Sussex Regiment failed to utilize opportunities which did occur to eliminate recurring weaknesses before active operations intensified. According to the Weapons Training Officer (WTO) of the 4th Royal Sussex Regiment, some improvement was demonstrated post-deployment, but

> the same old fault still remained – namely, the almost complete lack of section commanders with the capacity to lead and control their men. This disturbed me at the time; and later we felt the effect of this terrible weakness. When we were 'up against it', there were very few section commanders who did their job properly,

such was the inadequate standard of training in this Territorial battalion. Perhaps more shocking is that this flaw occurred during training in Dorset, training in France and in battle without ever being satisfactorily rectified. According to the WTO, junior leadership cost the Battalion unnecessary casualties and hampered its performance throughout the campaign. The importance of training to the average BEF soldier was immense, for his reliance on it was absolute and his ability to improvise solutions negligible; Sergeant Johnson, 4th Royal Sussex Regiment remarked during Phoney War training the men 'aven't the imagination of a gnat'.[167] Standards of training within Territorial units could be improved, if given appropriate guidance and the opportunity to increase experience, and this required the determination of a superior formation to create conducive conditions. Superiors were not always willing or able to create such circumstances.

In spring 1940, with BEF training compromised by an acute shortage of field engineers, the untrained 12th, 23rd and 46th Divisions were belatedly deployed to France to provide additional manual labour. They had received virtually no training for their unexpected employment, because as late as 16 December 1939, BEF Adjutant General had been informed by 'AG WO that low category Territorials could not be sent out for labour duties, and that it will be necessary to employ foreigners resident in France'.[168] CIGS Ironside had also vehemently opposed the deployment, prophetically arguing it was disingenuous to believe 'the men would not be put in the front-line if they were in France. They would have to be put in in a crisis'.[169] However, political desire to free up regulars for training overrode such views, leading to their deployment to the rear-echelon without artillery or signals, on a much reduced scale of transport and equipment, and with limited post-deployment training expectations.

The official campaign history has stated: 'While they were largely for labour duties, a balanced programme of training was carried out so far as time permitted'.[170] In reality, with minimal equipment, limited time and no foundation to build upon, the untrained TA divisions could offer only elementary guidance. 12th Division training guidance, issued on 3 April 1940, stated: 'If any units have men below eight weeks' standard of Intake after arrival, this must be attended to first'.[171] Having spent the majority of the Phoney War dispersed in small detachments for guard duty, 36th Brigade pre-deployment training had been restricted to two officer-only TEWTs and 20 rounds per man musketry practice for the subordinate 6th Queen's Own Royal West Kent Regiment.[172] For example, the pre-deployment duties of 5th Buffs Regiment Company Quartermaster Sergeant G. Anderson consisted largely of guarding decoding stations throughout Kent.[173]

Deployed on 20 April 1940, with so many deficiencies, Acting Brigadier Roupell planned for each battalion to carry out a fortnight's section and platoon training in rotation; hardly sophisticated, but vital for battalions previously confounded by guard duty. Even this was not straightforward as NCOs of insufficient quality and number forced Roupell to organize cadre courses for NCOs whilst personally overseeing elementary training. Without any training or knowledge of the duties involved, Sergeant C. Garratt was appointed 5th Buffs Regiment 'NCOi/c AA Pl and A/CQMS HQ Coy' solely on the basis of having served 12 years overseas with the regulars.[174] When 36th Brigade entered combat (as predicted by Ironside) 5th Buffs Regiment had only received a fortnight of basic training in France, 7th Queen's Own Royal West Kent Regiment had seven days and 6th Queen's Own Royal West Kent Regiment had not completed any training in France, this following nearly eight months in England with minimal training.[175] Influenced by his study of Anglo-French strategy, Nick Smart has suggested improvements in BEF organization, equipment and manpower ensured it was not 'unprepared for a first-class war'; experiences of 36th Brigade clearly undermine this.[176] The numerous sources of training guidance and the BEF's attempts to create a uniform standard had little relevance to these units, particularly as pioneer duties retained precedence over ensuring units were capable of self-defence until 15 May. Crucially, this was after the German invasion, highlighting how little oversight there was of labour division activities.

The ability of inspection systems to oversee training and establish a metric standard was hampered by under-trained personnel being dispersed throughout the BEF, rather than retained in the labour divisions. Frequent arrivals of reinforcements meant training schedules could never be completed, duplication was often required and solitary snap inspections became almost worthless. Over ten days in March, 4th Royal Berkshire Regiment were forced to absorb two separate drafts totalling 128 personnel, all of whom had experienced only rudimentary training.[177] It was unfair to expect battalions to absorb so many new recruits so late in the Phoney War and at the same time maintain their combat capability. Nevertheless, with no pre-war experience and having missed most of the Phoney War training in France, these conscripts were reliant on their new unit to improve on their basic training. This was not always forthcoming, for example, when 80 conscripts with five months service joined 7th Worcestershire Regiment on 24 April, Lieutenant Colonel Parkes stuck to his prearranged schedule, proceeded on leave the same day, and from 1–9 May the 'Bn employed on wiring, building of pill boxes and generally improving frontier defences'.[178]

The creation of a Royal Artillery training metric should have been as simple as comparing accuracy and reaction times of equivalent units. However, training continued to be affected by pre-war problems such as a lack of facilities, a lack of experienced personnel and the sheer cost of making an artillery unit operational. Although created in mid-November, 52nd Heavy Regiment RA did not test its 12 9.2" howitzers until early January 1940; even then each gun was only allowed to fire six rounds. With imperial policing the Army's main pre-war role, large-calibre guns were of little relevance in the inter-war period, as demonstrated by Signaller L. Cannon's comment: 'everyone was very interested, as not one man in the regiment had witnessed a 9.2" shoot before'.[179] Once deployed to France, as with other BEF arms, formation training proved difficult, although with the RA, it was due to freezing winter weather, the subsequent spring thaw and GHQ's restrictions on training with wireless for security reasons.[180] Some units were eventually able to concentrate, for example, 58th Medium Regiment trained at Vermelles from 22 January to the end of February under Corps

Commander Royal Artillery II Corps and from early March to mid-April at Pozières under GHQ Artillery Group.[181] Many units experienced limited accessibility to the wisdom of senior officers, as their late deployment and the antisocial nature of their guns meant they were denied involvement in formation training. Based at Fleurbaix from 5 April, 52nd Heavy Regiment were restricted to guard duty and basic training; only a few regimental specialists were sent to a distant anti-tank rifle-range from where they fired five rounds each before returning.[182] The RA carried out some creditable training during the Phoney War, although formation training remained elusive for many, the need for greater combat training was not foreseen and agreed inter-unit communication procedures were never tested.

Since GHQ had prioritized training in mobile warfare, the Royal Armoured Corps should have been one of the most intensively trained arms during the Phoney War, yet throughout there was a lack of urgency and focus. Scarce Royal Tank Regiment personnel were frequently diverted to stationary manual labour; 4th Royal Tank Regiment 'supplied 45 ORs to assist digging anti-tank obstacles' during October and November for a total of 38 days. Establishing a mechanized training metric was difficult because so few had experience of armour in combat; GHQ was forced to utilize 4th Royal Tank Regiment in experiments ranging from testing a new machine-gun to, in December 1939, a 48-hour 'Demonstration to representatives of GHQ and 1 & 2 Corps of devices for crossing anti-tank obstacles'.[183] Largely isolated Royal Armoured Corps units were reliant on superior formations for collective training; the best 2nd Division could offer the 4/7th Royal Dragoon Guards was to assist in the arrangement of skeleton exercises with 1st Division's 13/18th Royal Hussars.[184] Although equally reliant on superior formations to arrange training with armour, many infantry formations used internal solutions to avoid disruption to training schedules. With the arrival of 20th anti-tank Regiment on 1 November 1939, 8th Brigade used its three subordinate Bren gun Carrier Platoons to simulate 'a tank attack & test A-TK defences'.[185] Few Territorials and conscripts had any comprehension of what armoured formations were capable of and even many long-serving regulars had minimal experience due to overseas tours. In these circumstances, the improvised use of carriers was a dangerous solution as they only partially dispelled misconceptions of the strengths/weaknesses of armour, whilst simultaneously exaggerating the invincibility of carriers. Affiliation between the RTR and individual infantry formations was fleeting, with the closest links forged by 3rd Division and 4th Royal Tank Regiment in three overnight exercises, each ending in a dawn attack by armour. These were so deficient in developing tactics and close working relations that, post-war, Montgomery mischievously suggested: 'There was somewhere in France, under GHQ, one Army Tank Brigade. For myself, I never saw any of its tanks during the winter or during the active operations in May'.[186] Despite increasing awareness of the importance of combined operations, GHQ never provided conditions conducive for the practice and development of armour/infantry tactics, leaving both infantry and armour under-prepared.

During the Phoney War the BEF was heavily involved in the creation of extensive defensive positions along the Franco-Belgian border, in an attempt to extend the Maginot Line and protect northern France from invasion. In his instructions to all newly arrived BEF units, written in September 1939, Gort directed: 'During this period it is desirable to allot 50% of the available time to training, as against 50% to work on defences'.[187] However, when these instructions were revised and amended on 7 May 1940, the clause demanding BEF units devote half their time to construction of defensive positions was left in. This was in spite of a military conference of senior Allied officers at Vincennes on 9 November 1939, where Supreme Allied Commander General Gamelin had announced his Dyle plan and his intention to abandon the frontier defences to confront any German invasion in Belgium.[188] Three days before the German invasion and eight months after informing BEF units, GHQ was still demanding 50 per cent of time be allotted to manual labour to improve a position the BEF anticipated abandoning on the first day of significant fighting. This was not considered a contradiction at GHQ for as CGS Pownall noted in his diary on 25 October 1939, the establishment of defensive positions along the Franco-Belgian frontier was 'excellent training for the troops, much more so than if we had stayed in a back area practising battles. What better practical training than the preparation of a defensive position?'.[189] The limited value of this so-called training is demonstrated by the experiences of a detachment of 2nd East Yorkshire Regiment, which spent a month installing barbed wire between blockhouses and logging fields of fire in a wood in front of a Chateau along a 1000 yard front. The compensation bill from the landowner was ten times the 3rd Division estimate due to damage to the entire wood caused by the over-enthusiasm and malicious vandalism of under-supervised men attempting to alleviate the monotony of the job.[190] It should be noted that despite all these efforts this particular section of front was breached by German forces in half an hour.

Although the official campaign history believed the performance of frontier defences justified the considerable effort spent on them, reservations had existed amongst senior officers.[191] Lord Gort's concerns extended to warning against assuming that any forthcoming operations would closely resemble the Great War.[192] However, GHQ failed to discourage officers from using defence construction as an excuse for not organizing structured training programmes. Second Lieutenant C. Barker despaired that even his regular battalion (1st Gordon Highlanders) dug trenches on a daily basis, irrespective of weather conditions; defences which were later outflanked and, ultimately, proved useless.[193] CIGS Ironside's reservations concentrated on the ruler-straight defensive line, which disregarded all tactical thinking in order to shadow the frontier and protect every inch of French soil.[194] The failure to confront the fallacy of French thinking proved disastrous for the BEF, forced to use such flawed defences during the retreat to Dunkirk. On 24 May 2nd Bedfordshire and Hertfordshire Regiment retreated to the frontier defences on the Tourcoing-Monscron road; despite the numerous pill boxes and trenches of the position and the physical exhaustion of his men, Lieutenant Colonel Birch ordered A and B companies to be 'hard at it day and night improving the defences of their localities' because 'the MOUSCRON ridge was not far away and gave the Bosche full view of all our front'. The flawed location of the defences, right on the frontier, was the consequence of Belgian Phoney War neutrality and the Allied desire to establish defensive positions and keep men occupied. Birch's primary concern was a devastating artillery bombardment which 'would be accurate without previous registration, because I suspected our frontier defences had been "surveyed" from the "neutral" frontier months before'. However, such information could have been passed to the Germans by fifth column in a nearby block of flats which was still occupied with 'the people sitting at their windows watching the fun!'.[195]

The BEF took advantage of the Franco-German border by detaching formations for brief spells on the active Saar front. C-in-C Gort hoped in the process many inexperienced BEF personnel would benefit from their first taste of combat and junior leaders would gain valuable training in their day-to-day duties when in combat with the enemy. Gort's Despatches at the time noted: 'The British Army contains to-day very few regimental officers and other ranks who fought in the last war; much that was common knowledge and accepted practice then, must therefore be learned again'.[196] From 4 December 1939, BEF infantry brigades were deployed in rotation to the Saar front, increasing to three week tours from March 1940, and expanding to whole division deployments from 7 May.

One of Gort's greatest concerns was that

> conditions in the BEF, in the absence of actual hostilities, have been, to a certain extent unreal, and more similar to peacetime training than to warfare: there is a danger that those who have no war experience may not readily clear their minds of peacetime conditions where fire was represented by tokens.[197]

Hugh Sebag-Montefiore has argued activities on the Franco-German border were dominated by the Allies' 'live and let live' policy which restricted aggressive, confrontational action and prevented an escalation of hostilities.[198] This came at the expense of training opportunities and prevented acclimatization to high-tempo operations. Stretcher-bearer Ken Clarke recalled the tour of 1st Queen's Own Royal West Kent Regiment consisted of occasional shell-fire, a single self-inflicted injury and working parties in the Ligne de Contact. Battle-hardened by a week in WWI trenches, this battalion returned to the Franco-Belgian border, supposedly prepared for war and able to restart work on the frontier defences.[199] Despite this, the official campaign history agreed with Gort's viewpoint and stated the BEF units that served in front of the Maginot Line gained a 'most valuable experience'.[200] Modern historians are generally more critical of BEF Phoney War procedures, but even they can be lulled into a false impression by the facade of action and purpose. Sean Longden has argued: 'The notion that the BEF was idle from September 1939 until May 1940 was a fallacy. There was plenty of activity for the infantryman stationed in the Ligne de Contact seven miles in front of the Maginot Line' in the Saar region of France.[201] Longden failed adequately to recognize that virtually none of the activity was useful for preparing BEF troops for high-tempo operations and the German blitzkrieg advance.

It is important to understand how active a front had to be during the Phoney War for GHQ to believe it beneficial to BEF personnel and capable of enhancing a unit's capabilities in ways that could not be achieved on the Franco-Belgian border. During its Saar deployment 8th Infantry Brigade issued an intelligence summary to subordinate battalions for the period 1800hrs 13/01/40 to 1800hrs 14/01/40. It summarized one enemy patrol was possibly seen at 2100hrs but overall: 'Attacks NIL, Artillery NIL, Air Activity NIL'; it concluded: 'There has been more enemy movement than of late'. According to 8th Brigade Operational

Orders during the deployment, an explanation for the German inactivity was: 'The enemy has excellent OPs on his front from which the whole of the Bde front can be observed'.[202] This negated the need for any German offensive action whilst limiting the possibility of any BEF offensive action. Many BEF units experienced similar conditions during the winter of 1939–40, further reducing the training value of any deployment to the Saar.

In reality, deploying BEF units to the Maginot Line was less to do with acclimatizing personnel to new realities of modern warfare and more to do with bolstering and maintaining public opinion. The perceived lack of events during the Phoney War, particularly on the Franco-Belgian border where the BEF was based, led to Allied commanders desperate to be seen to be doing something and demonstrate the burden of war was being shared between BEF and French forces. Acts of bravery rewarded with decorations had a tremendous publicity and propaganda value. *The Daily Telegraph* reported on 13 January 1940: 'The first decorations in the field in this war were awarded by General Viscount Gort'; a Military Cross to Captain F. Barclay and a Military Medal to Lance Corporal H. Davies, both from 2nd Royal Norfolk Regiment, for bravery on a night patrol in front of the Maginot Line.[203] There is no doubting the bravery of these actions, but it is unlikely that medals would have been issued so quickly, if at all, had it not been for their propaganda value during the relative inactivity of the Phoney War. The desire to share any burden with the French and to convince the public and BEF personnel that the war was real took precedence over the organization of exercises on the Franco-Belgian border that could have assisted the training of the BEF.

In contrast to the limited methodical training within the BEF, the Germans 'carefully evaluated the lessons learned in Poland'; Light Divisions were proven to be insufficiently powerful and were converted to Panzer Divisions, unwieldy Motorized Infantry Divisions were stripped of an Infantry Regiment, and Panzer Divisions were re-equipped with a higher proportion of Panzer III and IV tanks. Many of the German units that participated in the invasion of France already had battle experience from the campaign in Poland and, therefore, during the Phoney War, COs did not have to work on basic training. War games were held at Koblenz on 7 February and Mayen on 14 February 1940, where multiple scenarios were examined and tested, after which senior officers and staff could be trained for their forthcoming tasks. Such was the thoroughness of German Phoney War training that when the Operations Department of XIX Army Corps issued orders for the attack across the Meuse on the night of 12/13 May 1940, subordinate divisions issued orders to their unit commanders which began: 'Attack in accordance with map exercise carried out on....'[204] Thorough preliminary studies meant previous map exercises could be used with only minor alterations, ensuring attacks could be carried out with very limited time for preparations. This demonstrates the benefit of proactive training compared to sitting on a quiet front, in front of the Maginot Line, and shows how the Germans were able to maintain a rapid tempo of operations which overwhelmed the Allies.

Whilst the Germans trained for invasion, British officers were frequently distracted by political interference and civilian curiosity. Referring to politicians in general and Hore-Belisha in particular, CIGS Ironside noted: 'Always, every civilian thinks he can run or even command an army. It takes up hours of our time and is most annoying'.[205] CGS Pownall complained on 25 October 1939, much of GHQ's time 'is taken up "liaising" with French officers – and not only officers for we have called on the Cardinal at Lille and the Prefects of Lille and Arras'. However, GHQ tolerated these distractions in the futile hope establishing contacts could overcome national interests in times of crisis. Such was the number of distinguished visitors to the BEF that on 5 April 1940, Gort ruefully informed War Minister Oliver Stanley that he had entertained 42 people in the previous ten days: 'They are mostly interesting, but one naturally longs occasionally for one free evening'. Gort might have added that he was being distracted from planning and overseeing BEF training. As CGS Pownall recorded in his diary on 12 October: 'With considerable distances and shortening days, to go up to the forward area can't be done in half a day before or after lunch'.[206] A tour of BEF positions and units for visitors meant the whole day was lost for the escorting officer, and the seniority of the escort increased with the importance of the dignitary. Rarely benefiting the BEF or the understanding of visitors, the superficial nature of these intrusions was demonstrated on 12 November 1939, when Dominion representatives visiting France inspected the line held by 2nd East Yorkshire Regiment, accompanied by Secretary of State for the Dominions Eden, HRH the Duke of Gloucester, the Corps and Division commanders, numerous staff officers and journalists. According to 8th Brigade HQ 'The visit took the form of half a mile above a very muddy lane on the wrong side of the tank obstacles. No defences were seen'; the War Diary entry concluded: 'It is hoped that the distinguished visitors ... were interested'.[207] The visits of dignitaries distracted senior officers, but also their subordinate units, from training for active operations.

BEF frequently experienced invasion scares and false alarms, which distracted senior officers and disturbed the training of subordinate units. On 1 November 1939, Lieutenant General Brooke wrote: 'At last October is gone and with it the chances of a German violation of Belgium this winter have receded'.[208] He subsequently started diary entries with an expectation of imminent invasion on eight days, 8–15 November. On occasions it was the sole focus of the diary entry, suggesting it absorbed almost all his time. Many of these false alarms forced BEF units to interrupt their current task or training to move into a position from which they could defend the Low Countries, yet, when the invasion did eventually begin on 10 May 1940, the BEF communication system was haphazard in its response and the BEF was not optimally placed to enter Belgium.

After trials within various units and battle schools, in October 1942 the WO accepted standardization of operating procedures by endorsing the creation and use of battle drills.[209] Army training remained flawed, but, after 1942, it at least had minimum standards it could rely on in combat. Attempts to establish a metric had begun in September 1939, when flexible pre-war training advice was replaced with detailed guidance for minor training, enhanced in October with the dissemination of mandatory training procedures for larger units. During the life of the BEF, problems continued due to the systemic nature of pre-war training flaws. Oversight, in its various guises, remained unsystematic and incapable of eliminating varied and incorrect training procedures. Each level of command had sufficient autonomy to vary how best to implement training and best use equipment, time and personnel, leading to an uncoordinated and unreliable skills-set. Recognition of the forthcoming threat remained vague at all levels, few grasping new air and mobile warfare tactics. Complex training was rare, attempts to utilize active fronts misguided, whilst basic training was commonplace but inadequate. To compound these failings a harsh winter, incessant construction of border defences, political interference and the visits of distinguished guests distracted all BEF units. The Phoney War offered time to intensify training and improve pre-war procedures; throughout the chain of command, the majority failed to seize the opportunity.

4
Communications: Prelude to Collapse

In September 1939, the British Expeditionary Force deployed to France with the naive belief that its communication system was capable of fulfilling any role modern warfare required of it. Accustomed to having sufficient communications for its imperial obligations, the inter-war army became unappreciative of its unglamorous support arm; the Royal Corps of Signals became undermanned and under-resourced as a result. The Army half-heartedly aspired to improve both hardware and overall capability, but never realised unfulfilled potential or the considerable lag between developing cutting-edge technology and available finance. Paradoxically, as the British Great War communication mix had proved such a stable foundation upon which to base inter-war operations, there was a natural pre-war disinclination to change a previously winning formula; this complacent belief only intensified when large-scale operations re-occurred in France in 1939–40. Within the high-volume, low pressure Phoney War environment, teething problems were not recognized as inherent signs of future unreliability. Whilst cable-based methods dominated communications, the overly complicated layout and inefficient procedures created bottlenecks which, in turn, placed unexpected pressure on more flexible methods. Although signals personnel lacked adequate experience, training or numbers to fully utilize the unexpected lull and develop beyond peacetime functionality, had GHQ recognized the tempo of operation was insufficient for combat, proactive action could have improved system resilience and lessened the risk of total collapse.

Whilst R. Nalder, official historian of the Royal Corps of Signals, has portrayed the British Army's system of communication in 1914 as slow, primitive and ineffective, Andy Simpson has argued the Western Front's prolonged period of stability allowed communications to experiment, develop in complexity and slowly implement lessons without risking undue vulnerability.[1] Brian Hall has argued a safety first approach in 1914 led to the Great War BEF favouring tried and tested cable, human messengers and visual signalling over excessively unreliable communication methods like wireless. Substantive development of wireless and an increasingly standardized approach only occurred when it was recognized a more technologically advanced and diversified communication system was necessary to achieve combined arms operations and restore mobility to the battlefield.[2]

Historians have shown how the momentum of advancement within communications was lost and replaced within the British Army during the inter-war period by quiet evolution and a degree of stagnation. Patrick Rose has illustrated how British units in inter-war India continued to use Great War cable-based communications, supplemented by visual signalling equipment which 'would have been familiar to Lord Roberts as he marched in 1880 from Kabul to Kandahar'; everyday imperial duties did not require a more mobile, wireless-based system.[3] Brian Bond has argued the greatest inter-war obstacle to developing the Army's capability, including its communication system, was indecision over whether its role as imperial policeman or first-class military force should be prioritized; qualified political and military support for development resulted in inconsistent funding sufficient for the former, but not the latter.[4] Similarly, I.F.W. Beckett has shown how for much of the 1930s, Chancellor Neville Chamberlain (later Prime Minister) hampered Territorial Army modernization with politically motivated financial restrictions, leaving it unequal to regular units in non-combat equipment such as wireless.[5] This indecisive action resulted in the BEF deploying to France in September 1939 with only 1st and 2nd Divisional Signals fully trained. According to R. Nalder the remaining regulars could 'in no military sense ... be regarded as trained units' whilst their Territorial equivalents 'had a proportion of men who had undergone virtually no military training'.[6] Even before expansion in 1939, it is clear British Army communications had numerous visible defects which were casually or forcibly accepted.

In their analysis of the France 1939–40 campaign, Brian Bond, David French and Simon Godfrey are amongst the few historians who have dedicated space to some aspects of the communication system that influenced BEF performance. In his study of the High Command, Brian Bond has concluded poor communications in both the political and military sphere, combined with the inadequate provision of liaison officers, all contributed to the cumbersome command and control structure that handicapped the BEF throughout the campaign.[7] In contrast, David French has emphasized the BEF used a well-established system which, regardless of flaws, provided fairly reliable Phoney War communications. When operations intensified, communications allowed just enough command and control to maintain BEF cohesion and expedite evacuation before system collapse became endemic on 26 May 1940.[8] Most recently, Simon Godfrey has contentiously argued criticism of BEF communications is 'unjustified', despite the frequent communication breakdowns, because most of the problems in signalling were 'a result of the defeat of the British Army, and not a cause of defeat'.[9] However, the following chapters show reliability issues occurred immediately upon deployment and throughout the chain of command, after which the advance to the Dyle River marked the beginning of comprehensive, system-wide collapse.

As with the Great War, the need for increasingly complex combined arms operations and additional battlefield mobility spurred the development of a faster, more flexible and robust system culminating in 1944–45 with a ubiquitous wireless-based system largely reliant on verbal orders to maintain high-tempo operations. David French has shown these developments made viable previously unachievable ground-air co-operation and artillery support techniques, but as a system, intrinsic flaws remained, namely the curbing of initiative amongst junior commanders. Although the Army's autocratic command and control had largely relented in its use of cable-conducive written orders, junior officers now hesitated when deprived of constant radio contact and the possibility of further instructions.[10] Once war recommenced in 1939, renewed impetus in improving technological development and manufacturing capacity allowed the required increase in tempo necessary for modern warfare; however, ending restraint of subordinate initiative through the communication system was never considered essential for achieving victory and, consequently, never occurred.

During this period several contemporary reports and reviews investigated army communications and concluded both procedures and theoretical capability were sound, although inter-war development was required to remove system imperfections; however, further analysis has revealed Great War appreciation of communications and their role in the high-tempo operations in 1918 dissipated over time, whilst a complacent fear of change was never satisfactorily overcome. The 1932 Kirke Report recognized effective communications were a crucial contributor to the formulation of 'useful plans' and the issuing 'of necessary orders', yet individual Committee members believed a widespread loss of 'signal sense' had occurred in the post-war army, causing a decline in the pace of operations; Major General A. McNamara bluntly recorded: 'We are getting slow'. The Report's aspirations included the replacement of cable communications forward of brigade headquarters with wireless and greater co-operation with civil manufacturers to ensure the regular inter-war army remained up-to-date with the latest scientific developments. However, fear of excessive controversy led to the promotion of verbal orders being qualified by the affirmation that top-down control through the use of detailed written orders was the 'difference between generalship and a mere dog fight'.[11] By 1935, the decline in importance of communications was illustrated by *Field Service Regulations* including the relatively trivial arrangement of rear-echelon guard detachments in the top six priorities of a commander, yet ignoring altogether the establishment of reliable communications throughout the chain of command. Furthermore, aspirations for development were reduced to hoping the liaison officer included in the 'establishments of Corps HQs and of GHQ' for each 'immediately subordinate formation' would be replicated for lower formations; until that time, divisions and brigades were encouraged to exert their authority and permanently borrow officers from subordinate units to assist the conveyance of information and orders.[12] The exploitation of subordinate resources was only rectified in July 1940 when establishments were increased to provide corps with six liaison officers, four for divisions and three for brigades. With the liaison issue resolved, the post-Dunkirk Bartholomew Committee attempted to justify pre-war procedures by declaring BEF communications in front of corps headquarters were theoretically sound with equipment satisfactory for both mobile and static warfare. In a blatant denial of inflexibility and a lack of responsiveness within BEF communications, the Bartholomew Committee concluded more diligent use of available wireless and written confirmation of all verbal orders, in accordance with official procedure, would have ensured system resilience against German pressure.[13] British Army communications did eventually become fit for purpose, but only after the complacent acceptance of the status quo and the trend of dwindling aspiration was reversed; this required the Army's wholehearted support of verbal orders and the dramatic expansion of wireless usage.

Established in 1920 as an independent formation the inter-war Royal Corps of Signals, with its unproven battle capability, compared unfavourably with the more glamorous and historical reputations of the combatant arms it served, and resulted in a continuous struggle for resources equivalent to other specialist arms. In September 1936, out of 10,789 British Army officers, only 457 (4.25 per cent) were members of the Royal Corps of Signals, leaving it unsurprisingly dwarfed by the infantry (4,890 officers) and the Royal Artillery (2,388 officers). However, considering the integral importance of communications in warfare, it is striking that the Army's signals were numerically inferior to the Royal Army Service Corps, 25 per cent smaller than the cavalry and approximately one third of the Royal Engineers' size (RASC – 495, cavalry – 569, RE – 1,281). Unlike every other front-line arm, the Royal Corps of Signals lacked a general ranking officer, further undermining its voice in the fight for resources; by comparison the Foot Guards alone had seven generals on active service in 1936.[14] These deficiencies were replicated amongst the rank-and-file; in 1932, seeking regular employment in a technical arm which could offer a post-army trade, T. Thomas was informed no vacancies existed at the Caernarfon Recruiting Office, except in signals where vacancies were plentiful. Similarly the Territorial Army struggled to attract people away from private sector employers; for example, 48th Divisional Signals operated on an improvised organizational structure to compensate for being less than 50 per cent of authorized peace-strength for much of the 1930s.[15]

In conjunction with manpower deficiencies, inertia in the implementation of Kirke Committee recommendations, especially the creation of close private sector links to maintain awareness of modern scientific developments, left the Army short of expertise in communications. Martin Alexander has already shown, when the French Army faced pressure in 1935 to end conscription for specialist units, the General Staff would only accept that operation of wireless apparatus 'could not be perfected by the military training it offered'.[16] In Britain, the Army's advanced practical training in telecommunication engineering was subcontracted to the General Post Office which provided a six-month course for eight officers per annum. In 1939, the Committee for Technical Training was appalled to learn this arrangement had been allowed to lapse for most of the 1930s, but with the Royal Corps of Signals suffering from a 68 officer deficiency in February 1939, the Committee acknowledged this opportunity would continue to be ignored. The Committee's report also highlighted the complete absence of military links with manufacturers, such as Marconi, thereby undermining efforts to provide practical engineering experience for signal officers.[17] In contrast, as part of their training in August 1939, the entire signals platoon of 1st Battalion, 1st German Parachute Regiment were shown around the Telefunken Radio Works in Berlin to help them understand the method of manufacture and internal workings of wireless sets they would be using in combat.[18] In Britain, most rank-and-file could only observe civil superiority from a distance; for example, upon joining 48th Divisional Signals in February 1939, Signaller W. Saunders noticed his unit's most gifted individuals all worked, at least part-time, for the Post Office.[19]

The Royal Corps of Signals did open its own School of Signals in 1920 and permanently located it in Catterick in 1925, but it had no involvement in developing new communication equipment or techniques. From 1925 to 1939, the School's principal function was to provide an 18 month course in signal training for young officers newly-commissioned into the Corps; despite having already completed basic training at Sandhurst or Woolwich, the course included three months mandatory tuition in drill and equitation. Infantry battalions, artillery batteries and similarly sized units were responsible for their own internal communications; to assist this, the School of Signals' secondary role was the provision of basic signal courses for the rank-and-file personnel who would carry out these duties. All other arms opted into the service except the Royal Tank Corps, which chose to create and undertake its own signals training. This left armoured divisional signals with signal troop commanders trained at two separate institutions using two different training methods; any hope of developing a common communication doctrine within 7th Armoured Divisional Signals was further undermined by only five of No. 1 Squadron's seven Signal Troops and only two of No. 2 Squadron's six Signal Troops being trained at Catterick.[20] This flawed division of responsibility continued throughout the inter-war period and into the BEF.

To some extent the Army did innovate and introduce new communication equipment to boost capability in the inter-war period; however, these were generally small progressions towards rapidly evolving cutting-edge technology which remained an aspiration, albeit financially out of reach. In 1934, a new mechanical cable dispenser that operated more effectively than manually laying cable was issued to divisional signals and, in 1937, this was supplemented by a new purpose-built, wheeled vehicle that incorporated the mechanical layer; in both cases it was hoped to assist communications between divisional headquarters and subordinated artillery. However, the post-Dunkirk Bartholomew Committee concluded 'the present line laying vehicle has poor cross country performance' with the result that cable was laid almost exclusively in roadside locations vulnerable to shellfire and saboteurs. The Committee reiterated long held aspirations to develop tracked line laying vehicles which would fulfil modern battlefield requirements, but was forced to acknowledge manufacturing capacity deficiencies, which had prevented this technically feasible development in the 1930s, remained in 1940.[21]

The short-range No. 1 set and the cumbersome, longer-range C set provided most British Army wireless capability in the early 1930s; for example, in Peshawar District, three C set wireless stations were semi-permanently installed for inter-garrison and inter-district communications, whilst infantry brigades utilized the No. 1 set for internal communications when on manoeuvres. The 1936 Arab Rebellion revealed this to be an inadequate capability; the post-campaign report stressed the need for an 'improved W/T [Wireless Telegraphy] set with more range than the No. 1 set and more mobility (for pack transport) than the C set'.[22] This gave renewed impetus to a development programme which had recently produced the No. 2 set and, by the end of the 1930s, the No. 3, 9 and 11 sets were theoretically available for issuing to units. Each one incorporated enhancements in mobility, robustness and range; for example, the No. 9 set for brigade-division communications relied on a large (four man crew) lorry for transportation, whereas the No. 11 set for divisional headquarter – artillery communications required only a high-powered, canvas-hooded Humber van with a two-man crew (the 'Gin Palace' and 'Bug' respectively).[23]

However, issuing of equipment to units, particularly Territorials, never kept pace with technological developments. In 1937, 48th Divisional Signals possessed just two elderly No. 1 sets and borrowed spare 3rd Division No. 1 and C sets for its annual training camp, yet its senior officers were teased at the Chief Signal Officer's February Conference with an introduction to the new No. 3 set. In 1938, 48th Divisional Signals still only possessed short-range No. 1 and 2 sets and were only able to briefly borrow No. 9 sets from newly equipped 3rd Divisional Signals; despite this, the unit's senior officers were forced to observe the latest No. 11 set at the February Signal Conference.[24] The reason for this discrepancy was the lack of spare manufacturing capacity; for example, addressing proposals to 'introduce the No. 11 [wireless] set into service', Army Training Memorandum No. 20A concluded they were currently impossible because of 'the delay in the manufacture of the necessary tools for mass production' which 'will prevent any sets being available in time for training in 1938'. Furthermore, ATM No. 20A revealed the Army's ultimate aspiration was a 'small portable wireless set, which can be carried in the field by man-pack' and used to equip infantry battalions; however, it acknowledged, in view of 'the many commitments in wireless sets the introduction of a set of this type cannot be contemplated for some considerable time'.[25]

Similarly, the Army aspired to equip signal units, particularly armoured divisional signals, with purpose-built vehicles designed for wireless transportation and operation. However, despite an agreed vehicle establishment, 1st Armoured Divisional Signals continued to be equipped with 'a varied collection of anything ordnance can supply', simply because 'industry could not meet the requirements'; many vehicles were so obsolete or unusual, the unit's Motor-Transport Sergeant had trouble obtaining spares through official channels and resorted to searching local garages. 1st Armoured Divisional Signals did receive over 100 new army vehicles on the eve of their May 1940 deployment, but such were the list of deficiencies, one improvised plywood armoured command vehicle was retained for operations in France.[26] After the removal of horse transport from establishments in 1934, Territorial signal formations were officially motorized formations; in reality, they were motorized for their annual camp only and their establishment depended on the price and availability of local hire companies. In 1934, 48th Divisional Signals could only afford a handful of unsatisfactory removal vehicles, but by 1936 sufficient funds had accumulated to hire 36 vehicles from the York-based Artillery Transport Company. With Brian Bond highlighting the inclusion of tanks, small arms and cordite on a list of numerically-deficient items within the War Office's final pre-war progress report, it is perhaps unsurprising the unglamorous, non-lethal signals equipment was also in short supply. However, the Army's aspiration for cross-country cable layers, man-pack wireless and purpose-built signal vehicles was technically feasible in the early 1930s, but they remained out of reach for signal units, as did much of the technology the Army did develop.[27]

Not only did the Army's equipment aspirations prove unachievable, but its signal training expectations proved unobtainable for many as well. Within the Royal Corps of Signals, each signaller was expected to master and qualify in a trade (for example, operator) with each trade graded into three levels (1–3). The higher the grading, the higher the pay and responsibility; this was important for promotion within the Army, but also post-army accreditation when joining a civilian trade group. However, in Territorial units 'it was considered impractical to test men on the standard qualification sheet' when equipment and instruction deficiencies prohibited good marks or even the regular army standard. In these circumstances each Territorial unit devised its own qualification exams, containing questions exclusively on equipment held and instruction given within the unit. Ultimately, units aimed to ensure all personnel were Group E Standard (regular army basic training before specialization into Group A-D: Mechanic, Operator, Linesman, Despatch Rider); subsequent module papers (when appropriate) could then provide gradual advancement towards regular standards in specialties.[28]

Paradoxically, there was substantial apprehension about the consequences of altering a previously successful communication formula and the possible unreliability of new technologies. Symbolic of this apprehension, during extensive field tests of the new No. 2 wireless set in 1936, 3rd Indian Divisional Signals achieved successful transmissions up to 450 miles in range on the plains of India's United Provinces. Yet, in autumn 1937, similar tests in mountainous Baluchistan by the same formation resulted in no successful transmissions and a three-day search involving RAF and local cavalry for a lost signal detachment.[29] With reliable communications between the High Command and field units considered essential for successful military operations, continuation of tried and tested methods was seen as satisfactory, even desirable. In his analysis of communications during the 1916 battle of the Somme, Brian Hall has highlighted the dominance of cable, but also 'of the supplementary methods of communication, visual signalling, carrier pigeons and runners were all given higher priority status than wireless'.[30] Order of precedence in India in 1939 was very similar; cable-based communications remained overwhelmingly dominant, but amongst supplementary techniques, wireless had only managed to leapfrog visual signalling. Although continuing faith in the effectiveness of carrier pigeons is striking, the most disturbing attitude of this communication guide was its description of the human messenger as the 'perfect machine' and 'at times the most reliable of any'. This statement completely ignores the vulnerability of the exposed human messenger on the modern battlefield, but it should not be seen as an anti-technological stance; it merely records satisfaction in the success of the existing methods. Within the British Army, willingness to include wireless in a diverse communication portfolio was matched by a lack of inclination to deviate from routine; in 1939, Peshawar had a state-of-the-art government radio station capable of long-distance communications with Quetta or Delhi, but since cable was never interrupted, it was mothballed and maintained in case of emergency.[31] Equally, the Army was loath to discard methods from its communication portfolio simply because they were old-fashioned; for example, in

1935, major exercises were still being held in Britain in which visual signalling was allocated the central communication responsibility, whilst cable and wireless received only secondary roles. In India, where visual signalling had a long unbroken history, there was even greater unwillingness to abandon viable methods; for example, in 1939, Peshawar District Command issued subordinates 19 pages of bearings, distances and descriptions of each outpost's visual contacts; its only caveat to usage was 'during the hot weather, from May to September, visual signalling is rendered almost impossible by heat haze'.[32] Whilst unnecessary consolidation of its communication portfolio was logically avoided by the Army, its failure to become increasingly accustomed to wireless and its determination to promote continued usage of obsolete visual signalling demonstrates the Army's inability to prepare for first-class war during imperial duties.

For all its aspirations, the complacent acceptance of pre-existing communications, particularly if the predominant method was satisfactory, meant little changed on the ground in the 1930s. In north-west India, where cable was dominant, 13 principal telegraph lines, 83 telegraph offices and 105 post offices in Peshawar and Mardan Districts alone connected virtually every police, military and civil post to the communication network; multiple connections to any one post merely added to the resilience of the system. Beyond the borders of British-administered India, cable could not reach the Empire's most isolated mountain outposts, but as previously demonstrated neither could wireless; with civil aircraft prohibited from north-west India, the most rapid and reliable form of communication was an airborne messenger service provided by local RAF squadrons.[33] Whilst this mix worked well in India, it was difficult to replicate in theatres with fewer resources and was impossible to replicate in a conflict against a first-class enemy. It is worth noting cable was not dominant everywhere and this complacent attitude meant there was no concerted inter-war drive to change this. In his analysis of Great War communications, Brian Hall has revealed: 'In Mesopotamia the less intense nature of the fighting, the long distances involved, and the initial absence of rigid security procedures meant that wireless quickly became an efficient, reliable and accepted primary means of communication'.[34] Similarly, the Report into the 1936 Arab Rebellion concluded:

Distances were usually too great to permit military lines being laid, while the civil lines were continually cut by saboteurs and were constant source of leakage of information. Despatch riders were far too vulnerable to ambush; and in fact W/T [Wireless Telegraphy] became of necessity the only safe and really effective means of communication.[35]

This shows the pre-war army was not afraid of wireless per se, but only trusted its usage in isolated theatres where, for historical, topographical and practical reasons, it was already the dominant form of communication.

Out of necessity and historical precedent, wireless was used as the primary communication method during the Arab Rebellion, but the campaign also illuminated 'the scale of W/T provided for signal units in Palestine was insufficient for the purpose' and future conflict involving first-class opponents would require an increase in wireless provision.[36] However, War Office complacency towards communications allowed this request to be knocked into the long grass, rather than actively pursued. Patrick Rose has highlighted how even in the early 1940s there existed no standing establishment for wireless communication between battalion and brigade levels; units were expected to adapt to whatever equipment they possessed.[37] Although the Kirke Committee envisaged a significant increase in wireless usage forward of brigades, battalion standing orders reveal how an inability to develop exclusively wireless-based communications left vulnerable loopholes where human exposure to danger was unavoidable. With no wireless allocated for administrative duties, a British battalion's Quartermaster, as officer in charge first line 'B' Echelon, was expected to 'anticipate feeding requirements' within his unit; discounting both distances and dangers on the modern battlefield, fall-back standing orders required the Quartermaster to 'visit Battalion Headquarters if the situation is obscure'. The complacent dismissal of the need for wireless within battalions also meant runners had to risk their lives to facilitate the exchange of position details between rifle companies and battalion headquarters; standing orders authorized no other method. A complacent attitude to communications took many forms, but it was pervasive within the pre-war British Army.[38]

The BEF deployed to France in September 1939 with several deeply entrenched and misguided views. Its imperial duties had given the misleading impression that British Army capability was sufficient for modern warfare. The creation of a stand-alone signal arm and gradual inter-war technical improvements gave the BEF a supposed advantage over its 1914 predecessor, without destroying its solid foundation of cable communications. Just as avoidable assumptions had coloured the BEF's response to Germany's Great War invasion, so incidents of questionable reliability and delayed communications in 1939 were labelled teething problems befitting any recently deployed and expanded military force; they were actually evidence of underlying weaknesses which would eventually collapse the system.[39] Flexible communication methods were used to bypass needless bottlenecks, rather than build system resilience and improve force mobility. The BEF lacked the ability or desire to rigorously test communications during the Phoney War, preventing the force ever moving beyond peacetime functionality before the German invasion of May 1940.

Inadequate communications was a major issue for the BEF from the moment it deployed to France in 1939 and throughout the campaign; on 4 September, Deputy Adjutant General J. Whitehead and his GHQ advance party disembarked at Cherbourg, only to find 'We were neither expected nor welcome, an atmosphere quite unlike the disembarkation scenes of 1914'.[40] The official signals history records how many BEF signal units initially deployed without the bulk of their equipment, leaving the BEF heavily reliant on the co-operation of the French Postes, Télégraphes et Téléphones (PTT). The first choice GHQ location of Doullens was quickly ruled out because the French had accidentally 'dug the cables up', removing the opportunity for the BEF to operate independently, so the BEF opted instead to locate its GHQ near Arras, where it could tap directly into the underground international telephone system.[41] With Arras itself ruled out as too vulnerable to espionage and aerial attack, from October 1939, GHQ was established in a series of villages west of the town; the central village of Harbarcq housed Commander-in-Chief Gort, Operations and some Intelligence personnel, whilst surrounding villages were occupied by Services, and other departments of varying importance. Accommodation in these villages being very limited, GHQ had to be spread over an area of some 80 square miles and communications involved an elaborate system of lines, with at least half a dozen sub-exchanges, supported by considerable numbers of despatch riders and motorized liaison officers. Having established his office within this network on 1 October 1939, Adjutant General Brownrigg informed subordinates 'the smooth working of this arrangement must depend upon the efficiency of the communications that can be established'; within a fortnight Brownrigg conceded defeat and 'arranged for bi-weekly liaison officers with [GHQ] 2/Ech owing to poor communications'.[42]

The post-Dunkirk report on GHQ organization reveals proactive efforts were made to rectify communication system layout inadequacies; in December 1939 the whole General Staff and key advisers moved into Arras, leaving the remaining GHQ personnel in situ. By geographically extricating themselves from the spider's web, the Report records General Staff business was notably speeded up, but the underlying problems of a strained telephone system and the frequent need for personal contact with distant administrative staff remained. The Royal Army Service Corps Department of GHQ had 'difficulty in obtaining reports' on unit locations and needs, both upon deployment in September 1939 and, crucially, after the reorganization in January 1940; it blamed the 'considerable inconvenience and serious delays' on the communication system and the units within it.[43] Even after reorganization, the system remained, in the words of 3rd Division's Major General B. Montgomery, 'an amazing layout', within which it was difficult to know where anyone was and command from the top suffered throughout. The anticipated expansion to four corps and two army headquarters was factored into BEF establishments, resulting in an increasingly complicated layout and an unwieldy GHQ totalling 2400 personnel by 1 May 1940; at the end of the Phoney War the communication system was already close to breaking point.[44]

The communication system was further complicated by the need to establish lines of communication from the Franco-Belgian border, to the channel ports of Normandy and Brittany, and on to Marseille in the South; this covered almost one third of France. The BEF could have concentrated its rear-echelon around the channel ports near the Franco-Belgian border, such as Calais, but fears over the relatively unknown capability of the Luftwaffe meant supply bases were located away from the border and danger. *Field Service Regulations 1935* dismissed unorthodox communications which ran obliquely from the front as 'comparatively disadvantageous' and excessively vulnerable to attack and breakdown. However, *FSR* could equally be used to justify BEF dispositions; for example, 'it is important that strategical concentration should be completed with a minimum of interruption by the enemy', even if this involved lengthy supply lines.[45] In the absence of clear-cut guidance, GHQ attitudes were similarly contradicted, for example, Chief of the General Staff Pownall recorded: 'Our L of C is terribly long, some 500 miles to Nantes and the further north we go the worse it gets'; however, GHQ concluded the risk from aerial attack superseded this 'very dangerous and un-Napoleonic affair'.[46] Having settled on over-extended communications, Gort was forced to acknowledge in reports to the War Office: 'The degree of dispersion required in modern warfare has materially added to' the Royal Corps of Signals' difficulties 'in providing communications'. The official signal history was more explicit, arguing the multiplicity of dispersed headquarters and the unforeseen extent of the lines of communication had placed demands upon signal units which 'far exceeded the highest estimates on which the establishments were based, particularly in the rear'.[47] To integrate BEF communications into the existing infrastructure, No. 1 Line of Communication Signals was forced to undertake some construction projects; for example, the creation of an overhead line from the main PTT building in Cherbourg to a BEF wireless station six miles south. However, given the extreme distances, it was impractical to consider creating a truly independent system throughout France and, consequently, BEF signals were obliged to utilize any available civil communications, no matter how obsolete; not only was the half-manual, half-automatic Cherbourg telephone exchange unlike anything in Britain, but the BEF signallers assigned to it found it sufficiently 'strange' that it proved a source of frustration and confusion.[48]

In 1939 the British Army's communication system was still fundamentally the same as that which they had employed in 1918. The BEF possessed three main means of communication: cable (line telegraphs and telephone), wireless (either Wireless Telegraphy by Morse Key (W/T) or Radio Telephony (R/T)) and human messengers (despatch riders and liaison officers).

The BEF preferred communication method throughout the chain of command was cable because of its perceived superiority over wireless in terms of range, capacity and security; all of which remained so long as the static operations of Phoney War continued. The stability of the Phoney War allowed 8th Brigade, already the mainstay of brigade-battalion communications, to establish cable links to key positions in front of subordinate battalions, yet also report back to 3rd Division on the Franco-Belgian border when the brigade was briefly deployed hundreds of miles away in the Saar region of France. Similarly, GHQ was theoretically capable of contacting all subordinate formations through its cable network, but could also, via its connection to international telephone lines, communicate with its French Allies, the RAF and the War Office.[49] Accustomed to cable's ubiquitous presence and reliability, incidents of fallibility proved disorientating to individual officers and debilitating to communications in general, despite the availability of a broad communications portfolio. After yet another exercise involving underperforming communications, 2nd Division warned subordinates: 'Officers have become telephone minded ... The result is that telephone lines are badly blocked' through congestion. Furthermore, expectations of perfect communications meant 'when a line was cut 300 yards from a Brigade HQ Signal Office', the confusion this caused resulted in '1½ hours for communications to be restored'.[50] Despite this, general ignorance about the fallibility of cable continued throughout the campaign prompting, in June 1940, Army Training Memorandum No. 33 to state:

> Cables are not laid for the fun of the thing. If you see a cable cut or a route damaged, report the details, and the spot where it happened, to the nearest signal section, or signal office, as soon as possible … Damage to a cable may cause loss of life, or it may only delay the arrival of rations, but you may be certain that someone will suffer. It takes time to repair a break in a cable route even if the exact spot is known; it takes much longer if a search has to be made to discover the fault.[51]

This message was not a priority for most soldiers within the BEF, with needless disruption an inevitable consequence.

Conversely, cable responsiveness could be impacted upon by failures within other parts of the system; for example, during the extreme weather of winter 1939–40, RASC GHQ recorded: 'Great difficulty experienced in inter-communication between this HQ and RASC units as telephones are scarce, lines always engaged and DRs unable to operate'. Overwhelming preference for cable forced it to operate at the limits of capacity so frequently, when roads became 'practically impassable' and volumes surged unexpectedly, the system slowed down or broke down. When cable was disrupted, GHQ Petrol observed signal personnel 'have to bear with hasty officers yelling at them sometimes because they do not get a call immediately', regardless of fault or possible alternatives; this unconstructive narrow-mindedness was very alien to the oil industry specialists drafted into GHQ Petrol.[52]

Mindful of this overdependence, the BEF introduced phoneless days when cable-based communications were prohibited for 24-hour periods. First to respond to unhealthy phone habits was II Corps, who instituted one phoneless day per week (Wednesdays), starting 7 February 1940, 'when no telephone calls between themselves and Divs are allowed'. Left to the discretion of corps commanders, it was not until 21 March 1940 that I Corps 'decided that phoneless periods shall be observed once a fortnight between each formation HQ and the HQ immediately above it'; superior benefits from involving all subordinate formations were cancelled out by the belated introduction and fortnightly frequency, which meant I Corps had only four phoneless days before the German invasion of 10 May. Although few acknowledged it, these days

failed to diversify BEF communication activity because their predictability and briefness meant they were incorporated into work schedules; for example, internal analysis of 'phoneless days between HQ L
of C Area and certain Sub-Areas' concluded: 'No serious inconvenience
caused but increase in telephoning on days previous and following'.[53]
This was not a new problem; Brian Hall has argued many experienced
Great War British officers struggled to relinquish the habits of static
warfare when semi-open warfare restarted in 1918, for example, it was
noted at a 3rd Army Conference that, as a result of three years of trench
warfare, 'many commanders appear to be lost when separated from
their telephones'.[54] Fearful of a repeat in France 1939–40, yet daunted
by the possible disruption caused by rigorous testing, BEF commanders
opted for the compromise of timid pressure-testing and blind faith that
updated secondary methods would prove sufficient should cable fail.

In theory the primary means of communication within the BEF was
wireless, but in practice this was unrealistic for all but a few armoured
and artillery units. David French has highlighted how dependence
on wireless alone would have left divisional headquarters commanding three brigades using a single set, whilst a battalion's solitary set
would have been its only link with other units.[55] Another tenuous link
authorized by official regulations was the expectation that co-operation
between infantry and armour could be achieved through a single wireless link. *Field Service Regulations* informed formations: 'When army
tank battalions are cooperating with infantry, the responsibility for
intercommunication rests primarily with the tank commander, who is
provided with a wireless set for the purpose'. Infantry units were not
given additional sets and were forced to make do with their existing
establishments. With this in mind, GHQ training instructions concentrated on efficiency, stating: 'Commanders and Staff officers of formations and units provided with Radio/Telephony should practice its use
because it cannot be successfully employed by officers unaccustomed
to R/T' and is 'apt to be neglected during the present time'. However,
no amount of training could compensate for the gaping holes in BEF
establishments, for example, RASC Troop Carrying Companies were not
routinely provided with wireless sets, even when providing mobility to
infantry units operating with armoured formations; this made communicating on the move and the issuing of fresh instructions virtually
impossible.[56] A similarly ill-conceived procedure involved 2nd Division
instructing its divisional cavalry (4/7th Dragoon Guards) to establish
and maintain a permanent wireless link 'back to a Div Terminal'; this
could only be achieved by cannibalizing wireless from other duties

for, as the Bartholomew Report highlights, divisional cavalry were not issued with their 'own rear link wireless and anchor set'. Such procedural inconsistencies continued throughout the Phoney War, often without resolution, leaving co-operation between infantry and armour fundamentally undermined.[57]

Wireless was part of a communication portfolio which only worked efficiently if all elements pulled their weight; this did not occur because BEF formations did not utilize their wireless assets to alleviate alternative communication pathways. 3rd Division were perfectly comfortable communicating with 1st Division using their cable connection via II Corps Signal Office, even when the latter suggested admin would lessen and tempo increase if the direct wireless link was utilized. Similarly, despite sufficient proximity to contact 12th Lancers directly via wireless, 4th Division opted to contact II Corps using cable, in order to gain directions for its despatch rider.[58] The problem was reports from Poland had claimed German direction finding of wireless transmissions contributed significantly to Polish headquarters being forced to relocate every 24 hours to alleviate relentless bombing. Apprehensive that the BEF's larger wireless capability left it similarly vulnerable, use of long-range sets was severely restricted during the Phoney War and all sets were forbidden to operate at their permanent headquarters' sites; the history of signals concluded the months of inactivity had a 'very adverse effect on the efficiency of handling wireless and cipher traffic during the subsequent operations'.[59] The BEF actions on the Saar front were symbolic of its contradictory approach to wireless; aware that combat was a possibility on this semi-active front and determined to prevent subordinate isolation, 8th Brigade ensured each of its battalions received an additional two wireless sets upon entering the line. However, fearful of unintended consequences, brigade ordered 'wireless silence will be observed' at all times, and they were never used as a result. The post-Dunkirk Bartholomew Committee illustrated how 'an ingrained habit of wireless silence' developed during this period which proved hard to shake when combat began in earnest; rejecting the BEF's approach entirely, the Committee recommended minimum restrictions in all further campaigns, and 'once operations are joined, the maximum use of wireless should be made'.[60] The irony is the BEF was confronting an enemy who maximized wireless usage and largely transmitted in the clear, thereby swamping BEF Intelligence and nullifying any associated risks. Restricted to passive training techniques, Wireless Operator W. Saunders became adept at recording German signals, but 'we never learned what value, if any, attached to what we had intercepted'. At the other end of the process, frustrated staff officer P. Gribble received numerous intercepted German transmissions throughout the campaign, but with intercept information routinely encoded by BEF and French signals, 'by the time the message is coded by the sender and decoded by the recipient some hours will have elapsed and the fleeting opportunity target will no longer present itself for attack'. Post-Dunkirk, the Bartholomew Report summarized: 'We had no difficulty in intercepting information, but there was so much that it was rarely possible to extract items in time to take action on them'.[61] Inadequate pre-war provision was compounded by Phoney War mishandling, resulting in degraded wireless capability and an undermined overall communication system.

The human messenger remained a vital part of the BEF's communication portfolio, especially the despatch rider whose flexibility allowed him to travel between any two points, often quicker than more technological methods could achieve. However, their reliability was not guaranteed as their customary enthusiasm for speed combined with bad weather and busy roads within the BEF area of operations led to a disturbing number of serious accidents and lost messages. In November 1939, GHQ RASC complained motorcycles being 'driven without due care' had resulted in 'accidents in which 10 DRs were involved and 1 DR sustained injuries which have since proved fatal'. A BEF campaign encouraging riders to keep 'below the maximum speed, and DRs will at all times exercise due care, so as to obviate casualties' fell largely on deaf ears; for example, the despatch riders of 48th Divisional Signals were recognized as highly skilled motorcycle fanatics and 'a law unto themselves'.[62] Efforts to ensure the safe delivery of communications were not assisted by the speed enforcers of the Military Police displaying the same reckless enthusiasm for speed; for example, having deployed to France in late September 1939, 1st Division Provost Company lost five personnel to serious injury in separate motorcycle accidents by 22 October. These figures were by no means unique, nor did they reduce over time, as the perpetual presence of newly equipped and deployed despatch riders was an unintended consequence of the gradual expansion of the BEF during the Phoney War. Never-ending accidents depleted an already scarce resource; although constantly in demand, full-time despatch riders made up only a small proportion of Royal Corps of Signals personnel. At corps level signal units comprised a headquarters and three companies (one each for construction, operating and artillery) however, there were only two messenger sections, each of a sergeant and 24 messengers. At divisional level signals consisted of a headquarters, a headquarters company and four standard companies; of the 17 sections that made up these units, only one, Section D of No. 1 Company, had permanent despatch rider duties. The other sections may have used men on messenger duties on an ad hoc basis, but they had other duties and specializations. The BEF failed to recognize the vulnerability of this communication method or the pressure this service was placed under despite the relative stability of the Phoney War; a pressure and exposure to excessive dangers which only intensified during active operations as other signal methods collapsed.[63]

The motorized liaison officer was another communication method predominantly reliant on a human component, equivalent in flexibility to the despatch rider, but with the additional ability of being able to explain orders rather than just deliver them. This method was favoured by the BEF on occasions when developing events required complex orders to be delivered to unusual places; for example, as the Mechelen invasion scare broke on 14 January, II Corps opted to send out liaison officers to find, recall and prepare for deployment 5th Division and, in particular, 15th Brigade who were on exercise at an unknown location. The Bartholomew Committee heard evidence that the youth and inexperience of BEF liaison officers (known as Motor Contact Officers) undermined their authority and, subsequently, their ability to reliably fulfil the role asked of them. This problem was even more widespread than the Committee's Report makes clear because many BEF liaison positions were filled by senior NCOs who encountered similar prejudices. On 14 April 1940, the commander of a light anti-aircraft battery refused to relocate his unit overnight until he received telephone confirmation from the II Corps night-time duty officer, much to the chagrin of the senior NCO sent to deliver the orders and the duty officer who sent them. This demonstrates how large formations with diverse communication capabilities opted for human messengers over the more technological methods, risking inefficiency in the process. With fear of fifth column rife in Phoney War France, communications involving personnel travelling through military areas alone or in pairs inevitably aroused suspicions and made the pace of human messenger communications unpredictable. After a German air-raid and leaflet drop on 27 February, the heightened tensions led to both 3rd Division's liaison officers being 'arrested as spies by 33 Fd Regt', thereby delaying their progress for hours; in the confusion of battle, these mistakes became more catastrophic and more frequent.[64]

Fears of messages being intercepted or the communication system's integrity being compromised by German espionage and fifth column led to the BEF implementing excessive security measures, often in the most futile of circumstances; these procedures added little to BEF security as a whole, but had considerable impact upon the tempo of communications. Measures to prevent 'the passage of enemy agents, information, defeatist literature [and] communist propaganda' across the Franco-Belgian border included the joint operation of frontier control posts with French police, whilst some commanders used their discretionary powers to order supplementary military patrols along the border to prevent 'unauthorised traffic'. However, as Lord Gort's Despatches make clear, the BEF had no legal right to close the border with neutral Belgium and 'considerably more than twenty thousand local inhabitants passed the frontier daily on their normal business'; this flow of people made the leakage of information inevitable.[65] Military cable was a relatively secure form of communication, but such was the desperation to minimize German awareness of BEF operations, British battalions deployed to the Saar front were banned from speaking English on the telephone (their primary means of communication) in the forward lines, in the hope their presence would go unnoticed. In reality German Intelligence was sufficiently adept at locating targets that, during the Phoney War, German radio's Lord Haw Haw correctly announced: 'You imagine that we do not know where your GHQ is. Let me tell you it is at Arras and the Commander-in-Chief's telephone number is Arras...' much to the BEF's consternation.[66] As previously mentioned, fear of German intercept capability led to wireless being routinely encoded within the BEF, regardless of the message content and recipient's capability; for example, on 23 September 1939 GHQ 2nd Echelon, who did not possess any cipher personnel, decoding equipment or the BEF code book, received three cipher wires from the War Office and RAF. The wires were referred to nearby No. 2 Base Sub-Area for deciphering, delaying the reception of non-urgent, non-operational information at the BEF's record-keeping headquarters.[67] S.P. Mackenzie has shown the scale of cipher was so vast within the BEF that almost all the officers in the Army Education Corps and 50 per cent of its NCOs had to be drafted in for cipher duties just to stop the system seizing up; those units without an AEC representative were often incapable of dealing with cipher communications.[68] Paranoia about sensitive information being leaked through letters home from France resulted in all BEF personnel having their mail read, censored and approved by their directly superior officer. Daily post in both directions for most personnel meant junior officers such as RASC Second Lieutenant J. Finch 'had at least one hour's reading and initialling each evening'. In units where officers were sparse, this process could produce extreme workloads; for example, on 12 December 1939 alone 'over 400 letters and Christmas cards passed through the office for censoring' by Captain T. Cooper, 2nd Division Provost Company. Unfortunately for the BEF, French censorship guidelines were not as rigorous and largely undermined BEF efforts, for example, on a covert visit to Nice in December 1939, Deputy Adjutant General J. Whitehead was met at the station by local dignitaries and a French guard of honour and accommodated in the Royal Suite of the Hotel Rhul; Whitehead recalled: 'It was a trial to have my time detailed for various functions and my programme issued each morning in the local papers', but the French could not be persuaded otherwise.[69] Senior officers' distrust towards the rank-and-file was replicated within large headquarters who felt similarly apprehensive when distributing sensitive information to subordinate headquarters; for example, II Corps had a strict policy of not communicating any future plans 'below Div HQ and Inf Bde Commanders' as a precaution against unnecessary security breaches. Ironically, it was often in the larger headquarters that documents went inexplicably astray, such as on 9 December 1939, when GHQ learned a sensitive document on BEF gas munitions and precautions had been 'floating around' for six days without having its location logged and recorded.[70]

The flawed procedures of the British communication system, such as an over-reliance on written orders, contributed to its collapse as much as equipment, through their unnecessary complexity slowing the transfer of orders and information. During the Great War, the production of overly long written orders increased exponentially because time was frequently abundant, distrust of subordinates was prevalent and precautions against subsequent official inquiries were considered prudent. The inter-war army maintained written orders as its favoured communication tool for three main reasons. The first reason, highlighted by David French, was that umpires of peacetime exercises relied on written orders to follow events and pass judgment on the plans of participating commanders and staff; eventually the writing of lengthy orders became habitual, even amongst officers without Great War experience. Secondly, the hierarchical ethos and structure of the Army concentrated control of most support weapons in the hands of higher formations to which subordinates appealed for help. The 1932 Kirke Committee concluded as soon as an application had been made, 'centralised control and complicated orders naturally ensue. The fire plan is the forcing house of the voluminous order'; with insufficient support weapons to individually equip each unit, the Committee could suggest few plausible alternatives to the current procedure. Finally, many BEF officers had trained with *FSR 1929* earlier in their careers, which glorified 'the precise and formal written order'; this circulated the view that Great War failures had occurred because of individual errors rather than inherently flawed procedures, meaning alterations to army processes were unnecessary.[71]

The trend for prolific paperwork within the communication system continued after the BEF's deployment to France. I Corps standing orders gave all superior officers the discretionary power to demand copies of any subordinate operation orders in order to keep 'in touch with events'. III Corps was even more prescriptive, demanding 'three copies of all instructions and orders produced for major exercises and information as to suitable time and places for observing exercises'. This shows both an element of distrust in subordinates and a desire to use the communication system as a method of ceaseless supervision and control.[72] The *Field Service Pocket Book 1939–40* recommended 'orders, instructions, reports and messages will, whenever possible, be issued, or confirmed, in writing' by both the originator and, in some cases involving telephone messages, the recipient as well. Furthermore, each unit participating in an operation should receive not only their specific instructions, but the instructions of other participating units to ensure clarity of objective and to facilitate co-operation; documented communication was still considered an ideal method of preventing mistakes and future criticism. Such was the profusion of communication-related paperwork within the BEF, that by November 1939, the War Office was receiving multiple complaints about the chronic shortage of typewriters upon which most orders were produced. Initially, a similar shortage of personnel capable of producing this forest of documentation existed in France, compelling newly-formed BEF units to improvise; prior to the incoming transfer of a single RASC Clerk in late October, GHQ Petrol was forced to exploit its contacts with the Société Générale des Huiles de Pétroles to borrow the French short-hand typist necessary for the unit to operate.[73] At no point was the impracticality of this system in a high-tempo, high-pressure battlefield environment considered or acted upon.

The use of verbal orders within the BEF received only tacit support because of the risk of mistakes and misguided subordinates. Military Training Pamphlet No. 23, which reinforced FSR 1935, did not specifically rule out verbal orders, but it did demand every commander make a 'clear statement as to the task he proposes' and 'allot definite tasks to his subordinates' when issuing orders. Surreptitiously the system ensured written orders were the best way of achieving this, by protecting both the commander and his subordinates from future comeback.[74] In January 1940, Army Training Memorandum No. 28 actively encouraged infantry platoons to 'accustom men to receive and deliver verbal messages' through a slightly more structured version of Chinese whispers; rather than promote a tempo-enhancing, flexible communication method, the above suggestion was listed as an indoor activity for bored men in bad weather.[75] In general, BEF units only used verbal orders during the Phoney War when there was a profound sense of urgency, such as the Mechelen incident of January 1940, which prompted 2nd Division Provost Company to issue skeleton verbal orders to section commanders, albeit supported by 'an operation order [which] was prepared but not issued to sections'.[76]

The British Army's attitude to verbal orders was fairly consistent during this period because no single organization or group was prepared to unilaterally promote their stand-alone use. Without listing specific occasions when their usage was correct, the 1932 Kirke Committee supported the general idea of 'verbal orders confirmed in writing when time permits'.[77] During the France 1939–40 campaign, GHQ's preference was for procedures based on formal written orders; if time permits 'detailed operation instructions' should be issued, with 'short telegraph or telephone messages' only used to inform units of deviations to the orders. In instances of significant time pressure GHQ recommended the calling of a Commanders' Conference at which verbal orders (in the correct sequence and as short as possible) and tracings and maps (marked with relevant operational boundaries) could be issued. Even within this more flexible procedure, GHQ considered written orders an integral part of the process; upon leaving the conference, or by despatch rider soon after, all officers should be issued with written confirmation of their orders. If it was impossible to collect commanders and there was not time for the issue of detailed written orders, BEF procedure required one of three alternatives. Either short written orders in message form, covering essentials only, such as objectives and timings, with a tracing carried by a liaison officer who could expand on information upon which the orders were based, or verbal orders by telephone (confirmed in writing), or short orders by telegram. GHQ did not offer suggestions for when units were without cable communications, and pointedly did not recommend quick verbal orders without written confirmation.[78] Reviewing BEF operations in June 1940, the Bartholomew Committee heard evidence that in the heat of battle, many orders by higher formations did take 'the form of conferences and verbal orders which were not confirmed'. Concluding that 'as some people affected by the orders were not present, they received no orders or information on essential matters', the Committee argued this deviation from procedure was the root cause for significant combat communication problems. The Committee demanded that the requirement for all verbal orders to be confirmed in writing must be rigorously enforced by higher formations in future operations; after Dunkirk, the problem of inadequate tempo within communications became clear, but the solution remained obscure.[79]

Every BEF headquarters with a signal section operated a signal office and together they formed the backbone of BEF communication infrastructure. The duties of signal office personnel included receiving, recording, despatching and delivering messages, but crucially not the creation, filing and distributing of internal copies necessary for a headquarters to operate effectively; Signals personnel only facilitated communications and it was the responsibility of the originating staff officer to deal with the consequences of any signals. Signal offices were supplemented by signal centres, temporary signal offices which concentrated communications of two headquarters in a unique location; these could act as a bridge between headquarters with disrupted communications or an advance signal office for a relocating unit. Although these offices combined to form a main artery of communications along the chain of command, the system was further developed and strengthened by lateral connections between signal offices and centres; the burden of responsibility for lateral communications was right to left. Direct links were used on occasions where justified by the exceptional importance or capacity requirement of the connection, but in general, communication infrastructure outside the orthodox framework was frowned upon for the 'dispersion of effort' it caused. The multiple connections of this system formed a latticework of resilience theoretically capable of bypassing any breakage; however, reliance on such a regimented spine of communications meant a chain reaction of delays could occur from a single bottleneck.[80]

To speed the transfer of information, the *Field Service Pocket Book 1939–40* authorized the use of abbreviations, particularly for the titles of units and subordinate commanders within them; however, it warned these should 'only be used when no possibility of misunderstanding could occur'.[81] Fearful of incorrect usage and blighted by ingrained peacetime habits of inefficiency and ignorance, abbreviations remained an under-utilized communication tool within the BEF which, in turn, compounded delays as duplications echoed through the system. In June 1940, ATM No. 33 recorded:

> A battalion signal section of the BEF recently had to deal with 176 'out' and nearly 100 'in' messages during its first 24-hours in the line; 1000 message forms were used, and two signal clerks had to be kept on duty the whole time, working in eight-hour shifts. Most of the messages contained between 40 and 170 groups and could have been drastically abbreviated if the originators had taken more care. Little use was made of 'all informed' at the end of text to save addresses being signalled unnecessarily.

The June 1940 ATM demanded 'all officers should be given practice in writing messages during training', but this was far from original; in July 1939, ATM No. 23 observed: 'Command Individual Training Reports continue to show that officers are still poor at expressing themselves in speech and on paper ... Practice will be provided in the writing of appreciations, orders, etc.'. During the Phoney War, communication procedures were just one of the many forms of training neglected by BEF officers distracted by alternative duties and the benefits of being in France. Increased availability of wireless, especially Radio Telephony, may have alleviated the burden of signal office personnel by allowing officers to communicate directly and independently, but in reality, the BEF communication procedures were too slow and complex, even for efficient operation during the relatively benign conditions of Phoney War.[82]

The most extraordinary procedures existed at its busiest and most important nerve centre, Commander-in-Chief Gort's GHQ. The procedures for incoming messages to GHQ required the signal office to produce three copies of every message (Action, File and War Diary) and send them to Operations via an on-call GSO3. Rather than risk mistakes within the hectic GHQ Signal Office, adequate copies were produced at the source, for example, GHQ standing orders instructed the War Office, subordinate corps and missions 'to originate all [teleprinted] messages to C-in-C and G Ops in quadruplicate'. Once the signal office had copied out a message three times, the Action copy was taken to the GSO2 who supervised Operations communications, the File copy was put on a board for all to see, and the War Diary copy was placed in the War Diary tray. The on-call GSO3 made additional copies of messages where necessary, for example, if they were of interest to other branches of

GHQ. Furthermore, every time messages contained dispositions which were entered on the Operations Map, identical marks were made on a War Diary Copy Map. The complex procedures could only be bypassed for a few reasons; GHQ standing orders stated: '"Immediate", "Most Immediate" and "Emergency Ops" may be taken direct to Deputy Chief General Staff or GSO1 where a GSO2 is not immediately available. No other message will be short-circuited past GSO2s'. With hundreds of messages received on a daily basis, a mountain of paperwork could quickly accumulate within large BEF headquarters, especially if multiple copies had to be made; in these circumstances, vital paperwork could be mislaid, context could be lost and responses delayed indefinitely. All messages require urgent action if left long enough and, consequently, high priority message classifications may have been used unnecessarily to attract attention; an increase in this type of message would have further delayed standard messages being dealt with. In contrast, outgoing message procedures were relatively straightforward, with a GSO3 being assigned responsibility for the display and update of a 'Number' contact list of formations and headquarters; the officer originating the message would then obtain a number from it, pass the message to the signal clerks for despatch and ensure that the File and War Diary copies reached the GSO3 responsible.[83]

Within the BEF, Operations and Intelligence personnel had substantial influence over all aspects of communications at large headquarters. GHQ standing orders demanded headquarters personnel make every effort to assist in the daily production of a combined Operations and Intelligence Report, jointly written by a GSO3 from Operations and a senior Intelligence officer; the Report was published at 2000hrs daily. In addition, these officers had round-the-clock authority to collect any information required for supplementary 'special' reports, for example, publishing at '1200hrs if important operations have occurred at dawn'. Operations and Intelligence jointly ensured these reports received prioritization during despatch, in cipher (normally by teleprinter) to the War Office, military missions and corps headquarters. It was anticipated these reports would provide 'War Office branches a complete picture of the immediate situation and should eliminate many telephone enquiries; they will provide the basis for War Office Press Communiques; and they can be used for Corps to inform lower formations'. However, with great power came great responsibility, which, for reasons of complacency or time pressure, Operations and Intelligence were less willing to fulfil. Even in the relatively tranquil Phoney War, the copious paperwork involved in communication procedures caused concern; GHQ standing orders warned all branches, but particularly Operations, to 'reduce pressure on communications and cipher personnel as far as possible'. Furthermore, BEF Operations and Intelligence staff rather than signals personnel were made responsible for ensuring critically important incoming information was 'not crowded out by non-essential matters'.[84] When combat began, the removal of key Operations and Intelligence personnel from the GHQ nerve centre would render them incapable of performing this duty, to the detriment of the BEF.

The British Army failed to take advantage of the lengthy inter-war interlude or the unexpected period of Phoney War 1939–40, both of which offered opportunity to test, strengthen and modernize communications to a standard suitable for first-class war. In each case a complacent acceptance of existing techniques and satisfactory performance in a low pressure environment superseded all other concerns. The creation of a stand-alone signal arm, initially without senior officers who could advocate its needs, did little to energize communications development or recruitment during the inter-war period; grandiose aspirations failed to materialize and the Army was left with a communication capability comparable with the end of the Great War. Upon deployment, the BEF passively accepted an overly complex layout that disrupted headquarters operations and caused the tempo of communications to slow to a snail's pace. Such was the fear of aerial attack, dangerously expansive lines of communication were consciously developed as the lesser of two evils, placing tremendous strain on an already overstretched signal corps. Despite the presence of a broad communication portfolio, cable remained overwhelmingly dominant; as a result, delays and disruption proved disorientating and an unwelcome warning of events to come. More flexible communication methods such as wireless and human messengers were utilized on occasions, but their use as either a fall-back or method of choice was left to officer or unit discretion. All had their faults and were comparatively unreliable in the benign Phoney War conditions, undermining any attempt to usurp cable's primary role. The failure to develop and harness wireless was a singular error and in marked contrast to the German approach. Sensitive information remained vulnerable to espionage and, on occasion, casual observation, despite the enforcement of disproportionate and ill-conceived security measures which compromised the tempo of communications and the military response. Ignoring the volume of communications and the accompanying explosion in paperwork, the BEF remained unflinchingly loyal to traditional written orders and rigid communication procedures which had worked in peacetime. The clutter of unnecessary paperwork and unabbreviated messages suffocated signal personnel and left them ill-prepared to deal with the demands of their colleagues in Operations and Intelligence or, more importantly, the rigours of mobile warfare.

5
Communications: Collapse

From the first few hours of intensive operations on 10 May 1940, the BEF's communication system was unequal to the responsibilities placed on it, resulting in a rapid deterioration in performance for both it and the units it served. The structural reorganization spurred by combat proved too great a burden for a communication system already buckling under the strain of Phoney War routine; any benefits were dwarfed by massive duplication, the isolation of decision-makers and general confusion from infrequent reports. The fallacy of heavy reliance on cable communications disastrously materialized as vulnerable civilian networks failed, incessant manoeuvres minimized opportunities to develop independent infrastructure and, on the few occasions this did occur, signals personnel quickly exhausted themselves and their resources, establishing fleetingly used, cable-based communications. The BEF had attempted to retain wireless for emergencies only, but once combat began, its unique ability to bypass physical obstructions left it with an unexpectedly heavy burden of responsibility; despite this, usage remained erratic as tempo-enhancing, cipher-free messages were tempered by continuing fears of interception and direction finding. Exhaustion from long hours and long distances, compounded by combat, refugee-blocked roads and constantly relocating units, magnified exponentially the vulnerability of human messengers to accidents and death. Written orders were simplified and largely restricted to communications requiring a degree of authority, whilst increased usage of verbal orders helped slow, but could not prevent, the implosion of the communication system. Voids in information were filled by rumour, often without foundation, but occasionally a consequence of verifiable sabotage and fifth column activity which, in turn, further prevented the functioning of the communication system, thereby perpetuating the downward spiral. Although riddled with self-inflicted communication deficiencies, the BEF was also undermined by a French system with even greater defects; inherently slow and procedurally inefficient, it could provide the BEF with little information on the critical events happening within its area of operations. In contrast, widespread experience of verbal orders and wireless helped German forces to breach the Allied front-line with high-tempo operations and then maintain adequate communications during the advance across France; aerial reconnaissance and close air support were additional benefits of this communications edge. The initial BEF collapse in communications was self-inflicted and occurred before the German breakthrough at Sedan; the Germans exploited weaknesses within the BEF communication system and denied it the opportunity to recover, but this only compounded a dire situation in which confusion already reigned.

The Allied communication system failed to ensure a speedy or uniform response to the invasion of 10 May 1940 which, due to haphazard information distribution, was only slowly recognized. At 0010hrs 10 May, Belgian Grand Quartier General (GQG) became aware that invasion was imminent and began issuing alerts to both subordinates and Allies; however, deadened by months of false alarms, mass bombing of Belgian Aerodromes at 0400hrs took the Belgian Air Force by surprise and over half its aeroplanes were destroyed on the ground.[1] Within the BEF a minority of units were proactive in their response to unusual overnight activity. Spurred by the first reports of trouble, as early as 2300hrs 9 May, subordinates of 6th Infantry Brigade received advisory warnings of possible parachute landings and increased aerial activity; believing invasion imminent, 2nd Durham Light Infantry began preparations to advance into Belgium and, as a result, required only a further 30 minutes for final preparations when official confirmation arrived on 10 May. Several units did not require a phone call to tell them of invasion because they could hear and see it all around them; 2nd Divisional Signals and 1st Survey Regiment Royal Artillery both commented on the intense aerial activity that occurred from 0400hrs onwards and that 'something out of the ordinary had happened'.[2] In contrast, the majority of the BEF was caught napping, in some cases literally; GSO2 R. Tong (GHQ Operations) was woken by unusually heavy bombing at 0400hrs, but opted to go back to sleep, only to be woken again at 0530hrs with urgent orders to report for duty. Air Intelligence Liaison Officer P. Gribble believed this typical response was symptomatic of 'the old story of crying wolf' which, when multiplied, meant GHQ had 'been caught off guard'.[3] Acknowledging the general unpreparedness of the BEF, Chief of the General Staff Lieutenant General Pownall despaired: 'Being in no state of previous alerte [sic] we shan't be moving till 1 pm'. GHQ received official confirmation of invasion at 0600hrs and orders from French GQG to implement Plan D at 0700hrs; it was 0640hrs before II Corps received official confirmation of invasion and 1040hrs before it received orders to implement Plan D. Despite procedures being pre-arranged, Brigadier Utterson-Kelso (131st Brigade) felt the gravity of the situation compelled him to disregard cable and wireless communications and instead, laboriously summoned representatives from his subordinate battalions to repeat in person the orders on Plan D, route marches and conditions for breaking wireless silence.[4] Inevitably, the news spurred a flurry of activity that swamped the communication system and further slowed the passage of information; for example, 2nd Divisional Signals admitted: 'Signal Office Traffic was exceptionally heavy during the morning and telegraph, telephone and DRs were extended to the limit'. In many instances the official communication system was beaten to the announcement by the media; whilst 2nd Cameronians Regiment nonchalantly recorded breakfast wireless included news about a German invasion, 5th Royal Inniskilling Dragoon Guards actively complained: 'When the real invasion came we got no warning at all; merely hearing the news on the BBC'.[5] Paradoxically, information filtered haphazardly through to the rear-echelon; for example, Line of Communication Headquarters only learnt of events late on 10 May due to a courtesy message from GHQ Q Branch, whilst small groups of BEF personnel were still departing France on leave on the morning of 11 May, because 'either they didn't know, or else they didn't care much'.[6] Despite this being the pinnacle of BEF communication capability during the campaign, the system was immediately stretched informing its stationary subordinates, the BBC proved more responsive to events than the chain of command and hours after the invasion began BEF personnel were still awaiting their first instructions.

When the fighting started on 10 May, Lord Gort was fulfilling his Phoney War dual role of Commander-in-Chief and Army Commander; Gort had planned to relinquish the role of Army Commander to two subordinates when the BEF was increased to four corps, but the German invasion preceded this. Whilst reliable telephonic availability for War Office and military mission communications was deemed obligatory for a BEF Commander-in-Chief, it was felt an Army Commander's duties required close proximity to the front.[7] During the Phoney War, Lord Gort had extricated himself from excessive GHQ bureaucracy by relocating to an external site; the contradictions of being both Commander-in-Chief and Army Commander were considered solvable by a similar organizational restructure. Lord Gort's solution to a disconnect between an Arras-based GHQ and combat operations in Belgium was the creation of a Command Post (CP) which would join the advance towards the Dyle River, leaving behind the main GHQ. Communications with static institutions and headquarters were primarily maintained through Arras, whilst the CP established wireless communications with the three corps and the 12th Royal Lancers. These connections were tenuous at best, for example, one No. 3 set per corps was reserved for communications with I and II Corps whilst a No. 3 set relay via GHQ was maintained for III Corps; this surprisingly sparse arrangement was due to a shortage of equipment, a determination to keep the CP streamlined and the less prominent position of III Corps (the reserve formation). Decisions were taken at the CP and then implemented through the production and issuing of orders at GHQ. Arras also acted as a 'Clearing House' for information, keeping the C-in-C informed at one end and the War Office, French GQG and flank formations at the other; it also dealt with the RAF in all matters of air support and reconnaissance.[8]

Theoretically capable of implementing the Commander-in-Chief's decisions quickly and effectively, in reality the restructured system was an administrative disaster and a significant self-inflicted reason for communication collapse. It did not facilitate improved control over the front, for as the advance progressed the CP was moved to Wahagnies (10 May) and then Renaix (13 May); disappointing results prompted the establishment of a small Battle Post even further forward in Lennick St Quentin on 15 May. Thus for a short period there were three headquarters; the C-in-C and the CGS at Lennick St Quentin, the DCGS leading a small coordinating staff at Renaix, and the bulk of GHQ at Arras. The post-Dunkirk Bartholomew Committee heard evidence that the duplication required for information transfers between GHQ and Lord Gort's CP was so labour-intensive that the system 'never worked satisfactorily' in terms of reliability or tempo; Gort's last-ditch attempt to influence the front with an advanced Battle Post further exaggerated the problem to such an unsustainable degree that it could only be maintained for 48 hours before change became inevitable. The fallacy of this plan is personified by the C-in-C's link to the outside world being reduced to a handful of signal clerks at his tiny outpost, who had the impossible duty of dealing with the flood of information being forwarded by the remainder of the BEF communication system. Echoing his previous actions when confronted by congested communications, Lord Gort frequently removed himself altogether from his command infrastructure in search of clearer information at the front; CGS Pownall had actively supported the creation of an advanced tactical headquarters, but complained in his diary on 14 May, that his Commander had been away for eight hours visiting that day, 'too long in difficult times'.[9]

Conversely, just as communications involving the Commander-in-Chief were imploding, the size and importance of his CP was increasing significantly. The official report on GHQ recorded the moment when a divided GHQ became clearly unsustainable;

> It was soon found inadvisable to rely on the slender civilian telephone communications and military wireless sets available to maintain the essential link between these three headquarters [GHQ, CP and BP], and it became necessary to issue all orders and instructions from the CP itself. This was not easy at first, owing to the limited staff available there.

The list of personnel operating beyond Arras-based GHQ initially consisted of the C-in-C, the CGS, personal staffs, a significant proportion of Operations, but only representatives of Intelligence, Administrative and Q branches; these were serviced by an Assistant Camp Commandant, a small administrative staff and various small detachments, including Signals. Over time more and more people found reason to be in close proximity to the C-in-C so that, in the words of Major General Montgomery, 'the size of the Command Post grew and grew'; this eased decision-making processes, but did little to alleviate pressure on the communication system as information continued to be sent to Arras-based GHQ and excessive information transfer obligations between GHQ's disparate parts remained. With searing honesty, the post-campaign report admitted 'not until Premesque [21 May] was the Command Post able to function with its full operational resources; while both "A" and "Q" branches suffered throughout in their communications with their rearward services'. Explaining how every hour counted during the campaign, in June 1940 Brigadier General Staff Oliver Leese informed the Bartholomew Committee: 'Where you may have a stable situation in the morning, by seven o'clock or eight o'clock in the evening, if you did not act and do something, the situation might be irretrievably lost'. The communication system was in crisis from day one of intensive hostilities because the decision-makers and organizers of GHQ Operations were not unified in a single location until Premesque, whilst other service branches were never unified; in the interim, 11 irreplaceable days were wasted in relative ignorance and isolation at a time of fast moving events.[10]

Internal communications between GHQ branches had faltered at times in the Phoney War due to insular staff officers, watertight operating procedures and narrow department-based allegiances, but the restructuring of GHQ compounded these failings, leaving unglamorous departments without access to critically important information. At 1700hrs 13/05/40, Q (Maintenance) Branch of GHQ complained: 'Information particularly from "G" [Operations] and "I" [Intelligence], gradually dried up and from this date became more or less obscure'. At this time, German forces had yet to comprehensively break through in the Ardennes and the BEF was still confidently advancing into Belgium; the collapse of internal GHQ communications predated outside factors. Campaign events remained 'generally obscure' until, on 17 May, Q Branch learnt 'enemy has broken through on the MEUSE front'; within three hours of receiving this information, this prudently located rear-echelon service headquarters was compelled into an immediate evacuation because the enemy was 'approaching Arras'. To ensure the security of GHQ non-combatants, 50 per cent of Q Branch and the majority of A Branch were relocated to Boulogne amidst a 'complete lack of information regarding situation'. The GHQ campaign report admitted unforeseen enemy advances ultimately forced these personnel to be repatriated 'prematurely to England, at a moment when their services would have been of great value to the C-in-C'; all because unglamorous departments were not kept up-to-date and provided with time to plan contingencies.[11] Other elements of GHQ were equally detached from events; for example, on 21 May, with the bulk of the BEF surrounded, GSO3 R. Page described GHQ and, in particular, Anti-Aircraft Command, as 'pretty slack and dull'. Having previously described his posting as 'at the centre of things', Page's department had been becalmed by the total failure of 'phone and wireless' communications, preventing contact with AA units throughout the theatre or other GHQ branches. With his determination to do something matched only by his superiors' determination to offload him, Page was transferred to liaison duties. Although it is unfair to expect a GSO3 in AA Command to be fully versed in the positions recorded on the GHQ Operations Map and information board, Page's 21 May belief that 'the BEF was still far to the east in Belgium', when in reality imminent evacuation beckoned, indicates a level of ignorance that could only have been shared or encouraged by senior officers; clearly certain departments were struggling to follow events, never mind participate in and orchestrate them.[12]

Cable was the preferred Phoney War method of communication within the BEF, but once in Belgium increased dependence on local civilian networks undermined both its previous level of reliability and security. Prior to the BEF's advance to the Dyle River, strictly enforced Belgian neutrality had prevented the Royal Corps of Signals developing any independent cable infrastructure within future areas of operation, thereby forcing, from 10 May onwards, the majority of communications to be facilitated by the civilian telephone network. Some disruption had been anticipated, for example, in November 1939, CGS Pownall admitted: 'The reorganization of our present administrative system necessitated by carrying the whole BEF 80 miles forward is no light business'; however, it was the scale and persistence of the disruption that surprised the BEF. A GHQ representative acknowledged in evidence to the post-Dunkirk Bartholomew Committee: 'It was sometimes very difficult to get calls through in a reasonable time and, of course, we had to be extremely careful what we said'.[13] The Flanders telephone network was an unsuitable provider of military communications in a combat environment, with civilian operators unwilling to stay at their posts when the German advance neared, or deviate from traditional shift patterns when high-volume traffic occurred outside office hours. It took over 24 hours of negotiation and effort for the newly established headquarters of II Corps to gain access to a section of Brussels telephone exchange dedicated to BEF formations and, even upon achieving this, Lieutenant General Alan Brooke complained, 'with great difficulty got through to GHQ' to discuss operations.[14] Unsurprisingly, combat operations caused a great deal of disruption to the high-visibility civilian cable infrastructure, which infected BEF units just when they needed reliable communications the most. By the end of 11 May, 2nd Division had settled into defensive positions on the Dyle River with cable communications established to I Corps in the rear and 4th and 6th brigades in front; on 12 May, the cornerstone of this communication network, the Wavre civil exchange, was completely destroyed by German bombing.[15]

Despite the best efforts of BEF signal personnel, the static nature of cable communications proved incompatible with the frequent movement that dominated the campaign. Corps headquarters were critically important to facilitating subordinate cable communications, yet between 10 May and evacuation, II Corps headquarters moved 12 times, making 'Command very difficult and normal communications impossible'; least affected was III Corps headquarters, but even this formation was forced to move a similarly disruptive seven times.[16] Further down the chain of command, the futility of laying cable on a volatile battlefield became clear quite quickly, for example, on 13 May, signallers from the 1st Survey Regiment laid '5½ miles of cable' to strengthen positions, yet the following day orders to relocate meant 'reeling in cable at first light'; this procedure could only be replicated a few times before men and material were exhausted.[17] Whilst some units, such as 48th Divisional Signals, rapidly concluded 'moves were made so quickly that there was often no time to lay lines', others persevered in hope more than expectation; for example, on 20 May, 36th Brigade Signal Section were still laying a line forward when they met retreating survivors of the recently overrun 5th Buffs Regiment.[18] It should be noted, these issues merely compounded the vulnerability of cable on the battlefield; for example, on the few occasions cable-based communications were available, 1st Duke of Wellington's Regiment complained telephone lines were 'constantly broken by shellfire and the signallers were kept very busy'.[19]

Even when it worked, long-distance cable communications between static headquarters was, according to Lieutenant General A. Brooke, a 'devastating process' dependent upon 'a long and poor system of telephone communication with very indistinct speech'. Inevitably, as the Germans advanced across France these physical lines of communication were severed, leaving static headquarters in the south of France increasingly isolated. Those headquarters that operated comparatively independently and minimized cable usage drifted into isolation; having received vague reports of enemy probing near Sedan on 15 May and Abancourt on 19 May, Line of Communication Headquarters suddenly realized intermittent GHQ communication had become no communication at an unrecognized point during the last four days. Putting the disruption down to 'GHQ possibly moving', it was a further 34 hours before this headquarters was convinced all communications had been cut by enemy action. Alternatively, those headquarters dependent on frequent contact with GHQ to coordinate operations were more alert to faltering communications. The British Air Force in France (BAFF) Headquarters recorded cable communications with GHQ ended at 2400hrs 17 May, forcing all information transfers to be diverted via the Air Ministry in London. Eventually conditions on the ground made cable impractical for even the most diligent of headquarters; for example, BAFF had a 'quiet night at headquarters' on 23 May, 'mainly due to the complete breakdown in communications'. Long-distance cable may have been flawed, but when it failed static rear-echelon headquarters were often left with nothing.[20]

When significant combat began, the BEF primarily intended wireless to be held in reserve for emergency use only; however, over time this method was forced to handle an unexpectedly high proportion of communications. This required the BEF to overcome habitual wireless silence, accept the threat from German direction finding and wireless interception, and streamline procedure to increase tempo; it only partially succeeded in achieving these objectives. On 10 May, a considerable proportion of BEF wireless sets were deployed in a relay chain along selected routes to the Dyle River to provide associated divisions with emergency communications in case of bombing or breakdown of civil communication networks. A wireless set was issued to each of the four traffic control posts, approximately 18–23 miles apart, that lined each route to the Dyle and divisions generally took two routes to avoid congestion and reduce the threat from aerial attack. Initially civil telephone facilities were adjudged 'sufficient' for traffic control, leaving wireless personnel with little to do; even after the move to the Dyle was complete, wireless remained in reserve until events compelled its involvement. Having entered Belgium on 10 May for relay duties, 48th Divisional Signals stayed silent in reserve until 12 May when it was asked to facilitate communication 'traffic as lines have failed'. Having previously maintained wireless silence, 2nd Buffs Regiment was able to portray the serious nature of Luftwaffe bombing on Courtrai on the night of 11/12 May, just by using wireless to report 'enemy action' to 131st Brigade.[21]

This determination to maintain wireless silence as long as possible was not entirely planned; for example, the post-Dunkirk Bartholomew Committee concluded many units failed to break wireless silence after crossing the frontier, despite receiving authorization to do so, to the detriment of BEF communications. A contributing factor not highlighted by the Committee was that the regulations enforcing wireless silence were never actually revoked; preparatory corps orders show the regulations were merely 'modified' to reduce the number of restrictions and increase usage. This subtle difference led to subjective interpretation of appropriate usage; for example, attempting to contact the neighbouring unit, wireless operators from 48th Divisional Signals called 'every 10 minutes for 3 hours' only to find 'other station ordered at their end not to open up'.[22]

Fear of German direction finding and subsequent bombardment also affected when and how BEF units used wireless during combat operations. 2nd Divisional Signals opted to locate its No. 11 sets 400 yards from divisional headquarters from 11 May onwards, in the hope this early prudence would minimize future disruption and casualties. Many units adopted this policy during the course of the campaign and used either cable or human runners to cover the remaining distance, both of which proved vulnerable to shellfire. There were good reasons for these precautions; for example, 48th Division Signallers, sent to reinforce 144th Brigade on 26 May, discovered the resident signal officer had virtually vetoed further wireless usage, after recently being 'DF'd' and suffering a six-hour bombardment and multiple signaller casualties as a result. In his written evidence to the Bartholomew Committee, Major General B. Montgomery argued it was inadvisable to use wireless after 24 hours in static contact with the enemy, as after this 'accurate fire was brought to bear on the set in a very short time'. Montgomery also argued that if continuous use was unavoidable, the only method of minimizing casualties was by diligent observance of the 400 yard exclusion zone which, in his opinion, should include all troops, not just the relevant headquarters; this was easier said than done in the congested battlefields of northern France.[23]

Having prepared for the distribution of high priority rather than high-volume communications, BEF wireless faced a sudden and unexpectedly heavy burden of responsibility when cable failed after only a few days of intensive fighting. The lack of practice amongst wireless operators, the deficient range, reliability and mobility of their equipment and the high-level insistence that virtually all wireless traffic be encoded before transmission, all combined to slow the BEF tempo of operations to a crawl. GSO2 R. Tong, who worked in Operations at the Commander-in-Chief's CP, despaired that important decisions by his department were being delayed by information awaiting processing at GHQ; 'Bombing targets appeared again and again but there were only bombers from home and they could not be informed in time'.[24] Similarly, when a German attack occurred at 0400hrs on 5 June, staff officer P. Gribble complained after only receiving wireless notification at 1115hrs; too late to salvage the situation. Furthermore, the delays in wireless could not be made up elsewhere, for example, Gribble was able to produce paraphrased translations of ZOAN (Zone des Opérations Aériennes du Nord) directives within two hours of receiving the wireless transcript each morning; by the time his superiors viewed them, they were already routinely 75 per cent 'out of date'.[25] Some formations felt compelled to abandon cipher in a desperate effort to keep on top of events; with its front buckling to enemy pressure on 16/17 May, 48th Division urged subordinate signallers to transmit operation orders 'at all costs, oiiu [Most Immediate Priority], in plain language'.[26] Other formations were proactive in concluding time-sensitive information could never be transmitted effectively if it went through the encoding process; II Corps unilaterally abandoned cipher on 14 May and instructed subordinate divisions: 'If fighter support required in case of serious emergency wireless 2 Corps Ops in clear as follows: Air Support required Area. Give time. Ack'. Even without cipher the responsiveness of BEF communications remained pitifully uncompetitive, for example, requests for air support still went via the Air Ministry in London and, under these procedures, the BAFF headquarters acknowledged 'A minimum of 3 hours lapses between the moment of spotting a target and the possible arrival of an Allied formation to engage it'; intercepted German wireless shows the quickest German equivalent response time occurred on 20 May and was ten minutes between initial request and action.[27] The rejection of cipher was not universal within the BEF, for example, on 20 May, Line of Communication headquarters in Le Mans began drafting in 'further cipher personnel' from subordinate units as its existing team was drowning in encoded messages and becoming seriously 'overworked'; Line of Communication headquarters only ended its involvement with cipher on 25 May, when GHQ 2nd Echelon informed it 'Cipher must be treated as compromised'.[28]

One of the problems of primarily relying on wireless for communications was that it was not universally accessible to units within the BEF. Understandably, improvised units formed mid-campaign were devoid of wireless; on 18 May, Vickforce was informed: 'No communication equipment or personnel [were] available' to keep it up-to-date with fast moving events. Less understandable was the absence of wireless within unglamorous, but critically important service units; for example, Second Lieutenant J. Finch's RASC ammunition column 'had no wireless link and orders were either passed by Despatch Rider or, more frequently, by personal summons to Company Headquarters'. The absence of wireless was not restricted to the BEF backwaters and could be found in the most surprising of locations. In his evidence to the post-Dunkirk Bartholomew Committee, Major General N. Irwin (2nd Division) complained: 'I had no wireless connection with Corps because I was given no set' [to contact them with]. Such was the Committee's bewilderment that Committee Member and Director of Military Training Major General C. Malden stated his personal incredulity that I Corps had not a single set they could issue 2nd Division and forced Irwin to confirm his statement. Such was the hit and miss availability of wireless that it could never be comfortably relied on as a primary source of communication by the BEF during the France campaign.[29]

The wireless that was used by the BEF in France proved mechanically unreliable throughout the campaign, but especially in the maelstrom of combat around Dunkirk. On 27 May, there was a complete breakdown of high-level BEF communications when GHQ, now reunited with Commander-in-Chief Gort's CP, moved from Premesque to Houtkerque (near Dunkirk). Lord Gort's Despatches make clear cable communications were impossible since all corps headquarters were on the move simultaneously, yet the wireless set that was present with each corps commander failed to compensate, resulting in an information blackout. On 1 June, the previously reliable wireless link between 1st Duke of Wellington's Regiment and 3rd Brigade broke down in heavy shellfire that disrupted signals and unsettled both operator and set. Similar circumstances had severed the wireless connection between 58th Medium Regiment Royal Artillery and III Corps on 26 May; however, once broken the intensity of fighting and frequency of moves never relented sufficiently for communications to be re-established.[30] Another technological difficulty with wireless was that in areas with a high density of sets, mutual interference made signals impossible to distinguish and read; Brian Hall has highlighted how this problem was commonplace in the Great War, particularly 1917–18. Although much more fleeting, the same issues recurred in May 1940; on 23 May, Brigadier Claude Nicholson began transmitting to his Calais Garrison, only to be bluntly informed by Lieutenant Colonel Keller (3rd Royal Tank Regiment) via wireless: 'Get off the air, I am trying to fight a bloody battle'. Lieutenant Colonel Keller's mood had not been helped by the discovery that his unit's sets had not been properly netted into the same frequencies before beginning their first enemy contact, just outside Calais; despite virtually every tank possessing wireless capability the action was marred by continual communication difficulties.[31]

For all its many faults, wireless was occasionally the last method of communication open to BEF units and commanders treasured the access to information, help and advice it offered, no matter how intermittently. Throughout the campaign, 8th Brigade deliberately kept their wireless link with subordinate battalions in reserve, but utilized it when the fluidic front made travel by human messenger too hazardous. Similarly, on 18 May, 48th Division fell back on wireless to maintain communications with subordinate brigades who had become geographically detached during the retreat from the Dyle River. Under pressure at St Eloi on 28 May, Lieutenant Colonel J. Birch (2nd Bedfordshire and Hertfordshire Regiment) never strayed far from his wireless truck, from where he was able to update superiors of developments and keep up-to-date himself. This personal, almost physical, attachment to wireless was replicated up the chain of command; for example, when Birch found Brigadier E. Barker (10th Brigade) wandering on Dunkirk beach, the Brigadier had lost most of his Brigade, but still carried 'his wireless set from which he would not be parted'. III Corps were evacuated in bits and pieces between 26 May and 3 June, but from 28 May its communication capability was reduced to a single Wireless Telegraphy Section; this was selected on grounds of availability, practicality and adequacy for diminishing requirements.[32] It is worth noting that the longevity of wireless was not unique to the BEF, but was consistent with experiences within Allied forces; Belgian GQG's last 'means of communication with the RAF and the French Air Force was by wireless', whilst the last communication between French First Army and French First Army Group was also by cipher wireless.[33]

During combat operations, despatch riders retained their place as a valuable part of the BEF communication portfolio for their flexibility, speed and perseverance; however, with full-time despatch riders scarce within the Royal Corps of Signals, there was a determination that they should not be misused in trivial or excessive duties. Until the numbers of despatch riders within the BEF were increased, III Corps Signals demanded they only be released 'when messages on hand justified their use'. Similarly 2nd Divisional Signals was very protective of its elite detachment of signal despatch riders and, upon entering Belgium, insisted on measures to prevent personnel being hijacked for traffic control and other non-communication duties.[34] No matter how agile, un-armoured human messengers travelling at speed within a combat area were at high risk of injury or death; 5th Brigade reported the death of a despatch rider as early as 11 May. On 12 May, Second Lieutenant P. Hadley (4th Royal Sussex Regiment) recalled a motorcycle running 'right into the back of our truck with an almighty wallop', resulting in a bad head wound for the despatch rider; this was 'the first of innumerable motorcycle casualties' Hadley witnessed during the course of the campaign.[35] The minimal technological complexity of a despatch rider allowed this method to have a prolonged role in the campaign. Under ceaseless air attack and significant pressure on the ground, on 27 May, III Corps recorded: 'Communication only possible now by DR'; although limited wireless capability was re-established at Dunkirk human messengers had dominated corps communications up to this point. Having seen marginally less combat, the communication portfolio of II Corps on 27 May still consisted of liaison officers, despatch riders and wireless; by 30 May, this communication portfolio had contracted to just despatch riders and liaison officers, although the scarcity of cars and the multitude of motorcycles made despatch riders the overwhelmingly dominant method of communication as II Corps neared evacuation.[36] Adjutant E. Brush, 1st Battalion, Rifle Brigade, has argued the mutually trusting relationship between officers and despatch riders enabled this method of communication to remain effective for much of the campaign, but gradually this was undermined by intensive combat, battlefield casualties and increasingly impermeable fronts.[37]

The other version of human messenger used for communication purposes was the liaison officer; these ranged in rank from Major General T. Eastwood (the C-in-C's personal trouble-shooter) to newly-commissioned second lieutenants (known as Motor Contact Officers). Lord Gort argued in his Despatches: 'They were of real value in settling matters of detail and reconciling points of view which did not always at first coincide'; they ascertained situation reports from forward and flank units and delivered the majority of Operation Instructions within the BEF during May 1940.[38] Brigadier C. Woolner briefed all officers assigned to liaison duties in 8th Brigade that 'the liaison officer was the top method of communication still for security, reliability, flexibility and [implementing] brigade leadership'; in Woolner's opinion, cable, wireless and visual methods of communication were 'very insecure' ... 'very impersonal' and he would minimize his use of them. Alongside orders, liaison officers delivered background information and encouragement direct to the front-line, but their versatility also allowed them to perform unanticipated roles; for example, in May 1940, 8th Brigade liaison officers delivered ammunition and rounded up stragglers.[39]

Liaison officers were used throughout the entirety of the fighting; for example, a GHQ representative informed the post-Dunkirk Bartholomew Committee, Corps always 'let us know where they were' by ensuring daily 'somebody always came in to see us'. This was not out of preference, but merely through a lack of alternative; for example, II Corps claimed the disruption caused by frequent moves could only be overcome by use of numerous liaison and motor contact officers. In the first few hours of combat on 10 May, Motor Contact Officer Second Lieutenant Colbeck was sent to the Dyle River to ascertain the situation and monitor 3rd Division's arrival, before reporting back to II Corps on 11 May. After taking control of the remnants of II Corps on 31 May, the final act of 4th Division headquarters on 2 June was to despatch motor contact officers to organize the last few brigades and direct them to the Dunkirk Mole for evacuation. Human messengers and, in particular, liaison officers proved sufficiently resilient to the rigours of combat to enable continuous operation during the campaign, unlike the technologically superior, but mechanically fragile, cable and wireless.[40]

In May 1940, the travelling requirements and need to interact with unfamiliar units made liaison a particularly hazardous profession, as the prevalence of nervous and exhausted units meant individuals or small groups in BEF uniform could easily be misidentified as Germans. On 13 May, GHQ warned units to be on the lookout for suspicious individuals in British uniform; this advisory warning evolved in parallel with the deteriorating military situation. David Orr and David Truesdale have highlighted the 2nd Royal Ulster Rifles' response to rumours that the Germans were infiltrating BEF positions disguised as staff officers, as that of everyone wanting 'to have a shot at a staff officer'; such rumours risked the lives of genuine liaison officers. Similarly, on 22 May, Vickforce instructed subordinates: 'Enemy are about in British uniforms. All ranks to be warned not take any orders from any officers they do not know'.[41] This procedure negated the use of liaison officers as a method of communication. Brian Bond has argued relying solely on liaison officers for inter-unit communication was dangerous because if they failed in their mission, crucial positions could be fundamentally undermined and relations between officers, units and even nations could be strained to breaking point by thoughts of betrayal.[42] In separate incidents, both 2nd Buffs Regiment and 2nd Durham Light Infantry were captured virtually en masse because orders to withdraw, carried by liaison officers, failed to reach their destination or arrived too late to be effective.[43] As the military situation declined, the missions issued to human messengers became increasingly precarious for individuals on foot or in staff cars and, as a result, BEF liaison officers were provided with ever greater armour protection in the hope that this would facilitate their continued involvement in the communication system. During its withdrawal from the Escaut River on 22 May, widespread open ground necessitated 1st East Surrey Regiment to provide all liaison officers with carrier transportation and still A Company could not be contacted and was left behind. On 28 May, even the provision of an armoured car escort and transportation for liaison personnel between 48th Division and 145th Brigade proved inadequate for the distribution of withdrawal orders for personnel in Cassel; when withdrawal was eventually attempted, less than 100 men from 145th Brigade reached the safety of Dunkirk. On 1 June, 3rd Brigade successfully distributed withdrawal orders to subordinate battalions, but only because they borrowed a light tank to transport Second Lieutenant Miller, and the orders he carried, around the Dunkirk pocket.[44]

As a method of communication, liaison officers were very labour-intensive and vulnerable to wasted effort. The simplest question took hours of travelling, for example, I Corps Liaison Officer E. Thornhill took most of a day to find out 1st Division and another unidentified Division were 'quite all right for both food and ammunition'; also there was no guarantee of an answer on arrival, for example, GSO2 Thornhill spent 29 May seeking situation reports from subordinate brigades and was 'unable to find out much information'. Liaison officers were at risk of events developing whilst they were in transit; on 8 June 1940, the liaison officer of 1st Survey Regiment RA was returning to 51st Division with his latest situation report, only to discover the divisional head-quarters had relocated to an unknown destination in the interim. It should be acknowledged, once combat began, liaison officers were also often the only form of communication capable of reuniting units which had been scattered whilst in transit. On 18 May, 2nd Bedfordshire & Hertfordshire Regiment got split between their original destination of Wortegem and their new destination of Avelghem; only informed liaison officers were able to traverse between the two, pick out unit transport and guide personnel and vehicles to unification.[45] Within the chaotic and dangerous retreat to Dunkirk, a handful of British Army officers, assigned to liaison duties without specific training, produced extraordinary feats of bravery distributing critical information to units which the BEF communication portfolio had failed to reach. During this retreat, 150th Brigade had no communications with battalions and, consequently, Brigade Major K. Chavasse was sent at night, alone and without lights, to deliver orders personally to subordinate battalions whose whereabouts were unknown; such was Chavasse's success that 150th Brigade was delegated the role of organizing the evacuation of its counterparts within 50th Division on 2 and 3 June. Even more incredibly, on 28 May, Captain Beck (III Corps Liaison Officer) single-handedly distributed III Corps Operation Order No. 6 (regarding the withdrawal into the Dunkirk perimeter) to 1st, 2nd, 44th and 46th Divisions and also 137th and 138th Brigades; these last two were particularly impressive as they had been out of contact for three days and believed lost before Beck bumped into them.[46] Whilst orders did, on occasion, still manage to reach their destination during this period, the use of individual officers to blunder around a geographical area until they bumped into the recipients did not make a reliable, or even credible, communication system.

As the BEF communication portfolio collapsed and the use of human messengers became more prevalent, a by-product of this transformation was the expanded use of verbal orders. Having previously suffered great difficulty in distributing written orders to its constituent parts, 58th Medium Regiment RA experienced a notable increase in tempo from 22 May onwards, when its Commanding Officer began attending III Corps Officer Conferences to receive and subsequently pass on verbal orders. With inadequate maps, uncertain positions and a declining combat situation, 4th Royal Sussex Regiment found little point in issuing written orders which were liable to be inaccurate and impossible to implement; instead the Battalion operated solely on verbally issued 'rough instructions' with subordinates only required to understand 'the main gist of the order'. As the campaign continued and exhaustion played an increasing factor in BEF decision-making, Lieutenant Colonel J. Birch argued had he not switched to issuing verbal orders at hastily called Officer Conferences, his battalion would have ceased to function; even with this measure Birch recalled, by the end of the campaign, 'not one of us seemed able to keep awake' even when discussing 'important orders'.[47] Written orders continued to play a role in the communication system, mainly where they were needed as evidence of authorization. On 20 May, Major MacKinlay, a member of Quartermaster General Lindsell's small staff at Lord Gort's CP, was procedurally compelled to issue written orders to 1st Troop Carrying Company, Royal Army Service Corps, 'for them to lift 4000 gallons petrol from Beaumont to rv [rendezvous] at Vimy for 50 Division'. However, the BEF had still not entirely rid itself of the pre-war belief that the presentation of written orders was more important than the implementation of their instructions; on 7 June 1940, the BEF's Beauman Division, operating south of the Somme River, spent so long preparing movement orders that, when they were finally issued at 1010hrs to 2/6th Duke of Wellington's Regiment, the Battalion had only 20 minutes to break camp and travel to nearby Bruz station, as they were expected to be entrained by 1030hrs.[48] Although the deteriorating military position forced BEF commanders to use more verbal orders, they were at a distinct disadvantage to their German counterparts, who knew when and how to use verbal and written orders from their experiences in Poland. On 9 September 1939, annoyed at the inability to transport 10th Panzer Division's armour across a lightly defended water obstacle, General Guderian (XIX Panzer Corps) issued forceful, clear 'verbal and written orders' to the engineer responsible that 'bridges over the Narev were to be built with all possible speed since they were urgently needed' to continue the advance. The Germans used verbal orders to speed the tempo of operations and written orders for authority; Guderian's actions succeeded in re-energizing a stalled attack without increasing casualties.[49]

The majority of occasions when the BEF's communications portfolio collapsed in its entirety were because of self-inflicted failings; the most striking and possibly important of these involved the attempted transportation of 1st Army Tank Brigade by train, from the Bassilly railhead in Belgium to Arras, France between 16–19 May. On 16 May, 1st Army Tank Brigade went into action, occupying the Forêt de Soignes to protect the flank of I Corps from German mechanized forces; although the post-Dunkirk Bartholomew Committee was told this operation was 'extremely successful', CGS Pownall recorded in his private diary that incorrect intelligence, poor communications and faulty judgment by local commanders had led to the only available tank brigade wasting its time in an operation which 'proved to be almost completely a canard'.[50] The relocation to Arras proved difficult as the BEF had rejected the use of mainline stations and depots because of their obvious vulnerability to aerial bombardment. The backwater of Bassilly was selected as the loading point, but Captain Byron, the local Rail Transport Officer, operated from a public call-box three miles away (the nearest communication facility). This recipe for disaster resulted in four separate aborted attempts to load the brigade, which cascaded down the line of retreat, as either the tanks, trains or train crews could not be found or moved. With this situation consistently described as 'very obscure owing to a lack of communications', the crisis would eventually involve the entire Q Branch officer contingent at the CP (four officers ranked Major and above), a number of Operations personnel and, at one point, even the DCGS. Confusion reigned unabated, frustrations grew and tempers frayed; complex written orders were replaced by simple verbal orders such as 'find trains', 'rescue tanks' and 'sort mess out'. Despite possessing more wireless than virtually any other BEF unit, wireless communication was never established between the tank brigade and the CP or even GHQ. Over the three-day period, nine separate trains were kept busy without ever transporting a single tank; eventually patience snapped and, Lord Gort's Despatches record, 'the remainder of the move was carried out by road [105 miles]; this gave rise to the inevitable mechanical trouble later'. On 21 May, the tank brigade went into action for the second time, in support of 6th and 8th Durham Light Infantry, south of Arras; its strength had already been reduced from 100 infantry tanks to just 74. Furthermore, each remaining tank was in desperate need of an overhaul after its ordeal and led to the Durham Light Infantry diplomatically describing their supporting armour as 'runners'.

This prized and once pristine military asset was reduced in strength by 25 per cent, not by enemy action, but simply because of the collapse of the communication system. Branches of GHQ failed to coordinate or even communicate with each other, oversight proved impossible, conflicting orders were issued, cable was not available in key locations, wireless failed completely and human messengers struggled to travel the distances involved and locate recipients. It is important to recognize that the BEF had the capability and the capacity required to transport this valuable asset by rail, thereby preventing mechanical degradation. An attack south of Arras was still carried out and caused significant casualties and a great deal of panic amongst the overextended Germans, but its impact would have been magnified had the BEF's communication system not wasted 25 per cent of its only available tank brigade.[51]

In addition to standard communications, the BEF was subjected to a multitude of unorthodox communications; some had a positive effect, but many were negative in their intent and outcome. 2nd Buffs Regiment described rumours as 'the curse' of the campaign, wasting energy and, because of their frequently unfounded nature, causing mistrust in the official communication system that reported them.[52] The most prevalent rumours were about parachute landings and some units, such as 1/8th Middlesex Regiment, repeatedly searched 'miles of country' in the hope of confronting these fictitious paratroopers. Other units were more wary of the risk of wild goose chases; for example, in response to a 12 May telegram regarding nearby parachute landings, 12th Division Provost Company merely warned all sections to keep a 'sharp look-out'. Rumours were often connected to common sightings, giving BEF units little opportunity to counteract them; warned by superiors that red blankets were a sign of fifth column loyalties, 2nd Durham Light Infantry confirmed it was preventing loitering, but also that more than 50 per cent of refugees in its vicinity were carrying red blankets.[53] As the military situation deteriorated, rumours became more debilitating to tired troops and the chain of command became increasingly terse in its response. 1st Duke of Wellington's Regiment were cut off by imaginary Germans on so many occasions that on 18 May, Lieutenant Colonel S. Kington issued special orders demanding his Battalion 'only believe in the existence of the enemy when they saw him'. Similarly, when the BEF garrison commander in Le Havre rang Line of Communication Headquarters in nearby Le Mans at 0330hrs on 21 May seeking permission for the immediate evacuation of personnel, the responding GSO1 chastised him for believing rumours that 'the enemy was at the gates'.[54]

Brian Bond has argued the campaign was notable for the pervasive obsession with spies who 'were said to be contacting the enemy in ingenious ways, for example, by hanging out washing in semaphore fashion'; Bond concluded the few cases of genuine treachery were dramatically outweighed by the number of innocent people manhandled or shot. Bond's conclusions were evident among some BEF personnel; for example, Second Lieutenant P. Hadley, 4th Royal Sussex Regiment gave orders that 'I was not to be woken up in the small hours of the morning simply because someone looked slightly suspicious'.[55] However, the sentiment amongst most BEF personnel was that fifth column was present, active and deliberately targeting communications in France. Staff officer P. Gribble was convinced 'the Germans go in for false rumours through the Fifth Column', particularly 'reported gas attacks and warnings given with no cause'. Similarly, on 15 May, I Corps felt duty-bound to warn subordinates about reports of civilians firing on British troops in the rear, which coincided with intensive cutting of telephone lines.[56] Although Brian Bond is fairly dismissive of spies 'ploughing give-away patterns in the fields', there is no doubt that this is what the BEF believed was occurring. III Corps was convinced that German saboteurs were following its movements; the most obvious sign of their presence was that wherever III Corps relocated, both military and civilian cable was immediately cut, Corps insignia was scythed into the ground nearby and aerial bombardment soon followed. This view was also prevalent within the BEF's lower ranks; for example, Corporal Edgar Rabbets, 5th Northamptonshire Regiment, observed two farmers 'ploughing a field down two sides so that the corner pointed towards our headquarters' in the form of an arrow; certain this was the reason for daily aerial bombardment and that 'no farmer ploughs his land that way', Rabbets summarily shot both farmers without reference to higher authority.[57] The validity of this act is open to question, but fifth column were not figments of imagination and did communicate valuable information to advancing German forces. In Rouen, 1st Armoured Division found hidden directions beneath every advertisement for Pernod Fils, 'detailing the best route to take southwards in order to avoid Allied strong-points'.[58] Rumours are inevitable in conflict, especially those with rapid movement and volatile fronts; however, it does appear a number of rumours were manufactured and communication systems targeted by genuine fifth column in an effort to disrupt the Allied defence of France.

As previously mentioned, the press continued to operate and remained a sought after source of information throughout the campaign, despite its vague and occasionally misleading nature. 4th Royal Sussex Regiment advanced into Belgium on 11 May listening to the cheerful BBC News which, by painting 'too rosy a picture of the situation', lured the Battalion into a false sense of security. During the subsequent retreat, 1st Duke of Wellington's Regiment did not realize the gravity of the situation until 27 May when the BBC News announced the enemy had broken through and that the British Army was on the run. Even at big headquarters, personnel starved of information relied on press reports to supplement their understanding of events; for example, on 1 June, the breakdown of all orthodox methods of communication at BAFF headquarters left personnel dependent on BBC News, 'the *Continental Daily Mail* and the French press generally'.[59]

The BEF was only capable of manning a small section of the Allied front and, therefore, was totally reliant on the French for information about events occurring in other sections of the front. Only French formations neighbouring the BEF were provided with British liaison officers who identified information relevant to GHQ and communicated it via cable, wireless or human messenger, depending on what was most convenient at the time. The official campaign history has described the information retrieved from these formations as 'scanty, vague and often inaccurate'; the paucity of information was more to do with the absence of information within these sources, rather than a lack of effort on behalf of the BEF liaison officers embedded with them. Such was the intermittent and unreliable nature of information from these sources that on 19 May, CGS Pownall recorded in his diary: 'There was a complete void on our right with only a disorganized mass of "fag ends" from the First Army to fill it'; however, after lunch 'Reports became not so bad, then almost good' and 'The First French Army reappeared from somewhere'. In mitigation the BEF was, on occasion, equally at fault for these communication breakdowns, for example, on 16 May, GSO2 R. Tong admitted failure in his temporary assignment of coordinating formation boundaries, stating: 'For some days I had on my conscience that the junction points between 2nd Division and the French [First Army] for which I was largely responsible, had gone astray'; leaving his superiors ignorant of this fact, the blame was incorrectly placed on the French.[60]

The overwhelming majority of the Allied front was manned by French formations which did not have a British liaison officer and it was from these units that information was virtually non-existent. Commander-in-Chief Gort was diplomatic in his analysis of French efforts to communicate important information from distant fronts, but when the front at Sedan broke on 15 May, even Gort was forced to acknowledge 'I was unable to verify that the French had enough reserves at their disposal ... to warrant the expectation that the gap would be closed'. More condemnatory of both arrangements and outcome, Major General B. Montgomery complained the absence of a BEF liaison officer within French Ninth Army resulted in an inability to obtain independent situation reports from what proved to be the most critical sector of the entire front; 'GHQ was not given details about the breakthrough at once. It was clear that GHQ (Intelligence) was not getting proper information from the French about the situation of either their own troops or of the enemy'. Although the BEF communication system was itself collapsing, on this occasion, the problem was at the source of the information; for example, even Chief of the Imperial General Staff Ironside complained from his well-connected War Office: 'I can find little out about the way the French are fighting'.[61]

Structurally and procedurally the French communication system was inept, with deficiencies even more widespread than within the BEF; Supreme Allied Commander General Gamelin's personal headquarters at Vincennes (near Paris) lacked a radio, telephone or even carrier pigeons. Upon visiting Vincennes, General Charles de Gaulle compared the Supreme Commander's headquarters to a convent in which few officers disturbed Gamelin from metaphorically 'testing the chemical reaction of his strategy in a laboratory'. With such a limited communication portfolio available, communication between GHQ and French GQG relied solely on human messengers; depending on availability a BEF liaison officer or NCO courier left the Operations Registry at GHQ with accumulated correspondence at 1000hrs daily and returned from GQG at approximately 1700hrs the following day. This procedure, which produced a minimum response time of 31 hours, began in October 1939 and continued during the combat operations of May 1940. In practice, responses routinely took far longer as GQG's disparate parts were spread over 70 kilometres, internal communications were also conducted by human messengers and inevitable thinking time for responses often meant a further 24 hour delay as the BEF courier would often not receive an answer until his next visit. Purely from a French viewpoint, General de Gaulle considered this 'an arrangement which might work as long as nothing was happening, but would certainly become untenable if battle were joined'; from a British perspective it was even more impractical.[62] An alternative approach to information gathering and inter-nation communications was to utilize the GHQ-based French Military Mission which, led by General Raoul Voruz, had been created to assist the BEF with these issues. The 15 officers and 50 rank-and-file of the French Mission could theoretically communicate with any French military formation directly, but their ability to obtain information was equally dependent on the ability to contact the relevant formation, the attitude of the formation to distributing information and the availability of the required information. Procedurally forced to contact civil ministries via the bureaucratic War Ministry, and with only their tiny, Paris-based, Anglo-French Liaison Section of the War Cabinet Secretariat (within the Supreme Council for National Defence) capable of expediting requests for information 'on urgent and important matters', the French Mission at GHQ was restricted in its ability to offer alternative sources of information to the BEF.[63] The use of communication procedures detrimental to the tempo of operations was prevalent throughout the French chain of command. In his post-campaign report, Captain Miles Reid commented on his time as a liaison officer at French First Army headquarters: 'No proper system of communications or records of communications existed and, strange though it may seem, French Army Headquarters had no recording telegraphic apparatus to work to its immediately lower or higher formation'. With the exception of a few typewritten operation orders, all orders were issued by senior officers in unrecorded telephone conversations, largely kept secret from the rest of the department; incoming messages were recorded hurriedly by the duty officer in an unstructured format and frequently illegible writing. The result of these chaotic procedures for the First Army was that it was difficult to obtain any information out of the Operations Section and that by 17 May, the department had effectively ceased to function; only the most senior Operations officers, Colonels Alombert and Vignal, continued to offer anything to the war effort.[64]

In a campaign where every hour counted, the French tempo of operations was simply too slow at communicating critical information up the chain of command and across to the BEF. At 2300hrs 12 May, German infantry crossed the Meuse River at an undefended weir and lock at the village of Houx; awareness of this catastrophe dawned only gradually on French commanders, diminishing the possibility of an effective counterattack. At 0500hrs 13 May, Commandant Boulanger (66th Regiment) became aware of the German crossing and informed General Camille Duffet (18th Division) sometime between 0600–0700hrs. General Julien Martin (XI Corps) heard the news between 0800–0900hrs, but onward progression to General Andre Corap (Ninth Army) was delayed by the failure of cable communications; communication to Corap was restored by 1100hrs, but it was still 1205hrs before it reached General Georges's staff, over 13 hours since the initial German crossing. Not only was this shockingly slow, but the failure to read the details of the incident had progressively tempered the urgency of the message as it travelled up the chain of command; consequently on 13 May, the summary of events issued by General Georges to Supreme Commander Gamelin and GQG included reassurances such as 'Defence now seems well assured on the whole front of the river'.[65] It was this combination of French internal communication failures that prevented Lord Gort and the three BEF corps from discovering a breach in the front had occurred until 15 May; as previously mentioned, this was then compounded by the BEF's own internal communication problems that left Q branch, GHQ ignorant until 17 May, five days after the German crossing. In his study of the French Army, Julian Jackson has argued it was no surprise that inherent communication problems resulted in the successive disintegration of French command structures from regiments up to Gamelin himself; under these conditions, those units that continued to fight operated in 'a kind of fog'.[66] Failure of French communications led to a collapse of command and control and, in turn, contributed to the collapse of BEF communications.

One of the reasons for the collapse of the BEF communication system was that it could not cope with the tempo of operations that the Germans imposed on it. This did not happen by accident, but because of the superior capability of the German communication system, which they took advantage of at every opportunity. The ubiquitous nature of wireless within the German Army meant it was readily used on occasions when cable was impractical and the battlefield was too dangerous for human messengers. When 10th Panzer Division crossed the Meuse River on 13 May 1940, its three crossing points were provided with communications by 90th Armoured Signal Battalion through the establishment of wireless stations on each side of each crossing. Whilst bridges were built by the Division's engineers, this set-up maintained the link with superiors for personnel on the far bank far better than what could be achieved by cable or human messengers. To ensure against any gap in wireless coverage, 'the operators with the attacking groups' were expected to 'cross the Meuse with the foremost infantry'. Wireless was utilized by all front-line units, including infantry, to maintain communications beyond an initial advance, and assist the exploitation of any breakthrough opportunity. Colonel Koelitz's infantry regiment began its advance across the Meuse River at 1600hrs 13 May as part of the larger attack by XIX Panzer Corps; despite significant geographical gains, at 1300hrs 14 May, Koelitz recorded he was 'still in radio contact with all battalions' and that 'we will have the required bridgehead very soon'. Such was the flexibility of German wireless that, when Koelitz's 2nd and 3rd battalions began forming a bridgehead over the next water obstacle (the Bar River), their regimental commander was still able to simultaneously communicate with them and also the 1st Battalion (held in reserve behind the Meuse River), even when he was geographically detached from all three. For all its advantages, wireless remained only a part of a diverse German communication portfolio, within which various methods were accorded roles depending on their suitability; for example, XIX Panzer Corps retained an entire signal battalion for maintaining secure cable communications between corps and divisional headquarters during the advance across France.[67]

One of the biggest divergences in capability between British and German forces was the German ability to provide hard-pressed troops with close air support; this occurred because of a difference in mentality towards wireless, combined arms operations and empowering subordinates. W. Jacob has illustrated how contemporary RAF thinking considered close air support 'both unprofitable and unacceptably dangerous'; as a result, no reliable ground-air wireless capability was developed for BEF infantry units, no standard operating procedure was devised and the fiercely independent RAF operated largely separately from GHQ in France 1939–40. In contrast, the Germans developed procedures to utilize their assets for surgical strikes supplementary to predetermined strategic operations. Each German division had an Air Liaison Officer who acted as a bridge between the Luftwaffe and troops in need. They worked in conjunction with air guidance units (three-man, mobile wireless units led by a Luftwaffe officer) who acted as forward air controllers within front-line units. Once a request for assistance was received at divisional headquarters, Luftwaffe liaison would arrange support from the appropriate Luftwaffe formation and coordinate with the forward controllers; once over the battlefield, the air guidance officer would guide aircraft onto local targets, thereby reducing the risk of friendly fire and lost momentum.[68] There was sufficient inter-service goodwill for ground troops to receive spontaneous advanced warnings, from unattached Luftwaffe aircraft flying overhead, about forthcoming attacks. At 0650hrs 14 May, intelligence from a reconnaissance plane told Lieutenant General Friedrich Kirchner (1st Panzer Division) that a French counter-attack consisting of armour and infantry was forming up; shortly after 0700hrs the first German tanks set out to meet the threat. It had taken the French over 19 hours to concentrate forces for a counter-attack on the Meuse Crossings and a further 12 hours to actually start the attack; German command, control and communications were sufficiently strong that they began their own counter-attack within ten minutes of identifying the approaching target. Neither the French nor the BEF communication system was capable of matching this responsiveness, nor were they designed to be; the speed of modern warfare was far beyond what had been anticipated pre-war, or even experienced during the Phoney War.[69]

The campaign culminated in the evacuation of the BEF, largely through Dunkirk, and later through a variety of Channel ports further west. Although ill-discipline played a part, at Dunkirk the dysfunctional nature of BEF communications had reached the point where it was incapable of reliably distributing and enforcing a simple blanket order within a small geographical area. On 27 May 1940, Dunkirk Perimeter Commander Lieutenant General Sir Ronald Adam attempted to restrict vehicular access within the perimeter to those strictly necessary for tactical, supply or medical purposes in the hope this would prevent chaotic traffic congestion. Lord Gort's Despatches acknowledged 'the few troops who could be spared for the traffic control did not, however, prove sufficient for the purpose, and consequently a great number of British and French vehicles entered the perimeter' when they should have remained outside. Ironically, one of the units to receive the orders was 2nd Division Provost Company who, having done such a thorough job destroying their vehicles and unit documentation, were only considered suitable for immediate evacuation; they could quite easily have assisted in enforcement, had the communication system been capable of issuing them specific orders in time.[70] Desensitized by inaccurate information and contradictory orders, their faith in the communication system was at an all-time low; many BEF personnel opted to disregard dubious orders in favour of their own personal interests and that of their subordinates. On 30 May, Brigadier N. Whitty (133rd Brigade) was observed disregarding instructions that 'the road was blocked to traffic', before continuing on his ultimately successful mission of delivering a staff car full of wounded to the Dunkirk beaches. The previous day, Brigadier E. Barker (10th Brigade) occupied a Military Police checkpoint with a combination of threats and platitudes just long enough for two of his three subordinate battalions to pass through Furness with their transport intact; only 2nd Bedfordshire and Hertfordshire Regiment was forced to march the remaining eight miles carrying all weapons, ammunition and tools. Even junior officers were successful in their subversive efforts, for example, Second Lieutenant J. Finch passed his redundant RASC supply column off as an 'AA Ammunition' convoy in order to bypass the Military Police barricades on the perimeter; Finch acknowledged that as an officer he should have acted differently, but justified his actions by arguing his subordinates would have struggled to travel the final ten miles on foot. For many BEF personnel, the communication system had lost its relevance; if they were going to get evacuated, it was up to them and those they trusted.[71]

Further south, the severance of GHQ from its lines of communication had left a considerable body of BEF manpower without the effective communication necessary for coordinating operations and also evacuation. The units cut off from GHQ on 20 May included 1st Armoured Division, 51st (Highland) Division, 12 partially-trained infantry battalions and an assortment of improvised and rear-echelon units. Upon returning to France on 13 June 1940 to assume command of the remaining BEF, Lieutenant General Alan Brooke reflected: 'To my consternation I found that there was still some 100,000 men' and masses of supplies.[72] Although Lord Gort's Despatches stated that since 17 May, Major General P. de Fonblanque (Lines of Communication Commander) 'had been taking energetic steps for its defence', the experience on the ground was somewhat different.[73] During the period 28 May-11 June, 1st Survey Regiment RA complained information 'was always difficult to obtain', especially as 'secrecy always seemed to overrule the passing on of information in even the highest circles'. After an intensive period of manoeuvre in which superior headquarters frequently relocated without informing subordinates, 1st Survey Regiment summarized on 10 June: 'Information had been very scarce and control nil. Our group was entirely on its own'. The neighbouring 51st Medium Regiment RA had also been left to its own devices and its commander's understanding of events was restricted to 'what he found out on his own initiative'. During the period 19 May-11 June 1940, 4th Buffs Regiment, who had been based on the lines of communication throughout the campaign, carried out a series of conflicting and meaningless manoeuvres simply because 'normal communications were non-existent'. Futile orders from a multitude of sources, all of whom had 'no information as to enemy movements', squandered the battalion's energy and resources without purpose. After a month of gruelling operations, 4th Buffs Regiment had sustained 139 casualties out of an original strength of 782 personnel, despite having been in action for just a matter of hours. Throughout this period the lack of information about the enemy, the sudden withdrawals at instant notice, the rumour, counter orders and general confusion, were caused almost entirely by a collapse of the BEF communication system. For small units and isolated groups of stragglers, through both circumstance and possibly choice, the collapse in BEF communications proved comprehensive and prolonged. Lance Bombardier William Sweeney was a 19-year old Territorial serving with 158th Battery when it was cut off from the remainder of 53rd Brigade RA in May 1940. Sweeney recalled

> We had no idea really what was going on and we got on our trucks and wandered off towards St Nazaire and, after a few days, we eventually arrived there. What we weren't aware of at that time, Dunkirk had happened and it was all over and the French had already asked for an Armistice.

Evacuated from St Nazaire on 19 June 1940, two days after an armistice was requested, the group of BEF personnel which included Lance Bombardier Sweeney spent 30 days without contact from a superior headquarters or instructions what to do. In comparison, from the German invasion on 10 May to the end of the Dunkirk evacuation to save the bulk of the BEF on 4 June was only 25 days. This shows how extensive communication collapse was and how comprehensively it affected BEF command and control.[74]

On 10 May 1940, the BEF reached the pinnacle of its communication capability; never again during the France campaign would this level of capacity be achieved, this variety of communication options be available and this many BEF units have the relative ease of communicating from static, pre-prepared positions. Despite this the German invasion caused a flurry of activity which swamped the BEF communication system, slowed the tempo of operations and, in some cases, allowed the media to pre-empt official military channels distributing news of invasion. Structural reorganization designed to assist operations in a new combat environment merely undermined the system by isolating decision-makers, imposing massive duplication and generally causing confusion. From the moment the BEF entered Belgium, its various methods of communication both individually and collectively became less reliable, less effective and less able to assist BEF operations. Pre-existing civilian cable networks quickly failed, whilst the speed and distance of operations prevented any significant independent cable infrastructure being developed. The use of wireless was hampered by confusion over operating practices, the use of cipher, the fear of German direction finding and subsequent bombardment, and the unreliability of equipment in increasingly chaotic battlefield conditions. Human messengers were used to bypass technological failings, but their capacity was limited and they remained vulnerable to accidents, death and the setting of impossible objectives. Although not uniformly accepted, the balance between written and verbal orders shifted to try to assist the tempo of operations; this helped prolong the functioning of the communication system, but could not prevent the system collapsing. Units compensated for a lack of official communications by searching for information from more unorthodox channels, such as the functioning media and, less wisely, rumours circulating the battlefield. The campaign was also symbolized by an active fifth column who sabotaged Allied communications, whilst surreptitiously communicating valuable information to advancing German forces. Self-inflicted deficiencies within the BEF communication system were compounded by the even more procedurally inept French; equally, superior wireless capability, ground-air cooperation and experience in verbal orders assisted the German Army in its exploitation of these failings. The BEF communication system only functioned when its portfolio of methods shared the burden; although isolated examples of each of the methods remaining in use exist all the way up to final evacuation, these were increasingly sporadic and the portfolio had become unrecognizable compared to its Phoney War state. The communication system had moved beyond inefficiency and the dysfunctional and had become a few randomly available disparate parts; units and commanders recognized the system had collapsed.

6
Discipline

From GHQ to the lowliest NCO, the chain of command consciously under-recorded levels of ill-discipline within the BEF. Despite this a significant number of the BEF's professional regulars and dedicated pre-war Territorials were involved in ill-discipline. Generally, rear-echelon units experienced the worst disciplinary levels and Territorial infantry battalions the best, although there were exceptions in both cases. Levels of ill-discipline depended on length of deployment, amount of officer supervision and proximity to temptation. The bureaucratic paperwork, the damage to a unit's reputation, awareness of limited detention capacity and the potential loss of precious manpower actively encouraged commanders to turn a blind eye to all but the most serious breaches of discipline. Instead, internal solutions, such as unofficial punishment and transfers to alternative positions were used to indicate the displeasure of the disciplinary system. The Army failed to deal with endemic inappropriate alcohol consumption and proved incapable of dealing with widespread black marketeering, leading to drunkenness and theft being two of the offences most under-reported in the BEF. Failure to clamp down on these relatively trivial offences led individuals to commit further, more serious crimes against colleagues, superiors and civilians. Combat operations only led to an increase in under-reporting as the tempo of operations weakened the ability to maintain discipline and enthusiasm to investigate and record infringements. As fatigue grew and unit cohesion reduced, unrecorded ill-discipline increased exponentially, culminating in chaotic scenes in and around Channel ports.

The official history of discipline 1939–45 defined discipline as the 'maintenance of proper subordination in the Army' through artificially created attributes of 'self-control, orderliness, obedience and capacity for cooperation'.[1] It also argued good discipline was 'a primary and indispensable factor' to British success during 1939–45.[2] Subsequently, historians have shown how methods of creating and maintaining good discipline, as well as incidences of ill-discipline, were issues of concern for British commanders throughout the war. David French has demonstrated army commanders felt sufficiently concerned about ill-discipline in spring 1940 (France), April 1942 (North Africa) and February 1944 (Italy), that they campaigned for the reintroduction of the death penalty as a deterrent.[3] Jonathan Fennell has highlighted General Auchinleck's alarm when arguing disciplinary measures clearly did not restrain soldiers from deserting in large numbers, since 88 per cent of Eighth Army casualties during summer 1942 were designated missing or surrender personnel.[4] Christine Bielecki has argued concerns about ill-discipline continued to overshadow the Army during the Italian campaign as war-weariness led to an unstoppable escalation in desertion despite increasingly punitive measures.[5] These three studies make clear that discipline was a constant concern for the Army throughout the war; as the war progressed these concerns inspired an increasingly thorough and scientific approach to discipline.

Army personnel were likely to become destructive elements, both individually and within their primary group (immediate associates), when unhappy in their posting or incapable of the tasks being asked of them. As the Army expanded and discipline became less predictable, Adjutant General Ronald Adam established, in June 1941, the Directorate of Selection of Personnel to assign jobs dependent on individual capability and to retrospectively examine army personnel for incorrect allocations during the first years of war. Formed in April 1942, the Directorate of Army Psychiatry assisted selection procedures, also sending subordinates into theatres to proactively weed out problem cases from front-line units.[6] The process of installing systems that scientifically prevented individuals incapable of sustained discipline from reaching the front-line was completed in April 1942, when War Office Selection Boards (WOSBs) began overseeing candidates for Officer Cadet Training Units. WOSBs rejected the traditional view that leadership was socially inherited and sought to ensure candidates' intelligence and leadership skills through testing in a high-pressure environment.[7]

Despite lacking this scientific approach to discipline, many official sources have lauded the BEF for exemplary discipline during the testing conditions of the France campaign. The official history of discipline recorded 'the discipline instilled into them [BEF personnel] as soldiers before the War had enabled them to fight and endure all that they encountered in the face of the enemy'.[8] In his Despatches, BEF Commander-in-Chief Lord Gort suggested the 'firm discipline' displayed had proven old-fashioned virtues were as important in modern warfare as they were in the past.[9] Focusing on the withdrawal from the Dyle River, the official campaign history concluded: 'The British withdrawal to the coast will rank high in military annals by any test of planning, discipline or performance, notwithstanding some local confusion'. The campaign history unsurprisingly celebrated BEF disciplinary standards because the war diaries and commanders' despatches, upon which its account was based, rarely recorded courts-martial proceedings or anecdotal incidents of ill-discipline.[10] Similarly, regimental histories and archives proudly promote their associates' greatest achievements, whilst skirting over evidence of more dishonourable events.

However, modern historians, such as John Ellis, have also maintained the view that ill-discipline occurred in isolated instances due to the exceptional pressures. Assured that the successful BEF evacuation required unceasing majority acceptance of hierarchical discipline, Ellis has dismissed any lapses, stating 'it is hardly surprising that some men broke down under the strain'.[11] David French is one of the few historians to examine incidents of ill-discipline away from high-pressure situations; between the outbreak of war and March 1940, during which time British troops had hardly seen a shot fired in anger, French has identified 'four cases of desertion into Belgium, numerous instances of men going absent without leave and 114 cases of soldiers being grossly insubordinate or striking a senior officer'.[12] Despite this, French has argued generalized judgments on BEF discipline, particularly critical judgments, should not be made using an excessively narrow range of evidence.

This book aims to complement the current historiography by examining the true level of ill-discipline in the BEF, through quantitative analysis and comparison of courts-martial records in combination with a more qualitative assessment of memoirs and war diaries. In particular, this chapter will highlight how unrecorded ill-discipline, adapted procedures, and an inability or unwillingness to prosecute led to an artificially low official record of ill-discipline. This was why the Army sought the security of a more scientific approach to discipline and selection from 1941 onwards.

Pre-war levels of ill-discipline within the volunteer-based British Army were sufficiently low and stable for the Government to consider them worth highlighting in Parliament. In February 1939, Secretary of State for War Hore-Belisha informed Parliament: 'The discipline of the

Army continues to be maintained at a high standard'.[13] The number of courts-martial in 1938 was slightly higher than the preceding year, but remained below 1936 levels. Throughout the British Army, home and abroad, there were 1876 courts-martial involving non-commissioned personnel in 1936, 1712 in 1937 and 1726 in 1938 (less than 0.5 per cent of total personnel); resulting in 1705, 1542 and 1561 confirmed convictions respectively.[14] S. Mackenzie has suggested the perception of British discipline, as highlighted by these figures, convinced the innately conservative senior ranks that reform was unnecessary. David French has argued the inter-war Army relied almost exclusively on the regimental system, the primary group and the ethos of paternal officership to prevent ill-discipline; a system which was maintained until 1942 when defeat compelled reform.[15] However, some of the disciplinary data is of questionable validity.

For the year ending 30 September 1937, there were only 23 courts-martial of non-commissioned personnel for drunkenness, despite British Army rank-and-file actual strength of over 400,000 (including reserves and the Territorial Army).[16] Although the figure does not include individuals disciplined internally by the Commanding Officer, it does include individuals officially punished by field punishment for drunkenness. Even if this figure records only the most serious examples of drunkenness, it seems an implausibly low figure for an army garrisoned around the world in areas of low living costs. The integrity of drunkenness figures is further undermined by the 554 courts-martial convictions of British non-commissioned personnel for drunkenness, between 1 September 1939 and 31 August 1940.[17] Although the Army roughly trebled in size, this does not explain the 24-fold increase from 1937 figures. The overlapping jurisdiction of military and local justice systems makes analysis of pre-war civil offences by military personnel exceptionally difficult, particularly in non-garrison towns. However, the obscurity of these cases in contemporary local papers suggests courts-martial records were only slightly distorted by their absence.

A possible explanation for how official figures were kept artificially low was that the delegation of authority restricted the progression of offences through the hierarchical Army legal system whilst ensuring a swift disciplinary outcome. Many NCOs used a combination of intimidating appearance and soothing words to prevent disorder occurring or escalating. This approach was personified in 1939 by Company Sergeant Major Kellet, C Company 2nd Middlesex Regiment who, despite being nearly 50, had never placed a soldier on a charge, 'being quite happy to give any offending soldier a good nagging'.[18] Within the official disciplinary system, the threshold of evidence necessary for a conviction was as high as a civilian court, leading to only the most blatant cases being pursued. In spring 1940, despite vocal insubordination in front of an entire section, a Royal Engineer Corporal of 225th Field Company had his case dismissed after both he and the offended Lance Sergeant produced equally favourable, yet conflicting, junior NCO witnesses; the word of the more senior NCO was not enough to prove guilt.[19] Once a disciplinary case became official, the Judge Advocate General's office demanded faultless legal procedures and complex paperwork if a conviction was to be successful. Consequently legally inexperienced officers frequently requested JAG office reassurance over the validation of charges and evidence in important cases. Exposure of this inexperience further disinclined COs to deal with ill-discipline officially.[20]

It should be noted the Army's method of reporting disciplinary statistics changed frequently in the pre-war period. The annual report for the year ending 30 September 1937 distinguished between types of courts-martial and types of offences in its breakdown of courts-martial data. For 1938, the reporting period was changed to the year ending 31 December to ensure up-to-date information, whilst the breakdown of offences was removed to streamline the report. No report was made in 1939 due to the outbreak of war, but when relevant courts-martial statistics were collated and published, they were for the year ending 31 August.[21] The changes may be a coincidence and a consequence of staff turnover in the War Office, but they do not make accurate comparisons easy, and contribute to the mystification of the true standards of discipline.

Analysis of courts-martial statistics relating to the period 4 September 1939, when BEF advance parties first arrived, to the official end of the campaign on 18 June 1940, has revealed 1761 individuals were court-martialled for 2650 separate offences. Of these, 209 individuals (12 per cent) were found not guilty, a surprisingly high figure, possibly due to officers enforcing regulations more rigorously without fully understanding the complexity of disciplinary procedures. Upon the completion of their courts-martial, no less than 518 soldiers (29 per cent) had their sentences altered; 381 (22 per cent) had sentences reduced by the confirming officer, whilst a further 137 convictions (8 per cent rounded) were, at least partially, quashed by the JAG.[22] By comparison, Timothy Bowman's study of 5645 courts-martial involving personnel from Irish Regiments on the Great War Western Front has shown 1917 (34 per cent) had their original sentence altered of which 161 cases were quashed.[23] Although there are similarities between the two sets of figures, British military justice had evolved between the wars. Boards of courts-martial retained sentencing options ranging from small fines to capital punishment (for treason, mutiny and murder) but unlike World War One, when 346 British soldiers were executed for a multitude of offences, only two BEF personnel were sentenced to death during the France campaign. Lance Corporal R. Goulding, 5th Royal Inniskilling Dragoon Guards and Private H. Taylor, 2nd Duke of Cornwall's Light Infantry were both sentenced to death for separate incidents of murder. In both cases C-in-C Gort commuted the sentence to penal servitude for life. The ability of courts-martial boards to sentence individuals to death safe in the knowledge that a higher authority could intervene was indicative of the military justice system. Having participated in several courts-martial in 1940, Major E. Thornhill noted: 'I had no qualms about giving very heavy sentences. I knew that these would be reviewed at a later date by the convening officer and reduced if they were considered too harsh'.[24] The exploitation of this legal failsafe by courts-martial boards was commonplace within the Army and explains why senior officers were neither shocked nor concerned at such a high percentage of altered convictions.

On 20 September 1939, a 2nd Cameronians Private became the first BEF soldier to be court-martialled when he was sentenced to 90 days field punishment for miscellaneous civil offences. The last member of the BEF to be court-martialled was an Auxiliary Military Pioneer Corps (AMPC) Pioneer for drunkenness on 8 June 1940. Seventeen courts-martial occurred in September 1939, 113 in October, 157 in November, 267 in December, 240 in January 1940, 270 in February, 332 in March, 283 in April, 71 in May and 11 in June.[25] Throughout these fluctuating figures, the only moment of concern recorded by the Adjutant General was the dramatic increase in courts-martial between November and December, within which occurred a similar increase in insubordinate offences. The GHQ response was to tentatively investigate further restrictions on alcohol and to accelerate the arrival of philanthropic bodies, but concern soon dissipated as this trend did not continue.[26] In late 1939, a steep rise in disciplinary infringements also occurred in the German Army; for example, 12th Infantry Division held 17 courts-martial in September 1939, 32 in October and 63 in November. Omer Bartov has illustrated the German High Command's contrasting response of increasingly punitive sentencing including greater enforcement of the death penalty. This stabilized court-martial levels within 12th Division to a monthly average of 18, which may explain Gort's attempts to reinstate the death penalty as a traditional deterrent.[27]

BEF personnel committed 25 types of offence in the following numerical order: Miscellaneous Military Offence (468), Drunkenness (446), Violence Against/Striking Superior (273), Absent without Leave (243), Disobedience (221), Theft (209), Insubordinate/Threatening Language (189), Sleeping at/Left Post (129), Miscellaneous Civil Offence (107), Offence against Property of an Inhabitant (62), Offence against Person of an Inhabitant (57), Desertion (49), Resisting Escort (38), Guilty of Absence (30), Escaping (26), Losing Property (26), Indecency (20), Mutiny (13), Injuring Property (12), Fraud (10), Manslaughter (9), Murder (6), Scandalous Conduct (4), Self-Inflicted Wound (2) and Rape (1). Whilst the frequency of some offences was remarkably similar to pre-war levels (219 investigated thefts and 153 alleged incidents of insubordination in 1937), other more serious offences such as murder, manslaughter and mutiny became more prevalent in the France campaign, having been almost non-existent pre-war; offences against the person of an inhabitant increased nearly 1400 per cent on 1937 levels.[28]

The largest numbers of BEF courts-martial were attributable to multi-unit, multi-location regiments and corps whose sheer numerical strength and decentralized deployment made incidence of ill-discipline inevitable. The AMPC was most ill-disciplined during the campaign, with 262 attributable courts-martial, although the quality of its officers, rank-and-file personnel and living conditions contributed heavily to this. The AMPC was led by the worst officers in the BEF, with the Adjutant General demanding on 19 November 1939, the transfer of all officers too elderly or incapable for combatant units to 'AMPC units'. Although all AMPC personnel were theoretically healthy men aged 35–50, a Phoney War GHQ investigation into high sickness rates within AMPC units concluded not only were rates genuine, but also they were a direct consequence of ubiquitous 'poor physique' and an average age of almost 50 amongst the men.[29] Formed with the objective of easing the manual labour workload of BEF units in training, just three weeks after downing civilian tools, AMPC recruits were deployed to France with no uniform and no combat training. With this raison d'être, it is unsurprising the AMPC came last when further resources were distributed. Whilst these conditions encouraged ill-discipline, it should be noted they were also recognized as extenuating circumstances. When the No. 1 Military Prison Commandant visited 47th AMPC Company at Doullens, he found conditions sufficiently 'appalling' that he unilaterally exonerated two imprisoned soldiers and transferred three others to a more hospitable detention facility.[30] Sympathy for individual circumstances should not be mistaken for an acceptance of widespread ill-discipline.

When the Adjutant General demanded the War Office deploy untrained TA divisions to solve the BEF's labour crisis, he did so because 'untrained and undisciplined AMPC personnel would be most unacceptable', particularly as they 'undoubtedly cause a serious deterioration in our relations with the French'.[31] To emphasize the gulf in disciplinary standards, no courts-martial occurred in the 12th, 23rd and 46th TA Divisions during the France campaign. In contrast, the poor discipline of AMPC units deteriorated further in close proximity to combat, for example, the HMS *Whitshed* demolition party reported on 23 May having to drive back at bayonet point a drunken, panic-stricken rabble of AMPC officers and men who attempted to rush the ship.[32]

High levels of ill-discipline within the AMPC units was inevitable due to poor officers incapable of enforcing discipline, the creation of any esprit de corps being severely restricted by the amorphous and temporary nature of the AMPC and its constituent units, the age and health of personnel meant career prospects were limited, whilst equally bleak pioneer duties and living conditions offered minimal incentives for staying within the rules. Despite this, the 262 AMPC courts-martial were not significantly worse than 256 courts-martial in the more stable, technical and disciplined Royal Artillery; 161 courts-martial occurred in the RE and 135 in the Royal Army Service Corps. It should be noted the courts-martial records do not distinguish between units in non-infantry regiments, making impossible more in-depth analysis of the unit types and geographical factors. With less officer supervision, greater opportunity for crime and, in some cases, a lack of unit pride, John Ellis has argued multi-location units were more vulnerable to ill-discipline. However, within the BEF, several dispersed units had very good disciplinary records; for example, the Royal Army Pay Corps had only one court-martial, whilst the Military Provost Staff Corps (MPSC) had no courts-martial irrespective of 62 other ranks for every officer. Also, when GHQ Provost Marshal requested in October 1939 that MPSC units be broken up and their personnel used to augment the Corps of Military Police, MPSC Commandant Lieutenant Colonel J. Gordon successfully objected on the grounds that they were entirely separate units and that the identity of the MPSC could be lost completely; this suggests esprit de corps was high in at least some non-combatant units.[33] Formed from the regular staff of Aldershot military detention facilities, BEF MPSC units had a strong, pre-existing bond, which gave them a disciplinary advantage over newly created AMPC units.

There were 690 courts-martial within the 151 rifle, machine-gun and motor-cycle battalions of the BEF, meaning the average disciplinary record was 4.56 courts-martial per battalion during the France campaign. There were 33 courts-martial between the eight battalions of Foot Guards, resulting in a superior average of 4.125 courts-martial per battalion; however, without the brief courts-martial-free deployment of the 20th Guards Brigade (2nd Irish and Welsh Guards) for the defence of Boulogne, courts-martial per battalion rises to a surprisingly inferior average of 5.5. Due to the small number of Irish battalions, the 12 courts-martial sustained by the 2nd Royal Inniskilling Fusiliers unfairly distorts the four Irish battalions' average of five courts-martial. In contrast, the already high average of 6.13 courts-martial for each of the 30 Scottish battalions is favourably distorted by the belated courts-martial-free deployment of the 52nd (Lowland) Division; excluding 52nd Division, the average rises to an even more disorderly 8.76 courts-martial for the 21 remaining Scottish battalions. The three Welsh battalions averaged 4.33 courts-martial, whilst the 113 English battalions average 4.23 courts-martial per battalion.[34]

This analysis demonstrates that Scottish and Irish battalions had a disciplinary record worse than the BEF average during the France campaign. However, excluding anomalies such as 20th Guards Brigade and 52nd Division, as well as accepting that the small sample unfairly distorts the Irish battalions' disciplinary record, a fairer analysis of BEF courts-martial records suggests the Scottish and Guards battalions had the worst disciplinary records. Since only 82 out of 1761 BEF courts-martial occurred in May and June 1940, the involvement of these battalions in some of the fiercest fighting cannot be used as an excuse. As the Guards were exclusively regular battalions and the Scottish battalions 33 per cent regulars, a possible extenuating factor might be their early arrival in France and subsequently lengthy deployment. However, many English battalions were deployed to France early and maintained below-average levels of ill-discipline, suggesting Scottish and Guards' disciplinary records were due to factors within the battalions rather than discriminatory external factors.[35]

The 4.56 battalion average hides a vast gulf in standards between the best and worst disciplined battalions in the BEF. The worst five battalions for discipline were 5th Division's 2nd Cameronians Regiment (43 courts-martial), 1st Division's 1st King's Shropshire Light Infantry (28), the GHQ Machine-Gun Battalion 4th Gordon Highlanders (22), 44th Division's 1st Queen's Own Royal West Kent Regiment (20) and 3rd Division's 2nd East Yorkshire Regiment (20). In terms of UK origin, locality once deployed to France, chain of command and type of battalion, the diversity of these units suggests above-average ill-discipline was not restricted to particular sections of the BEF. Internal factors within a battalion, in combination with length of deployment, are more likely to have precipitated overall high ill-discipline. Amongst the worst five battalions, some experienced significant spikes in ill-discipline; for example, 2nd Cameronians Regiment held one court-martial in February 1940, 12 in March and only two in April. In contrast, the 1st Queen's Own Royal West Kent Regiment averaged approximately three courts-martial per month throughout the Phoney War, deviating only in April with five. The courts-martial trend in the other three battalions was less clear-cut, falling between the two extremes, but generally experiencing a rise in official ill-discipline in the cold winter months. Despite being responsible for far more courts-martial than the overwhelming majority of BEF battalions, these units' charge sheets were not filled with trivial offences considered by other commanders too mundane for official proceedings. During the France campaign 4th Gordon Highlanders court-martialled only one person for drunkenness, but 13 individuals for offences involving violence or insubordination against a superior. The other four battalions had similarly undesirable charge sheets, although the ratio between serious and unforgivable was less striking; for example, 2nd Cameronians Regiment court-martialled 13 soldiers for drunkenness and ten individuals for violence or insubordination against a superior.[36]

Some personnel within these battalions have suggested their commanding officers rigorously enforced discipline to a higher standard than other BEF units, and this consequently impacted on courts-martial figures. 1st King's Shropshire Light Infantry Bugler A. Gaskin described his CO as a WWI disciplinarian who believed in severe haircuts and strict adherence to regulations.[37] According to 2nd East Yorkshire Regiment Second Lieutenant J. Ogden, Lieutenant Colonel Given controlled 'his battalion with a rod of iron', enthusiastically supported by company commanders such as 'veritable tyrant' Captain Spencer of B Company.[38] These views are strikingly similar to those of Private L. Arlington, 2nd Middlesex Regiment, who felt his battalion was unwaveringly subjected to excessively high standards of discipline and appearance; this made Lieutenant Colonel Haydon 'the most disliked man in the whole regiment'.[39] This unnecessarily petty approach to discipline did not correlate with a high courts-martial rate, as 2nd Middlesex Regiment achieved an admirable disciplinary record of only one court-martial during the entire campaign. In reality, most soldiers believed no officer could match their CO for toughness, just as they believed in the superiority of their battalion. Other than the number of courts-martial, there is no evidence to suggest that the COs of the five worst disciplined battalions were significantly less tolerant of ill-discipline, or more liable to use official disciplinary proceedings.

During the France campaign, there were 59 rifle, machine-gun and motor-cycle battalions who had no courts-martial, including the entire 12th, 23rd, 46th and 52nd Divisions. Seven out of nine infantry battalions in 42nd Division had no courts-martial, nor did the six TA battalions of 44th Division. Although the official disciplinary records of these battalions are identical, their staggered deployment to France allows differentiation on the basis of time deployed. Deployed in October 1939, 1st Suffolk Regiment (3rd Division) served the longest tour in France without sustaining a courts-martial. The 8th Worcestershire Regiment, 4th Oxfordshire & Buckinghamshire Light Infantry and 1st Buckinghamshire Battalion, The Oxfordshire & Buckinghamshire Light Infantry (all 48th Division) arrived in January 1940. 6th and 9th Durham Light Infantry (both 50th Division) share fifth place, having deployed simultaneously in February 1940.[40] Nothing in the 1st Suffolk Regiment war diary suggests disciplinary regulations were more flexibly interpreted or that the CO was prepared to turn a blind eye to ill-discipline. With BEF personnel based in a foreign country, often in intense discomfort and only limited opportunity for home leave, it is unsurprising many units were proud of their good disciplinary record. The anonymous author of *Infantry Officer*, a Second Lieutenant in a regular BEF battalion, noted: 'It speaks well for our troops that there was little or no crime – at least so far as I saw. During those eight months in France I don't remember more than one court-martial in my unit'.[41] Similarly the official history of the Duke of Wellington's Regiment noted with pride that apart from one internally dealt with uncensored letter posted on arrival at Cherbourg, no other military offence of any kind occurred during the whole of the Territorial 2nd/6th battalion's participation in the campaign.[42] Commendably, some BEF units genuinely had negligible ill-discipline throughout the campaign.

Formation commanders did not infringe the independence of subordinate battalion commanders by scrutinizing disciplinary procedures. 8th Infantry Brigade contained the impressive 1st Suffolk Regiment and the more disorderly 2nd East Yorkshire Regiment. Brigadier C. Woolner was a fit, aggressive commander, who as President of a General Courts-Martial Board, was personally responsible for one of only two BEF personnel sentenced to death during the campaign (later commuted to penal servitude for life). Minimal brigade intervention in subordinate affairs is a more plausible explanation than the suggestion that tough disciplinary oversight could paradoxically encourage overzealous enforcement in 2nd East Yorkshire Regiment as well as acting as a deterrent in 1st Suffolk Regiment. The only mention of Woolner being dissatisfied with 8th Brigade discipline was in October 1939, when 3rd Division highlighted the need to improve deteriorating turnout; Woolner was forced to admit 'the men are becoming slovenly' and implemented corrective drills.[43]

The most frequent identifiable offence within the BEF was drunkenness, for which 446 personnel were court-martialled; the top four offenders were the multi-unit AMPC (74 courts-martial), RA (60), RE (49) and RASC (27). Amongst easily differentiated infantry battalions, 2nd Cameronians Regiment were worst with 13 courts-martial for drunkenness, 1st King's Shropshire Light Infantry (11), equal third were 1st Gordon Highlanders and 1st Border Regiment (both 7).[44] With two of the top three, it appears drunkenness was a particular weakness within Scottish battalions; this is also supported by anecdotal evidence. GHQ GSO1 Lieutenant Colonel Bridgeman considered 51st Division one of the BEF's worst because they spent much of their time 'drinking whisky instead of training'.[45] During the Phoney War, the 8th Durham Light Infantry were deployed to St Remy to replace a hard drinking Scottish battalion, whose personnel had stolen the village estaminet's entire wine-cellar, forcing the battalion mess officer to pay for the wholesale stock at retail prices; the owner failed in her attempts to get 8th Durham Light Infantry to repeat the process.[46] Such was the infamous reputation of Scottish drinking habits, many BEF personnel were cheered by the implausible 24 May rumours that a half-drunk Scottish battalion 'without orders made a bayonet charge and wiped out 500 Germans'.[47]

Brian Bond has argued there is ample evidence that excessive alcohol consumption was commonplace throughout the BEF, but has not contextualized how great this temptation was, or examined the response of the High Command.[48] Unlike many imperial outposts, alcohol was easily accessible in France; for example, 2nd Middlesex Regiment personnel discovered approximately 33 per cent of all properties in Gondecourt officially or unofficially sold alcohol. 52nd Heavy Regiment RA utilized Fleurbaix estaminets for alcohol, cheap dining out, sources of fresh produce and for off-duty entertainment, for there were few alternatives. The Phoney War effectively forced BEF personnel to frequent establishments selling cheap alcohol for many of their non-military needs.[49]

All types of alcohol in France were extraordinarily cheap and sold at prices never before experienced by most serving soldiers. Answering parliamentary questions on 14 March 1940, War Secretary Oliver Stanley responded English draught beer costing sixpence a pint, imported by all Palestine-based NAAFI stores, was not only good value, but competitively priced compared to British retailers.[50] Whilst it was competitive with a 6d Bass on Third Class Rail, and similar to a 4.5d pint in a public-house, it was distinctly uncompetitive to Phoney War France where British soldiers could 'get very drunk on two franks [3d]' (sic) a night.[51] Impoverished new recruit W. Saunders (48th Divisional Signals) could only afford two half-pints per evening in Britain, whilst long serving Company Quartermaster Sergeant T. Thomas (1st Armoured Divisional Signals) had ten shillings disposable income to spend each Saturday. Serving in the BEF encouraged drinking habits because of a beneficial exchange rate of one franc = 1.36d (176.5 francs = £1), as well as fortnightly pay issues in 20 franc notes. In France 48th Divisional Signals rank-and-file 'quickly resolved to try every bottle on the [Yvetot] Café's display shelf', whilst CQMS Thomas's consumption of four-franc glasses of cognac was limited only by how much he could drink.[52] John Keegan has argued ill-discipline could not be localized to solitary individuals because groups always emulate trendsetters. Consequently when W. Saunders drank '23 drinks of 11 different varieties' in a single session, others copied; inevitably many in the unit were 'incredibly ill' and rendered unfit for duty, although no action was taken against them.[53] BEF officers were equally indulgent, for example, 2nd East Yorkshire Regiment junior officers 'stuck to champagne every night; one bottle per person, per night, at one shilling a bottle'.[54]

In the context of BEF alcohol intake, official drunkenness figures remained low despite the continual discovery of cheap alcohol by newly-deployed units. Many incidents went unbeknown to commanders, but in more blatant events the soft-touch disciplinary system only intervened if personnel were rendered completely incapable, and operated officially only if compelled to. 2nd Middlesex Regiment rejected courts-martial proceedings for two privates guilty of unauthorized absence from Roubaix Barracks and returning drunk; unofficial discipline – '24 hours guard duty on the main gate'.[55] Specifically asked for by MPSC GOC, the BEF tour of highly regarded Aldershot-based Royal Scots Captain A. McDonald MC nevertheless lasted only four days in December 1939 before repatriation; continually rendering 'himself unfit for duty through excessive drinking' forced the Adjutant General to issue an unofficial tour-ending severe reprimand.[56] When it became clear 2nd East Yorkshire Regiment patrols in the Baisieux area routinely 'disappeared like needles in a haystack, drinking themselves silly as fast as possible', junior officers consciously chose to introduce surprise spot-checks, rather than bring charges for dereliction.[57] However, on 28 October 1939, the Adjutant General ordered an extension of estaminet hours to 2130hrs, officially 'to allow troops to hear 9 p.m. BBC News', unofficially to legalize soldiers drinking after 2100hrs curfew; indeed self-policing units continued to purchase alcohol as desired, blatantly ignoring the restrictions.[58] Self-policing was particularly difficult for newly-commissioned officers, because as RASC Second Lieutenant J. Finch recalled: 'Subalterns were always lectured on keeping hard spirits from the troops but not how to do it'.[59] On his own initiative, Finch implemented a policy of announcing disciplinary charges to stop ongoing acts of excessive drinking, but never followed up on them, for fear of damaging unit morale; if replicated elsewhere in the BEF, this policy further brings in to question courts-martial statistics as a true indicator of disciplinary levels.

Placing urban centres off-limits proved no deterrent to determined alcohol/entertainment seekers. A 13 January 1940 sweep of out-of-bounds Valenciennes by 2nd Division Provost Company led to three BEF officers and 29 rank-and-file being charged and unofficially disciplined, but not court-martialled. The number of BEF personnel visiting Lille, particularly in the evening, justified the permanent presence of a Deputy Assistant Provost Marshal and over 50 military police from I and II Corps, yet their law-enforcement raids were so infrequent that senior officers felt comfortable drinking until they 'could hardly stand' in the city's Le Miami nightclub. Rather than embarrassingly prosecute senior officers, Le Miami was conveniently, albeit legitimately, closed by order of the High Command, as a centre of German spying and Nazi propaganda.[60]

The BEF's unwillingness to enforce regulations rigorously, combined with undue leniency for alcohol-induced dereliction, encouraged repeat offending and more serious crime. Although 171 individuals were court-martialled purely for drunkenness, a further 275 personnel were simultaneously court-martialled for other offences along with drunkenness. These offences included mutiny, scandalous conduct and striking a superior; serious crimes that might not have occurred had the offender been sober. Interestingly, Omer Bartov has shown once the occupation of France was complete, the German Army experienced a spike in drunkenness, but also theft, sexual offences, brawls with officers and civilians. In an assessment strikingly similar to many BEF officers, the GOC 12th Infantry Division argued that 'the long rest period in a rich land' had led astray 'many soldiers whose character is not strong enough to resist temptation'.[61]

Failure to deal with inappropriate behaviour during the strategic lull of the Phoney War meant complacent attitudes towards alcohol were maintained until the German invasion and beyond. Second Lieutenant J. Finch noted his RASC ammunition column was worryingly hung-over from the previous night's festivities, when it advanced into Belgium on 10 May.[62] Having responded to the German invasion on an hour's sleep, many Queen's Own (132nd) Brigade officers found marching 55 miles in two days harder than in previous practice route-marches; on 9/10 May, the newly-formed brigade's celebrations were 'somewhat protracted and many officers were rather late getting to bed'.[63] Inevitably, on any night of drunken revelry, there will be instances of self-inflicted injury. During the Phoney War, these trivial incidents cumulatively undermined the quality and quantity of training; on 9 May 1940, the consequences were much more significant. As a direct result of the officers and NCOs of B Company, 2nd East Yorkshire Regiment partying in Lille until 0300hrs 10 May, Company Commander Captain Spencer was rendered unfit for duty by what was conveniently deemed an unfortunate accident. Captain Spencer resumed command on 22 May, having missed several engagements and over ten days of critical, active operations. Spencer's last-minute replacement, by his own admission, 'had never done Company Commander's duties before' and, worryingly, he asked his subordinates 'to tell him if he did something wrong'.[64]

The complacent attitude towards alcohol continued during combat operations; for example, 2nd Buffs Regiment Intelligence Officer Edlmann felt it was appropriate to buy beer for battalion headquarters personnel during a lull in the advance to the Dyle.[65] Widespread availability and frequent personal consumption insidiously nullified BEF personnel's awareness of the possible catastrophic consequences of drinking alcohol in combat situations. On 18 May, despite holding crucial riverbank positions, No. 11 Platoon led by Second Lieutenant Blackburn succumbed to temptation, until they were all horribly drunk, weapon-less and incapable. To save No. 11 Platoon from 'condign punishment' and to safeguard BEF positions, junior officers conspired 'an excellent cover-up' by replacing them with No. 10 Platoon without informing battalion headquarters.[66] With twisted logic, self-enforcing disciplinary procedures were undermined by the desire to preserve company honour; predictably on 19 May, Second Lieutenant Blackburn broke down in combat, further endangering BEF positions. The incompatibility of alcohol and peak performance was never fully realized by the BEF during the France campaign.

Theft was another offence significantly under-recorded by the disciplinary system in 1939–40. Officially, 209 individuals were court-martialled for theft; prolific offenders were AMPC (43), RASC (38) and RE (35). With theft courts-martial in infantry battalions totalling only 27, multi-unit corps and regiments did not top offending rates simply because their units were indistinguishable in courts-martial records.[67] Rear-echelon formations had the most sustained, under-supervised access to virtually untraceable commodities such as rations, tools and, above all, petrol. The vast scale of the supply chain added to its vulnerability; for example, No.2 Base Ordnance Depot in Le Havre had 858,250 ft.^{2} of covered stores and 44 acres of stores open to the elements, but only a handful of office-based officers to supervise operations.[68] As the BEF expanded, it is unsurprising this arms-length supervision led to an 'increasing amount of pilfering ... principally at Base Ports and from goods in transport to railheads'.[69] When I Corps HQ arrived at Cherbourg in September 1939, so much equipment was stolen during disembarkation, the entire complement of 40 staff cars had to be pushed off the docks to marshalling areas; senior officers were not informed and suspected nothing, despite the cars being non-operational for over 24 hours.[70] By November 1939, endemic pilfering forced C-in-C Gort to demand provost personnel prioritize investigations into the 'sale of petrol to civilians', both from 'petrol dumps and possibly by persons authorized to draw petrol'.[71] These investigations were not very successful, illustrated by the only significant Phoney War success for 1st Division Provost Company being the discovery of 236 gallons of British Army petrol in a January raid on a Le Pavé estaminet. However, the failure of the Provost branch to identify either the source of stolen supplies, or more importantly, the British perpetrators in most cases, led to responsibility for black-market investigations being transferred to the GHQ Intelligence branch in February 1940. It is unclear how much progress was made by the Intelligence branch in reducing the level of pilfering because on 7 May 1940, War Secretary Stanley informed an MP no centrally collated figures existed, as their creation would require an unviable level of inquiry and it was the duty of individual COs to safeguard stores.[72] Omer Bartov has identified German theft statistics as being equally under-recorded, but only because senior officers were complicit in systemic plundering of occupied territories. In October 1940, German police investigating 12th Division discovered stolen Polish and French goods had been 'distributed in the presence of senior officers to officers, NCOs and soldiers'.[73]

The BEF petrol supply chain was particularly open to abuse due to a lack of accurate records, the absence of meaningful supervision, the vulnerability of army containers to leakage and the value of the commodity. The GHQ branch of RASC demanded each unit record all petrol received, issued and consumed throughout their deployment in France. Most units failed to achieve the standard; for example, after its first substantive stock-take on 4 January 1940, 1st Base Sub-Area admitted high volumes and insufficient staff had resulted in 'a very inaccurate record' over preceding months. To prevent fraud and unit exploitation by French retailers, the BEF ordered and paid for petrol from a centralized office at GHQ. With hundreds of units consuming over 600 tonnes of petrol a day by spring 1940, a staff of three officers led by a Lieutenant Colonel was woefully inadequate for supervising such a vast organization. As all three had been plucked from civilian employment and had no military experience, they could only defend the BEF from outlandish requests disproportionate to the majority, rather than widespread over-ordering. In November 1939, the petrol black-market became sufficiently endemic for the French to threaten imposing duty on BEF petrol in order to protect diminishing French Treasury returns. The main flaw in the system was the British Army's continued use of compressed cardboard four-gallon cans for all transportation and storage purposes; its vulnerability to breakage if stocked sideways or five cans high or left exposed to the elements provided a ready-made excuse for the incompetent and corrupt. As the BEF also sourced petrol from the UK, it was equally vulnerable to British profiteers; for example, in late December 1939, 23rd Field Regiment RA received a consignment of virtually empty fuel-cans. GHQ requests for a UK investigation led to suspiciously prompt WO replies on 24 and 27 December which ended the investigation; the implausible explanation was that leaking cans had been emptied, repaired, refilled and then re-leaked before delivery to the BEF had been completed. It should also be noted petrol could be lost to negligence amongst BEF rear-echelon personnel as well as theft. On 15 December 1939, I Corps Petrol Dump caught fire and was allowed to burn by the Commanding Officer for a further 56.5 hours in case the duration provided GHQ with valuable information. The fire started as BEF personnel, working without officer supervision, completed stacking a delivery of fuel-cans. No disciplinary action was taken, as the proximity of a rarely used road over 50 yards away meant the GHQ investigator could not conclusively prove whether a cigarette from BEF personnel or French farmers was to blame. The official report concluded further restrictions on BEF dump personnel were necessary, rather than on the nearby road, a clear indication of where the report's author felt blame lay.[74]

Whilst BEF wholesale pilfering was usually carried out by unidentifiable individuals, at the other end of the spectrum, minor thefts were an unreported fact of life in the Army. Even in the well-disciplined TA, soldiers quickly learnt the 'art of taking care of and guarding one's bed-space, kit and possessions'; unprotected by shared pre-war employment and friendship, BEF Signaller W. Saunders recalled: '[I] had a knife and my cap pinched, so of course the only thing I could do was pinch someone else's. They'd pinch the milk out of a blind man's tea'.[75] Minor thefts occurred in plain sight of officers; for example, Private A. Notley, 1/7th Middlesex Regiment openly admitted in a Phoney War letter censured by his platoon commander, chicken rustling was a favourite hobby amongst his colleagues.[76] Combat merely increased the possibilities; whilst evacuating troops at Dunkirk, Little Ship owner Alan Barrell recalled that 'one of them took my revolver from under my nose, it's a way they have in the army'.[77] In any large organization, minor thefts are inevitable, but in the BEF the majority of these went unreported due to the victim's disillusion with the official disciplinary system, or a preference for self-sufficient solutions.

The criminal offence senior officers feared most was desertion, as it signified a total breakdown of an individual's acceptance of the chain of command and its disciplinary system. In 1937, desertion was the most common military offence with 472 incidents (167 within three months of enlistment), followed in third place by 299 individuals going absent without leave. David French has argued low pay, inadequate leave, the Army's image problem and difficulty obtaining compassionate leave all contributed to making desertion an issue in the pre-war, UK-based army. Desertion remained a problem throughout World War II, with 30,740 occurrences in 1939–45, second only to 75,157 incidents of rank-and-file unauthorized absence. Although there were multiple reasons for desertion, Christine Bielecki has argued the main reason for wartime desertion was not cowardice, but the temporary loss of physical and mental stamina necessary to endure army life. In the BEF the almost exclusive reliance on volunteers, the large proportion of career regulars and the absence of sustained combat meant desertion occurred an infrequent 49 times whilst 243 individuals were court-martialled for unauthorized absences. Although the Channel formed an insurmountable obstruction to the temptations of home, the unique circumstances of the Phoney War meant the overwhelming majority did not even contemplate desertion. On 5 March 1940, Second Lieutenant P. Martin, 2nd Cheshire Regiment, informed his parents his enjoyment was tempered only by the fear of being sent home for a training course. In a letter home, Private A. Notley, 1/7th Middlesex Regiment recalled an immediate improvement in unit discipline after warnings that offenders and troublemakers would be returned home. Unlike the pre-war and post-Dunkirk periods, desertion was not a major concern for BEF commanders and had limited impact on the campaign.[78]

Statistically, though, official disciplinary procedures openly assisted the retention of low desertion rates and consequently undermined the validity of the figures. Under BEF reporting procedures, units were only obligated to inform an officer of the Provost branch on the eighth day of absence, whilst the Provost Marshal and French Mission were only advised of an individual's desertion on the tenth day of absence; until this point, units could treat any desertion as an internal matter and presumably prosecute under the lesser charge of unauthorized absence. When an intoxicated 48th Divisional Signals reservist, disgruntled at unit discipline, absconded whilst in possession of a vehicle, it was openly acknowledged within his unit that his capture by one of his own officers before the time limit, along with the recovery of the vehicle intact, all contributed to the insignificant sentence of 14 days field punishment. Low desertion rates were also assisted by the willingness of personnel to give deserters the benefit of the doubt. On 29 May 1940, 4th Royal Sussex Regiment, including Second Lieutenant Hadley's platoon, came under intensive artillery bombardment, resulting in the disappearance of Lance Corporal Biggs. Christine Bielecki has suggested deserters found the need to escape an untenable situation so overwhelming no threat could sway them.[79] The Biggs case seems to typify this, for having found the Lance Corporal alive and in excellent spirits at Dunkirk, Hadley hypothesised: 'I suspect that the bursting of the shell almost on top of him was too much for his nerves and he may have temporarily lost his memory'.[80] For reasons of regimental honour, or possibly in recognition that further disciplinary proceedings were futile, Lance Corporal Biggs was given the benefit of the doubt, as were many other BEF personnel. This figure-distorting approach even extended to incidents involving senior ranking, well-trained regulars. After witnessing an erratically-behaving lone Captain whilst patrolling the Dunkirk perimeter on 31 May, the same officer visited Second Lieutenant Ogden in England 'wanting to know what I was putting in my report about him. This revealed to me that he was actually running away when I bumped into him, and at once beetled off down to the beach to get a ship for England'.[81] There can be no doubt that Ogden knew the Captain's identity after the meeting in England, and yet he failed to inform his superiors or record the details in order to preserve the honour of the individual and his unit. Decisions such as this helpfully maintain a false impression about BEF absence and desertion which, although good overall, was far from flawless.

When crimes occurred units could issue fines, sentences of guard duty or up to 28 days field punishment (rank-and-file only); sentencing was dependent on the Commanding Officer's attitude and varied from unit to unit. Serious crimes and those involving NCOs and officers were dealt with by courts-martial; sentencing guidelines were identical for all courts-martial, but since the adjudicating board for each court-martial was unique, variation in sentencing was inevitable. The vast majority of convicted soldiers were sentenced to field punishment, although the World War I approach of tying men to gun-limbers had been abolished during inter-war modernization. In 1939, field punishment entailed hard physical labour such as filling sandbags, carried out at the double, throughout daylight hours, plus a daily non-stop two hours of drill with full kit; this usually occurred at a specialist camp run for each Corps by MPSC staff. Sentencing was not made in isolation, but dependent on capacity, for example, for four months courts-martial of II Corps personnel conveniently ensured soldiers sentenced to field punishment did not exceed the II Corps Field Punishment (FP) Camp capacity of 28; within 11 days of camp capacity expanding to 84, the number of detainees increased to 78. On 30 November 1939, I Corps FP Camp had an occupancy rate of 48/50 places whilst 27/28 places were filled at II Corps FP Camp. These manipulated figures prevent analysis of crime rates or preference for field punishment as a sentence, and merely indicate that I Corps had nearly twice II Corps capacity and courts-martial sentenced accordingly.[82]

The BEF's response to prisoner returns was equally pragmatic and varied. I Corps standing orders required unit repatriation of soldiers under sentence (SUS) every time the BEF came to four hours' notice or upon invasion; II Corps sought SUS repatriation only on the fourth day of any advance into Belgium.[83] Senior officers were frequently ambivalent about soldiers completing their sentences. On 6 September 1939, 5th Division GOC Major General H. Franklyn requested the JAG Office Judicial Department arrange 'all men now serving sentences' be 'automatically returned to their units' and that 'after 1/9/39 all sentences should be either remitted or suspended' regardless of the crime.[84] This request was resisted, but it highlights the inability of commanders to be impartial law enforcers, when their overriding concern was unit strength and capability. It also explains why GHQ was surprised when the War Office ordered overseas deployment of No.1 Military Prison.

For such a serious subject, the BEF approach to post-sentence disciplinary procedures was amateurish and improvised. In November 1939, II Corps HQ naively believed convicted soldiers would not try to escape if 'confined in rooms with open windows and unlocked doors'; these views contributed to the decision to remove day-to-day FP Camp administration from Corps to the MPSC. FP Camp rules were not formalized until the MPSC Commandant took the trouble of writing them on 28 March 1940; similarly the implications of a 'life sentence' were not considered until the GHQ administrative branch was questioned on them in January 1940.[85] When a UK-based Assistant Provost Marshal came to study BEF procedures for issuing, confirming and implementing a death sentence, he was forced to inform the Adjutant General 'nothing is laid down'.[86]

Subtlety of the BEF response to disciplinary incidents could be much greater than court-martial sentences imply. Echoing Gerry Rubin's analysis of the military justice system 1940–66 through 21 detailed example courts-martial, this chapter has examined the most striking courts-martial of officers during the France campaign. On 21 February 1940, four officers of the Territorial 1/7th Royal Warwickshire Regiment (a Major, an Acting-Major and two Second Lieutenants) were placed under open arrest for their part in the death of a Private. They were variably charged with mutiny, unauthorized absence and miscellaneous military offences on a day when 1/7th Royal Warwickshire Regiment were practising the use of assault boats on a river swollen by melting snow. These officers were not immovable troublemakers, but acknowledged future prospects, for example, on 17 February, Acting-Major H. Tedder had been promoted to command A Company. The rank of the individuals involved guarantees the CO was disobeyed regarding the river practice, whilst the charge of absence indicates the officers were not on the river at the time of the death. The not guilty pleas of the officers, the seniority of rank involved and seriousness of the alleged offences led to an unusually lengthy two-day courts-martial, at the end of which all four officers were found guilty. Even more unusually, sentencing was delayed five days, presumably to allow the court-martial board to consult both GHQ and the JAG office; the two senior officers were eventually issued severe reprimands, whilst the two Second Lieutenants were issued reprimands.[87]

However, the courts-martial do not tell the full story, for there was clearly a catastrophic breakdown in the relationship between Lieutenant Colonel Siddeley and his subordinate officers. Whilst the four officers may have been found technically guilty, it did not significantly impact on their careers. Major R. Cox remained second-in-command 1/7th Royal Warwickshire Regiment, the two Second Lieutenants continued virtually unscathed and Acting-Major H. Tedder was attached to the superior, regular 2nd Royal Warwickshire Regiment on the instructions of Major General Montgomery. In contrast, Lieutenant Colonel Siddeley was informed of his removal as early as 27 February and was sidelined to the position of Town Major, St Nazaire on 5 March. The swift removal of Siddeley compared to the non-existent punishments for the four prosecuted officers shows where the Army Establishment felt the real responsibility for this incident lay and also how an examination of BEF discipline based only on courts-martial statistics can be misleading. Regiments had an unwritten desire to deal with incidents internally, as highlighted by the 17 March inspection of 1/7th Royal Warwickshire Regiment (48th Division, I Corps) by Warwickshire veteran Major General Montgomery (3rd Division, II Corps) along with Lieutenant Colonel P. Dunn, 2nd Royal Warwickshire Regiment. Acceptance of alleged ringleader Acting-Major Tedder into Dunn's 2nd Warwickshire Regiment and the appointment of a 2nd Royal Ulster Rifles Major (3rd Division) to command 1/7th Royal Warwickshire Regiment, all point to backroom deals designed to restore stability within the regimental family.[88]

The sidelining of Lieutenant Colonel Siddeley was not an isolated incident of commanders being blamed for their subordinates' actions. In 1939, the officers of an RASC ammunition column detailed Mess staff to cut wood daily to heat the Officers' Mess. When the landowner submitted a large compensation claim to the BEF, it was the CO who was held accountable, court-martialled and subsequently committed suicide.[89] It should be noted the higher-profile a disciplinary incident, the more likely it was to be dealt with unofficially. The British Army had tremendous capacity for subtlety, allowing it to show disapproval of legal actions not in keeping with a CO's position. On 1 June 1940, Lieutenant Colonel R. Boxshall, 1st East Surrey Regiment, was seeking embarkation orders for his battalion when he accidentally boarded the departing HMS *Esk*, forcing him to abandon his command. With his battalion demonstrating exemplary performance during the campaign, Boxshall had expected the pre-agreed standard recognition of a Distinguished

Service Order similar to other battalion commanders in 4th Division. When this failed to materialize, Boxshall caused a fuss which eventually led to a belated Mention in Despatches. The only event that fully explains the apparent loss of paperwork recommending decoration and the intransigence of the Army to fully correct the situation was Boxshall's understandable, but equally unacceptable, premature evacuation from Dunkirk. The establishment was fully capable of admonishing officers without recourse to official disciplinary procedures.[90]

Brian Bond has argued BEF discipline was generally good, dependent on units remaining coherent bodies and only deteriorated during the chaos of Dunkirk.[91] However, in a number of areas including bridge demolitions, prisoner welfare and concern for civilians, the BEF was prone to rumour and fatigue-based ill-discipline. Rear-echelon ill-discipline remained most prevalent, but even in front-line units, both regular and TA, discipline was far from blemish free. Once evacuations began discipline deteriorated markedly at all levels and in all areas; this decline continued until the end of the campaign. In the fog of war much of this went unrecorded or was committed by supposedly unidentifiable personnel, but illustrations of the reality can be found in detailed examples.

In his post-Dunkirk analysis, C-in-C Gort noted the BEF quickly established the paramount importance of bridge demolitions on water obstacles as a means of imposing even a short delay on the German advance: 'The BEF destroyed over 500 bridges and there were few failures'.[92] The official campaign history records effective demolitions 'helped considerably to delay the enemy advance' whilst noting only a couple of instances where 'bridges were destroyed before the last troops across'.[93] The lesson learnt by those on the front-line was the under-reported propensity to panic within unsupervised demolition teams. On 18 May, Lieutenant Colonel S. Kington, 1st Duke of Wellington's Regiment reassured the nervous officer responsible for the Tournai bridge demolition no enemy were in sight and that the whole 3rd Brigade rearguard (a carrier platoon and several anti-tank guns) were still to cross. The regimental history recorded: 'This information was apparently discounted by the officer, for no sooner had the Commanding Officer and Adjutant departed to catch up with the Battalion, than the bridge went up with a resounding crash'.[94] No disciplinary action was taken, despite the loss of the rearguard, because the demolition team had successfully fulfilled its orders. Compelled by an absence of faith, many infantry commanders attempted to usurp control of demolitions in order to safeguard their subordinates. 4th Royal Berkshire Regiment standing orders encouraged any subordinate officer to attempt to assume control of any bridge required by the battalion to ensure its safekeeping.[95] Despite sending a liaison officer to seize control of the Heerstert bridge on 21/22 May, Lieutenant Colonel Birch, 2nd Bedfordshire and Hertfordshire Regiment, admitted 'being of a distrustful nature and thinking the bridge might go before I got back I carried in my pocket my air-cushion'.[96] Premature demolitions were not just a symbol of rear-echelon ill-discipline; the unexpected loss of carefully conserved equipment and additional physical exertion could trigger ill-discipline in previously steady units. On 29 May, with their assigned bridge prematurely destroyed, orders to march eight additional miles in full kit and assume positions on the Dunkirk Perimeter were met with severe protests from 2nd Bedfordshire and Hertfordshire officers, NCOs and rank-and-file. Discipline deteriorated to such an extent, Brigade informed Lieutenant Colonel Birch that 'thoughts of evacuation were to be kept quiet' for fear of mass desertions.[97]

To those responsible for bridge demolition the strategic importance of delaying the enemy's advance took precedence over possible military casualties and ethical considerations. On 19 May, Lieutenant Colonel Hugh Swinburne, 1st Tyneside Scottish, discovered the demolition of a bridge over the Canal du Nord had been postponed due to the constant flow of refugees across it. Having seen German tanks briefly on the previous day, alternatives such as holding the refugees back with a small patrol were dismissed. Lieutenant Colonel Swinburne ordered the immediate demolition, whereupon the junior officer responsible burst into tears. According to Swinburne's account: 'I had to push down the plunger myself, much as I hated to do it with people still on the bridge. But orders were orders, and sentiment comes nowhere in war'.[98] The decision to destroy a refugee-covered bridge, despite the Germans being out of sight and despite the Canal du Nord being easily fordable by a car, never mind a tank, in close vicinity to the bridge, displays a misguided sense of discipline. A determination to follow orders to the letter, and minimize risk to his command by any means possible, led to an incorrect analysis of the situation by Lieutenant Colonel Swinburne; delay would have moderately increased the risk to the 1st Tyneside Scottish, but in war risk has to be managed, it cannot be removed.

The execution of prisoners, collateral damage and friendly fire incidents are all types of ill-discipline which occur in most wars and the BEF campaign in France was no different. Incidents such as these are usually open to interpretation, but even in the most blatant examples of ill-discipline commanders were far from condemnatory and often did little to formally advise higher authority.

Military law authority Gerry Rubin has argued the January 1941 conviction (later appealed) of Captain J. Savage for ordering the shooting of a German internee, demonstrates the impeccable integrity of the British military justice system, especially considering the wartime situation and reports of German brutality. The court-martial acts as 'a powerful reminder of those principles for which Britain was fighting' and is undiminished by the conviction not being upheld by the confirming officer.[99] In contrast, the treatment of prisoners by BEF units was often ruthless, bordering on criminal, even if contemporaries believed the execution of suspicious individuals and prisoners of war could be uncontroversial and justified. Initially the BEF had high aspirations of prisoner welfare; for example, during an April 1940 I Corps Manning Exercise, 2nd Division Provost Company ensured its 16 simulated prisoners-of-war received humane interrogation from the divisional intelligence officer, a hot meal, and a haversack ration for sustenance en-route to the rear-echelon.[100]

However, once BEF survival was threatened, the logistics of guarding and feeding prisoners was frequently considered an unnecessary burden and risk. By 11 May, battalion obligations had been reduced to ensuring prisoners were 'handed over by the quickest possible means to nearest Route Regulation Post'.[101] On 19 May, after interrogating a suspected spy in his 1st Tyneside Scottish HQ, in anticipation of a rapid withdrawal, Lieutenant Colonel Swinburne ordered the individual's immediate execution by Sergeant Dick Chambers; according to Company Sergeant Major C. Baggs 'It was done okay'.[102] 2nd Division Provost Company also had no problem acting as judge, jury and executioner when 'four spies were shot' in Cysoing on 21 May.[103] Although official policy was to execute known spies, snap decisions by fatigued officers in high-pressure situations does not tally with Rubin's portrayal of impartial British military justice. Black-and-white judgments were commonplace; for example, when 2nd Middlesex Regiment occupied positions on the Dendre, it concluded 'the whole area reeked of 5th Columny', simply because a few inhabitants did more 'than scowl at us'.[104] In these situations incorrect identification was a permanent danger; for example, 1st Survey Regiment RA were considering shooting a captured parachutist when he was identified as the nephew of the local Burgomeister and a refugee from Louvain. Unfortunately mistakes were made, as illustrated by the confirmed parachutist captured and shot by French troops on 23 May, being belatedly identified as a bailed out RAF pilot.[105]

Regarding clearly identifiable enemy combatants, most killings were not premeditated, but extreme reactions to battlefield trauma. On the outskirts of Dunkirk, having sustained several casualties to air attack, a 2nd Middlesex Regiment Corporal instinctively executed the sole Luftwaffe survivor of a crashed DO17 in an act of revenge. Colleague L. Arlington recalled this was later regretted as 'most of them had very serious misgivings about this sort of behaviour, towards Germans who were giving themselves up'.[106] This supports Brian Bond's argument that 'some German prisoners, or soldiers intending to surrender were killed in the heat of battle, [but] it seems most unlikely that any were murdered in cold blood after they had surrendered and been handed over to higher authorities'.[107] In fact spur-of-the-moment illegality affected all ranks. On 23 May, 2nd East Yorkshire Regiment received orders from 'some windy staff officer' that 'all prisoners would in future be shot'; officially designed to conserve men and material, the unspecified superior formation clearly issued this calculated order to achieve an element of retribution upon the Germans.[108] Although there is no evidence this order was ever carried out, Second Lieutenant Ogden's memoirs acknowledge that on 30 May, when a visiting staff officer was informed 8th Brigade HQ was holding suspected fifth column, he ordered the IO (Intelligence Officer) 'to shoot them all or he would shoot the IO'. Surprisingly Ogden attempted to justify the officer's reaction by stating: 'The British Army was in extremis, and this officer was also in the extremis. Those who are about to die do not mind who they kill' before adding approvingly 'only England could produce a ball of fire like that one'.[109] The fate of the prisoners is unclear, but it is clear discipline amongst all sections of the BEF deteriorated during the campaign, and that action considered unacceptable at the beginning was considered increasingly justified by the time of Dunkirk, both by the ill-disciplined and their contemporary witnesses.

Despite the best efforts of disciplined, civilized armies, collateral damage is an almost inevitable consequence of intensive fighting in built-up areas where the local population is unwilling or unable to evacuate. However, during the France campaign the subordination of civilian interests, and even civilian casualties, were tolerated as justifiable tactics to reduce BEF casualties. At Courtrai, 2nd Buffs Regiment had to force out civilians and 'post sentries to keep them away in case of espionage'.[110] On 22 May, 2nd Division Provost Company patrols actively sought to prevent the return of refugees into the strategically important town of Cysoing.[111] Having selected positions to defend the Furness Canal, 2nd Middlesex Regiment undertook the 'unpleasant task of clearing the civilians from the farms that we were occupying'.[112] On 23 May, a counter-attack by 8th Brigade at Wattrelos was authorized after the local Mayor's assurances that all civilians had been evacuated. Consequently many civilians discovered in the attack were killed to the extent that it was said 'there would soon be none left in the world'; a Corporal justified the actions to an officer stating: 'They might be Germans, sir. So of course I reluctantly had to say carry on'.[113] The Mayor was tragically wrong in his assurances and, although it can be understood BEF personnel did not want to take any chances, the number of civilians encountered must have made them question those assurances. However, it was not unjustifiable insensitivity; for example, on 18 May, 4th Royal Berkshire Regiment recorded that their positions included the village of Exembodegen which 'was infested with snipers dressed as civilians', thereby creating an ethical dilemma BEF troops were not trained for.[114] With respect to illegal killings, targeting of civilians and immoral battlefield actions, at no time during the campaign did the BEF sink to the unjustifiable level of brutality within the German Army, especially SS units, as demonstrated by the Wormhoudt and Le Paradis massacres.

Friendly fire incidents can occur in any conflict, but were particularly frequent in France due to the inadequate night training, inexperienced personnel, the confused nature of operations and the inadequate communications of the BEF. Even pre-planned routes and timings during the advance to the Dyle River could not prevent an unexpectedly close proximity between a Middlesex battalion and an unidentified unit from 2nd Division; one officer admitted 'we had mistaken one another for Germans', resulting in a 0300hrs fire-fight, casualties and lost pride.[115] Inexperienced troops did not have the discipline to hold their fire until positive identification had been made, especially at night when the process could be lengthy and dangerous. Paradoxically, the Germans were aware of BEF inexperience and tried to exploit fears of being involved in a friendly fire incident. On 22 May, as 4th Royal Sussex Regiment began a 2115hrs withdrawal from the Escaut, the Germans launched a surprise attack during which phrases such as 'Don't fire – We're the Jocks' were shouted. Second Lieutenant Hadley recalled 'every man in my platoon seemed to be calling out to them, or else to be shouting to his neighbour to tell them not to fire', contributing to an atmosphere of confusion, the wounding of Corporal Duvall and the shambolic implementation of withdrawal procedures.[116] This example shows the fragility of BEF discipline, where a few choice words can reduce a silent platoon awaiting orders to an arguing mass of men, acting independently of the chain of command. Incidents such as this compelled the post-Dunkirk Bartholomew Committee to demand greater discipline to reduce vulnerability to 'every conceivable ruse [which] has been employed'; greater discipline would also reduce friendly fire.[117]

In spring 1940, BEF brigades were reorganized, inter-mixing battalions. Designed to strengthen battlefield discipline in Territorial battalions, the effect was to undermine combat capability in regular battalions. Witnesses observed it, HQs were aware of it and officers were scathing when recording it in their memoirs, and yet it often went unreported. The official history's only comment on BEF reorganization was to note: 'As a measure of unification some Regular battalions were transferred to Territorial brigades and vice versa'.[118] Brian Bond has argued stiffening TA brigades was a wise decision although some regular officers resented being associated with Territorials they perceived as inferior.[119] When 2nd Buffs Regiment marched into Belgium with Territorial 44th Division, Intelligence Officer Edlmann personally 'regretted not going off with 1st Corps [regulars] with whom we'd been for so long'.[120] On 23 May, Lieutenant Colonel J. Birch, 2nd Bedfordshire & Hertfordshire Regiment feared his battalion's good march discipline could be undermined by the mere proximity of the exhausted Territorial 1/6th East Surrey Regiment.[121] Birch felt the heavier casualties sustained by 1/6th East Surrey Regiment, when confronting German infiltration on 25 May, justified his viewpoint. Unexpectedly transferred from 132nd Brigade, 44th Division to 10th Brigade, 4th Division, 1/6th East Surrey Regiment found itself advancing to the Dyle after just six days with its new formation, and having been deployed in France for less than a month. It is little wonder that the Territorials were out of their depth and the regulars felt they had been burdened with a liability.

Some officers felt the differences between regular and TA battalions were sufficiently stark for the Germans to notice. Second Lieutenant Ogden, 2nd East Yorkshire Regiment observed during the campaign: 'The brilliant German intelligence services sought out the [4th] Royal Berkshire's as the only Territorial Army battalion in 3rd Division to be softened up for the breakthrough. Hence they were under terrific pressure throughout'.[122] This perception is not entirely accurate; for example, on 29 May, 4th Royal Berkshire Regiment positions were undermined by the enemy-enforced withdrawal of neighbouring 9th Brigade. However, having begun the campaign with 774 all-ranks, only 47 able-bodies were evacuated on 1 June and only 152 rank-and-file could be mustered on 6 June. In comparison with the 424 all-ranks mustered by 1st Suffolk Regiment on 5 June, 4th Royal Berkshire Regiment losses were clearly exceptional. They symbolize its inferior training and discipline and explain its removal from reforming 8th Brigade on 10 June 1940. Having been transferred 'almost overnight' to the regular 3rd Division, 4th Royal Berkshire Regiment were clearly the divisional weak link and casualty figures suggest this was known and exploited by the Germans.[123]

However, regular commanders were not averse to criticizing anyone, even regulars, who failed in battle. On 28 May, personnel from 2nd Duke of Cornwall's Light Infantry were observed fleeing a burning barn in the St Eloi area. Lieutenant Colonel Birch, 2nd Bedfordshire & Hertfordshire Regiment noted: 'I don't believe the Bosche were close and it was another case of tired men giving way under the effects of a sudden "Blitz". If the officers and NCOs had done their job and "got hold" of the men that panic would not have occurred'.[124] Birch's comments are filled with contempt for regulars who fled bombardment when his men held in similar circumstances the previous day. Clear examples of ill-discipline did not always feature in courts-martial records.

Ill-equipped for combat, many rear-echelon units were involved in significant ill-discipline, all of which went unrecorded or unpunished; however, it did engender a multitude of responses from front-line troops, ranging from sympathy to physical violence. Retreating from the Dyle on 15 May, 1st Survey Regiment RA lost unit cohesion and became scattered traversing through the Forest of Soignes. Soon after, approximately 30 1st Survey Regiment personnel staggered into the positions of 2nd East Yorkshire Regiment, 'in a state of considerable shock and alarm. It appeared they had already lost half their men [of one battery] by sniping and mortaring from irregulars behind the lines'.[125] The regular battalion did little more than humour the vivid imaginations of these panic-stricken men before sending them on their way. In contrast, on 31 May, 1st Suffolk Regiment sent their second-in-command to rally fleeing Royal Engineers and, through encouragement, return them to defensive positions on the L'Yser Canal which they had abandoned under intense mortar-fire. The most hostile response to rear-echelon ill-discipline came when it endangered the lives of others. When unidentified corps troops led by their panicking officer 'lost all semblance of control' on a UK-bound, under-fire troopship, regular personnel from the Royal Tank Regiment and an army chaplain maintained order with pistol butts and lead pipes until the panic subsided.[126]

As the BEF was forced into a decreasing geographical pocket around Dunkirk, the increased risk to life, a lack of supplies and the confused intermingling of BEF personnel with French soldiers and civilians led to an increasingly widespread deterioration in BEF discipline. Examining events in the vicinity of Dunkirk, Brian Bond has argued, 'though there were honourable exceptions', the majority of the BEF was reduced to 'a myriad of small "*ad hoc*" groups, all too often without their officers ... sustained by a vision of evacuation to Blighty'.[127] Highlighting that most personal accounts of Dunkirk stress exhaustion, a lack of sleep, uncertainty and moments of overwhelming terror, Bond portrays a scene of impenetrable chaos. However, within this chaos, disciplinary standards varied and this had a direct result upon embarkation processes. Having arrived on the Dunkirk beaches on 28 May, 58th Medium Regiment RA were not fully evacuated until four days later on 31 May; with each passing day their number became fewer, their appearance more shambolic and their discipline more fragile, all of which had a detrimental effect on their place of precedence in the evacuation process.[128] 52nd Heavy Regiment RA also faced delays after their arrival at Bray-Les-Dunes at 0700hrs 28 May; their absence of kit, dishevelled appearance and obvious tiredness meant they were not fully evacuated until 1000hrs 30 May.[129] In contrast, those groups which retained discipline and obvious fighting spirit were fast-tracked to embarkation, for example, on 30 May Second Lieutenant Hadley's group of 4th Royal Sussex Regiment personnel 'marched the last 200 yards in fine style, in step, to the evident satisfaction of a Brigadier whose eyes lit upon us'; Hadley's group had reached the water's edge within four hours and boarded a boat within six hours of arriving at Dunkirk. Hadley believed his swift embarkation bypassed, rather than delayed, those 'who were too exhausted to care whether it was their turn or not, [and] lay huddled together in a disorderly and exhausted multitude'.[130] Also on 30 May, concerned at being associated with the preceding rabble, Captain T. Marks, 1/8th Middlesex Regiment informed the observing Brigadier, 'This is the Middlesex Regiment', before marching his Company, in formation, onto the beach, whistling the regimental march; Marks' group was evacuated the same day.[131]

Another method of identifying those most suitable for prompt evacuation was by examining their ability to maintain personal grooming in such difficult conditions. In 1937, infantry training manuals insisted disciplined soldiers were soldiers who kept 'themselves, their clothes and their weapons in good order'.[132] With no food and minimal sleep, many 48th Divisional Signals personnel dispensed with shaving, fatalistically assumed the worst and required several attempts before being successfully evacuated. On 31 May, 4th Royal Berkshire Regimental Adjutant Captain F. Waldron recommenced shaving after being condemned for his appearance by his superior, Brigadier C. Woolner; this symbolized 4th Royal Berkshire Regiment's crumbling discipline and hints at why the 47 battalion survivors were evacuated in dribs and drabs during the following 48 hours. In contrast, arriving at La Panne on 2 June, Second Lieutenant Ogden felt superior BEF training and discipline was symbolized by his 2nd East Yorkshire Regiment subordinates being shaved, fed and cheerful, and also explained their prompt evacuation. Despite cumulative hunger, fatigue and threat of injury, BEF personnel with high discipline levels were able to recover quickly and return to routine; for example, Second Lieutenant Hadley felt 'a new man' after shaving on the journey home.[133]

It is difficult to be critical of BEF discipline at Dunkirk because the conditions on the beach were not conducive to unit cohesion and made the maintenance of good order virtually impossible. A 2nd Middlesex Regiment Platoon Sergeant Major concluded, in the last 200 yards of beach, unit cohesion at even the most basic level was 'impossible for as soon as I found one, so the shells and confusion broke us up again'.[134] Officers evacuating their subordinates via the Dunkirk Mole found primary group integrity equally difficult to maintain, for example, Second Lieutenant Finch (RASC) recalled: 'There was no chance of keeping your unit together; men were seated twenty deep across and you just filed into your place as the others moved forward'.[135] The magnitude of the chaos is best demonstrated by the experiences of 1st Suffolk Regiment, statistically the most disciplined infantry battalion in the BEF. Having arrived at La Panne with few officers and a multitude of evacuation options, ranging from little ships to the Mole, at 0400hrs 1 June, the final order issued by battalion HQ in France was 'every man for himself'.[136] David French has argued the effectiveness of primary group loyalty in persuading men to remain disciplined depended on the human stability of each primary group and on the fact that leaders and men knew each other intimately.[137] However, the disintegration of the primary group on the Dunkirk beaches indicates how important they were to the maintenance of discipline during BEF combat operations. Where unmanned whalers were used to transfer troops from the beaches to larger ships, Second Lieutenant Hadley, 4th Royal Sussex Regiment, observed 'others who had reached the water's edge later than we had, rushing into the water and seizing the boats which should rightly have carried us'.[138] Sergeant Leonard Howard, 210th Field Company RE, was another witness to the breakdown of discipline at the water's edge. Howard recalled: 'I saw British men shoot British troops'; on one occasion an officer shot dead a panic-stricken man to prevent a boat capsizing, resulting in no contemporary 'reaction at all. There was such chaos on the beach that didn't seem to be out of keeping'.[139] Overall, these were isolated instances, as demonstrated by the successful evacuation of 338,226 Allied personnel including 198,315 British; a remarkable feat which could not have been achieved without courage, skill and a degree of discipline.[140]

Events after Dunkirk until the end of the France campaign are frequently under-reported, yet the widespread collapse of discipline and morale during the largely unopposed evacuation of the remaining 150,000 BEF personnel is more worthy of criticism than the extreme events of Dunkirk. Mark Connelly and Walter Miller have demonstrated the BEF fought with good discipline and high morale up to Dunkirk; isolated units only surrendered when further resistance appeared futile. Connelly and Miller have argued: 'Factors that undermined morale – lack of communication and clarity of orders, hunger and tiredness – all applied and yet did not in themselves fatally undermine the will to resist'.[141] However, the will to resist was catastrophically undermined by these same factors amongst BEF personnel after Dunkirk. Although the Royal Navy successfully evacuated a further 144,171 BEF personnel from south of the Somme, the official campaign history acknowledges rapid evacuations caused confusion and lack of control in the matter of stores and equipment; considerable quantities of precious guns and vehicles which could have been brought away were destroyed or abandoned. The sanitized official history suggests 'it is difficult to apportion blame, for in those days no one knew what was happening or where the enemy would appear from'.[142] In contrast, the November 1940 report on the same evacuations was not so diplomatic; its scathing conclusions included: headquarters were too easily panicked by 'unauthenticated reports and rumours', officers of all ranks were not prepared to accept any risk to personnel in order to preserve war materials, and perhaps most damning, troops widely developed 'the fatal habit of looking over their shoulders and of thinking in terms of a good get-away'. Although the report questioned the willingness to fight of all ranks and all units, it recognized the prioritized embarkation of fighting troops fatally undermined the determination of non-combat units to remain and resist. Senior officers believed any German advance would be 'hotly pressed' and withdrew accordingly. In effect the majority of the BEF still in France retreated faster than the enemy could advance, thereby preventing the mass surrenders befitting its disorganized state.[143]

Despite sufficient time, facilities and vehicle transports, at Le Havre, fear of a German attack that never came led to total disregard for the considerable accumulation of stores and vehicles. 17th Field Regiment RA alone needlessly sacrificed 80 vehicles and 16 25pdr guns during the panic-fuelled evacuation. The actions of Assistant Adjutant M. Cummings, 75th Field Regiment RA, illustrate what could be achieved at Le Havre when individuals retained their fighting spirit. Having rendered his guns useless as ordered and safely embarked his men, Cummings and a French liaison officer remained to almost single-handedly collect, load and repatriate via French ships 13 25pdr guns, 13 vehicles and a small arsenal of infantry support weapons. At St Malo, without dockside cranes or purpose-built transportation, initiative and determination amongst a significant minority of personnel enabled the recovery of 100 vehicles, 400 motorcycles and 250 tonnes of stores. The Channel ports evacuation could have been significantly more successful had the discipline applied at St Malo been replicated elsewhere.[144]

With the official history of morale 1939–45 defining morale as the 'attitude of the soldier towards his employment', it is clear fighting spirit plummeted post-Dunkirk.[145] A possible explanation provided by Brigadier A. McPherson was that 'on no account should troops be allowed to feel that the particular campaign in which they are engaged is a side-show of small significance'.[146] Post-Dunkirk, the fear of being left behind, particularly amongst some of the more obscure rear-echelon units, explains the enthusiasm for rapid withdrawals. On 17 June 1940, the 1st Armoured Division Signals rearguard of two NCOs and 20 rank-and-file were ordered by Brest Garrison HQ to 'proceed soonest to dockside on foot'; to avoid attracting German attention and prevent further delays to embarkation, orders included '*Nothing to be destroyed by fire or gunfire*'. Passing drunken and fatigued British soldiers lying on the pavement, the final half-mile to the docks was carried out at 'Quick march', then 'Double march', before becoming a run.[147] On 18 June, No. 1 Line of Communication Signals personnel were evacuated from Brest, leaving Signaller R. Cowan annoyed that his unit's carefully conserved equipment was considered expendable and that no room was made available despite being ready for embarkation for over 36 hours.[148] Despite there being 150,000 British personnel south of the Somme, in 18 tense days of June 1940, only 11 BEF courts-martial were convened and these were largely for incidents relating to the previous month. With a collapsing front and a desire to return home, senior officers did not have the enthusiasm or inclination to follow up reports of criminal and military misdemeanours. In late May, 12th Division Provost Company was subordinated to Deputy Assistant Provost Marshal Nantes sub-area, after becoming separated from its divisional headquarters. Despite a virtually complete complement of men and equipment, this unit was retained for guard duties until embarkation, at the expense of more traditional law and order duties.[149] The absence of significant courts-martial statistics and reports by investigating provost companies makes any analysis of offences below the Somme after Dunkirk too superficial for comparison with the Phoney War BEF.

This book has no desire to vilify the decisions of individuals, made under extraordinary pressures in the heat of battle, nor does it seek to portray the BEF as a rampaging army, capable of great brutality against friend or foe alike. The BEF was a professional military force, made up largely of volunteers, and was capable of consistently high discipline in extreme conditions. However, casual acceptance of courts-martial statistics as the sole, accurate indicator of disciplinary levels, fails to appreciate the complexity of the disciplinary system. Courts-martial statistics do show discipline was proportionately worst in Scottish and, surprisingly, Guards battalions. Regulars and Territorials were equally capable of exemplary disciplinary records, although the longer deployment of regulars often left them disadvantaged. The charge sheets of the worst disciplined battalions were not dominated by trivial infringements, but included significant levels of serious crimes as well. A lack of adequate supervision, inferior officers and large establishments meant multi-unit corps and regiments topped the tables for most disciplinary offences. Despite difficulty to police against and prosecute, as well as the propensity of individuals and units to seek self-sufficient solutions, theft and drunkenness were officially amongst the most frequently recorded offences and, in reality, even more prevalent than statistics show. Within the BEF, experienced veterans were just as vulnerable as raw recruits to the temptations of Phoney War France, notably cheap alcohol. Ill-discipline fluctuated during the Phoney War, but officially tailed off in May and June 1940, as commanders became too distracted by the deteriorating military situation to properly investigate and record criminal incidents. Examination of bridge demolitions, treatment of enemy combatants and incidents of friendly fire all highlight higher levels of ill-discipline than officially recorded. At Dunkirk, the break-up of units frequently led to the breakdown of discipline, even in previously exemplary units. Post-Dunkirk, discipline and morale plummeted in the large remnant BEF as fear of being left behind took precedence over a determination to perform at the highest levels. Beneficial accounting methods, the widespread failure to actually record incidents of ill-discipline and the tremendous subtlety of the application of the disciplinary system all encouraged an under-representation of the true level of disciplinary problems in the BEF. As awareness of the true level of ill-discipline within this volunteer professional force increased, it helped shift the Army towards a scientific approach to discipline and morale. This was especially important as the Army transformed into a mass conscript force capable of even more dramatic and dangerous fluctuations in discipline.

7
Headquarters and Staff

Although awareness of the need for effective, professional and qualified staff officers and commanders increased during the inter-war period, staff work remained an undervalued, under-practised and under-managed function of the British Army. To disseminate knowledge of staff functions and headquarter responsibilities, the Army used the mixed approach of vague training manuals, overly strategic Staff College courses and the practical experience of UK training and imperial postings. This lack of uniform training led to supposedly equal headquarters varying in organization, working environment and productivity as well as the quality and quantity of personnel. Phoney War staff training was equally flawed as the British Expeditionary Force proved resistant to external assistance, whilst internal measures were met with disinterest among participants and providers. Inadequate Staff College capacity allowed only 50 officers per annum to be trained for inter-war imperial duties; the legacy of this policy was insufficient Camberley graduates for even a full strength volunteer army. The belated introduction of a shortened Staff College course in January 1940 allowed 180 officers to graduate every 17 weeks and produced 4000 graduates before the end of the war; too late for the immediate and urgent needs of the BEF. Such were the shortages in the France campaign, over half of all infantry brigadiers were appointed from alternative sources; inevitably this involved the old, the unqualified, and for five officers, a recall from retirement. Weaknesses in the staff system occurred throughout the chain of command, compounding the effect flawed communications, training and discipline were already having on the BEF's tempo of operations and capability. In combat, the cumbersome BEF system quickly buckled, forcing the responsibility for command function and personal survival to be passed down to subordinates, regardless of preparedness or ability. The shock of these events affected British Army thinking for years to come as it hastily sought to increase flexibility through reorganization, rather than a re-evaluation of its command principles.[1]

Staff College historian F.W. Young has argued by being responsible for offering solutions to decision-makers, solving military and administrative problems in an orderly manner and, ultimately, ensuring the welfare of the rank-and-file, the staff officer is of critical importance in modern warfare.[2] Despite the turbulent nature of the France campaign, contemporaries considered the efforts of the BEF staff worthy of praise. With the notable exception of the intelligence branch, Commander-in-Chief Gort highlighted the ability of all GHQ branches of staff 'to bear a specially heavy and prolonged strain of responsibility'.[3] BEF Chief of the General Staff Lieutenant General Pownall argued his subordinate BEF staff were more resilient under pressure, more practical and more flexible than their French counterparts, particularly when faced with unexpected events. Pownall concluded only by the fine leadership of headquarters personnel, 'good staff work' and, above all, magnificent fighting spirit, was the BEF saved.[4] Corroborating Gort and Pownall's view, the official campaign history noted when 'normal procedure was interrupted by events and reliance on individuals took the place of orthodox administration', senior commanders and their staff 'were not confounded'.[5] Since the military consultant for the official history was Lieutenant General Pownall, it is unsurprising its conclusions were sympathetic towards BEF staff performance.

Given the alleged effectiveness of BEF staff during the campaign, it could be expected that the British Army would retain its long-standing organizational framework within which staff officers directed operations. In contrast, a sudden rejection of the pre-war status quo compelled the Army to begin fundamental reform to match German flexibility and mobility. However, a failure to correctly analyse pre-war and BEF staff flaws undermined army capability for several years; only through bitter experience was an acceptable balance between mobility and controllable firepower achieved.

Andy Simpson has demonstrated how the formal role of corps headquarters evolved through the Great War, from post-box for GHQ orders, to the engine room of planning and directing operations, before assuming a coordination and oversight function for newly empowered divisions. Though corps headquarters rarely existed during the inter-war period, their theoretical functions of planning and coordination were considered equally critical on the resumption of large-scale operations in 1939.[6] However, post-Dunkirk, operational command by such a high formation was comprehensively rejected by the July 1940 Bartholomew Committee, which stated: 'It has been suggested by some that the Corps should be regarded as the basic fighting formation. The Committee does not take this view'. Rejecting divisions as equally cumbersome and battalions as too militarily insignificant, the Committee concluded: 'The brigade therefore seems to be the best to organize as the lowest self-contained fighting formation, in the form of a brigade group, within the division'.[7] In his study of the North African campaign, David French has argued the post-Dunkirk reorganization prevented higher formations exploiting battlefield opportunities, caused the dispersal of firepower, particularly in multi-armed detachments known as Jock Columns, and ultimately contributed to heavy casualties as individual brigades became isolated and overwhelmed by entire German divisions. The inferior tempo of the British Army, which had first become evident during the France campaign, continued to undermine operations; the flaws in pre-war staff training inhibited a rapid tempo of operations and remained unaddressed.[8] During the Normandy campaign, Timothy Harrison Place has illustrated how a high operational tempo within the British Army was achieved by better communications, more experienced staff officers, superiority of equipment and the ability to transfer operational command to the most suitable formation headquarters (depending on the speed of advance).[9] In his analysis of why the British Army was able to carry out operations in 1918 more successfully, efficiently and rapidly, Andy Simpson came to almost identical conclusions; this highlights the irreplaceable importance of wartime experience to efficient staff operations.[10]

Flaws in the British Army command and control systems were, however, allowed to develop and fester during the inter-war period. The vagueness of training manuals, the façade of excellence provided by the Staff College and the absence of sufficient opportunities to gain realistic experience lulled officers into complacency about their individual and collective resilience under pressure. Weaknesses amongst headquarters personnel were partially exposed by Phoney War before being brutally exploited by German mobile warfare. Amidst the confusion of rapid retreat system flaws became obscured, forcing the Army into years of trial and error before credible solutions could be found.

The 1935 *Field Service Regulations*, written by Major General Archibald Wavell, provided the pre-war foundation upon which staff training was based and BEF decision-making was ultimately guided. All officers were provided with a general operations edition promoting 'information regarding each arm [and their interaction on the battlefield] that officers of other arms should possess'; prospective senior officers were encouraged to study a supplementary version which concentrated on the tactical employment of larger formations.[11] When writing *FSR 1935*, Wavell was forced by the inter-war programme of army modernization to balance the development of a contemporary training guide with the need to ensure long-term relevance. Imminently redundant advice, for example, 'marches should be comparatively short until men and animals are hardened' was tempered with the acknowledgement that the growing prevalence of mechanization meant mechanical movement required 'increasing attention'. Equally, whilst *FSR 1935* was designed to prepare the Army for war with a first-class enemy, it could not ignore current army operations, particularly on the semi-active front of north-west India. Consequently it contained guidance on covering forces when concentrating on hostile frontiers and advice for column commanders on how to influence their subordinates effectively when in hostile territory.[12] Although Wavell was saddened that several of his more unorthodox ideas were eliminated from the final draft by the Army Council, Victoria Schofield has highlighted how Wavell supported the long-standing orthodox premise that detailed specifics be avoided in *FSR*; in January 1935, Wavell corresponded with his friend Basil Liddell Hart: 'There is nothing fixed in war, except a few elementary rules of common sense'.[13] Similarly, John Connell has stressed Wavell's preponderance towards common sense rather than prescriptive battle instructions by highlighting comments previously made to prospective Staff College attendees in 1932: 'For heaven's sake don't treat those [*FSR*] as holy writ...They are merely a set of common sense maxims'.[14] Andy Simpson has identified *FSR* as 'a set of principles for application by trained and experienced officers, which specifically avoided going into too much detail, since those applying them should, through experience and training, know what detailed actions to perform within their framework'.[15] Whilst this flexibility allowed *FSR 1909* to endure the Great War's tactical revolution, it also weakened the ability to adopt best practice, a weakness *FSR 1935* perpetuated.

A few of the more obvious divisions in responsibility were identified in *FSR 1935*; for example, brigades, divisions and corps were classified as local formations responsible for checking hostile advances, organizing local counter-attacks, protecting threatened flanks and rotating subordinate units to prevent exhaustion. In contrast, General Headquarters were responsible for organizing large-scale offensives and using the general reserve to extend a flank or cover a withdrawal. However, as a combat aid, *FSR 1935* was almost useless due to its use of cryptic advice; for example, unspecified 'special measures' should be used to defend rear areas from marauding tanks. It also avoided passing judgment on difficult issues by using the policy of commander's discretion as a shield. Acknowledging some sectors of the front would have terrain disadvantageous to defence, *FSR* simply stated it was for the commander 'to decide' whether to make the best of it, or advance to a better position. This did not identify which commander should decide, which headquarters should be consulted or whether there was a right of appeal. Worst of all, the deliberate vagueness of *FSR* 1935 meant it was riddled with contradictions which allowed a commander and his staff to justify virtually any decision. *FSR 1935* paradoxically demanded 'a Commander must be prepared to revise his ideas', but must not be 'too easily diverted from his original purpose by finding a situation not exactly in accordance with his anticipations'. It undermined the view that 'the Commander can influence the battle only by his original dispositions and directions', by stressing 'the detailed tactical plan will only be formed after actual contact'. Finally, warnings against undue interference in subordinate activities conflicted with demands that all commanders maintain constant vigilance and 'be prepared to intervene personally in the conduct of battle where necessary'.[16] Although officers were supposed to only supplement the foundation offered by *FSR*, in reality commanders and their staff were totally reliant on alternative sources to guide their administrative and command duties. In mitigation, the inconsistencies of *FSR 1935* merely replicate the lack of consistent teaching within the Army as a whole; for example, Wavell attended Staff College (1909–10) during the term of strategically minded Commandant Henry Wilson and his antithesis, the practically minded Commandant William Robertson. These two officers symbolize the indecision within the British Army as to whether Staff College should be a stepping stone to high command or a training establishment for staff officers; this indecision continued to overshadow the Army when Wavell rewrote *FSR*[17].

The duties of a regimental staff officer involved the collection, collation and dissemination of information on both friendly and enemy forces, the submission of plans for operations and the issuing of orders translating their commanders' wishes into action. However, these duties mainly related to training exercises and periods of war; as Lieutenant A. Walch, 2nd Loyal Regiment noted, a regimental officer 'could not study one's profession seriously on Salisbury Plain all the time'.[18] In peacetime, staff work focused on more routine matters concerning the provision, pay and records of subordinates.[19] Already hampered by under-strength units, the brief distraction in an officer's day caused by routine paperwork did not prepare individuals for the critically important and frantic nature of staff work in modern war. Inter-war Deputy Company Commander A. Walch's argued 'genuine company work lasted a few minutes' in 2nd Loyal Regiment, whilst Captain E. Brush, 2nd Battalion, Rifle Brigade despaired the monotonous nature of his staff duties as 'absolutely soul-destroying' regardless of their length.[20] Adjutant T. Durrant, 54th Field Brigade RA, recalled: 'I could complete the adjutant's office duties in an hour or so', although the additional duties of a Territorial officer in a TA unit 'occupied a lot of time in the evenings and weekends'.[21] In his explanation that Major Jewel, 8th Worcestershire Regiment, was the sole officer directly responsible for the half-company based at Upton-upon-Severn Drill Hall, Private S. Beard also hints at the difference between isolated Territorial Army officers relentlessly involved in additional staff work, and the equivalent garrison-based regular officers who often benefited from a rota system.[22]

In comparison, individuals allocated staff roles with minimal face-to-face troop contact were vastly overworked compared to their combat-orientated colleagues. David French has briefly highlighted the inappropriateness of pre-war 1st Division having only three permanent staff officers attached to its Aldershot headquarters and, equally, Territorial divisions being allocated only two.[23] In reality, overworked staff personnel were commonplace throughout the chain of command and not just at divisional level. With the assistance of just a driver and a storeman, Company Quartermaster Sergeant T. Thomas, 1st Armoured Divisional Signals, was responsible for all MT vehicles and stores, maintenance of all connected ledgers and liaison with the Ordnance workshops at Tidworth. In comparison to the orthodox hours of his colleagues, Thomas gloomily recorded 'it was an onerous job and on most days I worked well into the evenings in order to reorganise the stores and records'. To emphasize the excessive pressures of peacetime staff positions, upon deployment to France in May 1940, the role was filled by a Royal Army Ordnance Corps Captain supported by a Warrant Officer II and several technicians.[24] In 1939, as pre-war Deputy Assistant Adjutant and Quartermaster for Chatham, Major E. Thornhill accepted 'duty from 8am to 8pm and every third night' as the unfortunate consequence of being 'the only regular officer in the Headquarters'; an unsustainable work schedule, only alleviated by the recruitment of several retired officers after mobilization.[25] Even in the generously staffed War Office, the paperwork overload produced by the bureaucratic peacetime system could only be sustained by excessive work schedules. In spring 1939, the Training by Arms Section Office of the Directorate for Military Training was a hive of activity with 12 officers and 13 phones; yet Staff Officer J. Faviell continued to 'burn the midnight oil because really important issues could not be worked out in the din' of the office.[26] Ironically, in mid-1938, it was 'the pressure of day-to-day work in the War Office' which meant 'no branch had time to produce anything in the form of a workable plan' for the possible deployment of British troops to France.[27] It should be noted, at all levels of the British Army, this intensive staff activity did not equate to guaranteed productivity or preparedness for modern war, even amongst the individuals involved.

Whilst pre-war naval officers sought to serve on and subsequently command bigger and bigger ships, there was no desire amongst most pre-war army officers to serve in stationary and largely under-used formation headquarters.[28] With both Sandhurst and Staff College encouraging active lifestyles and energetic outside recreations, few officers aspired to be office-based administrators working antisocial hours. In 1936, Major G. Richards was 'not interested' in administrative duties and consequently used every means at his disposal to avoid a posting as an Area Command A Branch GSO3; rather than face disciplinary procedures, Richards was rewarded for his persistent intransigence with the outdoor-orientated 'plum job' of Brigade Major for the Army's only UK-based Tank Brigade.[29] In order for subordinates to overcome fear of boredom and isolation from the regimental family, in 1938–39, Adjutant A. Walch's 1st Loyal Regiment, was frequently forced to threaten disciplinary action to ensure personnel of all ranks took up headquarter postings which they did not like.[30] Many officers did not feel like soldiers unless they were out in the field; for example, learning of his post-Dunkirk appointment as GSO2 (Staff Duties and Training) at Eastern Command, Major K. Chavasse summarized the forthcoming 'long hours of office work with occasional trips out' as the 'bottle washing' position of his new headquarters.[31] Even experienced staff officers, such as Brigadier J. Whitehead, (who uniquely served as Assistant Adjutant General in both 1918 and 1939–40), admitted the unpopularity of unglamorous staff work. Whilst chiefly tasked with disciplinary and personal issues, Whitehead summarized the perpetual role of A Branch as dealing with 'all and sundry that other people did not fancy'.[32] Although wars are not won by the side with the most paperwork, it is equally important to recognize victory is not exclusively achieved by personnel with exciting or unpredictable roles. In the pre-war British Army too many officers sought to avoid large headquarter roles rather than gain experience which would have proved invaluable in France.

David French has suggested the overwhelming majority of officers were unfamiliar with formation headquarter duties because during pre-war manoeuvres, staffs had to be improvised around an inadequate nucleus.[33] More in-depth study has revealed regimental officers temporarily assigned staff duties or positions in exercises were frequently utterly disconnected from the less fashionable staff activities that made operations viable. The 1934 *Training Regulations with special reference to Manoeuvres* betrayed the cost-pressures of the inter-war period by recommending in its sample one-sided Training Exercise Without Troops (TEWTs) for both brigade and division formations the minimum number of staff positions needed for tactical understanding. In the brigade TEWT this meant the absence of a Quartermaster, Medical Officer, Transport Officer and any representative of the Royal Army Service Corps or Royal Army Ordnance Corps from both brigade directing staff and battalion headquarter syndicates. In the divisional TEWTs there were similar absences and, with the unavoidable exception of signals personnel, the remaining support arms of divisional artillery, Royal Engineers and cavalry were only included because of their importance to offensive operations.[34]

Whilst on individual occasions this was of no great importance, perpetually repeated it undermined understanding of the realities of war and allowed the development of an inherent weakness in the thought processes of British officers. No experience of transport issues during large-scale manoeuvres led to Major J. Haydon's Staff College syndicate being criticized for formulating a divisional exercise plan using transport to simultaneously move two entire brigades. The syndicate's assumption that 'the scheme still holds good, but the training may become rather slower' if sufficient MT was unavailable contrasted considerably with the convener's view that 'it is most doubtful whether you would get [sufficient] MT' and consequently 'this scheme would need a lot of aberration'. The Directing Staff's overall conclusion that 'this is quite a suitable scheme' demonstrates the low priority given to non-combat staff issues compared to the accurate and neat presentation of operation orders.[35] Similarly, no comprehension of medical matters left second-year student Captain C. Barclay exposed to criticism after his first attempt at a corps medical evacuation scheme evacuated all dead personnel as well as wounded. Belated attempts to correct this resulted in only a 'slight reprimand' from Staff College Directing Staff.[36] On 3 September 1939, Second Lieutenant J. Finch, the night-time duty officer at Aldershot Headquarters, was totally dependent on his experienced Staff Sergeant for issuing any orders; Finch was 'completely untrained' in how an out-of-hours headquarters operated and his sole qualification, a BA degree in classics, did not help.[37] Similarly, GHQ staff officer P. Gribble expected his pre-war training to have prepared him for his role as Air Intelligence Liaison Officer at British Air Forces in France (BAFF) Headquarters. However, there were 'quite a lot of people away on leave. The contrast between the real thing and the opening phase of an exercise is very forcible'. The unexpected absence of key individuals resulted in 'no news of our own troops or aircraft. No messages, no intelligence summaries, no telephones'.[38] Post-Dunkirk, BEF CGS Pownall accused the stereotypical French staff officer of being only interested in projects, etudes and hypotheses before concluding: 'It is in the *practical* staff duties and organization that the French fail'; it is arguable pre-war staff training left British officers vulnerable to the same accusation.[39]

The experiences of the British Army during inter-war overseas service also provided minimal opportunity for officers to master staff duties relevant to combat in Europe. Many full strength, relatively well-equipped, regular battalions were sent overseas only to be broken up into small detachments for manning isolated garrisons. Throughout 1936, 2nd Royal Berkshire Regiment was divided between up to six geographical localities, based simultaneously in Cyprus and Egypt, and found even basic administration challenging. Ordered to guard 50 miles of vulnerable Palestinian railway throughout winter 1938/39, 1st Buffs Regiment separated into ten widely dispersed outposts, forcing platoons to act independently for long periods and leaving battalion headquarters largely redundant. This was more than an inconvenient hindrance to effective administration by battalion and company headquarters; similar to previously discussed effects on battalion training, prolonged dispersal degraded staff capability, leaving it lethargic in times of crisis. On 16 October 1936, it took 2nd Buffs regimental headquarters in Acre four hours to organize armoured car support for an ambushed platoon near Nahariya, despite operating in Palestine as part of 15th Brigade and despite the relatively small distance of six miles.[40]

The contrasting tactic of using brigade strength mobile columns to traverse hostile territory in 1930s Waziristan similarly degraded staff capability in British battalions, albeit by making combat staff duties unproductively easy. The absence of hostile heavy weapons allowed column commanders to unnaturally compact their brigades, ensuring constant control with just a handful of wireless sets. With Waziristan roads considered unacceptably dangerous after 1600hrs, Wazirforce headquarters took advantage of unchallenged air supremacy to air-drop daily written orders and intelligence reports to its distant brigades; an equally unlikely tactic in a European theatre.[41] Deployments to the Middle East and Waziristan proved poor training environments for British officers in need of building their staff capability, albeit for contrasting reasons.

Despite its flaws, Waziristan was the only continuous semi-active front in the inter-war British Empire and could have proved of benefit to the future BEF. However, the minimization of British involvement in the fighting, the exposure of British officers to varied guidance and the failure to ensure the lessons of experience were transferred to BEF personnel, all led to an under-utilization of this asset. Predominance as the reserve battalion in Anglo-Indian brigades minimized opportunities for British Army officers to master staff techniques under fire; for example, despite an exemplary record in the Nowshera Brigade 1934–37, 2nd Duke of Wellington's Regiment regretted it was frequently used as force reserve and had more than its fair share of labour duties. During this period Nowshera Brigade Standing Orders recommended ensuring additional headquarters personnel 'be on duty' when confronted with long orders and instructions.[42] This fell well short of inter-war advice given to British rifle battalions which emphasized the importance of reducing 'operation orders in length' through pre-arranged standing orders and abbreviations, 'thus enabling time to be saved'.[43] Even if less efficient staff techniques were sufficient in Waziristan, it would have been advantageous for best practice to be enforced throughout the Army to ensure it was second nature by 1939–40. None of the six battalions who participated in the Waziristan Rebellion 1936–37, nor any of their late 1930s replacements, served with the BEF in France 1940. Their experiences were recorded in the annual report every Command sent to the War Office each November. Information was collated and innovations approved by the Army Council were incorporated into future training material. However, with individual training memoranda issued in May and collective training memoranda for formations the following January, it was 13 months minimum before ideas on staff issues filtered back to Home Commands, if they were accepted at all. Factor in the right of generals to issue their own training memoranda or to alter, at least in tone, War Office training material, and it becomes clear staff officers of the future BEF had excessive difficulty benefiting from the experiences of personnel in Waziristan.[44]

Once war was declared in 1939, *FSR* were amended to reduce the accounting obligations many officers laboured with in peacetime. The

concise BEF reference guide *Field Service Pocket Book 1939–1940* stated:
'Office work in the field is to be restricted to what is absolutely indispensable'; in particular 'equipment accounts will not be kept'.[45] The
failure of the Army to acknowledge the warlike conditions in peacetime theatres such as Palestine and Waziristan provided personnel
with undue emphasis on accurate record-keeping rather than tempo
of operations and combat effectiveness. The official report into the
1936 Arab Rebellion concluded the campaign's 'chief administrative'
lesson was the difficulties of conducting operations on active service
under conditions of peacetime accounting; the War Office failed to
address this issue until a state of war was officially recognized.[46] As
illustration, all pre-war 2-inch mortars were issued to infantry platoons
with a large foolscap cardboard folder designed to record the weapon's
target, ammunition usage and performance. On experiencing combat
for the first time in May 1940, Second Lieutenant Peter Hadley, 4th
Royal Sussex Regiment, doubted whether he would have complied with
this pre-war regulation, before noting 'as the fighting becomes more
intense the number of army forms grows correspondingly smaller'.[47]
Such accounting was designed to keep track of costs and help provide
information to formulate best practice guidelines. In reality it slowed
the tempo of operations, led to unrealistic expectations of battle and
contributed to those officers fortunate enough to serve overseas being
as flawed as their home-based counterparts.

The final mechanism for training personnel in the advanced duties
of staff officers and commanders was through supplementary education
provided by elite institutions. The earliest of these was the Staff College
which, founded in 1858, was expected to correct the more obvious deficiencies in British Army staff work, as witnessed in the recent Crimean
War. The institution was deliberately called the Staff College to emphasize its primary function; an increasingly vital role when, in 1860, the
War Office recommended only Staff College graduates be appointed in
future staff postings. The production of educated, professional officers who were capable of command was a beneficial by-product which
grew in importance as the Staff College diversified into its dual role.
Whilst this duality became embedded in the Staff College syllabus, the
balance between the two roles remained un-reconciled, shifted with
each new commandant and caused perpetual uncertainty; Sir George
Barrow, who taught at both Camberley and Quetta in the early 20th
Century strikingly concluded he did not understand 'the real purpose
of a Staff College'.[48] There had been, however, increasing realization of
the Staff College's potential, as witnessed by the success of the Prussian

General Staff in the 1870s. It should be acknowledged no Staff College develops in isolation, but instead is influenced by the institutions of other countries, if only by their presence. Brian Bond has argued from 1904, the growing threat from Germany gave Staff College a 'direct sense of purpose' as the supplier of officers for the newly formed British General Staff and as the centre for continental strategy formulation. Karl Demeter has shown this academic arms race was a two-way process; for example, in November 1919, Reichwehr Colonel General Hans von Seeckt began surreptitiously and unofficially re-establishing the German Staff College previously forbidden at Versailles, to ensure Germany remained intellectually competitive with its enemies, if not materially.[49]

By orchestrating the increasing professionalism of military leaders, 'both in command and staff positions', Brian Bond has argued the Staff College ensured the 1914 BEF was better organized, trained and led than its 1854 and 1899 predecessors.[50] With its benefit judged irrefutable, for both the Army and the individual officer, it was inevitable the inter-war Staff College would continue to grow in influence. The dual function remained, as demonstrated by the stated aim in the Staff College Charter to train officers for war, for 'staff employment and with further experience for command'. In the inter-war period this was achieved with a two-year course theoretically featuring one year's tuition on divisional staff and command duties and a further year's study devoted to corps and army operations as well as the political and strategic issues faced by imperial defence planners.[51]

David French has argued the Staff College was an elite training institution as only the most ambitious and best educated officers could pass the highly competitive, broad ranging, ten-day academic examination. Increasingly seen as a way of bypassing a promotion system based on seniority, in 1904 there were four candidates for each Staff College vacancy, but by 1928 the ratio was nine to one.[52] In June 1913, 185 candidates competed for only 36 places, whilst in 1929, 409 British Army officers applied for only 56 positions at Camberley and Quetta combined.[53] Over time the competitive nature of the entrance examination became exaggerated in the minds of participants; for example, in 1933 Captain E. Brush despaired at being one of 700 candidates for supposedly only 20 vacancies.[54] However, the credibility of Staff College as an elite institution is diminished by the number of resits taken by successful applicants. Captain E. Thornhill failed the 1929 and 1930 exams before eventually passing in 1931, whilst Captain J. Faviell's previous failure meant he retained an 'inferiority complex' even after entering the Staff College in 1935.[55] Captain C. Barclay had failed so many times a multitude of regulatory and financial factors meant he would have been 'debarred from any further attempts', had he not passed in 1929.[56] All these officers were eventually adjudged to have reached the required standard, but their identification as elite officers must be questioned considering their selection came at the expense of officers who passed first time. Prior to application, Captain E. Brush boosted his academic capability with a specialist correspondence course and enhanced his service record with a voluntary, month-long staff attachment; despite passing the 1933 exam, Brush was not allocated a place and never reapplied.[57] Given enough tuition and attempts, most competent officers could eventually achieve the relatively low pass-mark and, inevitably, perpetual applicants could demonstrate greater determination and longer service records than first-time applicants; this should not have made them the Army's elite.

The Staff College's elite academic status was also undermined by the alternative method of entry; the process of nomination annually reserved a proportion of places for successful applicants with exceptional service records. After the Great War, the nomination process was considered an ideal method for enabling distinguished field officers to supplement their battlefield experience with formal, theoretical training, without forcing proven combat veterans of high rank to participate in a demeaning entrance exam. Reopened after 4½ years in April 1919, the first two years of Staff College courses were exclusively for nominated officers in an effort to clear the Great War backlog; included amongst the students were 20 Brigadier Generals, three Brevet Colonels, 77 Brevet Lieutenant Colonels, five holders of the Victoria Cross and 170 holders of the Distinguished Service Order.[58] By 1921 the need for these extraordinary measures had diminished, an entrance exam was re-established and an increasing number of Staff College places were opened up to competition. Inevitably the quality of nominated candidates declined with each passing year, but the Army remained convinced nominated officers were comparable with, and possibly superior to, those officers who gained competitive vacancies through their test scores; as a result, nominated personnel remained a significant minority of each year's intake. In 1927, only 31 out of 60 places at Camberley were competitive vacancies open to the most academically gifted; of the remaining 29 places, 19 were allocated to nominated British Army officers, whilst the remainder went to personnel from overseas dominions and other services. Inter-war nominations were used to correct 'undue preponderance' towards specific arms in any year group; for example, if Royal Artillery officers dominated the competitive vacancies, nominations would deliberately favour less academically gifted personnel from other arms. This can be seen as a prudent measure for ensuring diversity of background and viewpoint within each year group, but also as a politically correct measure for preventing discord between the Army's separate arms. The contradiction at the centre of this process was that selection through academic competition was viewed with perpetual suspicion, whereas the nomination process and, more specifically, the judgment of senior officers who selected nominees was sufficiently trusted that academically inferior, preselected officers who scraped a pass-mark were still considered worthy of a Staff College education. In 1927, Staff College Commandant Major General Gwynn informed colleagues undeserving officers could gain entry via the entrance exam, but were unable to deceive the discerning eye of experienced area commanders. Paradoxically, not only did Commandant Gwynn welcome nominated officers who had scraped through the entrance exam, but he also naively believed officers worthy of Staff College could fail to meet the low academic threshold because of their dedication to their inter-war regimental duties. Similarly, in 1927, the Director of Staff Duties (DSD) wrote to the CIGS to argue that the nomination process should be held in isolation from the exam result, otherwise some nominated officers 'may be excluded in favour of less able men who passed the competitive nomination'.[59] The academic credentials of Staff College were further diminished when, in 1928, nominated personnel were excused from the annual requirement of achieving the entrance exam pass-mark. The DSD vehemently opposed this policy, stating a previously qualified officer might 'do no more work for 2 or 3 years' in the hope his day-to-day activities might earn him a nomination and, also, that an officer poorly versed in army regulations would fail to fully benefit from Staff College. The Army Council dismissed these objections and voted through the rule change, thereby allowing officers to reach the Army's elite educational establishment without having academically proven themselves for several years.[60] The initially sound use of nominations to utilize Great War talent reduced in value over time, until it reached the point of undermining the credibility of the Staff College graduate.

The acceptance of persistent regular army failures was in stark contrast to the unequivocal exclusion, until 1937, of Territorial Army candidates from higher education military establishments such as the Staff College. In September 1939, British Army strength included 18,900 Territorial officers supported by 7750 Territorial Reserve officers; regardless of age, rank or experience, this substantial part of the inter-war officer corps had been denied access to all but the few Staff College places available between 1937 and 1939.[61] The absence of any positive discrimination to theoretically hasten Territorial development meant the majority of places continued to go to the regulars from regiments with historic links to Staff College, or those with overseas records; this only changed post-mobilization, for example, on 15 September 1939, No. 1 War Course (a brief, crash course in the Staff College syllabus), assembled at Camberley with 105 Territorial students, nine regulars and one Canadian Army officer.[62] David French has correctly argued exclusion from Staff College meant many Territorial officers lacked the skills to advance their careers, solve unexpected problems or deal with complex combined arms operations.[63] However, denial of the existence of Territorials equally disadvantaged regular graduates of the Staff College. In his two years at Camberley (1935–36) Major J. Haydon had no Territorial colleagues to interact with during syndicate work, nor did any of his exercises or essay assignments comprehend command of two-tier infantry formations. Most exercises were historical recreations where Territorials were not present (the 1917 defence of Palestine by Turkish forces) or fictional confrontations involving unspecific, uniform infantry formations; (brigades in Southland/Northland, divisions in Westland/ Eastland and corps in Mercia/East Anglia). When a degree of realism was required the exclusively regular pre-war 1st Division was used, thereby further avoiding the study of staff and command problems in mixed or exclusively Territorial formations.[64] Devoid of theoretical interaction with Territorials, Staff College graduates found themselves unprepared when posted to the real thing. The tactical exercises, lectures and written essays of his Camberley course left Major K. Chavasse convinced he had been comprehensively taught how to command a brigade and how to be a good staff officer. His appointment in January 1940 as Brigade Major to 150th Brigade left Chavasse struggling to relate to Territorial colleagues, shocked at the training deficiencies of all formations personnel for which he (the Brigade's Camberley graduate) rather than a syndicate, was responsible.[65]

Regardless of its flaws, the Staff College was an opportunity for intellectual self-development, free from the burden of regimental and administrative duties. In 1958, Chief of the Imperial General Staff Gerald Templer (an inter-war student) described Staff College as 'an opportunity to the individual officer' to 'learn to think – logically, hard and if possible with originality'.[66] This echoed inter-war directing staff, such as Colonel B. Montgomery (Camberley 1926–29 and Quetta 1934–37), who saw 'an opportunity for three years hard study', and also students, for example, Major G. Richards (Camberley 1934–35) who felt 'fortunate' to have access to 'first-class' instruction.[67] Paradoxically the Army retained a distaste for theoretical narrow intellectualism, preferring instead intuitive decision-making and personal leadership of subordinates; Nikolas Gardner has demonstrated this ethos was at its height in the 1914 BEF.[68] Even after Dunkirk, Commander-in-Chief Home Forces Ironside was arguing: 'The namby-pamby people that have grown up in late years are not to be trusted in an emergency. Character and guts. That is what is wanted. Not all brains'.[69] Amongst 1930s Staff College students this materialized as a complacent apathy and a failure to fully utilize the opportunities available to them. During exercises with specific roles, Captain J. Faviell always felt 'great relief [when] mine was a minor administrative task with little responsibility'; however, this was not always achievable as so many officers 'looked for some simple job'.[70] Disillusioned by compulsory involvement in the weekly drag and the strong emphasis on recreational sports at which he was not adept, Captain E. Thornhill endured his uneventful Camberley course without motivation or aspiration. Reviewing his time at Camberley (1930–31) Captain C. Barclay recalled: 'I had always been told by "old boys" that the course was extremely strenuous and that only the most robust and quick-thinking officers could hope to avoid a nervous breakdown … I don't think it was true'. In fact, the release from regimental life, the plentiful leisure time and organized recreation meant, had Barclay been given the opportunity of repeating the course, 'I would have accepted'.[71]

Although entry to Staff College was a competitive process, the alleviation of time and performance-based pressure once at Staff College contributed to the lackadaisical attitude of many students. Summarizing the time pressures he worked under, Captain J. Faviell commented students were provided with up to a week to produce written answers to written papers, which 'presented no great difficulty to me' due to the 'first-class' College library full of references.[72] A study of Major J. Haydon's written work (1935–36) shows three days were allowed for brief tactical appreciations, reduced to a single day after a year of study; weekly deadlines for more strategic exercises reduced to five days by the end of Staff College course. Performance-based pressure was virtually absent from Staff College because it was felt talented students were still learning even when failing. In March 1935, supervisor Lieutenant Colonel Hawkesworth criticized Major J. Haydon's written work for failing to identify the correct objectives and for missing the 'whole point' of the brigade based exercise; Hawkesworth concluded: 'This appreciation is on the right lines … In spite of all the red ink'.[73] The consequence of this lenient marking was a near 100 per cent pass rate. In 1931, three out of 60 anticipated officers failed to graduate; one officer resigned his commission for a lucrative business appointment, one left for an unrecorded disciplinary offence and only one officer was considered 'below standard professionally'.[74] Even more unrealistically, on 7 September 1939, Commandant B. Paget eulogized: '[You] are just as good fish in the Staff College pool as ever came out of it', after all 120 officers on the inaugural 12 month course graduated three months prematurely to meet mobilization demands.[75] In contrast, the German system ruthlessly applied pressure to ensure students were kept motivated; this pressure was maintained until capability was proven beyond doubt and habitual. In December 1937, a British Intelligence Report on the two-year German Staff College course revealed 'a number' of each 125 annual intake were dismissed after 12 months, whilst a further group were 'failed' at the end of the course. To ensure performance levels did not dip after graduation, all surviving students entered a 12-month probationary staff position after which their qualification could still be denied for unsatisfactory performance.[76]

David French has argued by taking officers largely too young to have commanded more than a company and training them to control armies, the inter-war Staff College syllabus was excessively strategic.[77] French has not fully conveyed the extent to which officers, desperately in need of training on formation staff duties, wasted their Staff College opportunity receiving guidance on dealing with governments. During his opportunity, Major J. Haydon spent five days intensively working on a Cabinet paper on the Army's role in imperial defence, only to be criticized for being vague on budgetary considerations and for suggesting the Army's global role had diminished with the expansion of air-power. Most strikingly, Haydon's supervisors felt it was unacceptable that a Major in the Irish Guards with 16 months Staff College training had written a paper which the Secretary of State for War 'would not learn much from'. This was despite a 1935/36 syllabus with week-long student assignments as diverse as the British Board of Trade or a liaison officer at Austrian GHQ in 1915.[78] Captain C. Barclay felt his year group wasted time on non-military visits to Morris Motor Works in Cowley or listening to political lectures, for example, by Lord Hankey, Secretary to the Cabinet. In 1931, Barclay anticipated it would be 12 years before such information became relevant, however his retirement ranked Brigadier meant it never did.[79] Arguably, these superficially elite officers were the most likely to reach the highest military echelons and they were unlikely to repeat such an intensive period of self-development.

However, these issues should have been secondary to preparing sufficient officers to effectively staff an expeditionary force, never mind a large conscript army.

More importantly, both tactically and strategically, Staff College teaching concentrated on what was theoretically sound, rather than what was practically necessary or even achievable in war. Nikolas Gardner has already identified a degree of detachment from the practicalities of warfare prior to the Great War; for example, a Camberley instructor attached to 4th Division was incapable of formulating a practical operational order, unable to perform routine staff duties and under time pressure 'was a hindrance rather than a help'.[80] Assuming Great War experiences would have eliminated any realism deficiency, in 1932, Director of Military Training A. McNamara informed colleagues: 'It may be safely stated that the Army is better trained (academically, at any rate) than ever before'.[81] However, by focusing on what was theoretically sound, students were deterred from risk-taking and boldness by directing staff who unintentionally encouraged cautious responses. After being comprehensively briefed on the parameters of a divisional exercise, in 1935, the cautious atmosphere allowed acting divisional commander (Captain) J. Faviell to simply state: 'I would go forward and talk to my Brigade commanders'; judged a 'very sensible' answer by directing staff.[82] Within the same year group, Major J. Haydon was assigned the simulated defence of Palestine in 1917; his generalized objective of preventing the annihilation of his force led to criticism about its vagueness, but Lieutenant Colonel Christison was forced to admit 'your object is quite sound'.[83] Asked to formulate proposals for alleviating Turkish military pressure on Russia in 1915, a 1936 Staff College syndicate of one Major and seven Captains recommended: Six divisions 'landing on GALLIPOLI Peninsula, gaining control of STRAITS and seizing CONSTANTINOPLE – The whole to be a combined operation with the Navy'. Superficially bold to propose a campaign which ended in catastrophic failure and 138,000 Allied casualties (including 73,000 British), the syndicate actually eliminated risk of criticism by replicating plans judged theoretically sound in 1915; this detachment from reality was assessed 'a very good bit of work' by Lieutenant Colonel McConnell.[84] Had the France 1940 manoeuvres of 3rd Division, in particular 27 May, been proposed to Major General Montgomery during his spell with Staff College directing staff, he freely admitted they 'would have been considered mad' and unachievable, including by him; this highlights how Staff College could not replicate wartime conditions, no matter how theoretically sound the training.[85]

The Staff College failed to take simple, cost-effective steps to improve the relevance of the syllabus and the preparedness of its graduates for war against Germany. Despite France being considered an inevitable ally in any future European war, no French officers actively participated in a 1935 one-day, first-year exercise effectively simulating conflict between Germany and an Anglo-French alliance, nor a more substantive 1937 continental war exercise with competing syndicates representing French and German forces.[86] In both instances, French Army involvement would have added realism by illuminating similarities and differences in both procedure and mentality. A post-war realization of the desire to avoid future conflict without pre-established military links led to the internationalization of Staff College students and directing staff from 1945 onwards. By 1958 students came from Britain along with 19 other Commonwealth and Allied nations (including France), whilst directing staff expanded to include permanent positions for Canadian, Australian, American and French Lieutenant Colonels. Furthermore, 'the Organization and Methods of French and US Armies' became a specific module of the syllabus, taught to all students by officers from the relevant nations.[87]

Whilst Camberley students learnt about the French from British officers, the French Army ignored British techniques altogether. Victoria Schofield has highlighted how British attendees of the Ecoles des Marcheux staff course in December 1934 were not asked about the British Army, its methods or equipment and were not permitted to participate in any exercises. Although disappointed by the French Army's lack of progression since the Great War, Major Generals Wavell, Freyburg and Marshall-Cornwall were more frustrated by the lack of co-operation; 'If they had asked our opinion at times it would have been of value from their point of view'.[88] The impartial perspective of the visiting British delegation enabled them to more easily identify weaknesses in the French system, namely an arrogant, insular attitude that discounted the possibility of alternative, possibly superior, doctrines being developed beyond French borders; J. Connell has shown this view was perpetually indoctrinated amongst new officers and became increasingly damaging with each passing year.[89] Martin Alexander's analysis of unco-operative French behaviour has deduced political unwillingness to acknowledge Britain's importance when it possessed only a 'parade-ground' army, political and military preference for closer links with Italy's superficially imposing army and an aspiration to transfer 16 French North African divisions to the Franco-German border, thereby eradicating the need for unpredictable allies.[90] The 1935 Italian-Abyssinian War may have shifted French foreign policy to an increasingly pro-British stance, but it did not transform military doctrine, nor did the transfer of power from General Weygand to General Gamelin in the same year. Belief in the traditional French policies of a conscript army, maximum detente and an outwardly unified High Command remained ubiquitous; Gamelin's aspirations for modernization, mechanization and experimentation were largely nullified by an officer corps content with strategic and tactical concepts of 1914–18.[91] With France culturally different and militarily inflexible, it is unsurprising Britain and its Staff College failed to fully understand or benefit from French pre-war thought processes.

The absence of French involvement at inter-war Staff College was disastrous, but not entirely the fault of Britain; however, infrequent and ineffective interaction with the RAF was a criminal failure of inter-arm co-operation. Pre-war, army students were not guaranteed direct interaction with RAF equivalents as only two RAF officers attended Camberley each year. Few exercises had RAF roles and, when they did, the preparatory teaching was often faulty; in 1935 first-year students were informed army co-operation squadrons were restricted to photographic, reconnaissance and communication roles only. However, in 1936, Waziristan Army Co-operation Squadrons provided continuous close-air support to assist hard-pressed British brigades, for example, between 5 and 24 December offensive air action was taken on 45 separate occasions, despite highly restrictive rules of engagement; similar co-operation was lacking in France in 1940.[92] Post-1945, RAF student numbers were increased to guarantee each army officer at least a whole term of syndicate work with a serving RAF officer, combined arms exercises became firmly entrenched and an RAF viewpoint was more authoritatively taught; these reforms were possible in the 1930s.[93]

Apart from letters on the Army List, J.P. Harris has argued that during the inter-war years 'Camberley products were not obviously distinguished from brother officers who had never attended the institution'.[94] Although Staff College graduates were not guaranteed to have benefited from their opportunity for self-development, they were undoubtedly idolized as elite officers equipped with the latest thinking which pre-war units and headquarters could utilize. However, as this book has shown, these officers were liable to influence the Army with flawed teaching as much as best practice. In 1935, on his first regimental posting post-Camberley, Captain E. Thornhill was quickly detached from his tranquil hill station to join month-long discussions on Ceylon rearmament programmes and, later, primarily because of his Staff College credentials, became the most senior staff officer in Ceylon. Thornhill recalled:

'It was felt that as an officer who had recently passed out of the Staff College I could be of some use'. His next posting, in April 1937, as Staff Captain Southern Command was less prestigious, because of the higher domestic prevalence of Camberley graduates. Strikingly, not only was this post responsible for mundane activities such as dealing with traffic accidents, postings and courts-martial, but Thornhill had to become a self-taught staff officer; his duties were 'not something of which I had had experience in the past', either at Staff College or in Ceylon.[95] In February 1940, Deputy Adjutant and Quartermaster J. Faviell found the boredom and futility of seeking scarce resources for 9th Scottish Division was alleviated by 'the fact that as "PSC" I was regarded as an expert on tactics. This I played on and hoped I did some good in their battle training'. Since his Staff College graduation five years before, Faviell's only combat experience was a brief deployment to Palestine in 1936, where he was promptly shot and invalided home. Even with skills deadened by two years' work at the War Office, Faviell's experience and knowledge was still considered equal to anyone in the entire division, demonstrating both the revered status of Staff College and the desperate state of Territorial staff training.[96]

A less revered military institution to provide service personnel with supplementary education and equally neglect the Territorial Army was the Imperial Defence College (IDC). Formed in January 1927, its founding charter stated its aim was 'the training of a body of officers and civilian officials in the broadest aspects of Imperial Strategy and the occasional examination of concrete problems of Imperial Defence referred to them by the Chiefs of Staff Committee'. The IDC syllabus was 33 per cent lectures by high-profile public figures and 67 per cent exercises studying hypothetical wars; the work was exclusively strategic in nature, for example, students were specifically told 'not to concern themselves with the detailed planning of operations'. From its formation, the actions of Dominion governments, the military services and the UK civil service undermined the IDC's credibility and its ability to fulfil its charter; short-term cost and loss of control trumped potential long-term gains. Dominion governments baulked at the £350 per student annual cost and rarely filled their 12 place allocation; in 1929 and 1932 only one Dominion officer joined the 12 month course, whilst in other years, vacant places were filled by less militarily significant Dominion governments with dubious need for tri-service understanding, for example, landlocked Rhodesia in 1929. With 30 places available in total each year, the Army and Navy picked up some of the slack, but the RAF signalled its true attitude by steadfastly refusing to increase its five officer allocation until 1936; as a result the student body fluctuated between lows of 20 (in 1928) and highs of 32 (in 1938).[97] Dissemination of tri-service limitations and capability required all three services to take the IDC seriously; the Navy's selection process undermined these efforts. In 1929, Royal Navy Captain A. Cunningham was uncertain of best naval practice after two years overseas, 'had never undergone a staff course, and was largely ignorant of staff organization in a big fleet'; he was, however, available when the course began.[98] Army support for the IDC was illustrated by the inclusion of future highfliers Lieutenant Colonels A. Brooke and C. Auchinleck in the first year's intake. However, the Army naturally prioritized the development and success of its own institutions and units, thereby preventing the involvement of some passionate IDC enthusiasts. Upon discovering his next posting was to the prestigious 2nd Division rather than his preferred appointment as IDC instructor, heartbroken Major General A. Wavell acknowledged 'no one else seemed to rate the IDC very highly'.[99] The equal status for civilians implied by the founding charter belied the fact that this was unequivocally a military establishment; civilians were prevented from becoming Commandant and the civil service was denied place numbers equal to any of the fighting services. Furthermore this was an establishment for professional soldiers, with only two part-time Territorial officers allowed entry in the first 50 years. With uncertain benefits for either the individual or their employer, the civil service did not prioritize its role at the IDC. Unlike military teaching posts, the position of civilian tutor was not filled until 1929 (two years late), uniquely it remained part-time until 1935, and, upon the post-holder's retirement in 1937, the position was left unfilled. Throughout the pre-war period, civilian student numbers fluctuated between three and seven, but by 1946 the charade could continue no longer; the civil service terminated student participation, citing it was 'too busy' for such non-essential postings. Enhancing military/governmental understanding required wholehearted support from each participating service to succeed; the tempered support received up to 1939 prevented the IDC consistently examining the incompatibility of military principle and political compromise. The last major exercise of the 1938 course was a Europe-wide conflict emanating from the 'Sudeten problem'. The IDC predicted six weeks' effective Czechoslovakian resistance after which international intervention would escalate or end the conflict. When the real thing coincidentally occurred soon after, the political compromise reached rendered all the previous decade's lectures and exercises meaningless; the evidently bitter IDC Commandant A. Longmore recorded: 'We could not forsee, in

our setting the virtual hamstringing of Czechoslovakia by the unopposed German occupation of Sudeten territory'.[100]

Although the IDC's influence on the BEF paled into insignificance
when compared with the Staff College, neither institution dominated
BEF thought-processes in France. Superficially the prestige of the Staff
College was maintained during the France campaign with the views of
its directing staff sought on equipment and training, its course places
filled with the BEF's finest prospects and its graduates dominating the
upper ranks of the BEF. In reality, its visiting delegations were considered just another distraction, the preparatory work of future attendees
was considered low priority and its graduates formed merely a thin crust
of the senior officer corps.

Once war was declared, the Staff College was temporarily mothballed
before reopening in January 1940 with a condensed 17 week course
accommodating 180 officers at a time.[101] In preparation for Staff
College reopening, a delegation of directing staff led by the new
Camberley Commandant Major General R. Collins visited the BEF
between Christmas and early January, to observe best practice and offer
their thoughts. Staff Duties and Training (SD & T) was the GHQ branch
which advised on BEF best practice, yet the Camberley instructors spent
barely 30 minutes with this integral training unit before moving on
to front-line units; Major General Collins opted to remain, but it is
unclear if he got to speak with the unit's Commanding Officer, as he was
inconveniently inspecting training in the field with C-in-C Gort. In a
more blatant example of BEF personnel being passively unco-operative,
the efforts of a Staff College instructor to discuss provost issues within
2nd Division were largely prevented by the relevant Deputy Assistant
Provost Marshal uncharacteristically devoting himself for two whole
days to the area visit of Sir J. Simon and Lord Hankey.[102] Between 4
and 8 January, Commandant Collins officially spent four days touring
II Corps positions, inspecting units and imparting wisdom to commanders. Lieutenant General Brooke admired Collins for being 'full of
go and energy', but appears to have been uncertain what to do with
him; foiled by severe frost in his 5 January attempt to show off 3rd
Division's concrete defences, Brooke took Collins to see some interesting 'stained glass windows' in nearby Bouvines Church. Possibly in
need of respite, the following day Brooke dumped Collins on Major
General Johnson, suggesting an all-day inspection of 4th Division; afterwards Brooke went for a haircut and watch shopping in Lille. Although
Collins spent 24 hours with each division within II Corps, his tour was
carried out at a frantic pace, illustrated by Collins arriving in Bethune

at 1500hrs to inspect 15th/19th King's Royal Hussars and interview its Commander; by 1545hrs, not only had the interview concluded, but Collins was in Loos inspecting 'No. 3 A. Fd [Ordnance] Wkshop'. Whilst superficially appearing cooperative, by deliberately keeping Collins on the move, II Corps staff minimized the risk of unwanted interference, whilst ensuring the formation was portrayed in a good light at the Staff College; Brooke, having 'neglected' his regular routine, avoided exposing to criticism or comment some nine hours' office work which he did as soon as Collins left.[103] Feigning co-operation whilst filling time was not exclusive to II Corps; for example, on 29 December 1939, the Camberley instructor visiting I Corps's 6th Brigade was 'shown round defences by Bde Comd' before being ushered into a lecture on '2nd Div in Last War' given by a serving Major with Great War experience.[104] Formation head-quarters, their personnel and routine were always protected from the prying eyes of supposed staff experts.

With Staff College directing staff having gleaned so little on mod-ern staff methods from their BEF tour, the preparatory work of future attendees took on even greater significance, as the more experienced and knowledgeable BEF candidates were, the more beneficial Staff College would be, for them and the Army as a whole. GHQ did ensure all BEF officers attending Staff College in January 1940 toured round the whole force, including the lines of communication. However, this apparent concern for the development of future staff officers and commanders hid senior officers' disinterest and lethargy, for example, the tour pro-gramme was planned and implemented by SD & T GSO2 Captain C. McNabb; a heavy responsibility for an officer who had only passed the Staff College course himself in summer 1939.[105] This inexperience was demonstrated by the decision to base the tour of rear-echelon adminis-trative areas in Paris; consequently, after three months on the front-line, officers such as Adjutant A. Walch, 1st Loyal Regiment were inevitably more interested in 'watching night shows' than a northern France mili-tary tour in mid-December.[106] The involvement of corps headquarters staff was limited to ensuring departing candidates 'undergo a short period of attachment to other arms', yet even this proved too much work. Not only did corps devolve this responsibility down to division, but by instructing divisions this action was 'desirable', rather than com-pulsory, they offered units an excuse for retaining officers in post until the last moment; for example, Adjutant A. Walch's did not go on any attachment before joining the BEF tour and Staff College.[107]

In January 1940, by focusing exclusively on immediately relevant material, a new, intensive Staff College syllabus allowed the British

Army to dramatically increase the output of professionally trained staff officers without demonstrably affecting their short-term capability. Compared to the inter-war average of 50 army officers per year, the shortened 17 week course allowed Staff College to produce 4000 graduates during the war. The official history of training 1939–45 shows contemporaries still held the belief that only the lengthy pre-war syllabus could produce the 'perfectly trained staff officer well versed in tactics and organization'. However, there was a general acknowledgement that the Army's numerical requirements had changed and such a standard 'could not be achieved without slowing down the output below the numbers sorely needed in numerous headquarters'. By following a syllabus that focused on the 'essentials' necessary for divisional staff work, each graduate still attained the ability to become 'a useful component of a headquarters'. Although the Army did begin increasing the course again post-1945, the official history judged the war course so successful that 'given afterwards practical staff experience as well as regimental duty, he [the Staff College graduate] need attend no further centralized staff course'.[108] The war course was also successful because its intensity focused the minds of students, its refined syllabus had clear purpose, and the shortage of staff officers ensured any skills learnt would be quickly applied. Adjutant A. Walch appreciated the 'hard work' and absence of 'time off' of the January 1940 course, because he believed it left him and his colleagues better prepared for their imminent staff postings.[109] The war may have made students less lackadaisical, but the intensive workload, transparent course objective and immediate post-course staff posting could all have been introduced pre-war had the Army been inclined; the BEF would have been better prepared if they had.

In 1939, in the absence of significant field experience within the Army, the logical outcome of selection procedures for BEF Commands was that officers trained at the Staff College specifically for this role would predominate. This had occurred in the Great War; for example, within the senior command and staff positions of the 1914 BEF (down to divisional level), 'no less than 40 out of the 45 who held these appointments in the first three months of war were PSC'.[110] Without looking specifically at the France campaign, David French has demonstrated the increasing inter-war dominance of the Staff College by highlighting 49.1 per cent of Great War divisional commanders were Staff College graduates, increasing to 64 per cent in 1930 and averaging 79.4 per cent in World War Two.[111] Had the Army Council and War Office decided to rigorously pursue this policy when forming the BEF, the selection procedures were in place to implement it. From December 1937, all officers appointed to command and staff positions between the ranks of Lieutenant Colonel and Major General were identified and approved by the Army's Senior Selection Board (Secretary of State for War, Adjutant General, and three Generals from Home Commands); consequently, there were no accidents or surprises amongst officers selected for the BEF.[112] Despite these factors, the idea of the relatively small volunteer professional expeditionary force of 1939–40 being staffed by the Army's academic elite is undermined at divisional level and disappears upon examination of BEF Brigadiers.

Admittedly, the BEF 1939–40 followed trends by ensuring C-in-C Gort, his most senior staff officers at GHQ and all corps commanders were Camberley graduates. Discounting individuals who commanded divisions for a few hours during the evacuation process, just 16 officers were needed to command infantry divisions in France. Of those, 15 had passed Staff College, the exception being Major General D. Johnson VC (4th Division) who had reached high office due to his Great War reputation rather than academic qualifications. With H. Loyd (2nd Division) assuming command in June 1939 and B. Montgomery (3rd Division) appointed in August 1939, it was considered sensible to balance the first two corps sent to France with two established commanders; 4th Division's Johnson (since January 1938) and 1st Division's H. Alexander (since February 1938). Nevertheless, for all his competence, Johnson was so old, he was compulsorily retired from field service in 1941. This appointment betrays a dearth of high-quality divisional commanders within an inter-war army unprepared for and unable to respond to large-scale operations.[113] In contrast, due to pre-war association and the Polish campaign, XIX Panzer Corps Commander H. Guderian knew his three subordinate divisional commanders well enough to have 'complete trust in their competence and reliability'. The benefit of this long-term approach was the absence of fear regarding the inability to issue 'orders for long periods of time once the attack was launched'; Guderian's divisional commanders could be trusted to act independently because they 'knew my views and shared my belief' in blitzkrieg tactics.[114]

The idea of the BEF being commanded by elite, specially chosen officers completely disappears at brigade level. Of the 37 officers in command of infantry brigades within the BEF on 10 May, only 17 (46 per cent) had passed Staff College, whilst 20 had not. Including the four combat replacements, the belatedly deployed 52nd Division, 20th Guards Brigade at Boulogne and 30th Brigade at Calais, 46 officers commanded infantry brigades in combat during the France campaign; of these 20 officers (44 per cent) had passed Staff College, whilst 26 had not. It should be noted these figures do not include officers suddenly given temporary command as their units were wound down and their superiors evacuated. The appointment of four officers, including Brigadier E. Warren of 4th Brigade, who had neither staff qualifications, military decorations nor significant Great War records, shows officers without distinguishing features were needed to command in the BEF. The impression that command positions were filled by any available officer is supported by the selection of five officers for BEF brigades who in August 1939 were either unemployed or fully retired. Even amongst the Camberley graduates there were officers of dubious quality; the modern thinking implied in Brigadier R. Chichester-Constable's PSC qualification actually referred to his August 1921 graduation. Having retired from the Royal Tank Regiment to work for the York (East Riding) TA and Air Force Association, officer shortages led to his re-commissioning on 14 September 1939, and later his appointment to command 139th Brigade. Regardless of an officer's activities at Camberley, the value of a Staff College course must inevitably diminish over time, particularly if the skills learnt are not updated and continually used, leaving many of the BEF's theoretically qualified officers unprepared for modern, mobile warfare.[115]

Although the BEF High Command sought to improve the quality of subordinate brigadiers, pre-deployment efforts were dismissed as too blunt, whilst post-deployment efforts were largely too late. In November 1939, C-in-C Gort asked the Army Council to ensure no officer over 45 was appointed as a brigadier in the BEF. David French has suggested the Army Council only refused on the grounds that every brigadier in the next five divisions due to go to France would be ineligible.[116] French failed to highlight amongst the individuals rejected by Gort were four officers with PSC qualifications, including Brigadier E. Miles (126th Brigade); Miles was an experienced serving officer who had attended Camberley, completed a supplementary year-long course at the Imperial Defence College and had previously received the Distinguished Service Order and Military Cross for bravery.[117] Untested in wartime formation command, the Army Council was nevertheless unwilling to remove so many officers who had met the pre-war requirements for brigade command. Age alone was an inadequate tool for defining capability, but the absence of any pre-deployment test of competency passed the burden of quality control to the subjective impressions of field commanders.

Deployed to France in February 1940, the three brigades of 50th Division were assessed by their Corps Commander Lieutenant General Brooke for deficiencies in men and material. Brigadier H. Kreyer (150th Brigade) was quickly judged unfit for command, but was not removed from post until 9 April, and his permanent replacement, the newly-promoted Brigadier C. Haydon was not appointed until 26 April 1940. This was despite Brigade Major K. Chavasse of 150th Brigade acknowledging his Brigadier was a 'rather elderly man', who may have been 'an ideal commander of a Territorial Brigade in peace time', but was clearly 'not fit' and 'too old for the job in war'. Noting how Kreyer's replacement 'shook things up', Chavasse concluded 'it was obviously for the best', but equally, the intensification of hostilities so soon after upheaval shows the elevated risk of changing commander in the field.[118] On 14 April 1940, 50th Division was only saved from the removal of two further brigadiers and the Division's GSO1 Lieutenant Colonel M. Everett by the objections of Major General G. Martel; Brooke despaired in his diary, Martel 'does not quite agree with me in this respect, but I am certain that a change is very desirable'.[119] Brooke was particularly dismissive of Everett's abilities, despite the latter having unusually passed both the Staff College and Royal Navy Staff College courses, possibly because of his age and pre-war retirement; it shows the prestige of staff qualifications, no matter how impressive, was quickly dismissed by capable field officers. Invasion intervened before a final decision could be taken, but this demonstrates how senior officers were still frustrated with the quality of their field commanders even after nine months of Phoney War. It also highlights the failure of Staff College to be the sole provider of middle-ranking officers destined for field command.

In September 1939, GHQ led the BEF deployment to France and quickly established, west of Arras, 42 square miles of dispersed head-quarters. Eventually covering over 50 square miles, C-in-C Gort justified the expansion as prudent preparation for eventually commanding a fully deployed BEF of two army headquarters and four corps in June 1940. Diverging from this view Chief of the Imperial General Staff Ironside felt early expansion merely meant more people to worry the C-in-C, whilst Lieutenant General Brooke believed there were 'too many cooks' among the 'vast herd' of GHQ staff.[120] Although CGS Pownall blamed 'teething troubles' on the pre-war understanding of 'GHQ as a compact unit in a town or camp', Major General Montgomery believed the overly-complicated layout established fundamental and permanent staff problems, for example, 'it was difficult to know where anyone was and command from the top suffered from the beginning'.[121] Brian Bond has highlighted how the layout of French GQG was even worse, with four Bureaux (Sections) divided between three geographical locations and three separate commanders; for example, 4th Bureau 'stays with [General] Georges, but is under [Supreme Commander] Gamelin'.[122] The BEF maintained a cohesive Phoney War GHQ under Gort, but this did not prevent organizational flaws.

The multitude of BEF GHQ addresses meant correspondence continually went astray; for example, Colonel E. Birch, BEF Commander Royal Army Service Corps, informed all units 'correspondence intended for this Headquarters is being dispatched incorrectly addressed and consequently arrives at the wrong destination causing delay and annoyance'. With errors and omissions incompatible with the needs of wartime, Birch despaired at the idleness and incompetence of his fellow staff officers, for the correct address of 'CRASC, GHQ Troops' was hardly complicated.[123] Expansion, dispersal and duplication all exponentially increased the level of paperwork and communication within GHQ; in December 1939, the Adjutant General received 5360 letters and issued 6666 letters, whilst GHQ 2nd Echelon received 1288 official envelopes in the post on 11 December alone.[124] Amongst the abundant paperwork, small but crucial sections of GHQ were overlooked or under-prioritized. Astonishingly, the petrol section of Royal Army Service Corps 'never had an office' permanently assigned to them; their specific war diary noted instead 'we slip in where we can when someone goes on leave'.[125] GHQ Paymaster-in-Chief and his staff were assigned an office with indifferent lighting, no heating, and practically no stationary, but accepted 'this was the case with most GHQ offices'. Despite informing the War Office of the absence of 'essential Army forms' in early September, the Pay Office records show the first delivery of office stationery from Britain did not arrive until 16 November 1939; this shows more conclusively the low priority given to this department.[126] When Staff Duties and Training (SD & T) GHQ complained to a visiting War Office staff officer in November 1939 about the failed despatch of 5000 copies of the September Army Training Memoranda, it discovered not only had they been vaguely despatched to 'GHQ, BEF' a month before, but also that no one in GHQ had thought or known to inform SD & T of their arrival; most embarrassingly, Armoured Fighting Vehicles GHQ had discovered them by chance and was already using them without the knowledge of SD & T.[127]

Faulty information sharing within an expanded GHQ was compounded by the insular attitude of many staff officers, the watertight nature of many departments and the absence of loyalty to the British Army as a whole. Nikolas Gardner has shown BEF GHQ in 1914 worked in 'watertight compartments', ignorant of each other's duties and jealous of each other's influence; the poor inter-branch relations within GHQ in 1914 had led to GHQ Operations actively conspiring to destroy, manipulate or sideline the work of GHQ Intelligence.[128] Fear of crippling jealousies returning in 1939 led CGS Pownall to handpick four of his previous Camberley students to act as senior staff officers in GHQ Operations and Intelligence. Despite demanding his staff form a 'team that will pull well together and without jealousies', Pownall did not always practise what he preached; for example, he criticized CIGS Ironside for expecting 'Swayne [Gort's Liaison at GQG] to dig out all sorts of information for him too. Swayne hasn't time nor is it his job'.[129] Rather than rivalries, the majority of isolation occurred because of undue deference to regulations, inexperience or incompetence. In January 1940, requests by GHQ petrol section for a copy of all move-ment tables involving newly arrived units were bluntly rejected by Q Maintenance on the grounds RASC Transport had already received their single allotted copy. Unwilling to accept slow information transfers when troop mobility was at risk, Petrol opted to continue the policy of stealing the document for five minutes to take 'hasty extracts', just as they had always done, as they had 'not been caught yet'.[130] Regardless of inappropriateness or the effect on tempo, intelligence personnel preferred to approach their own staff, both at GHQ and the War Office, before contacting alternative departments.[131] Many BEF officers oper-ated in watertight compartments because their pre-war experiences had led them to associate staff work with internal office work. Frustrated by yet another outdated and narrow-minded interdepartmental message, Staff Officer P. Gribble despaired at younger officers determined to fol-low 'the process of sending elaborate minutes through a central registry' rather than the infinitely quicker and more productive face-to-face dis-cussion, often with an office next door or upstairs.[132] Captain M. Reid has highlighted the impenetrable nature of incompetently run French headquarters as being equal to British watertight compartments. With the exception of formally typewritten operation orders, at French First Army all outgoing orders were issued in unrecorded telephone conver-sations leaving Liaison Officer Reid 'no means of knowing what orders had been given'. All incoming messages were received on the telephone and recorded in various exercise books by the duty officer. However, Reid recalled no master copy of messages was kept: 'It was difficult to get a view of these books and when I did get access to them, in nine cases out of ten the entries were illegible'.[133] British staff methods may have been slow and inefficient, but they were vastly superior to incompetent French procedures.

Under significant time pressure for the first time in their careers, many staff officers were unable to maintain the standards of accuracy they had achieved in peacetime. When GHQ SD & T complained a letter from the Anglo-French Liaison Section was riddled with sufficient errors to undermine both intention and credibility, the originator openly admitted 'the letter was dictated in a terrible hurry with several interruptions and had to be despatched without reasonable time for checking'.[134] The occasional error in an organization the size of the BEF is inevitable, but perpetual inaccuracy undermined trust, caused operational chaos and disrupted the supply chain. Misled again on the availability of building materials at the GHQ dump in Maroeuil, a disillusioned 2nd Division informed GHQ 'this is a typical instance of written orders from High Comd as regards availability of material being almost entirely at variance with facts; there have been many instances of this so far since arrival in France'.[135] Some officers deliberately kept inaccurate records as a method of disguising their personal failures. Although the senior officer of 1st Base Sub-Area acknowledged keeping a 'very inaccurate record' eased his workload, an inspection of his facility found 'weak' organizational skills had led to a daily discrepancy in operating capacity of 150 tonnes of petrol compared with the virtually identical 2nd Base Sub-Area. With no foreseeable alternative, GHQ was forced to accept this officer as an example of the variable quality of rear-echelon staff officers and hope a more standardized level of performance would be achieved over time.[136] Paradoxically, many units were so trusting of GHQ staff work that destructive errors filtered down through the chain of command before the dangers were recognized. An attempt by GHQ to highlight common staff errors with an example message almost collapsed BEF transport schedules as multiple headquarters accepted the error-strewn drill communication as genuine; on 25 October 1939, the GHQ RASC Adjutant was forced to spend 'hours running around trying to square things up and pacify people'.[137] These errors were the fulfilment of pre-war failure to train sufficient staff officers properly, particularly for rear-echelon and High Command duties, and also to maintain their skills with frequent exercises realistic in timescale and pressure.

The automatic response of Phoney War BEF formations to increasing work pressure and inaccurate staff work was to continuously request expansions to their establishments. This culminated in February 1940 with all BEF units receiving an Army Council communiqué highlighting 'grave concern' at the number of requests for new and increased establishments, 'especially in connection with staffs'. Not only did the Army Council argue mobilization increases should have been sufficient, but it re-emphasized a number of basic staff principles warning against laziness, ego and empire building. The promotion of obvious staff principles, for example, 'in war the duties of all ranks becomes more arduous', combined with the suspension of further emergency commissions a fortnight later, did not stop the continued expansion of headquarters staff, particularly large headquarters, within the BEF.[138] The most striking increase was in GHQ 2nd Echelon, the headquarters which dealt with reinforcements, along with records and statistics. A mobilization strength of 19 officers and 141 rank-and-file in early September 1939 was authorized to expand to 24 officers and 372 rank-and-file in December, before eventually reaching 38 officers and 886 rank-and-file in May 1940. Although the BEF expanded substantially during the Phoney War, as did the paperwork it produced, the doubling of officers and 614 per cent increase in non-commissioned strength within the headquarters that supervised BEF reinforcements, does appear unjustified and in conflict with Army Council instructions. It should be noted that for security and accommodation purposes GHQ 2nd Echelon had relocated to Margate by early 1940, allowing the inclusion of four officers and 329 rank-and-file from the Auxiliary Territorial Service. However, this accounts for less than half the expansion and does not prevent the impression that a well-connected headquarters, which remained under BEF control throughout, was overstaffed at the expense of other more deserving headquarters.[139] In contrast, during the Phoney War, the isolated No. 1 Line of Communication headquarters, based in Le Mans, varied only marginally from its May 1940 peak of 36 officers and 132 rank-and-file. With strength leached away to reinforce rear-echelon units, just 28 officers at No. 1 L of C HQ were available for operational staff duties, once the link with GHQ was severed on 20 May; approximately 150,000 BEF personnel still in France after Dunkirk were reliant on this unsatisfactory arrangement for nearly a month of combat operations.[140]

At corps headquarters, officer establishments increased approximately 20 per cent and rank-and-file approximately 10 per cent during the course of the Phoney War. The Army Council warning seems to have been ignored as corps establishments continued inexorably towards their May peaks without any sudden increases enforced by imposed deadlines; for example, II Corps HQ officer strength was 53 in January,

58 in April and 64 in May.[141] It should be noted the brief deployment of III Corps combined with the loss of its original war diary during the retreat to Dunkirk, prevents analysis of trends within III Corps HQ establishments. The overstaffing of corps headquarters during the Phoney War left many officers ill-deployed or simply redundant when significant combat began. Major E. Thornhill was appointed Deputy Assistant Adjutant General at I Corps in April 1940, to assist the search for new Army headquarters. When invasion occurred before their introduction, Camberley graduate Thornhill filled his days as a liaison officer, running errands and, on one memorable day, as a signpost; despite his best efforts, Thornhill still had prolonged periods when 'I had absolutely nothing to do'.[142]

Strangely, the expansion of staffs passed uneventfully at divisional headquarters, the formation upon which most army operations were based, regardless of deployment date or type. The regular 4th Division deployed in October 1939 and the Territorial 50th Division deployed in February 1940; both maintained a relatively stable headquarters staff of approximately 19 officers throughout the Phoney War.[143] In its assessment of BEF divisional faults, the SD & T branch of GHQ concluded staff errors occurred due to the inexperience of existing staff, rather than deficiencies in establishments. In March 1940, on its first divisional strength exercise since 1935, 4th Division found it contained so many headquarters that congestion consumed several locations, including one village which had 'no less than five headquarters'. Scheduling errors such as assigning the battalion withdrawn first from a defensive position to join the rear section of a convoy were partly due to inexperience; the failure to issue orders, or in the case of 12th Brigade, a commander, to B Echelon headquarters, and the inability to efficiently utilize troop carrying companies, was a legacy of pre-war TEWTs excluding rear-echelon activities. The absence of staff and signals from divisional rearguards was not due to insufficient establishments, but ignorance as to whether such personnel were necessary. SD & T also found inexperience at divisional level was replicated down the chain of command and was a major contributor to staff difficulties amongst subordinate formations. The 5th Division exercise of 24–28 March 1940 included a combined infantry/armour attack generously scheduled for 1830hrs. Despite advanced notice of this attack, the divisional commander's orders were not issued until 1030hrs, whilst the relevant brigade and battalion commanders took a further 7½ hours to complete their plan and orders. With company commanders receiving only 30 minutes to find, brief and position their platoons, SD & T observed it was inevitable that 'men in the sections had no idea of what they were supposed to be doing'. Furthermore, SD & T concluded 'it was purely the machinery of reconnaissance and orders referred to by divisional commanders which caused the delay', since supporting artillery and armour had completed preparations by 1630hrs. Both Major General D. Johnson and Major General H. Franklin gave suggestions at the end of their exercises for removing staff rustiness and increasing the smoothness of operations, but few opportunities to implement the unrecorded ideas presented themselves before the German invasion on 10 May; strikingly, neither divisional commander complained about lack of staff.[144]

David French has argued the distinct personalities of BEF corps commanders directly impacted upon their staff and how their headquarters functioned; for example, II Corps benefited from Lieutenant General Brooke outwardly appearing 'imperturbable' regardless of events, whilst I Corps suffered when Lieutenant General Barker became 'too excitable' in combat to command efficiently, or even effectively.[145] Further investigation has revealed significant differences in how BEF corps commanders controlled their headquarters and interacted with their subordinates. Brooke was the most outdoor-orientated Corps Commander, averaging approximately two site visits per day (40 visits in 19 days on duty in April 1940), although periods of extreme weather could reduce this (35 visits in 28 days on duty in January 1940). The geographical dispersal of corps formations in 1939–40 made improvements on this unsustainable in the long-term, although there were exceptions; on 25 April 1940, Brooke visited five subordinates or associates. Crucially, by bypassing staff reports and observing units in person, Brooke helped ease the 'very heavy strain on the A/Q staff' who were 'seriously overworked' on the occasions they simultaneously administered five separate divisions during the Phoney War. Furthermore, Brooke was able to have an immediate impact on the ground, for example, readjusting all 3rd Division artillery positions after a two-day inspection in early November 1939. To prevent the need for further Phoney War interventions, each time II Corps received a new division or position, Brooke walked over the terrain with the relevant subordinate commander. When invasion occurred, the passage of multiple formations through single geographical locations and the compaction of the BEF overall, allowed Brooke to intensify his routine; six different units benefited from his reassuring presence on both 12 and 21 May 1940.[146] For all his efforts, Brooke never got close to the Great War record of Lieutenant General A. Hunter-Weston, the energetic commander of VIII Corps, who visited 16, mostly rear-echelon, units on 28 July 1918.[147]

In comparison, the Phoney War routine of Lieutenant General Dill usually involved only visiting subordinate units when accompanying the C-in-C, visiting dignitaries or when touring the Saar front. Although there were exceptions where the Corps Commander's presence was of particular benefit, for example, a March 1940 practice anti-aircraft shoot, attended by Dill, his Brigadier General Staff and Corps Commander Royal Artillery, the overall trend was for Dill to coordinate from his corps headquarters. Unlike Brooke's hectic schedule, during the Mechelin invasion scare, Dill left his headquarters only once between 14–31 January 1940 (to visit GHQ on 15 January); Dill preferred instead to repeatedly summon subordinate commanders and staff from 1st, 2nd and 48th Divisions for regular corps conferences and meetings. On occasions, in common with Brooke, Dill did seek to bypass staff bureaucracy, albeit by more surreptitious methods. Rather than carry out intrusive inspections, Dill uniquely appears to have utilized dates of regimental significance and the routine Sunday church parade, usually in combination, to observe subordinate rank-and-file away from a combat environment. St Patrick's Day on Sunday 17 March 1940 gave Dill the opportunity to observe the 1st Royal Irish Fusiliers on parade and address the battalion, under the guise of the traditional issuing of shamrocks.[148] Another Dill method of bypassing staff bureaucracy which proved popular with all BEF Corps Commanders was the Corps Commanders' Sunday lunch. Brooke described them as a 'good clearing house' for all disputed staff issues and sought their continuation after Dill's departure. Little is known of the Phoney War routine of Lieutenant General M. Barker (Dill's replacement) due to the loss of I Corps War Diary for April 1940; however, it is known he continued Dill's policy of working lunches because he invited Brooke and Lieutenant General Adam (III Corps) to I Corps headquarters on 5 May to discuss recent GHQ orders.[149] Whilst it is understandable that informal, unrecorded discussions between people of authority was quicker than alternative forms of inter-corps communication for solving staff issues, this ad hoc approach could not be replicated during mobile warfare.

The least outdoor-orientated Corps Commander was Lieutenant General Adam whose belatedly deployed III Corps headquarters became fully operational on 9 April 1940. In contrast to his colleagues, Adam only left his headquarters to attend GHQ or visit fellow corps commanders; his supervision of subordinates appears to have been restricted exclusively to relying on unit reports from his staff and divisional commanders who visited frequently. This culminated in some units, for example, 2nd Buffs Regiment, being observed by Lieutenant General

Adam for the first time as they marched into Belgium on 10 May 1940. Adam's actions appear out of step with his superiors who showed immediate interest in the newly-deployed units of III Corps. Not only did 44th Division receive two solo visits in quick succession from C-in-C Gort, but on their first day in charge of a front-line sector on the Franco-Belgian border, they were personally welcomed and inspected by General Georges (Allied Commander for north-east France).[150] Whilst Adam may have been willing to trust the information-gathering skills of his headquarters staff and the command skills of his divisional commanders, his superiors preferred the subjective insights, at least in part, of personal visits, no matter how well rehearsed an inspected unit's actions might be.

BEF corps commanders even varied in how they wanted their headquarters and staff to function whilst they were on leave. Being obliged to hand over temporary command to their most senior divisional commander appears to have directly influenced the instructions of corps commanders departing on leave. Still uncertain about the competence of Major General D. Johnson (4th Division), Brooke continued his unit inspections until the eve of his departure and began them again almost immediately upon his return. In the intervening period of 2–12 April, II Corps headquarters was effectively placed in tick-over with no visitors entertained, no exercises supervised and only essential staff work carried out. In 11 days of duty as Acting Corps Commander, Johnson was only required to represent II Corps headquarters once, at a GHQ conference on 10 April; he was thoughtfully provided with an adviser (chaperone) in the form of the Brigadier General Staff II Corps.[151] In contrast, when Major General H. Alexander (1st Division) assumed temporary command between 2–14 January, I Corps headquarters functioned virtually as normal. The relentless conveyor-belt of visitors was allowed to continue in a clear show of faith in Alexander's military competence and diplomatic skills. Alexander personally escorted distinguished visitors Clement Attlee and Sir Victor Warrender on separate all-day tours of the I Corps sector, whilst other attendees included a party of Canadian officers led by Major General A. McNaughton and a seven man group from the Staff College. To prevent Alexander being placed in a difficult position of criticizing an officer of equal rank, only Alexander's own division carried out exercises during the period, allowing the Acting Corps Commander and his new staff to comment with impunity. The most plausible reason for why I Corps conferences proceeded as scheduled, along with joint reconnaissance of positions with key personnel from newly-deployed divisions, was that both Alexander and Brigadier

General Staff A. Percival had served under Dill in the same positions since 1938; this created a degree of understanding which could not be replicated in the more recently formed II Corps.[152]

At all levels of BEF Command the ability of Chiefs of Staff, or their equivalent, to ensure smooth operations was restricted by the British rejection of any headquarter-based authority figure other than the Commanding Officer. David French has argued this left British commanders overburdened with coordinating the work of their own headquarters when their presence on the edge of battle may have been more useful.[153] However, during the France campaign, BEF commanders frequently nullified the ability of their senior staff advisers to implement orders by isolating them from their subordinate staff. Between 10–21 May, CGS Pownall could not fulfil his responsibilities after following C-in-C Gort to a series of isolated Command Posts away from the expertise and knowledge of subordinate operations and intelligence staff; the situation was compounded by Gort ignoring Pownall for up to 'eight hours' a day, further isolating the most senior staff officer in the BEF.[154] In contrast, Brigadier C. Haydon kept Brigade Major K. Chavasse in charge of 150th Brigade headquarters, but assigned new roles as messengers, observers and guards to all other personnel. Without authority, a commander or staff, Chavasse refused to act on orders for a general withdrawal until receiving the personal reassurance of Major General Martel (50th Division).[155] By comparison, German willingness to delegate headquarter operations to Chiefs of Staff prevented staff paralysis, whilst ensuring commanders had freedom of movement. The close links between these key officers remained, for example, at XIX Panzer Corps, General Guderian and his Chief of Staff Colonel Nehring worked so closely together that they shared the same desk. However, when Guderian spent 12 May 1940 advancing to the Meuse River with 10th Panzer Division, Nehring was left behind to supervise the establishment and functioning of the newly-relocated XIX Panzer Corps and its staff. Similarly, on 15 May, General Schaal only retained freedom of movement on the day his 10th Panzer Division transferred control of the Meuse bridgeheads to XIV Army Corps, because he entrusted the handover briefing to his 'excellent' GSO1 Lieutenant Colonel Freiherr von Liebenstein.[156]

Despite over 2000 headquarter personnel rendered virtually redundant in the rudderless Arras-based GHQ, efforts to direct BEF operations from the C-in-C's Command Post used only a limited number of operations staff and were condemned in the official report into GHQ organization as 'not very satisfactory'.[157] The resulting staff work to coordinate the withdrawal of BEF forces from the Dyle River was rated as 'appalling' by CGS Pownall.[158] In the absence of senior officers, attempts to create a clearing house at Arras for incoming information and outgoing orders failed comprehensively. To compound this, standing orders issued by GHQ and corps headquarters delegated responsibility for deciding what information should be passed up the chain of command to the subordinate headquarters. Consequently, subordinates flooded GHQ with detailed information in order to protect themselves from future criticism; on 23 May, CGS Pownall despaired: 'All today we have been troubled with minor flaps and local situations which we should never even hear about till all had been put right'.[159] With insufficient staff, procedures and communications to respond efficiently or effectively to the German advance, Deputy Chief of the General Staff Oliver Leese concluded his evidence to the post-Dunkirk Bartholomew Committee: 'GHQ were not the proper people to run this battle'.[160]

During the confused fighting of August-September 1914, Andy Simpson has demonstrated the two British corps in France disregarded their administrative subordination to the malfunctioning GHQ and began acting independently to protect the interests of their subordinates and themselves.[161] In May 1940, independent thinking and action to ensure self-preservation was a requirement of divisional commanders. Responsibility for the 21 May counter-attack on German forces south of Arras, theoretically using an army tank brigade along with 5th and 50th Divisions, was assigned entirely to Major General H. Franklyn (5th Division). However, with 'no special staff' to assist him run his 'own show', Franklyn gradually 'lost all control of his staff' and became 'not himself' under the unexpected burden. During his evidence to the Bartholomew Committee, Major General N. Irwin bitterly recalled a hectic 24-hour period within which higher headquarters' confusion led to 2nd Division receiving orders from Pol Force, Eastwood Force, III Corps and Dunkirk Perimeter Commander Lieutenant General Adam; Irwin solved the problem of receiving orders from up to three different commanders at a time by unilaterally deciding to ignore illegitimate or impossible orders. The barrage of out-of-touch higher formation orders paradoxically produced an overwhelming sense of isolation; Irwin emphasized this by stating: 'Divisional Commanders were fighting their battles by the light of God'.[162] These sentiments were echoed by Major General E. Osborne, whose neighbouring 44th Division headquarters received no further written orders from III Corps after 27 May 'except for about three messages which in each case had been so delayed as to be out of date'. In some respects, Osborne's predicament was even worse as his divisional staff were scattered by German armour early on 28 May, leaving the divisional commander to supervise the withdrawal of his subordinates to Dunkirk virtually single-handedly. Left to its own devices, 44th Division was suffering from a weak strength and shortage of officers when it evacuated from Dunkirk.[163] Some divisional commanders were ideally suited to this level of independence; for example, by allowing Major General B. Montgomery (3rd Division) a free hand as to how orders were carried out, Lieutenant General A. Brooke (II Corps) eradicated the transfer of unnecessary information between their respective headquarters and ensured he was not bothered by trivial details.[164] A visiting liaison officer observed this approach enabled Montgomery to preside over his headquarters like 'some great Renaissance Prince ... calmly discussing problems and sending his subordinates about their business with crisp clear orders'. In his evidence to the Bartholomew Committee, Montgomery sought greater ring-fencing of the divisional commander's right to 'fight the local battle', otherwise their unique ability to coordinate smaller units, maintain morale and achieve success on the battlefield would be lost.[165]

Having provided only written evidence that could not be cross-examined, Montgomery's support for division-based operations was overlooked amongst the mass of evidence heard by the Bartholomew Committee. The absence of C-in-C Gort, CGS Pownall or any of the BEF corps commanders from the witness list also undermined the Committee's ability to recognize the importance of higher formations in coordinating units and concentrating firepower. Nine BEF divisional commanders gave evidence, but there is no indication the Committee gave extra consideration to their words compared to the evidence of numerous brigadiers and battalion commanders; this may have had a distorting effect on the Committee's conclusions. Furthermore, from Montgomery's belief that his dispositions had been consistently sound to Irwin's statement that he had saved his division only with the help of God, BEF divisional commanders concentrated on protecting their own reputation and future prospects, rather than shaping the Committee's conclusions. The overwhelming fear of the Committee was that in a war of extended frontages and fluidic battlefields, units could quickly become isolated. By relatively painlessly reallocating corps and division anti-tank and machine-gun resources to brigades, the Committee believed it could maximize the number of formations capable of operating independently and surviving on a confused battlefield. The Committee acknowledged its report was formulated exclusively from exhausted eyewitnesses, and without any analysis from unit war diaries, but argued little else could be done if immediate conclusions were to be drawn; the error was to rely on this flawed report in the medium to long-term, when a less frantic reassessment may have produced alternative proposals.[166]

The use of ad hoc, multi-arm groups to defend isolated positions had already been tried in the France campaign with mixed results. The turning point in the campaign, where orthodox military procedures were no longer considered sufficient, occurred on 17 May 1940, when GHQ discovered a 40 mile gap in Allied lines that could not be filled by conventional formations. Over the next few days, multiple improvised formations were created on the BEF's south-west flank to provide a series of defensive stops at road centres and river crossings, culminating in 85 miles of canal line between Gravelines and St Amand being theoretically occupied. As demonstration of the multi-arm brigade groups, Macforce was created on 18 May and consisted of 127th Brigade, two field regiments of artillery, an anti-tank battery along with a handful of engineers, signallers, medical and service personnel.[167] Pre-war army regulations provided begrudging approval for this unorthodox policy in another example of their vulnerability to interpretation; whilst *FSR 1935* stated 'every detachment weakens the main body', it acknowledged a 'well-handled detachment may enable results to be achieved that could never have been obtained by keeping the whole force united'.[168] Similarly, the post-Dunkirk Bartholomew Committee highlighted the unavoidable extreme difficulty in coordinating, controlling and administering abnormal units in contrast to existing, fully staffed formations; however, it also acknowledged conditions were exceptional and that improvised formations had contributed in sufficiently delaying the enemy to enable evacuation.[169] Modern historians have implied strong criticism of improvised formations without ever being explicit as to why their creation was wrong, given the circumstances, or providing an alternative policy. After recording the official campaign history's questioning of the necessity in removing senior intelligence officers from staff duties to command scratch forces, and Montgomery's blunt criticism of this 'amazing' decision, Brian Bond only concluded that improvised formations could provide little more than a 'flimsy protective screen'.[170] Equally implicit, David French has revealed the 45 miles (and 44 crossings) of canal lines occupied by improvised formations on 22 May were actually defended by personnel equivalent to one battalion per 12,000 yards. French contextualized this by highlighting the Phoney War aspiration of GHQ that each BEF division would only have to hold 6000 yards; French concluded German tactics of high-tempo operations and concentrated firepower were well suited to exploiting this overstretched defence.[171]

Although historians have utilized contemporary sources and the official history to highlight the undeniable weaknesses of improvised formations, these sources are equally useful in revealing the level of desperation within GHQ and the lack of options open to the BEF. With no better alternative available, the official history has argued improvised formations provided valuable 'insurance' against the threat of German armour penetrating the BEF's undefended southern flank. Furthermore, by largely using rear-echelon units and depot-based personnel, GHQ created a measure of 'organisation and a fighting value' where previously there was none.[172] In admitting any orthodox defensive flank was 'utterly beyond our means', CGS Pownall was forced to acknowledge improvised defences were based on 'any old people' and 'anyone we can lay hold of thrown together, dished out with a few anti-tank rifles'. DCGS Oliver Leese more diplomatically informed the Bartholomew Committee 'the formation of these forces was because there were no other troops available to do it'.[173] Even improvised formations were aware of the unpalatable reasons for their existence; for example, on 18 May, Lieutenant Colonel Vickery (Vickforce) informed his five improvised battalions of RE personnel they were to be known as 'Last-ditchers'.[174]

Once orthodox staff procedures failed endemically, the extent to which GHQ abdicated command responsibility is demonstrated by CGS Pownall's note that Major General Eastwood, operating out of I Corps headquarters, had assumed overall control of all improvised formations, without the assistance of any GHQ staff; as explanation, Pownall recorded: 'We cannot deal here with so many units'. When cross-examined by the Bartholomew Committee about the makeup of improvised formations, senior GHQ officer Lieutenant Colonel Bridgeman revealed: 'I have not complete details because we never knew who was in and who was out'.[175] The effect of this abdication of responsibility was to dramatically alleviate the burden of staff work on GHQ whilst it struggled to organize an orderly withdrawal towards Dunkirk. In his Despatches, C-in-C Gort recorded it was easier to order improvised formations to rely on 'fortuitous sources of supply' and to 'live for a time on the country' than it was to establish reliable supply chains. BEF Quartermaster General Lindsell found it simpler to provide improvised formations with the location of supply and ammunition trains rather than guess the needs of units whose makeup, location and requirements were constantly changing.[176] This transformation of responsibility was not exclusively beneficial to higher formation headquarters; *FSR 1935* recommended detachment commanders be allowed greater initiative as compensation for reduced staff and communications. This allowed BEF commanders, such as Major L. Perowne (Perowne's Rifles) to issue dramatically simplified orders such as 'Hold everything' (21/05/40) and 'fire everything and when ammo expended withdraw' (22/05/40).[177] For all their weaknesses, improvised formations were a necessary evil which maintained or created capability, improved the tempo of operations and reduced the overall staff burden.

The inherent flaw in the inter-war army and the BEF was the failure to test under pressurized conditions the personnel, procedures and formations that would be used to confront German aggression. Laid out in the untested *FSR 1935*, the fundamentals of army training provided inadequate knowledge on the functioning and responsibilities of formation headquarters, as did the domestic and overseas experiences of regimental life. Conscious of unnecessary cost, pre-war TEWTs ignored the rear-echelon entirely, or paid it such limited attention that understanding of its integral role remained sketchy, even amongst senior officers. The credibility of the Staff College as an elite establishment for staff training was undermined by the acceptance of persistent failures, the exclusion of talented Territorials and the use of a curriculum which was too strategic and unrealistic for modern, mobile warfare. Instead of a high-pressure learning environment, the absence of performance-based pressure allowed students to apathetically drift through the Staff College course, leaving them qualified, but unprepared for their eventual roles. Failure to ensure the pre-war Staff College-based system could produce adequate formation commanders for an expeditionary force left the BEF reliant on the old, unqualified and unfit to fill some of its less glamorous positions. From the most senior commanders to the lowliest staff officer, flawed Phoney War procedures were considered obstructions to be worked round, rather than defects to be solved. Rather than headquarters prepared for the stresses of combat, newly-experienced wartime workloads overtook any prospect for improving staff work and it became increasingly inefficient, inaccurate and narrow-minded. When combat did occur, GHQ layout was found to be faulty, much of its staff work was proven flawed and much of its responsibilities had to be delegated.

8
Conclusion

The British Expeditionary Force's campaign in 1939–40 was the culmination of inter-war conflict preparation and the foundation experience upon which future structural overhaul and policy changes were based. Fundamentally undermined by its confused inter-war role and peacetime domestic inactivity, command and control within the British Army was overwhelmed during operations in France, before beginning the evolutionary process of becoming a military force capable of sustained victory. The British Army's pre-war training, communications, discipline, headquarters and staff were materially, procedurally, individually and collectively found wanting under the pressurized conditions of Germany's invasion in May 1940. Having identified why German victory made change within the British Army inevitable, this book has investigated how this transformation occurred and what defects were overlooked or incorporated in the haste to modernize.

Pre-war objections to a training metric were belatedly overturned, but half-hearted attempts to introduce a uniform standard proved insufficient for eradicating varied and substandard training. Aspirations to significantly improve Great War communication systems were unfulfilled, leaving the BEF with communications barely sufficient for Phoney War which collapsed almost immediately upon the commencement of high-tempo operations. BEF discipline, while not matching German brutality, was worse than official figures suggest with incidence of ill-discipline endemic, hidden from authorities and delaying the development of corrective policies. Expansion of headquarter and staff establishments obliged the BEF to use under-educated, antiquated and inexperienced officers to fill unglamorous command and staff positions, compounding the poor training of its misallocated headquarter personnel and the bureaucratic procedures they used; high-tempo operations subsequently forced an unexpected delegation of authority down the chain of command to a level capable of using it. These conclusions explain why the Army introduced battle drills, expanded its flexible communication capability, addressed the causes of ill-discipline more systematically and tried to boost tempo with brigade-based operations.

The pre-war Army considered a centrally imposed uniform standard of training undesirable because of its infringement of commanders' independence and unsuitable due to the diversity of terrain, opposition and rules of engagement which British personnel experienced around the world. With only those conversant in accepted military principle eligible for high rank, the Army misguidedly believed an inspectorate to oversee training was an unnecessary drain on resources, thereby allowing variation to proliferate. Hampered by deficiencies in manpower, instructors and equipment, UK-based units prepared for future conflict by occupying rank-and-file with repetitive basic training and maintaining high standards of drill. Officer training was theoretically expansive due to the use of TEWTs, but these only concealed the lack of genuine all-rank exercises where working relationships could be formed, problems identified and the unpredictability of war comprehended. With training frequently without obvious purpose, too monotonous or unrealistic, many personnel merely went through the motions, rather than striving for individual and collective capability enhancement. Defective training was a common theme throughout an officer's education, from excessive drill at Sandhurst, to Great War teaching methods post-commissioning, culminating in the overly strategic and narrow-minded Staff College; this impacted upon the officers involved, but also the subordinates they trained in peace and led in war.

The War Office, spurred by imminent war, set about introducing a metric standard via the publication of multiple training documents in late summer and early autumn 1939. Belated recognition that ubiquitous awareness of vague principles did not guarantee acceptable performance compelled the War Office to toughen its language and prescribe a mandatory skills set. Whilst commanders could not deviate from this syllabus, they retained discretion over the order and intensity of the training, thereby perpetuating the risk of variation and inadequacy. In France, BEF units seeking training guidance faced torn loyalties and confusion because of the failure to prevent the Army Council and the independently-minded GHQ competing for authority. Metric enforcement was also a diverse process, but one where an unwillingness to interfere, shortage of time or an absence of credible authority hampered those charged with enforcing standards. Variation between units remained commonplace with some units dedicated to improving themselves and others content with standards already obtained; the attitude of senior officers was integral to how their subordinates trained. Although nominally the BEF's top priority, in reality training had to compete for attention against the construction of static defences, illusory war zones and well-meaning, but time-consuming, political visitors. By 1942, the Army could bear the burden of widespread variation no longer and attempted to reverse the years of defeat through the creation of battle drills and minimum combat standards.

Despite being integral to the functioning of other arms and the co-ordination of higher formations, the inter-war Royal Corps of Signals was a relatively new, under-valued and under-resourced stand-alone arm of the British Army. New equipment was slowly introduced, but it did not guarantee a significant capability boost or provide a cutting-edge communications system; in some areas the impact on the ground was negligible. Throughout the Empire, tried and tested cable, visual signalling and even carrier pigeons continued to prove satisfactory, thereby lulling the Army into a false sense of security. Wireless was universally recognized as the future, but there was confusion about its role both in the inter-war Army and the BEF. Each theatre, arm, commander and unit utilized available equipment in accordance with their own preferences. Pre-war manufacturing deficiencies and inadequate coordination with civilian specialists compounded several self-inflicted flaws which became increasingly evident on deployment to France. Cost and security concerns restricted usage of the more flexible communication methods, whilst tempo was sapped by detailed written orders, excessive paperwork and formal procedures. Sufficient reliability and capability was maintained for the largely static operations of the Phoney War, but even then, many officers and headquarters sought unsustainable face-to-face encounters in preference to misunderstanding or even ignorance. When high-tempo operations commenced, the signal system proved too similar to its Great War predecessor to provide the flexible communications necessary for an expansive, volatile battlefield. The system collapsed almost immediately; information transfer failures rose to epidemic proportions at a time when the gravity of messages was increasing exponentially. To boost tempo, individual officers and headquarters improvised with verbal orders, expanded liaison officer usage and the occasional disregard of cipher and even security protocols. These could never fully compensate for institutional failures which combined to collapse the communication system and undermined BEF performance in the France campaign.

The British Army consciously under-recorded levels of ill-discipline to prevent individuals, units and the military being associated with reputation-damaging incidents. The most frequent offences and offenders have been identified through quantitative analysis of courts-martial records, but by incorporating a qualitative assessment of memoirs and war diaries, a more genuine picture of discipline within the BEF can be presented. Analysis of Field General Courts-Martial and the more serious General Courts-Martial has shown multi-unit corps and regiments topped the tables for the most disciplinary misdemeanours because of their inferior supervision, poor quality officers and larger establishments; however, the worst offenders proportionally were Scottish infantry and Guards battalions. Regulars and Territorials were equally capable of maintaining enviable charge sheets, but prolonged exposure to temptation left regulars at a disadvantage. The military justice system's complexity and obsessive desire for detail resulted in units officially prosecuting only their worst and most prolific offenders; the majority of offenders were dealt with in-house. Officially, theft and drunkenness were the most numerous specific offences due to a tendency for repeat offending; equally theft and drunkenness were the most frequent unofficial crimes because of the ease in avoiding detection and the trivial nature of many offences. By May and June 1940, the absence of stability or respite from intensive combat operations left the BEF unable to deal with misdemeanours using time-consuming and meticulously detailed official procedures; at this point the ability of courts-martial records to accurately portray BEF ill-discipline levels is minimal. To compound this, incidents of friendly fire, premature bridge demolition and immoral treatment of enemy combatants were not officially recorded, when qualitative analysis shows they were equally worthy of classification as ill-discipline. Ill-discipline was greatest at Dunkirk and south of the Somme River; however, whilst the pressurized conditions of the Dunkirk beaches can be used as justification for ill-discipline, BEF personnel remaining elsewhere in France post-Dunkirk frequently displayed inadequate discipline, poor morale and, worst of all, the absence of any will to resist. Furthermore, the adaptability of the disciplinary system allowed it to show leniency, enforce punitive punishment, minimize paperwork and sentence according to conditions. Flexible interpretation and deliberate disregard of regulations was widespread within the British Army and generally tolerated by senior officers; only defeat in combat and the introduction of conscription convinced the High Command they needed the security only available from science-based discipline and morale.

The average staff skills-set within the inter-war British Army was faulty and revealed to be a significant wartime liability once the BEF deployed to France in 1939. The method by which this handicap could be eliminated proved too obscure or unpalatable for BEF staff officers; defective staff capability only ceased to undermine performance when communications, experience and organizational flexibility developed sufficiently to compensate for pre-war deficiencies. Primary source analysis, most originally with the Army List, has highlighted no uniform qualification for staff positions existed; those with the most qualifications retained capability blind spots and, along with the entire staff system, operated under a cloud of peacetime bureaucracy. The British staff system was unprepared for high-tempo warfare because of the combination of training manuals devoid of examples, exercises without rear-echelon involvement, overseas deployments incompatible with European conditions or tactics, and elite training institutions which failed to provide practical, rounded and relevant education. Staff College undermined its elite status by allowing entry to persistent failures and rejecting first-time passes, whilst exclusion of Territorials merely made the number of graduates incompatible with staffing and commanding a large expeditionary force. When the BEF was formed, graduates isolated in Territorial units had an unexpected and unsustainable level of expectation and responsibility placed upon their shoulders; furthermore, neither the pressures they felt, nor the syllabus they had learnt at Staff College, prepared them for such a role. Inevitably the imbalance between positions and qualified staff officers meant front-line units had to be prioritized and unglamorous, largely rear-echelon units had to be content with the old, unfit and untested. Confronted by high-volume workloads, many headquarter procedures proved unsuitable for disseminating information efficiently or preparing units effectively for combat. When high-tempo operations became widespread, so did the inability of BEF staff to cope, forcing responsibility for individual and collective survival to be delegated down the chain of command.

Within the Army the variable beliefs of commanders were a critical factor when formulating training schedules and determining an acceptable level of accomplishment. Training idiosyncrasies were compounded by preference for particular communication methods diverging between military arms, units and even individual officers. Units differed in their willingness to invoke official disciplinary procedures, whilst court-martialled personnel were at the mercy of the unique mentality of their Board of Courts-Martial. Staff College provided merely one of the many sources of command and staff officers leading to variable qualifications, quality and approaches to headquarter operations.

Similarly, the Army can be portrayed as complacent in its preparations for war with a first-class enemy; for example, by retaining Great War communications and peacetime administrative procedures the Army knowingly condemned personnel to an obsolete pace of operations. Peacetime ill-discipline was minimized by reliance on a volunteer, professional army which dealt with offenders internally within units and external to the official disciplinary system; expectation that this would continue in wartime ignored the low pressure environment in which this impressive record was achieved. The Army also rejected the predictability of battle drills and complacently believed that commanders well versed in the principles identified within *Field Service Regulations* would instinctively know how to train their subordinates.

The scale of French Army failings and the size of the German invasion meant the BEF deployed to France in 1939–40 was too insignificant numerically to alter the eventual outcome of the campaign. However, the France campaign, its build-up and legacy are of critical importance to historians to explain both the early defeats and later victories of the British Army in World War Two. Physically embodying inter-war thinking and experience, the BEF's actions highlighted the deeply entrenched flaws within the British Army which had remained hidden or stubbornly resistant to reform during the inter-war period. The post-campaign changes to training, communications, discipline, headquarters and staff demonstrated the substantial legacy this campaign had on individuals, units and the Army as a whole. This study has revealed the fallacy of inexperienced and untested headquarter personnel directing operations with a variable training policy, an outdated communication system and an undiagnosed disciplinary problem. However, inter-war variation and complacency cannot be blamed for the entirety of failings because the BEF's command and control system inflicted many of its own with misguided priorities, for example, construction programmes for frontier defences and assignments to illusory war zones. The BEF's campaign substantially contributed to the standardization of training with battle drills, the creation of a modern, flexible, and responsive communication system, a centrally-monitored disciplinary system supplementary to traditional regimental support mechanisms and the evolution of operational framework, initially to brigade-based organization, before eventually culminating in an adaptable system capable of sustaining or stimulating British advances towards victory.

Notes

1 Introduction

1. Simon Godfrey, *British Army Communications in the Second World War: Lifting the Fog of Battle*, (London, 2013, Bloomsbury Academic); Timothy Harrison Place, *Military Training in the British Army 1940–1944: From Dunkirk to D-Day*, (London, 2000, Frank Cass Publishers); David French, *Raising Churchill's Army: The British Army and the War against Germany 1939–1945*, (Oxford, 2001, Oxford University Press); Jonathan Fennell, *Combat and Morale in the North African Campaign: The Eighth Army and the Path to El Alamein*, (Cambridge, 2011, Cambridge University Press); Christine Bielecki, *British Infantry Morale During the Italian Campaign 1943–45*, (University of London, 2006, Unpublished PhD)
2. D. French, *Raising Churchill's Army*, p. 12; Shelford Bidwell & Dominick Graham, *Fire-Power: The British Army Weapons and Theories of War 1904–1945*, (Barnsley, 2004, Pen & Sword Books Ltd), pp. 185–6; Brian Bond, *British Military Policy Between the Two World Wars*, (Oxford, 1980, Oxford University Press), pp. 327–8
3. D. French, *Raising Churchill's Army*, pp. 73–6
4. Jeremy Crang, *The British Army and the People's War 1939–1945*, (Manchester, 2000, Manchester University Press), p. 64
5. Lieutenant Colonel F.W. Young, *The Story of the Staff College 1858–1958*, (Camberley, 1958, Gale & Polden Ltd), pp. 10–17; TNA, WO 277/36, *The Official History of Training 1939–1945*, (Compiled by Lieutenant Colonel J.W. Gibb), p. 6
6. Gerry Rubin, *Murder, Mutiny and the Military: British Court Martial Cases 1940–1966*, (London, 2005, Francis Boulte Publishers), p. 57
7. Mark Connelly, *We Can Take It!: Britain and the Memory of the Second World War*, (Harlow, 2004, Pearson Education Limited), pp. 9–10, 14, 62, 67–74, 90
8. Philip Warner, *The Battle of France 1940*, (London, 2002, Cassell & Co), pp. 14–17; Major General Julian Thompson, *Dunkirk: Retreat to Victory*, (London, 2009, Pan Macmillan Ltd), pp. xiii–xiv, 21–2; Nicholas Harman, *Dunkirk: The Necessary Myth*, (London, 1980, Hodder & Stoughton), pp. 13–14, 253–5
9. TNA, WO 167/459, *4th Royal Tank Regiment War Diary, September 1939 – May 1940, (February)* p. 1, *(March)* p. 1
10. TNA, WO 167/721, *2nd Cameronians Regiment War Diary, September 1939 – May 1940, (March)* p. 1
11. TNA, WO 167/1076, *GHQ Supply Directorate Transport (Petrol) Royal Army Service Corps War Diary, September 1939 – May 1940, (March)* p. 4
12. Brian Hall, (2012), 'The British Army and Wireless Communication 1896–1918', *War in History*, Vol. 19, No. 3, p. 291
13. TNA, WO 90/8, *Judge Advocate General's Office: General Courts-Martial Register (Abroad) 1917–1943*, pp. 107–9; TNA, WO 213/35, *Field General Courts-Martial Register October 1939 – April 1942: (Abroad Only), Volume No. 35*, pp. 1–81;

TNA, WO 167/721, 2nd Cameronians Regiment War Diary, (March) pp. 1–8, (April) p. 1
14. Brian Holden Reid, *War Studies at the Staff College 1890–1930*, (London, 1992, HMSO), p. viii

2   Campaign Overview

1. Major L.F. Ellis, *The War in France and Flanders 1939–1940*, (London, 1953, HMSO), pp. 1–3, 5–6; G.C. Peden, *British Rearmament and the Treasury 1932–1939*, (Edinburgh, 1979, Scottish Academic Press Ltd), p. 137; Brian Bond, *British Military Policy Between the Two World Wars*, (Oxford, 1980, Oxford University Press), p. 309
2. IWM, Major General L.A. Hawes, 87/4/1, *Memoirs*, pp.W1–W6
3. B. Bond, *British Military Policy*, pp. 298, 305, 327–8; G. Peden, *British Rearmament and the Treasury*, pp. 147–50
4. Bernard Montgomery, *The Memoirs of Field Marshal The Viscount Montgomery of Alamein*, (London, 1968, Collins), pp. 51–2; Colonel R. Macleod & Denis Kelly (eds), *The Ironside Diaries 1937–1940*, (London, 1963, Constable & Company Ltd), pp. 90–4; L. Ellis, *The War in France and Flanders*, p. 11
5. J.R. Colville, *Man of Valour: The Life of Field Marshal The Viscount Gort*, (London, 1972, Collins), p.129; Major General Sir Francis de Guingand, *From Brass Hat to Bowler Hat*, (London, 1979, Hamish Hamilton Ltd), p. 3
6. Alex Danchev & Daniel Todman (eds), *War Diaries 1939–1945: Field Marshal Lord Alanbrooke*, (London, 2002, Phoenix Press), p. 18
7. B. Montgomery, *Memoirs*, p. 52
8. David French, *Raising Churchill's Army: The British Army and the War against Germany 1919–1945*, (Oxford, 2001, Oxford University Press), p. 182
9. Colonel R. Macleod & D. Kelly (eds), *The Ironside Diaries*, pp. 93–4; Brian Bond (ed.), *Chief of Staff: The Diaries of Lieutenant General Sir Henry Pownall – Volume One 1933–1940*, (London, 1972, Leo Cooper Ltd) p. 223
10. L. Ellis, *The War in France and Flanders*, pp. 11–12
11. Colonel R. Macleod & D. Kelly (eds), *The Ironside Diaries*, p. 77
12. B. Montgomery, *Memoirs*, p. 52–4
13. L. Ellis, *The War in France and Flanders*, pp. 15–21
14. LHCMA, BRIDGEMAN 1/1, *Lord Gort's Despatches of the Operations of the British Expeditionary Force*, p. 7
15. Julian Jackson, *The Fall of France: The Nazi Invasion of 1940*, (Oxford, 2003, Oxford University Press), p. 27
16. Brian Bond, *Britain, France and Belgium 1939–1940*, (London, 1990, Brassey's Ltd), pp. 29, 44–5
17. LHCMA, BRIDGEMAN 1/1, *Lord Gort's Despatches*, pp. 25–6
18. B. Bond, *Britain, France and Belgium*, pp. 29, 33, 44–5; J. Jackson, *The Fall of France*, pp. 28, 30, 37
19. L. Ellis, *The War in France and Flanders*, pp. 31–2; A. Danchev & D. Todman (eds), *War Diaries 1939–1945*, p. 30; B. Bond (ed.), *Chief of Staff*, p. 276
20. J. Jackson, *The Fall of France*, pp. 30–2
21. LHCMA, BRIDGEMAN 1/1, *Lord Gort's Despatches*, p. 16; J. Colville, *Man of Valour*, p. 163

22. E.T. Williams & H.M. Palmer (eds), *The Dictionary of National Biography 1951–1960*, (Oxford, 1971, Oxford University Press), p. 505
23. B. Bond (ed.), *Chief of Staff*, p. 256
24. E. Williams & H. Palmer (eds), *The Dictionary of National Biography 1951–1960*, p. 505; J. Colville, *Man of Valour*, pp. 158–60, 162
25. B. Bond (ed.), *Chief of Staff*, p. 262
26. A. Danchev & D. Todman (eds), *War Diaries 1939–1945*, p. 21
27. J. Colville, *Man of Valour*, p. 161
28. B. Bond (ed.), *Chief of Staff*, pp. 258–9, 264
29. E. Williams & H. Palmer (eds), *The Dictionary of National Biography*, p. 505
30. B. Bond (ed.), *Chief of Staff*, pp. 274–5; A. Danchev & D. Todman (eds), *War Diaries 1939–1945*, p. 29
31. J. Colville, *Man of Valour*, p. 166
32. J. Colville, *Man of Valour*, pp. 170–1
33. L. Ellis, *The War in France and Flanders*, pp. 32–3
34. B. Bond, *Britain, France and Belgium*, pp. 48–9
35. T.K. Derry, *The Campaign in Norway*, (London, 1952, HMSO), pp. 12–13
36. Colonel R. Macleod & D. Kelly (eds), *The Ironside Diaries*, p. 216
37. A. Danchev & D. Todman (eds), *War Diaries 1939–1945*, p. 40; TNA, WO 167/148, *II Corps War Diary, September 1939 – June 1940, (April Summary)*, p. 1
38. LHCMA, BRIDGEMAN 1/1, *Lord Gort's Despatches*, pp. 20–1; TNA, WO 167/21, *GHQ Staff Duties and Training War Diary, September 1939 – June 1940, Lord Gort's Letter to Under-Secretary of State for War, dated 12/02/40*, APPENDIX G.R./1151/50, pp. 2–4
39. J. Colville, *Man of Valour*, pp. 176–7; B. Bond (ed.), *Chief of Staff*, pp. 288–9, 294; A. Danchev & D. Todman (eds), *War Diaries 1939–1945*, p. 46
40. IWM, Major General L. Hawes, 87/4/1, *Memoirs*, p. GC8
41. J. Jackson, *The Fall of France*, p. 124; J. Colville, *Man of Valour*, pp. 181–5
42. L. Ellis, *The War in France and Flanders*, pp. 40, 49–51
43. B. Bond (ed.), *Chief of Staff*, p. 308; A. Danchev & D. Todman (eds), *War Diaries 1939–1945*, p. 60
44. John North (ed.), *The Alexander Memoirs 1940–1945*, (London, 1962, Cassell & Company Ltd), p. 75; Major General Sir Edward Spears, *Assignment to Catastrophe Volume 1: Prelude to Dunkirk, July 1939 – May 1940*, (London, 1954, William Heinemann Ltd), p. 137
45. Heinz Guderian, *Panzer Leader*, (London, 2000, Penguin Books), p. 97
46. J. Jackson, *The Fall of France*, pp. 34, 39; L. Ellis, *The War in France and Flanders*, pp. 43–6
47. Major General Julian Thompson, *Dunkirk: Retreat to Victory*, (London, 2009, Pan Macmillan Ltd), p. 38; L. Ellis, *The War in France and Flanders*, p. 46; J. Jackson, *The Fall of France*, p. 54; H. Guderian, *Panzer Leader*, p. 90
48. J. Thompson, *Dunkirk*, p. 40
49. L. Ellis, *The War in France and Flanders*, p. 42; J. Jackson, *The Fall of France*, p. 42, 85–6
50. L. Ellis, *The War in France and Flanders*, p. 40; A. Danchev & D. Todman (eds), *War Diaries 1939–1945*, p. 63; B. Bond (ed.), *Chief of Staff*, p. 317
51. LHCMA, BRIDGEMAN 1/1, *Lord Gort's Despatches*, pp. 35–6
52. LHCMA, BRIDGEMAN 1/1, *Lord Gort's Despatches*, pp. 35–6; B. Bond, *Britain, France and Belgium*, pp. 64–5

53. E. Spears, *Assignment to Catastrophe Volume 1: Prelude to Dunkirk*, pp. 148–9; B. Bond (ed.), *Chief of Staff*, p. 323; H. Guderian, *Panzer Leader*, p. 113

54. J. Thompson, *Dunkirk*, p. 84; B. Bond, *Britain, France and Belgium*, pp. 71–2; B.H. Liddell Hart (ed.), *The Rommel Papers*, (London, 1953, Collins), pp. 32–4

55. H. Guderian, *Panzer Leader*, p. 114

56. L. Ellis, *The War in France and Flanders*, pp. 138–9, 150, 350–1

57. B. Bond, *Britain, France and Belgium*, pp. 72–5, 79–80; J. Jackson, *The Fall of France*, pp. 89–91; LHCMA, BRIDGEMAN 1/1, *Lord Gort's Despatches*, p. 45

58. L. Ellis, *The War in France and Flanders*, p. 132

59. L. Ellis, *The War in France and Flanders*, pp. 141, 149, 199; Colonel R. Macleod & D. Kelly (eds), *The Ironside Diaries*, p. 334

60. A. Danchev & D. Todman (eds), *War Diaries 1939–1945*, p. 70

61. B. Bond (ed.), *Chief of Staff*, p. 342

62. L. Ellis, *The War in France and Flanders*, pp. 212, 245–9; B. Bond (ed.), *Chief of Staff*, pp. 355–6; A. Danchev & D. Todman (eds), *War Diaries 1939–1945*, pp. 72–4; LHCMA, BRIDGEMAN 1/1, *Lord Gort's Despatches*, pp. 82, 92

63. J. Thompson, *Dunkirk*, pp. 273, 279; L. Ellis, *The War in France and Flanders*, pp. 280–1, 294, 298; H. Guderian, *Panzer Leader*, p. 123

64. A. Danchev & D. Todman (eds), *War Diaries 1939–1945*, p. 80

65. Major General Sir Edward Spears, *Assignment to Catastrophe: Volume II – The Fall of France, June 1940*, (London, 1954, William Heinemann Ltd), pp. 291–2

66. A. Danchev & D. Todman (eds), *War Diaries 1939–1945*, p. 79; L. Ellis, *The War in France and Flanders*, pp. 301–5

3 Training

1. R. Callaghan, cited in Timothy Moreman, *The Jungle, The Japanese and the British Commonwealth Armies at War 1941–1945: Fighting Methods, Doctrine and Training for Jungle Warfare*, (London, 2005, Frank Cass Publishers), p. 8

2. Timothy Harrison Place, *Military Training in the British Army 1940–1944: From Dunkirk to D-Day*, (London, 2000, Frank Cass Publishers), p. 3

3. Timothy Moreman, *The Jungle, The Japanese and the British Commonwealth Armies at War 1941–1945*, p. 8

4. David French, *Raising Churchill's Army: The British Army and the War against Germany 1919–1945*, (Oxford, 2001, Oxford University Press), p. 282

5. Colonel R. Macleod & Denis Kelly (eds), *The Ironside Diaries 1937–1940*, (London, 1963, Constable & Company Ltd) pp. 21, 43

6. TNA, WO 33/1502, *February 1938 Cabinet Paper: The Organization of the Army for its Role in War – Memorandum by the Secretary of State for War*, APPENDIX 2, p. 1

7. IWM, H. Atkins, 92/28/1, *Memoirs*, p. 13

8. NAM, No. 1994-03-12, *Memoirs of L. Arlington, 2nd Middlesex Regiment 1939–1945*, p. 10

9. TNA, WO 33/1502, *February 1938 Cabinet Paper*, APPENDIX 2, pp. 4–6

10. TNA, WO 191/70, *Military Lessons of the Arab Rebellion in Palestine 1936: Written by General Staff, Headquarters, British Forces in Palestine and Trans-Jordan, February 1938*, pp. 1, 167

11. BL, *Official History of Operations on the N.W. Frontier of India 1936–37, (New Delhi, 1943, Manager of Publications)*, p. 3
12. TNA, WO 191/70, *February 1938 Report on the 1936 Arab Rebellion*, p. 1
13. BL, *Official History of Operations on the N.W. Frontier of India 1936–37*, pp. 233–6
14. Colonel R. Macleod & D. Kelly (eds), *The Ironside Diaries*, p. 39
15. TNA, WO 33/1305, *1933 Notes on Certain Lessons of the Great War (Extracts from the 1932 Kirke Committee Report)*, p. 27
16. BL, *Training Regulations 1934 (With Amendments) – With Special References to Manoeuvres*, p. 19
17. TNA, WO 191/70, *February 1938 Report on the 1936 Arab Rebellion*, p. 167
18. Colonel R. Macleod & D. Kelly (eds), *The Ironside Diaries, (APPENDIX 1 – Notes on Higher Organization to Ensure Better Preparation of the Army for War, 04/12/1937)* p. 392
19. John Baynes, *Far From a Donkey: The Life of General Sir Ivor Maxse*, (London, 1995, Brassey's Ltd) pp. 210, 214
20. Colonel R. Macleod & D. Kelly (eds), *The Ironside Diaries, (APPENDIX 1 – Notes on Higher Organization to Ensure Better Preparations of the Army for War, 04/12/1937)* p. 392
21. Brian Bond, *British Military Policy Between the Two World Wars* (Oxford, 1980, Oxford University Press) p. 332
22. Colonel R. Macleod & D. Kelly (eds), *The Ironside Diaries*, p. 76
23. IWM, *Field Service Regulations Vol. III (December 1935): Operations – Higher Formations*, p. 6
24. BL, *Right or Wrong? Elements of Training and Leadership Illustrated 1937*, p. 8
25. T. Harrison Place, *Military Training in the British Army*, p. 44; BL, *Infantry Section Leading 1938*, p. 1
26. TNA, WO 33/1305, *1933 Notes on Certain Lessons of the Great War*, p. 28
27. TNA, WO 33/1510, *Army Training Memorandum No. 20A, June 1938*, p. 1
28. TNA, WO 231/132, *Military Training Pamphlet No. 3: Notes on the Tactical Handling of the New (1938) Battalion, (April 1938)*, p. 4;
29. IWM, H. Atkins, 92/28/1, *Memoirs*, p. 16
30. David Rissik, *The DLI At War*, (London, 1953, Charles Birchall & Sons Ltd) p. 8
31. TNA, WO 231/239, *ATM No. 23 Individual Training Period (July 1939)*, p. 11
32. IWM, S.G.T. Beard, 06/99/1, *Memoirs*, p. 4
33. NAM, No. 1994-03-12, *Memoirs of L. Arlington*, p. 20
34. LHCMA, KIRKE 4/22, *Notes by J. Kennedy on Points to be Considered by Kirke Committee Including Peace Exercises and Whether they Replicate War Conditions and Training*, p. 18
35. TNA, WO 32/3113, *Training: General (Code 35(A)) Aldershot Command: Land for Training in the 1930s*, p. 1; *Letter dated 18/01/38, by Major General i/c Admin, Aldershot Command to the Under-Secretary of State for War*, p. 1
36. Brigadier C.N. Barclay, *The History of the Duke of Wellington's Regiment 1919–1952* (London, 1953, William Clowes & Sons) p. 7
37. Lieutenant Colonel Lord Birdwood, *The Worcestershire Regiment 1922–1950* (Aldershot, 1952, Gale & Polden Ltd) p. 10
38. Colonel R. Macleod & D. Kelly (eds), *The Ironside Diaries*, pp. 86–7
39. Brigadier C. Barclay, *Duke of Wellington's Regiment 1919–1952*, p. 9

40. BL, *Training Regulations 1934*, pp. 107–9
41. John Slessor, *The Central Blue*, (London, 1956, Cassell & Co Ltd), pp. 83–6; IWM, Major General J.C. Haydon, 93/28/1 JCH 3/1, *Paper 1 (23/01/36)* p. 1
42. TNA, AIR 2/1924, *Southern Command Combined Operations Exercise 25–29 August 1936: Draft Report by DSD*, p. 1; *Letter dated 27/04/37, from Lieutenant Colonel A. Nye (War Office) to Wing Commander C. Dearlove (Air Ministry)*, p. 1
43. TNA, WO 191/70, *February 1938 Report on the 1936 Arab Rebellion*, p. 168
44. BL, *Official History of Operations on the N.W. Frontier of India 1936–37*, p. 18
45. Lieutenant Colonel Lord Birdwood, *The Worcestershire Regiment 1922–1950*, p. 203; Brigadier Gordon Blight, *The History of the Royal Berkshire Regiment 1920–1947* (London, 1953, Staples Press Ltd), p. 160
46. LHCMA, KIRKE 4/22, *1932 Notes by J. Kennedy for the Kirke Committee*, p. 18
47. TNA, WO 163/600, *August 1938 Report by the Committee on Territorial Army Finance and Organization*, p. 66
48. TNA, WO 277/36, *The Official History of Training 1939–1945, (compiled by Lieutenant Colonel J.W. Gibb)*, p. 3
49. Brigadier G. Blight, *The Royal Berkshire Regiment 1920–1947*, p. 139
50. IWM, Major General L.A. Hawes, 87/4/1, *Memoirs*, p. GM3
51. Colonel R. Macleod & D. Kelly (eds), *The Ironside Diaries*, pp. 26–8
52. BL, *Training Regulations 1934*, p. 66
53. Colonel R. Macleod & D. Kelly (eds), *The Ironside Diaries*, p. 33
54. IWM, Major General L. Hawes, 87/4/1, *Memoirs*, pp. W4, W8
55. John Colville, *Man of Valour: The Life of Field Marshal the Viscount Gort* (London, 1972, Collins), p. 77
56. TNA, WO 33/1474, *Continental War Exercise for German Syndicates (Held at Staff College Camberley & Andover 1937)*, p. 2
57. Brigadier G. Blight, *The Royal Berkshire Regiment 1920–1947*, p. 145
58. B. Bond, *British Military Policy*, pp. 327–8
59. Colonel R. Macleod & D. Kelly (eds), *The Ironside Diaries*, p. 129
60. TNA, WO 277/36, *Training 1939–45 (Gibb)*, pp. 1–3; Ken Clarke, (spring 2007), 'Every Day A Bonus', (Account of his Service with the 1st Queen's Own Royal West Kent Regiment) *The Journal: The Regimental Association of the Queen's Own Buffs (PWRR)*, No. 14, p. 42
61. TNA, WO 163/456, *September 1937 Report by the Committee on the Supply of Officers*, p. 40
62. Colonel R. Macleod & D. Kelly (eds), *The Ironside Diaries*, pp. 23, 56; BL, *Training Regulations 1934*, p. 69
63. Brigadier G. Blight, *The Royal Berkshire Regiment 1920–1947*, p. 142
64. I.F.W. Beckett, *The Amateur Military Tradition 1558–1945*, (Manchester, 1991, Manchester University Press), pp. 255–6; Wilfred Saunders, *Dunkirk Diary of a Very Young Soldier*, (Studley, 2010, Brewin Books), p. 5
65. Brigadier R.G. Cherry, (1939), 'Territorial Army Staffs and Training', *RUSI Journal*, Vol. 84, p. 548
66. T. Harrison Place, *Military Training in the British Army*, p. 47
67. TNA, WO 191/70, *February 1938 Report on the 1936 Arab Rebellion*, p. 83
68. LHCMA, KIRKE 4/5, *May 1932 Notes by DMT McNamara: Lessons of War on the Western Front from the History of the Great War*, p. 10
69. BL, *Official History of Operations on the N.W. Frontier of India 1936–37*, p. 3; Tommy Thomas, *Signal Success*, (Lewes, 1995, The Book Guild Ltd), p. 80

70. D. French, *Raising Churchill's Army*, p. 174
71. Lieutenant Colonel Lord Birdwood, *The Worcestershire Regiment 1922–1950*, p. 156
72. Brigadier R. Cherry, (1939), 'Territorial Army Staffs and Training', *RUSI Journal*, Vol. 84, p. 552
73. A. Carton de Wiart, *Happy Odyssey*, (London, 1950, Jonathan Cape Ltd), p. 168
74. BL, *Training Regulations 1934*, p. 22
75. IWM, Major W.G. Blaxland, 83/46/1, *Memoirs*, p. 25
76. D. French, *Raising Churchill's Army*, p. 58
77. IWM, Major W. Blaxland, 83/46/1, *Memoirs*, p. 24
78. BL, *Training Regulations 1934*, p. 22
79. IWM, Brigadier C.N. Barker, 96/12/1, *Memoirs*, p. 12
80. IWM, Major W. Blaxland, 83/46/1, *Memoirs*, p. 50
81. Anon, *Infantry Officer*, (London, 1943, B. Batsford Ltd), pp. 16–17
82. BL, *Training Regulations 1934*, p. 22
83. NAM, No. 2011-10-8, Memoirs of E. Brown (2nd Middlesex Regiment & RA) p. 3
84. BL, *Training Regulations 1934*, p. 23
85. IWM, Major W. Blaxland, 83/46/1, *Memoirs*, p. 46
86. IWM, Brigadier C. Barker, 96/12/1, *Memoirs*, p. 13
87. IWM, Major W. Blaxland, 83/46/1, *Memoirs*, p. 51
88. IWM, Brigadier C. Barker, 96/12/1, *Memoirs*, pp. 14–15
89. IWM, Major W. Blaxland, 83/46/1, *Memoirs*, p. 50
90. TNA, WO 231/161, *MTP No. 23, Operations Part 1: General Principles, Fighting Troops and Their Characteristics (September 1939)*, p. 12
91. TNA, WO 231/132 *MTP No. 3*, p. 3
92. D. French, *Raising Churchill's Army*, pp. 58–9
93. D. French, *Raising Churchill's Army*, p. 32
94. TNA, WO 33/1305, *1933 Notes on Certain Lessons of the Great War*, p. 26
95. Major L.F. Ellis, *The War in France and Flanders 1939–1940*, (London, 1953, HMSO), pp. 20–1
96. D. French, *Raising Churchill's Army*, p. 174
97. Hugh Sebag-Montefiore, *Dunkirk: Fight to the Last Man*, (London, 2006, Viking), p. 9
98. George Forty, *British Army Handbook 1939–1945*, (Strood, 1998, Sutton Publishing Ltd), p. 5
99. Brian Bond, *Britain, France and Belgium 1939–1940*, (London, 1990, Brassey's Ltd), p. 13
100. IWM, *FSR Vol. III (December 1935): Operations – Higher Formations*, p. 6
101. TNA, WO 231/161, *MTP No. 23 (September 1939)*, p. 15
102. TNA, WO 231/239, *ATM No. 23 (July 1939)*, p. 6
103. TNA, WO 231/239, *ATM No. 23 (July 1939)*, pp. 11, 16
104. TNA, WO 231/240, *ATM No. 24, WAR, (September 1939)*, p. 9
105. LHCMA, KIRKE 4/5, *May 1932 Notes by DMT McNamara*, p. 10
106. TNA, WO 231/240, *ATM No. 24, WAR, (September 1939)*, p. 10
107. TNA, WO 231/240, *ATM No. 24, WAR, (September 1939)*, p. 6; TNA, WO 231/241, *ATM No. 25, WAR, (October 1939)*, p. 5
108. TNA, WO 231/240, *ATM No. 24, WAR, (September 1939)*, pp. 5, 8
109. TNA, WO 231/241, *ATM No. 25, WAR, (October 1939)*, p. 6

110. TNA, WO 231/241, *ATM No. 25, WAR, (October 1939)*, p. 14
111. IWM, H. Atkins, 92/28/1, *Memoirs*, p. 16
112. LHCMA, BRIDGEMAN 3/1, *Training Instructions for the BEF from CGS Pownall, Written September 1939, Amended 07/05/40*, p. 1
113. Colonel R. Macleod & D. Kelly (eds), *The Ironside Diaries*, p. 161
114. TNA, WO 167/148, *II Corps War Diary, September 1939 – June 1940: Minutes of II Corps Training Conference (29/10/39)*, APPENDIX RR, p. 4
115. Alex Danchev & Daniel Todman (eds), *War Diaries 1939–1945: Field Marshal Lord Alanbrooke*, (London, 2002, Phoenix Press), p. 18
116. TNA, WO 167/362, *8th Infantry Brigade War Diary, September 1939–June 1940 (November)*, p. 8
117. Colonel R. Macleod & D. Kelly (eds), *The Ironside Diaries*, p. 99
118. Colonel R. Macleod & D. Kelly (eds), *The Ironside Diaries*, pp. 164–5
119. TNA, WO 231/242, *ATM No. 26, WAR, (November 1939)*, p. 5
120. TNA, WO 167/21, *GHQ Staff Duties and Training Branch War Diary, September 1939–May 1940 (November)*, p. 5
121. TNA, WO 167/839, *2nd Royal Warwickshire Regiment War Diary, September 1939 – June 1940 (November)*, p. 1
122. TNA, WO 167/21, *SD & T GHQ War Diary (September): APPENDIX 1 – SD & T Staff Duties Agreed with DMT WO*, p. 1, (October), p. 10
123. TNA, WO 167/203, *2nd Division War Diary September 1939–June 1940:2nd Division Letter No. 148/G – Co-operation with RAF (16/12/39)* APPENDIX 116, p. 1, *I Corps Standing Orders for Mechanical Movement by Road 1939–Revised (16/12/39)*, APPENDIX A to APPENDIX 116, p. 1
124. TNA, WO 167/21, *SD & T GHQ War Diary: Report on Low Flying Attack on Move of 6th Infantry Brigade, 19/12/39, (Written 21/12/39)*, APPENDIX D, p. 1
125. TNA, WO 167/357, *6th Infantry Brigade War Diary, September 1939–June 1940, (December): Road Column Exercise 20/12/39*, APPENDIX 17, p. 2
126. TNA, WO 167/794, *2nd Royal Norfolk Regiment War Diary, September 1939–June 1940, (May)*, p. 3
127. H. Sebag-Montefiore, *Dunkirk: Fight to the Last Man*, p. 61
128. TNA, WO 231/161, *MTP No. 23 (September 1939)*, p. 15
129. TNA, WO 231/241, *ATM No. 25, WAR, (October 1939)*, p. 15
130. LHCMA, BRIDGEMAN 3/1, *Training Instructions for the BEF*, p. 1
131. TNA, WO 167/148, *II Corps War Diary: Minutes of II Corps Training Conference (29/10/39)*, APPENDIX RR, p. 1, *Minutes of Corps Commanders Conference No. 3*, APPENDIX OO, p. 2
132. TNA, WO 231/241, *ATM No. 25, WAR, (October 1939)*, p. 14
133. TNA, WO 167/169, *III Corps War Diary, April-May 1940: 3 Corps Training Instruction No. 1 (18/04/40)*, APPENDIX 5, p. 1
134. TNA, WO 167/148, *II Corps Summary of November War Diary*, p. 1
135. TNA, WO 167/169, *III Corps War Diary, (April)*, p. 3
136. TNA, WO 167/275, *44th Division War Diary, April-May 1940, (May)*, p. 1
137. TNA, WO 167/169, *III Corps War Diary: 3 Corps Training Instructions No. 1 (18/04/40)*, APPENDIX 5, p. 6
138. Peter Hadley, *Third Class to Dunkirk: A Worm's Eye View of the BEF 1940* (London, 1944, Hollis & Carter), p. 31
139. LHCMA, BRIDGEMAN 3/3, *Report Of The War Office Committee On Repair In The Field, February 1940*, p. 7

140. LHCMA, BRIDGEMAN 7/1, *Letter on BEF dated 10/10/1975*, p. 3
141. D. French, *Raising Churchill's Army*, p. 179
142. TNA, WO 167/357, *6th Infantry Brigade War Diary: Training Instruction No. 1, (01/12/39)*, APPENDIX 2, p. 1; TNA, WO 167/362, *8th Infantry Brigade War Diary: Operational Instruction No. 6, (20/10/39)*, APPENDIX Q, p. 1
143. TNA, WO 167/707, *4th Royal Berkshire Regiment War Diary, January-June 1940, (March)*, p. 4
144. TNA, WO 167/218, *3rd Division War Diary, September 1939–June 1940, (March)*, p. 2
145. A. Carton de Wiart, *Happy Odyssey*, p. 162
146. TNA, WO 167/203, *2nd Division War Diary, (December)*, p. 2
147. IWM, Captain J. Ogden, 67/267/1, *Memoirs*, p. 20
148. D. French, *Raising Churchill's Army*, p. 161
149. IWM, Captain J. Ogden, 67/267/1, *Memoirs*, p. 33
150. Ken Clarke, (spring 2007), 'Every Day a Bonus', (Account of his Service with 1st Queen's Own Royal West Kent Regiment), *The Journal: The Regimental Association of the Queen's Own Buffs (PWRR)*, Number 14, p. 43
151. TNA, WO 167/357, *6th Infantry Brigade Training Instruction No. 1 (01/12/39)*, APPENDIX 2, p. 1
152. TNA, WO 167/839, *2nd Royal Warwickshire Regiment War Diary, September 1939–June 1940: Routine Order No. 15 (03/11/39)*, APPENDIX 1, p. 1
153. TNA, WO 167/382, *36th Infantry Brigade War Diary April – May 1940: Nominal Roll of Officers on Strength (28/04/40)*, p. 1
154. Major General E.K.G. Sixsmith, (1982), 'The British Army in May 1940 – A Comparison with the BEF 1914', *RUSI Journal*, Vol. 127, p. 10
155. NAM, No. 1994-03-12, *Memoirs of L. Arlington*, p. 30
156. NAM, No. 2001-02-444, *Reports by Various Officers & NCOs on Buffs 1939–1945: Personal Diary of Captain E. Edlmann, 2nd Buffs Regiment, May 1940*, p. 2
157. IWM, Lieutenant Colonel J. Birch, MISC 105 ITEM 1667, *Personal Diary of Lieutenant Colonel J. Birch, 2nd Bedfordshire & Hertfordshire Regiment during the Campaign in France (May to early June 1940)*, p. 12
158. NAM, No. 1994-03-136, *War Diary of Lieutenant Colonel. E.W. Fane de Salis, 1/8th Middlesex Regiment*, p. 3
159. TNA, WO 167/846, *7th Worcestershire Regiment War Diary January-June 1940, (January)*, p. 2
160. TNA, WO 167/707, *4th Royal Berkshire Regiment War Diary: 4th Royal Berkshire Training Instruction for the Week Commencing 14/04/40*, p. 1
161. TNA, WO 231/239, *ATM No. 23, (July 1939)*, p. 17
162. LHCMA, BRIDGEMAN 3/1, *Training Instructions for the BEF*, p. 1
163. I. Beckett, *The Amateur Military Tradition*, p. 259
164. D. French, *Raising Churchill's Army*, p. 179
165. TNA, WO 167/707, *4th Royal Berkshire Regiment War Diary, (February)*. p. 2, *(March)*, p. 1
166. TNA, WO 167/846, *7th Worcestershire Regiment War Diary, (April)*, p. 1
167. P. Hadley, *Third Class to Dunkirk*, pp. 26, 38
168. TNA, WO 167/11, *BEF GHQ Adjutant General War Diary, September 1939– May 1940, (December)*, p. 6

169. Colonel R. Macleod & D. Kelly (eds), *The Ironside Diaries*, p. 137
170. L. Ellis, *The War in France and Flanders*, p. 21
171. TNA, WO 167/257, *A & Q 12th Division War Diary, April-June 1940*, (April), p. 1
172. TNA, WO 167/382, *36th Infantry Brigade War Diary*, p. 1
173. NAM, No. 1997-05-6, *Memoirs of CQMS G.W. Anderson (Buffs Regiment 1934–1946)*, p. 1
174. NAM, No. 2001-02-444, *Reports by Various Officers & NCOs (Buffs 1939–1945) – Account of Sergeant C. Garratt, 5th Buffs*, p. 1
175. TNA, WO 167/382, *36th Infantry Brigade War Diary*, p. 3
176. Nick Smart, *British Strategy and Politics During the Phony War*, (Westport (USA), 2003, Praeger Publishers), p. 174
177. TNA, WO 167/707, *4th Royal Berkshire Regiment War Diary (March)*, p. 3
178. TNA, WO 167/846, *7th Worcestershire Regiment War Diary, (May)*, p. 1
179. IWM, Signaller L. Cannon, 79/27/1, *Memoirs*, p. 11
180. General Sir Martin Farndale, *History of the Royal Regiment of Artillery, The Years of Defeat 1939–1941*, (London, 1996, Brassey's Ltd), p. 23
181. IWM, A. Towle, 84/33/1, *Memoirs*, p. 3
182. IWM, L. Cannon, 79/27/1, *Memoirs*, p. 17
183. TNA, WO 167/459, *4th Royal Tank Regiment War Diary, September 1939–May 1940*, (October), p. 3, (December), p. 2
184. TNA, WO 167/203, *2nd Division War Diary: Letter dated 23/12/39, from 2nd Div HQ to 4/7th DG, RE: Training Instructions for BEF Winter 1939–40*, APPENDIX 119, p. 1
185. TNA, WO 167/362, *8th Infantry Brigade War Diary, (November)*, p. 1
186. Bernard Montgomery, *The Memoirs of Field Marshal The Viscount Montgomery of Alamein*, (London, 1968, Collins), p. 50
187. LHCMA, BRIDGEMAN 3/1, *Training Instructions for the BEF*, p. 1
188. B. Bond, *Britain, France and Belgium*, p. 29
189. Brian Bond (ed.), *Chief of Staff: The Diaries of Lieutenant General Sir Henry Pownall, Volume One 1933–1940*, (London, 1972, Leo Cooper), p. 249
190. IWM, Captain J. Ogden, 67/267/1, *Memoirs*, p. 38
191. L. Ellis, *The War in France and Flanders*, p. 21
192. LHCMA, BRIDGEMAN 3/1, *Training Instructions for the BEF*, APPENDIX B, p. 1
193. IWM, Brigadier C. Barker, 96/12/1, *Memoirs*, p. 16
194. Colonel R. Macleod & D. Kelly (eds), *The Ironside Diaries*, p. 123
195. IWM, Lieutenant Colonel J. Birch, MISC 105 ITEM 1667, *Personal Diary of Lieutenant Colonel J. Birch*, pp. 7–8
196. LHCMA, BRIDGEMAN 1/1, *Lord Gort's Despatches of the Operations of the BEF*, p. 7
197. LHCMA, BRIDGEMAN 3/1, *Training Instruction for the BEF*, APPENDIX B, p. 2
198. H. Sebag-Montefiore, *Dunkirk: Fight to the Last Man*, p. 17
199. Ken Clarke, (spring 2007), 'Every Day A Bonus', (Account of his Service with the 1st Queen's Own Royal West Kent Regiment), *The Journal: The Regimental Association of the Queen's Own Buffs (PWRR)*, Number 14, p. 48
200. L. Ellis, *The War in France and Flanders*, p. 20
201. Sean Longden, *Dunkirk: The Men They Left Behind*, (London, 2008, Constable & Robinson Ltd), p. 96

202. TNA, WO 167/362, *8th Infantry Brigade War Diary: Intelligence Summary No. 2, (14/01/40)*, APPENDIX A2, p. 1, *Operations Order No. 11*, (10/01/40), APPENDIX A to APPENDIX AP, p. 1
203. David Marley (ed.), *The Daily Telegraph: The Story of the War 1939–1941*, (London, 1942, Hodder & Stoughton Ltd), p. 42
204. Heinz Guderian, *Panzer Leader* (London, 2000, Penguin Books), pp. 89–90, 476
205. Colonel R. Macleod & D. Kelly (eds), *The Ironside Diaries*, p. 134
206. B. Bond (ed.), *Chief of Staff*, pp. 243, 249; J. Colville, *Man of Valour*, p. 178
207. TNA, WO 167/362, *8th Infantry Brigade War Diary, (November)*, p. 5
208. A. Danchev & D. Todman (eds), *War Diaries 1939–1945*, p. 12
209. T. Harrison Place, *Military Training in the British Army*, p. 59

4   Communications: Prelude to Collapse

1. Major General R.F.H. Nalder, *The Royal Corps of Signals: A History of its Antecedents and Developments c.1800–1955*, (London, 1958, Royal Signal Institution), p. i; Andy Simpson, *Directing Operations: British Corps Command on the Western Front 1914–1918*, (Strood, 2006, Spellmount), pp. 222, 231–5
2. Brian Hall, (2012), 'The British Army and Wireless Communication 1896–1918', *War in History*, Vol. 19, Issue 3, pp. 290–1, 305–6, 319–21
3. Patrick Rose, 'Indian Army Command Culture and the North West Frontier 1919–1939', in Alan Jefferys & Patrick Rose (eds), *The Indian Army 1939–1947: Experience and Development*, (Farnham, 2012, Ashgate Publishing Ltd), p. 53
4. Brian Bond, *British Military Policy between the Two World Wars*, (Oxford, 1980, Oxford University Press), p. 7
5. I.F.W. Beckett, *The Amateur Military Tradition 1558–1945*, (Manchester, 1991, Manchester University Press), pp. 253–4
6. R. Nalder, *The Royal Corps of Signals*, p. 269
7. Brian Bond, *Britain, France and Belgium 1939–1940*, (London, 1990, Brassey's Ltd), p. 54
8. David French, *Raising Churchill's Army: The British Army and the War against Germany 1919–1945*, (Oxford, 2001, Oxford University Press), pp. 165–6, 183.
9. Simon Godfrey, *British Army Communications in the Second World War: Lifting the Fog of Battle*, (London, 2013, Bloomsbury Academic), p. 12
10. R. Nalder, *The Royal Corps of Signals*, p. i; David French, *Raising Churchill's Army*, pp. 282–3
11. TNA, WO 33/1305, *1933 Notes on Certain Lessons of the Great War (Extracts from 1932 Kirke Committee Report)*, pp. 4, 11–12, 17–18; LHCMA, KIRKE 4/22, *Notes by J. Kennedy on Points to be Considered by the Committee Including Peace Exercises and Whether they Replicate War Conditions and Training*, pp. 1–2; LHCMA, KIRKE 4/3, *Summary of Lessons from the Great War Western Front – Written by Director of Military Training A. McNamara – 18/05/32*, pp. 1–2
12. IWM, *Field Service Regulations, Vol. III (December 1935): Operations – Higher Formations*, pp. 18, 31
13. TNA, WO 106/1775, *Bartholomew Committee Report on the Operations in Flanders 1940 (July 1940)*, pp. 13, 20
14. TNA, WO 163/456, *Committee on the Supply of Officers (September 1937) – Number of Officers in Combatant Arms of the Army (30/09/36)*, p. 1

15. Tommy Thomas, *Signal Success*, (Lewes, 1995, The Book Guild Ltd), p. 40; Brigadier E.A. James, *The History of the 48th Divisional Signals, Territorial Army, Vol. II, 1933–1939*, (Birmingham, 1950, Unknown Publisher), p. 16

16. Martin Alexander, *The Republic in Danger: General Maurice Gamelin and the Politics of French Defence 1933–1940*, (Cambridge, 2002, Cambridge University Press), p. 39; TNA, WO 33/1305, *1933 Notes on Certain Lessons of the Great War*, p. 4

17. TNA, WO 163/408, *Report of the Committee on Technical Training of Officers & Men of all Arms of the Army (June 1939)*, pp. 10, 18, 57

18. Martin Poppell, *Heaven & Hell: The War Diary of a German Paratrooper*, (Staplehurst, 2000, Spellmount), p. 17

19. Wilfred Saunders, *Dunkirk Diary of a Very Young Soldier*, (Studley, 2010, Brewin Books), pp. 6, 10

20. R. Nalder, *The Royal Corps of Signals*, p. 639; BL, *Historical Record – Egypt Mobile Divisional Signals 01/01/39–31/03/39*, pp. 1, 3, 8

21. E. James, *48th Divisional Signals 1933–1939*, pp. 7, 16; TNA, *WO 106/1775, July 1940 Bartholomew Report*, p. 20

22. BL, *Military Report and Gazetteer on the Peshawar District 1939*, (Calcutta, 1940, Indian Army General Staff Branch), pp. 166–9; TNA, *WO 191/70, Military Lessons of the Arab Rebellion in Palestine 1936, Written by General Staff, Headquarters, British Forces, Palestine & Trans-Jordan, February 1938*, p. 169

23. W. Saunders, *Dunkirk Diary*, pp. 4–5

24. E. James, *48th Divisional Signals 1933–1939*, pp. 14–22

25. TNA, WO 33/1510, *Army Training Memorandum No. 20A: Developments in Organization and Equipment (June 1938)*, p. 21

26. T. Thomas, *Signal Success*, pp. 98–9, 105–6

27. E. James, *48th Divisional Signals 1933–1939*, pp. 7, 14; Brian Bond, *British Military Policy*, p. 328

28. W. Saunders, *Dunkirk Diary*, p. 4; T. Thomas, *Signal Success*, p. 63; E. James, *48th Divisional Signals 1933–1939*, p. 17

29. T. Thomas, *Signal Success*, pp. 73, 84

30. Brian Hall, (2012), 'The British Army and Wireless Communication 1896–1918', *War in History*, Vol. 19, Issue 3, pp. 301–4

31. D. Jackson, *India's Army*, (London, 1940, Sampson, Low, Marston & Co Ltd), pp. 203, 206; BL, *Military Report and Gazetteer on the Peshawar District 1939*, p. 169

32. E. James, *48th Divisional Signals 1933–1939*, p. 11; BL, *Military Report and Gazetteer on the Peshawar District 1939*, pp. 218–36

33. BL, *Military Report and Gazetteer on the Peshawar District 1939*, pp. 166–74

34. Brian Hall, (2012) 'The British Army and Wireless Communication 1896–1918', *War in History*, Vol. 19, Issue 3, p. 316

35. TNA, WO 191/70, *February 1938 Report on the 1936 Arab Rebellion*, p. 169

36. TNA, WO 191/70, *February 1938 Report on the 1936 Arab Rebellion*, p. 169

37. Patrick Rose, 'Indian Army Command Culture and the North West Frontier 1919–1939' in A. Jefferys and P. Rose (eds), *The Indian Army 1939–1947*, p. 53

38. TNA, WO 33/1305, *1933 Notes on Certain Lessons of the Great War*, p. 12; BL, *Battalion Standing Orders for War for Rifle Battalions*, (Aldershot, 1939, Gale & Polden), pp. 21–2

39. Nikolas Gardner, *Trial by Fire: Command and the British Expeditionary Force in 1914*, (Westport, USA, 2003, Praeger Publishers), pp. 40–6

40. IWM, Brigadier J. Whitehead, 97/10/1, *Memoirs*, p. 35
41. R. Nalder, *The Royal Corps of Signals*, p. 269; Brian Bond (ed.), *Chief of Staff: The Diaries of Lieutenant General Sir Henry Pownall, Volume One, 1933–1940*, (London, 1972, Leo Cooper Ltd), p. 235
42. LHCMA, BRIDGEMAN 2/8, *Report on the Organization of GHQ and HQ of Services with Recommendations*, pp. 1–2; TNA, WO 167/11, *GHQ Adjutant General War Diary September 1939–May 1940, (October)*, pp. 1–2
43. LHCMA, BRIDGEMAN 2/8, *Report on the Organization of GHQ*, pp. 1–2; TNA, WO 167/24, *RASC GHQ War Diary September 1939–May 1940, (September)* p. 4, *CRASC GHQ Troops Routine Orders (22/01/40)* p. 5
44. Bernard Montgomery, *The Memoirs of Field Marshal The Viscount Montgomery of Alamein*, (London, 1968, Collins), p. 52; LHCMA, BRIDGEMAN 2/8, *Report on the Organization of GHQ*, pp. 1–2
45. LHCMA, BRIDGEMAN 1/1, *Lord Gort's Despatches of the Operations of the BEF*, p. 14; IWM, *FSR Vol. III (December 1935): Operations – Higher Formations*, pp. 11, 15
46. B. Bond (ed.), *Chief of Staff*, p. 235
47. LHCMA, BRIDGEMAN 1/1, *Lord Gort's Despatches*, p. 15; R. Nalder, *The Royal Corps of Signals*, p. 271
48. IWM, Major R.T.B. Cowan, 07/25/1, *Reminiscences*, pp. 9–10
49. TNA, WO 167/362, *8th Infantry Brigade War Diary September 1939–June 1940, 8th Brigade, Warning Order No. 1, (25/10/39), APPENDIX R* p. 2, *(January)* p. 2; TNA, WO 106/1775, *July 1940 Bartholomew Report*, p. 4
50. TNA, WO 167/203, *2nd Division War Diary September 1939–June 1940, Points of General Interest in Connection with the Manning Exercise (06/12/39), APPENDIX 103*, pp. 3–4
51. LHCMA, BRIDGEMAN 3/8, *ATM No. 33, (June 1940)*, p. 10
52. TNA, WO 167/24, *RASC GHQ War Diary (January)* p. 1; TNA, WO 167/1076, *GHQ Supply Directorate Transport (Petrol) RASC War Diary September 1939–May 1940 (February)* p. 7
53. TNA, WO 167/218, *3rd Division War Diary September 1939–June 1940 (February)* p. 2; TNA, WO 167/124, *I Corps War Diary September 1939–June 1940: Phoneless Days in I Corps (21/03/40), APPENDIX 3* p. 1; TNA, WO 167/54, *Line of Communication Area Headquarters September 1939–June 1940, (February)*, p. 1
54. Brian Hall, (2012), 'The British Army and Wireless Communication 1896–1918', *War in History*, Vol. 19, Issue 3, p. 310
55. D. French, *Raising Churchill's Army*, p. 166
56. TNA, 355.6.FIE, *Field Service Pocket Book 1939–1940, Pamphlet 1–13, Pamphlet No. 2, Orders and Intercommunication (1939)*, p. 15; LHCMA, BRIDGEMAN 3/1, *Training Instructions for the BEF from Chief of the General Staff Pownall, APPENDIX E* p. 1; TNA, WO 106/1775, *July 1940 Bartholomew Report*, p. 15
57. TNA, WO 167/203, *2nd Division War Diary, 23/12/39 Letter from 2nd Division HQ to 4/7th DG, APPENDIX 119*, p. 1; TNA, WO 106/1775, *July 1940 Bartholomew Report*, p. 16
58. TNA, WO 167/148, *II Corps War Diary September 1939–June 1940, Duty Officer's Diary – Night of 13/14 April 1940*, pp. 1–2

59. TNA, WO 287/286, *Tactical and Technical Notes on the German Army (Issued Weekly): Series No. 2 (Based on information received up to 20/09/1939)*, p. 2; R. Nalder, *The Royal Corps of Signals*, p. 271

60. TNA, WO 167/362, *8th Brigade War Diary Operation Order No. 11 (10/01/40), APPENDIX AP* p. 4; TNA, WO 106/1775, *July 1940 Bartholomew Report*, p. 13

61. TNA, WO 106/1775, *July 1940 Bartholomew Report*, p. 13; W. Saunders, *Dunkirk Diary*, p. 51; P. Gribble, *The Diary of a Staff Officer*, (London, 1941, Methuen & Co Ltd), pp. 29–30

62. TNA, WO 167/24, *RASC GHQ War Diary: CRASC GHQ Routine Orders No. 5 (09/11/39)* p. 4; W. Saunders, *Dunkirk Diary*, p. 4

63. TNA, WO 167/201, *1st Division Provost Company War Diary September 1939–January 1940, (October)* pp. 1–3; George Forty, *British Army Handbook 1939–1945*, (Strood, 1998, Sutton Publishing Ltd), pp. 86–7

64. TNA, WO 167/148, *II Corps War Diary (January)* p. 7, *Duty Officer's Diary – Night of 13/14 April 1940*, p. 1; TNA, WO 106/1775, *July 1940 Bartholomew Report – Evidence of Brigadier Oliver Leese (12/06/40)*, p. 16; TNA, WO 167/218, *3rd Division War Diary (February)* p. 3

65. TNA, WO 167/275, *44th Division War Diary April – May 1940, 44th Division Operation Instruction No. 8 (27/04/40), APPENDIX 16* pp 1–2; LHCMA, BRIDGEMAN 1/1, *Lord Gort's Despatches*, p. 10

66. TNA, WO 167/362, *8th Brigade War Diary, Operation Order No. 11, (10/01/40), APPENDIX AP*, p. 4; IWM, Brigadier J. Whitehead, 97/10/1, *Memoirs*, p. 38

67. TNA, WO 167/1, *GHQ 2nd Echelon War Diary September 1939–June 1940 (September)*, p. 8

68. S.P. Mackenzie, *Politics and Military Morale: Current-Affairs and Citizenship Education in the British Army 1914–1950*, (Oxford, 1992, Oxford University Press), p. 56

69. IWM, Major J. Finch, 90/6/1, *Memoirs*, p. 6; TNA, WO 167/215, *2nd Division Provost Company War Diary September 1939–June 1940, (September)* p. 8; IWM, Brigadier J. Whitehead, 97/10/1, *Memoirs*, p. 37

70. TNA, WO 167/148, *II Corps War Diary – II Corps Conference Minutes 23/11/39, APPENDIX QQ* p. 1; TNA, WO 197/11, *Visits to BEF by War Office and other Staff Officers: Reports and Questionnaires – Letter dated 09/12/39*, p. 1

71. TNA, WO 33/1305, *1933 Notes on Certain Lessons of the Great War*, pp. 17–18; D. French, *Raising Churchill's Army*, p. 161

72. TNA, WO 167/124, *I Corps War Diary – Standing Orders*, p. 3; TNA, WO 167/169, *III Corps War Diary April – May 1940: III Corps Training Instructions No. 1 (18/04/40), APPENDIX 5*, p. 6

73. TNA, 355.6.FIE, *FSPB 1939-1940: Pamphlet No. 2*, pp. 2–3; TNA, WO 197/11, *Visits to BEF by WO & Other Staff Officers – Notes of Director of Staff Duties Visit to BEF (14/11/39)*, p. 3; TNA, WO 167/1076, *GHQ SDT (Petrol) RASC War Diary (October)* p. 7

74. TNA, WO 231/161, *Military Training Pamphlet No. 23, Operations Part 1 (September 1939)*, p. 13

75. TNA, WO 231/244, *ATM No. 28, January 1940*, p. 24

76. TNA, WO 167/215, *2nd Division Provost Company War Diary (January)* p. 2

77. TNA, WO 33/1305, *1933 Notes on Certain Lessons of the Great War*, p. 18

78. LHCMA, BRIDGEMAN 2/1, *Notes on the Operations in Belgium and Flanders 10th May – 3rd June 1940: Compiled by the General Staff of GHQ, BEF*, pp. 4–5

79. TNA, WO 106/1775, *July 1940 Bartholomew Report*, p. 13
80. TNA, 355.6.FIE, *FSPB 1939–40: Pamphlet 1*, pp. 10, 30, 46, *Pamphlet 2*, pp. 13–15
81. TNA, 355.6.FIE, *FSPB 1939–40: Pamphlet 1*, pp. 10, 30, 46
82. LHCMA, BRIDGEMAN 3/8, *ATM No. 33 (June 1940)* p. 10; TNA, WO 231/239, *ATM No. 23 (July 1939)*, p. 9
83. LHCMA, BRIDGEMAN 2/7, *GHQ, 1st Echelon, Standing Orders – Incoming Messages and Outgoing Messages*, pp. 1–2
84. LHCMA, BRIDGEMAN 2/7, *GHQ, 1st Echelon, Standing Orders – Situation Reports*, pp. 4–5

5   Communications: Collapse

1. The Belgian Ministry of Foreign Affairs, *Belgium – The Official Account of What Happened 1939–1940*, (London, 1941, Evan Bros Ltd), p. 33
2. David Rissik, *The DLI At War*, (London, 1953, Charles Birchall & Sons Ltd), pp. 9–10; TNA, WO 167/208, *2nd Divisional Signals War Diary, September 1939–June 1940, (May)*, p. 1; TNA, WO 167/571, *1st Survey Regiment RA War Diary, September 1939–June 1940, 1st Survey Battery Supplement, April – June 1940*, p. 2
3. IWM, Lieutenant Colonel R. Tong, 83/32/1, *Memoirs*, p. 1; P. Gribble, *The Diary of a Staff Officer*, (London, 1941, Methuen & Co Ltd), p. 3
4. Brian Bond (ed.), *Chief of Staff: The Diaries of Lieutenant General Sir Henry Pownall, Volume One, 1933–1940*, (London, 1972, Leo Cooper Ltd), p. 308; TNA, WO 167/148, *II Corps War Diary September 1939–June 1940 (May)*, p. 2; NAM, No. 2001-02-444, *Reports by Various Officers and NCOs on the Buffs Regiment 1939–1945 – Personal Diary of Captain E. Edlmann, 2nd Buffs Regiment (May 1940)*, pp. 1–2
5. TNA, WO 167/208, *2nd Divisional Signals War Diary, (May)*, p. 1; TNA, WO 167/721, *2nd Cameronians Regiment War Diary, September 1939–May 1940, (May)*, p. 5; General Sir Cecil Blacker & Major General Henry Woods, *5th Royal Inniskilling Dragoon Guards: Change and Challenge 1928–1978*, (London, 1978, William Clowes & Sons Ltd), p. 20
6. TNA, WO 167/54, *Line of Communication Headquarters War Diary, September 1939–June 1940, (May)*, p. 1; Anon, *Infantry Officer*, (London, 1943, B.T. Batsford Ltd), p. 29
7. B. Bond (ed.), *Chief of Staff*, pp. 262, 294
8. LHCMA, BRIDGEMAN 2/8, *June 1940 Report on the Organization of GHQ & HQ of Services*, pp. 2–3; TNA, WO 167/179, *III Corps Signals War Diary, April – June 1940, Wireless Map (APPENDIX 1) to III Corps Signals Operation Order No. 1, 12/04/40 (APPENDIX 3)*, p. 1
9. B. Bond (ed.), *Chief of Staff*, pp. 314–315; TNA, WO 106/1775, *July 1940 Report by the Bartholomew Committee – Evidence from 12/06/40*, p. 16
10. LHCMA, BRIDGEMAN 2/8, *Report on the Organization of GHQ*, p. 3; Bernard Montgomery, *The Memoirs of Field Marshal The Viscount Montgomery of Alamein*, (London, 1968, Collins), p. 57; TNA, WO 106/1775, *July 1940 Report by the Bartholomew Committee – Evidence from 12/06/40*, pp. 16–17

11. LHCMA, LINDSELL 1/3, *GHQ 'Q' (Maintenance) Branch War Diary (May 1940),* pp. 1–2; LHCMA, BRIDGEMAN 2/8, *Report on the Organization of GHQ,* p. 3

12. IWM, Lieutenant Colonel R. Page, 67/373/1, *Memoirs,* pp. 1–2

13. B. Bond (ed.), *Chief of Staff,* p. 255; TNA, WO 106/1775, *July 1940 Bartholomew Report – Evidence from 12/06/40,* p. 16

14. TNA, WO 167/148, *II Corps War Diary, (May),* pp. 3–4; Alex Danchev & Daniel Todman (eds), *War Diaries 1939–1945: Field Marshal Lord Alanbrooke,* (London, 2002, Phoenix Press), p. 60

15. TNA, WO 167/208, *2nd Divisional Signals War Diary, (May),* p. 5

16. TNA, WO 167/148, *II Corps War Diary – (May Summary),* p. 1; TNA, WO 167/179, *III Corps Signals War Diary, (May),* pp. 1–2

17. TNA, WO 167/571, *1st Survey Regiment RA War Diary – 1st Sound Ranging Battery Supplement, April – May 1940, (May),* p. 3

18. Wilfred Saunders, *Dunkirk Diary of a Very Young Soldier,* (Studley, 2010, Brewin Books), p. 91; Colonel C.R.B. Knight, *Historical Records of the Buffs,* (London, 1951, The Medici Society), p. 73

19. Brigadier C.N. Barclay, *The History of the Duke of Wellington's Regiment 1919–1952,* (London, 1953, William Clowes & Sons Ltd), p. 35

20. A. Danchev & D. Todman (eds), *War Diaries 1939–1945,* p. 87; TNA, WO 167/54, *Line of Communication Headquarters War Diary, (May),* pp. 1–16; P. Gribble, *The Diary of a Staff Officer,* pp. 24, 37

21. TNA, WO 167/208, *2nd Divisional Signals War Diary, (May),* pp. 2–3; W. Saunders, *Dunkirk Diary,* pp. 66–7; NAM, No. 2001-02-444, *Personal Diary of Captain E. Edlmann, (May 1940),* p. 4

22. TNA, WO 106/1775, *July 1940 Bartholomew Report,* p. 13; TNA, WO 167/179, *III Corps Signals War Diary – III Corps Signals Operation Order No. 1, 12/04/40, (APPENDIX 3),* p. 4; W. Saunders, *Dunkirk Diary,* p. 73

23. TNA, WO 167/208, *2nd Divisional Signals War Diary, (May),* p. 5; W. Saunders, *Dunkirk Diary,* pp. 73–4, 94; TNA, WO 106/1775, *July 1940 Bartholomew Report – Evidence of B. Montgomery 14/06/40 – 3rd Division Notes on Artillery (APPENDIX B),* p. 1

24. IWM, Lieutenant Colonel R. Tong, 83/32/1, *Memoirs,* p. 18

25. P. Gribble, *The Diary of a Staff Officer,* p. 59

26. W. Saunders, *Dunkirk Diary,* pp. 68–9

27. TNA, WO 167/148, *II Corps War Diary – II Corps Order to Subordinate Divisions (14/05/40),* p. 1; P. Gribble, *The Diary of a Staff Officer,* pp. 24, 29–31

28. TNA, WO 167/54, *Line of Communication Headquarters War Diary, (May),* pp. 16, 39

29. TNA, WO 167/1403, *Perowne's Rifles (Vickforce) War Diary, May – June 1940, (May),* p. 4; IWM, Major J. Finch, 90/6/1, *Memoirs,* p. 2; TNA, WO 106/1775, *Bartholomew Report – Evidence of 12/06/40,* p. 18

30. LHCMA, BRIDGEMAN 1/1, *Lord Gort's Despatches of the Operations of the BEF,* p. 73; Brigadier C. Barclay, *Duke of Wellington's Regiment 1919–1952,* p. 43; IWM, A. Towle, 84/33/1, *Memoirs,* p. 7

31. Brian Hall, (2012), 'The British Army and Wireless Communications 1896–1918', *War in History,* Vol. 19, Issue 3, pp. 312–13; William Moore, *Panzer Bait: With the 3rd Royal Tank Regiment 1940–1944,* (London, 1991, Leo Cooper), pp. 9, 11

32. IWM, Captain J. Ogden, 67/267/1, *Memoirs*, p. 132; W. Saunders, *Dunkirk Diary*, p. 70; IWM, Lieutenant Colonel J. Birch, MISC 105 ITEM 1667, *Personal Diary of Lieutenant Colonel J. Birch, 2nd Bedfordshire & Hertfordshire Regiment, May – June 1940*, pp. 12, 22–4; TNA, WO 169/179, *III Corps Signals War Diary, (May)*, p. 2; TNA, WO 167/169, *III Corps War Diary April – May 1940, (May)*, p. 3

33. The Belgian Ministry of Foreign Affairs, *Official Account 1939–1940*, p. 43; IWM, Lieutenant General E. Osborne, 785 Con Shelf, *Personal War Diary of Major General E. Osborne, (May 1940)*, p. 9

34. TNA, WO 167/179, *III Corps Signals War Diary – III Corps Signals Operation Order No. 1, 12/04/40, (APPENDIX 3)*, p. 5; TNA, WO 167/208, *2nd Divisional Signals War Diary, (May)*, p. 2

35. TNA, WO 167/208, *2nd Divisional Signals War Diary (May)*, p. 5; P. Hadley, *Third Class to Dunkirk: A Worm's Eye View of the BEF*, (London, 1944, Hollis & Carter Ltd), p. 37

36. TNA, WO 167/169, *III Corps War Diary, (May)*, p. 3; TNA, WO 167/148, *II Corps War Diary (May)*, pp. 20, 23

37. IWM, Lieutenant Colonel E. Brush, 85/8/1, *Memoirs*, p. 87

38. LHCMA, BRIDGEMAN 1/1, *Lord Gort's Despatches*, p. 85

39. IWM, Captain J. Ogden, 67/267/1, *Memoirs*, pp. 122–3, 143

40. TNA, WO 106/1775, *July 1940 Bartholomew Report – Evidence of 12/06/40*, p. 16; TNA, WO 167/148, *II Corps War Diary, (May Summary)*, p. 1, *(May)*, p. 3; TNA, WO 167/230, *4th Division War Diary, September 1939–June 1940, (June)*, pp. 1–2

41. TNA, WO 167/260, *12th Division Provost Company War Diary, April – May 1940, (May)*, p. 1; David Orr & David Truesdale, *The Rifles Are There: 1st and 2nd Battalions, The Royal Ulster Rifles in the Second World War*, (Barnsley, 2005, Pen & Sword Books Ltd), p. 20; TNA, WO 167/1403, *Perowne's Rifles (Vickforce) War Diary, (May)*, p. 5

42. Brian Bond, *Britain, France and Belgium 1939–1940*, (London, 1990, Brassey's Ltd), p. 80

43. IWM, Lieutenant General E. Osborne, 785 Con Shelf, *Personal War Diary*, p. 12; D. Rissik, *The DLI At War*, p. 21

44. IWM, Brigadier R. Boxshall, 84/41/1, *Memoirs*, pp. 1–2; TNA, WO 167/400, *145th Brigade War Diary, January – May 1940, (May)*, pp. 10–12; Brigadier C. Barclay, *Duke of Wellington's Regiment 1919–1952*, p. 43

45. IWM, Lieutenant Colonel E. Thornhill, 99/36/1, *Memoirs*, p. 66; TNA, WO 167/571, *1st Survey Regiment RA War Diary, April – June 1940 Supplement*, p. 4; IWM, Lieutenant Colonel J. Birch, MISC 105 ITEM 1667, *Personal War Diary*, p. 3

46. IWM, Colonel K. Chavasse, 98/23/1, *Memoirs*, p. 55; TNA, WO 167/169, *III Corps War Diary – Report of Captain Beck, 28/05/40, (APPENDIX D)*, pp. 1–2

47. IWM, A. Towle, 84/33/1, *Memoirs*, pp. 5–6; P. Hadley, *Third Class to Dunkirk*, p. 124; IWM, Lieutenant Colonel J. Birch, MISC 105 ITEM 1667, *Personal War Diary*, p. 22

48. LHCMA, LINDSELL 1/2, *Personal War Diary of Quartermaster General W. Lindsell, (May 1940)*, p. 13; Brigadier C. Barclay, *Duke of Wellington's Regiment 1919–1952*, p. 207

49. Heinz Guderian, *Panzer Leader*, (London, 2000, Penguin Books Ltd), p. 78

50. TNA, WO 106/1775, July 1940 *Bartholomew Report*, p. 14, *Evidence of 12/06/40*, p. 1; B. Bond (ed.), *Chief of Staff*, pp. 318, 331

51. LHCMA, LINDSELL 1/2, *War Diary of Quartermaster General W. Lindsell*, pp. 7–10; LHCMA, BRIDGEMAN 1/1, *Lord Gort's Despatches*, p. 36; D. Rissik, *The DLI at War*, p. 25

52. NAM, No. 2001-02-444, Personal Diary of Captain E. Edlmann, (May 1940), p. 3

53. NAM, No. 1994-03-136, *War Diary of Lieutenant Colonel E.W. Fane de Salis, 1/8th Middlesex Regiment, September 1939–June 1940*, p. 4; TNA, WO 167/260, *12th Division Provost Company War Diary, (May)*, p. 1; D. Rissik, *The DLI At War*, p. 11

54. TNA, WO 167/54, *Line of Communication Headquarters War Diary, (May)*, p. 18; Brigadier C. Barclay, *Duke of Wellington's Regiment 1919–1952*, p. 35

55. Brian Bond, 'The British Field Force in France and Belgium 1939–1940', in Paul Addison & Angus Calder (eds), *Time to Kill: The Soldier's Experience of War in the West*, (London, 1997, Pimlico), p. 43; P. Hadley, *Third Class to Dunkirk*, p. 44

56. P. Gribble, *The Diary of a Staff Officer*, pp. 22–3; IWM, Lieutenant Colonel M. Reid, 83/37/1 & Con Shelf, *Official Reports and Signals – I Corps BEF to French First Army (15/05/40)*, p. 1

57. B. Bond, 'The British Field Force in France and Belgium 1939–1940', in P. Addison & A. Calder (eds), *Time to Kill*, p. 43; TNA, WO 167/169, *III Corps War Diary, (May)*, pp. 1–3; Max Arthur, *Forgotten Voices of the Second World War*, (Haydock, 2004, The Book People Ltd), p. 53

58. Tommy Thomas, *Signal Success*, (Lewes, 1995, The Book Guild Ltd), p. 110

59. P. Hadley, *Third Class to Dunkirk*, p. 36; Brigadier C. Barclay, *Duke of Wellington's Regiment 1919–1952*, p. 37; P. Gribble, *The Diary of a Staff Officer*, p. 55

60. Major L.F. Ellis, *The War in France and Flanders 1939–1940*, (London, 1953, HMSO), pp. 63–4; B. Bond (ed.), *Chief of Staff*, pp. 322–3; IWM, Lieutenant Colonel R. Tong, 83/32/1, *Memoirs*, p. 14

61. LHCMA, BRIDGEMAN 1/1, *Lord Gort's Despatches*, p. 42; B. Montgomery, *Memoirs*, p. 57; Colonel R. Macleod & D. Kelly, *The Ironside Diaries 1937–1940*, (London, 1963, Constable & Company Ltd), p. 319

62. Charles de Gaulle, *War Memoirs Volume One – The Call to Honour 1940–1942*, (London, 1955, Collins), pp. 39–40; TNA, WO 197/23, *Demi-Official Correspondence Between GHQ & British Military Mission in France October 1939–January 1940, Letter from Major General P. Whitefoord to GHQ Branches (21/10/39)*, p. 1

63. TNA, WO 197/23, *Agreed Lines of Communication for the French Military Mission, October 1939*, p. 1, *Letter from French Ministry of Defence to British Military Attache on Composition of French Military Mission to GHQ (14/09/39)*, pp. 1–2

64. IWM, Lieutenant Colonel M. Reid, 83/37/1 & Con Shelf, *Post-Campaign Report (06/06/40)*, p. 3

65. Hugh Sebag-Montefiore, *Dunkirk: Fight to the Last Man*, (London, 2006, Viking), pp. 84–6

66. L. Ellis, *The War in France and Flanders*, pp. 63–4; A. Danchev & D. Todman (eds), *War Diaries 1939–1945*, pp. 63–4; Julian Jackson, *The Fall of France: The Nazi Invasion of 1940*, (Oxford, 2003, Oxford University Press), p. 222

67. H. Guderian, *Panzer Leader, 10th Panzer Division Order No. 5, (13/05/40)* & *XIX Panzer Corps Order No. 9, (19/05/40)*, pp. 484–6, 493–5; Alan Bance (Translated), *Blitzkrieg in Their Own Words*, (Barnsley, 2005, Pen & Sword Books Ltd), p. 108
68. W. Jacob, (December 1982), 'Air Support for the British Army 1939–1943', *Military Affairs*, Vol. 46, No. 4, pp. 174–6; John Ward, *Hitler's Stuka Squadrons: The Ju 87 1939–1945*, (Strood, 2004, Spellmount), p. 76
69. H. Guderian, *Panzer Leader*, p. 105; J. Jackson, *The Fall of France*, pp. 47–8
70. LHCMA, BRIDGEMAN 1/1, *Lord Gort's Despatches*, pp. 69–72; TNA, WO 167/215, *2nd Division Provost Company War Diary, September 1939–June 1940, (May)*, p. 3
71. P. Hadley, *Third Class to Dunkirk*, p. 134; IWM, Lieutenant Colonel J. Birch, MISC 105 ITEM 1667, *Personal War Diary*, p. 19; IWM, Major J. Finch, 90/6/1, *Memoirs*, p. 7
72. A. Danchev & D. Todman (eds), *War Diaries 1939–1945*, p. 79
73. LHCMA, BRIDGEMAN 1/1, *Lord Gort's Despatches*, p. 51
74. TNA, WO 167/571, *1st Survey Regiment RA War Diary, April – June 1940 Supplement, (June)*, pp. 1, 4–5; Colonel C. Knight, *Historical Records of the Buffs*, pp. 63–9; Richard Campbell-Begg & Peter Liddle, *For Five Shillings A Day: Personal Histories of World War II*, (London, 2000, Harper Collins Publishers), p. 26

6   Discipline

1. TNA, WO 277/7, *Official History of Discipline 1939–1945*, (Compiled by Brigadier A. McPherson, WO, 1950), p. 1
2. TNA, WO 277/7, *Discipline 1939–1945*, (McPherson), p. 21
3. David French, (October 1998), 'Discipline and the Death Penalty in the British Army in the War against Germany during the Second World War', *Journal of Contemporary History*, Vol. 33, No. 4, pp. 538–40
4. Jonathan Fennell, *Combat and Morale in the North African Campaign: The Eighth Army and the Path to El Alamein*, (Cambridge, 2011, Cambridge University Press), p. 266
5. Christine Bielecki, *British Infantry Morale during the Italian Campaign 1943–1945*, (University of London, 2006, Unpublished PhD), p. 349
6. J. Fennell, *Combat and Morale in the North African Campaign*, p. 285; C. Bielecki, *British Infantry Morale*, p. 23
7. David French, *Raising Churchill's Army: The British Army and the War against Germany 1919–1945*, (Oxford, 2001, Oxford University Press), p. 74
8. TNA, WO 277/7, *Discipline 1939–1945*, (McPherson), p. 5
9. LHCMA, BRIDGEMAN 1/1, *Lord Gort's Despatches of the Operations of the BEF*, p. 89
10. Major L.F. Ellis, *The War in France and Flanders 1939–1940*, (London, 1953, HMSO), pp. xvi, 326
11. John Ellis, *The Sharp End: The Fighting Man in World War II*, (London, 1993, Pimlico), p. 263
12. D. French, (October 1998), 'Discipline and the Death Penalty in the British Army in the War against Germany during the Second World War', *Journal of Contemporary History*, Vol. 33, No. 4, p. 538

13. [Cmd. 5950], *The General Annual Report on the British Army (for the Year Ending 31 December 1938), Parliamentary Papers,* February 1939, p. 20

14. [Cmd. 5950], *General Annual Report of the British Army 1938, Parliamentary Papers,* p. 26

15. S.P. Mackenzie, *Politics and Military Morale: Current-Affairs and Citizenship Education in the British Army 1914–1950,* (Oxford, 1992, Oxford University Press), p. 58; D. French, *Raising Churchill's Army,* p. 136

16. [Cmd. 5686], *The General Annual Report on the British Army (for the Year Ending 30 September 1937), Parliamentary Papers,* March 1938, pp. 22, 59

17. TNA, WO 277/7, *Discipline 1939–1945,* (McPherson): APPENDIX 1A – Comprehensive Summary of Courts-Martial Convictions 1939–45 (British OR), p. 1

18. NAM, No. 1994-03-12, *Memoirs of L. Arlington, 2nd Middlesex Regiment 1939–1945,* p. 12

19. IWM, F. Southall, 84/36/1, *Memoirs,* p. 19

20. TNA, WO 82/28, *Judge Advocate General's Office: Daily Register of Letters (Day Books) – Military Department, February 1939–January 1940,* p. 149

21. TNA, WO 277/7, *Discipline 1939–1945,* (McPherson), APPENDIX 1A, p. 1

22. TNA, WO 90/8, *JAG Office: General Courts-Martial Register (Abroad) 1917–1943. pp. 107–9;* TNA, WO 213/35, *Field General Courts-Martial Register: (Abroad Only), Volume No. 35, October 1939-April 1942,* pp. 1–81

23. Timothy Bowman, *The Irish Regiments in the Great War: Discipline and Morale,* (Manchester, 2003, Manchester University Press), pp. 16–17

24. Cathryn Corns & John Hughes Wilson, *Blindfold and Alone: British Military Executions in the Great War,* (London, 2001, Cassell & Co), p. 503; TNA, WO 90/8, *JAG Office: GCM Register (Abroad) 1917–43,* pp. 107–9; TNA WO 213/35, *FGCM Register: (Abroad Only), Vol. 35, 1939–1942;* IWM, Lieutenant Colonel E. Thornhill, 99/36/1, *Memoirs,* p. 69

25. TNA, WO 90/8, *JAG Office: GCM Register (Abroad) 1917–43,* pp. 107–9; TNA, WO 213/35, *FGCM Register: (Abroad Only), Vol. 35, 1939–1942,* pp. 1–81

26. TNA, WO 167/11, *BEF Adjutant General's War Diary September 1939–May 1940, (December),* p. 10

27. Omer Bartov, *Hitler's Army: Soldiers, Nazis and War in the Third Reich,* (Oxford, 1991, Oxford University Press), pp. 64–8

28. TNA, WO 90/8, *JAG Office: GCM Register (Abroad) 1917–43,* pp. 107–9; TNA, WO 213/35, *FGCM Register: (Abroad Only), Vol. 35, 1939–1942,* pp. 1–81; [Cmd. 5686], *General Annual Report of the British Army 1937, Parliamentary Papers,* p. 59

29. TNA, WO 167/11, *BEF Adjutant General's War Diary, (November)* p. 4, *(December)* p. 9

30. TNA, WO 167/1354, *Provost No. 1 Military Prison War Diary, September 1939–April 1940, (December),* p. 1

31. TNA, WO 167/11, *BEF Adjutant General's War Diary, (December)* p. 2

32. TNA, WO 90/8, *JAG Office: GCM Register (Abroad) 1917–43,* pp. 107–9; TNA, WO 213/35, *FGCM Register: (Abroad Only), Vol. 35, 1939–1942,* pp. 1–81; Nicholas Harman, *Dunkirk: The Necessary Myth,* (London, 1980, Hodder & Stoughton), p. 113

33. TNA, WO 90/8, *JAG Office: GCM Register (Abroad) 1917–43,* pp 107–9; TNA, WO 213/35, *FGCM Register: (Abroad Only), Vol. 35, 1939–1942,* pp. 1–81;

J. Ellis, *The Sharp End*, pp. 227–9; TNA, WO 167/1354, *Provost No. 1 Military Prison, (September 1939)* p. 1, *(October)* p. 2

34. TNA, WO 90/8, *JAG Office: GCM Register (Abroad) 1917–43*, pp. 107–9; TNA, WO 213/35, *FGCM Register: (Abroad Only), Vol. 35, 1939–1942*, pp. 1–81

35. TNA, WO 90/8, *JAG Office: GCM Register (Abroad) 1917–43*, pp. 107–9; TNA, WO 213/35, *FGCM Register: (Abroad Only), Vol. 35, 1939–1942*, pp. 1–81

36. TNA, WO 90/8, *JAG Office: GCM Register (Abroad) 1917–43*, pp. 107–9; TNA, WO 213/35, *FGCM Register :(Abroad Only), Vol. 35, 1939–1942*, pp. 1–81

37. IWM, A. Gaskin, 87/44/1, *Memoirs*, p. 19

38. IWM, Captain J. Ogden, 67/267/1, *Memoirs*, pp. 16, 19

39. NAM, No. 1994-03-12, *Memoirs of L. Arlington*, p. 27

40. TNA, WO 90/8, *JAG Office: GCM Register (Abroad) 1917–43*, pp. 107–9; TNA, WO 213/35, *FGCM Register: (Abroad Only) Vol. 35, 1939–1942*, pp. 1–81

41. Anon, *Infantry Officer*, (London, 1943, B.T. Batsford Ltd), p. 24

42. Brigadier C.N. Barclay, *The History of the Duke of Wellington's Regiment 1919–1952*, (London, 1953, William Clowes & Sons Ltd), p. 198

43. TNA, WO 90/8, *JAG Office: GCM Register (Abroad) 1917–43*, p. 107; TNA, WO 167/362, *8th Infantry Brigade War Diary, September 1939–June 1940, (October)* p. 11, *(December)* p. 6; IWM, Captain J. Ogden, 67/267/1, *Memoirs*, p. 36

44. TNA, WO 90/8, *JAG Office: GCM Register (Abroad) 1917–43*, pp. 107–9; TNA, WO 213/35, *FGCM Register: (Abroad Only), Vol. 35, 1939–1942*, pp. 1–81

45. LHCMA, BRIDGEMAN 7/1, *Letter on BEF, dated 10/10/75*, p. 3

46. David Rissik, *The DLI At War*, (London, 1953, Charles Birchall & Sons Ltd), p. 7

47. Wilfred Saunders, *Dunkirk Diary of a Very Young Soldier*, (Studley, 2010, Brewin Books), p. 73

48. Brian Bond, 'The British Field Force in France and Belgium 1939–1940', in P. Addison & A. Calder, (eds), *Time to Kill: The Soldier's Experience of War in the West*, (London, 1997, Pimlico), p. 42

49. NAM, No. 1994-03-12, *Memoirs of L. Arlington*, p. 25; IWM, Signaller L. Cannon, 79/27/1, *Memoirs*, p. 15

50. [Hansard], *Written Answers (Commons), 14/03/40, Parliamentary Papers*, p. 1

51. Tommy Thomas, *Signal Success*, (Lewes, 1995, The Book Guild Ltd), pp. 93–5; NAM, No. 1994-03-12, *Memoirs of L. Arlington*, p. 25

52. W. Saunders, *Dunkirk Diary*, pp. 27, 37–8; T. Thomas, *Signal Success*, pp. 95, 108; 'Exchange Rates in 1939', Times [London, England] 3 January 1940: p. 12, *The Times Digital Archive*. Web 16 July 2012; TNA, WO 167/840, *1/7th Royal Warwickshire Regiment War Diary January – May 1940, (January)* p. 1, *(February)* p. 2

53. John Keegan, 'Towards a Theory of Combat Motivation' in P. Addison & A. Calder, (eds), *Time to Kill*, p. 10; W. Saunders, *Dunkirk Diary*, p. 38

54. IWM, Captain J. Ogden, 67/267/1, *Memoirs*, p. 15

55. NAM, No. 1994-03-12, *Memoirs of L. Arlington*, p. 32

56. TNA, WO 167/1354, *Provost No. 1 Military Prison War Diary, (December)* pp. 1–2

57. IWM, Captain J. Ogden, 67/267/1, *Memoirs*, p. 41

58. TNA, WO 167/11, *BEF Adjutant General's War Diary, (October)* p. 5; W. Saunders, *Dunkirk Diary*, p. 44

59. IWM, Major J. Finch, 90/6/1, *Memoirs*, p. 7

60. TNA, WO 167/215, *2nd Division Provost Company War Diary, September 1939–June 1940, (January)* p. 2; TNA, WO 167/1345, *Deputy Assistant Provost*

Marshal (GHQ) War Diary, September 1939–April 1940, Minutes from 23/11/39 Provost Marshal's Conference, APPENDIX B p. 3; IWM, Captain J. Ogden 67/267/1, *Memoirs,* p. 44

61. TNA, WO 90/8, *JAG Office: GCM Register (Abroad) 1917–43,* pp. 107–9; TNA, WO 213/35, *FGCM Register: (Abroad Only), Vol. 35, 1939–1942,* pp. 1–81; O. Bartov, *Hitler's Army,* pp. 68–9

62. IWM, Major J. Finch, 90/6/1, *Dunkirk Memoirs,* p. 1

63. Lieutenant Colonel H.D. Chaplin, *The Queen's Own Royal West Kent Regiment 1920–1950,* (London, 1954, Michael Joseph Ltd), p. 127

64. IWM, Captain J. Ogden, 67/267/1, *Memoirs,* p. 53

65. NAM, No. 2001-02-444, *Reports by Various Officers and NCOs on Buffs 1939–1945: Personal Diary of Captain E. Edlmann, 2nd Buffs Regiment, 10–29 May 1940,* p. 2

66. IWM, Captain J. Ogden, 67/267/1, *Memoirs,* p. 93

67. TNA, WO 90/8, *JAG Office: GCM Register (Abroad) 1917–43,* pp. 107–9; TNA, WO 213/35, *FGCM Register: (Abroad Only), Vol. 35, 1939–1942,* pp. 1–81

68. IWM, Major General W. Richards, 84/32/1, *Accommodation Requirements of Field Force dated 01/04/40,* p. 1

69. TNA, WO 167/1345, *DAPM GHQ War Diary, Minutes from 23/11/39 PM Conference,* APPENDIX B, p. 1

70. IWM, Major J. Finch, 90/6/1, *Memoirs,* p. 2

71. TNA, WO 167/1345, *DAPM GHQ War Diary, Minutes from 23/11/39 PM Conference,* APPENDIX B, p. 1

72. TNA, WO 167/201, *1st Division Provost Company War Diary, September 1939–January 1940, (January),* p. 2; [HANSARD] *Written Answers (Commons) 14/03/40, Parliamentary Papers,* p. 1

73. Omer Bartov, *Hitler's Army,* p. 68

74. TNA, WO 167/24, *RASC GHQ War Diary September 1939–May 1940: CRASC, GHQ Routine Orders 12/10/39 and 26/10/39,* p. 1; TNA, WO 167/1076, *GHQ Supply Directorate Transport (Petrol) RASC War Diary September 1939–May 1940, (October)* p. 5, *(November)* pp. 15–16, *(December)* p. 7, *(January)* p. 1, *(February)* p. 7

75. W. Saunders, *Dunkirk Diary,* p. 7

76. NAM, No. 2000-11-55, *Papers of A. Notley, 1/7th Middlesex and 9th Parachute Regiment 1940–1944, Undated Letter,* p. 1

77. NAM, No. 1994-03-19, *Memoirs of A. Barrell,* p. 3

78. [Cmd. 5686], *General Annual Report on the British Army 1937, Parliamentary Papers,* p. 59; D. French, *Raising Churchill's Army,* p. 130; TNA, WO 277/7, *Discipline 1939–1945, (McPherson),* APPENDIX 1A, p. 1; C. Bielecki, *British Infantry Morale,* p. 348; TNA, WO 90/8, *JAG Office: GCM Register (Abroad) 1917–43,* pp. 107–9; TNA, WO 213/35, *FGCM Register: (Abroad Only), Vol. 35, 1939–1942,* pp. 1–81; IWM, Major General P. Martin, 07/7/1, *Manuscripts & Letters January 1939–November 1947, Letter dated 05/03/40,* p. 1; NAM, No. 2000-11-55, *Papers of A. Notley 1940–1944, Undated Letter,* p. 2

79. TNA, WO 167/1345, *DAPM GHQ War Diary, Minutes of 23/11/39 PM Conference,* APPENDIX B, p. 3; W. Saunders, *Dunkirk Diary,* p. 57; P. Hadley, *Third Class to Dunkirk: A Worm's Eye View of the BEF 1940,* (Bath, 1944, Hollis & Carter Ltd), p. 121; C. Bielecki, *British Infantry Morale,* p. 349

80. P. Hadley, *Third Class to Dunkirk,* p. 121

81. IWM, Captain J. Ogden, 67/267/1, *Memoirs,* p. 162

82. TNA, WO 277/7, *Discipline 1939–1945, (McPherson)*, pp. 25–7; TNA, WO 167/1354, *Provost No. 1 Military Prison War Diary, (November)* p. 6, *(December)* p. 3, *(January)* p. 1

83. TNA, WO 167/1354, *Provost No. 1 Military Prison War Diary, (January)* p. 2, *(April)* p. 4

84. TNA, WO 82/41, *JAG Office: Daily Register of Letters (Day Books), Judicial Department, September 1938–March 1940*, p. 155

85. TNA, WO 167/1354, *Provost No. 1 Military Prison War Diary, (November)* p. 5, *(January)* p. 1, *(March)* p. 3

86. TNA, WO 167/1345, *DAPM GHQ War Diary, (April)* p. 1

87. TNA, WO 167/840, *1/7th Royal Warwickshire Regiment War Diary January – May 1940, (February)* pp. 7–11, (March) pp. 1–9; TNA, WO 90/8, *JAG Office: GCM Register (Abroad) 1917–43*, p. 108

88. TNA, WO 167/840, *1/7th Royal Warwickshire Regiment War Diary, (February)* pp. 7–11, *(March)* pp. 1–9; TNA, WO 90/8, *JAG Office: GCM Register (Abroad) 1917–43*, p. 108

89. IWM, Major J. Finch, 90/6/1, *Memoirs*, p. 7

90. IWM, Brigadier R. Boxshall, 84/41/1, *Memoirs*, pp. 3–4

91. Brian Bond, 'The British Field Force in France and Belgium 1939–1940' in P. Addison & A. Calder (eds), *Time to Kill*, p. 47

92. LHCMA, BRIDGEMAN 1/1, *Lord Gort's Despatches*, p. 87

93. L. Ellis, *The War in France and Flanders*, p. 62

94. Brigadier C. Barclay, *Duke of Wellington's Regiment 1919–1952*, p. 35

95. TNA, WO 167/707, *4th Royal Berkshire Regiment War Diary January – June 1940, (April Standing Order)*, p. 1

96. IWM, Lieutenant Colonel J. Birch MISC 105 ITEM 1667, *Diary of the CO 2nd Battalion, Bedfordshire & Hertfordshire Regiment (May to early June 1940)*, p. 6

97. IWM, Lieutenant Colonel J. Birch MISC 105 ITEM 1667, *Personal Diary of Lieutenant Colonel J. Birch*, pp. 18–20

98. Hugh Sebag-Montefiore, *Dunkirk: Fight to the Last Man*, (London, 2006, Viking), p. 134

99. Gerry Rubin, *Murder, Mutiny and the Military: British Court Martial Cases 1940–1966*, (London, 2005, Francis Boutle Publishers), p. 57

100. TNA, WO 167/215, *2nd Division Provost Company War Diary, (April)*, p. 2

101. TNA, WO 167/707, *4th Royal Berkshire Regiment War Diary, Operation Order No. 7 (11/05/40)*, p. 2

102. H. Sebag-Montefiore, *Dunkirk: Fight to the Last Man*, p. 134

103. TNA, WO 167/215, *2nd Division Provost Company War Diary, (May)*, p. 2

104. NAM, No. 1994-05-188, *D Company, 2nd Middlesex Regiment War Diary, (May 1940)*, p. 2

105. TNA, WO 167/571, *1st Survey Regiment RA War Diary September 1939–June 1940, (May)*, p. 7

106. NAM, No. 1994-03-12, *Memoirs of L. Arlington*, p. 50

107. Brian Bond, 'The British Field Force in France and Belgium 1939–1940' in P. Addison & A. Calder (eds), *Time to Kill*, p. 46

108. IWM, Captain J. Ogden, 67/267/1, *Memoirs*, p. 121

109. IWM, Captain J. Ogden, 67/267/1, *Memoirs*, pp. 147–8

110. NAM, No. 2001-02-444, *Personal Diary of Captain E. Edlmann*, p. 3

111. TNA, WO 167/215, *2nd Division Provost Company War Diary, (May)*, p. 2
112. NAM, No. 1994-05-188, *D Company, 2nd Middlesex Regiment War Diary (May 1940)*, p. 9
113. IWM, Captain J. Ogden, 67/267/1, *Memoirs*, p. 120
114. TNA, WO 167/707, *4th Royal Berkshire Regiment War Diary, (May)*, p. 2
115. Anon, *Infantry Officer*, p. 40
116. P. Hadley, *Third Class to Dunkirk*, p. 86
117. TNA, WO 106/1775, *Bartholomew Committee Report on the Operations in Flanders 1940 (July 1940)*, pp. 2–3
118. L. Ellis, *The War in France and Flanders*, p. 19
119. Brian Bond, 'The British Field Force in France and Belgium 1939–1940' in P. Addison & A. Calder (eds), *Time to Kill*, p. 41
120. NAM, No. 2001-02-444, *Personal Diary of Captain E. Edlmann*, p. 2
121. IWM, Lieutenant Colonel J. Birch, MISC 105 ITEM 1667, *Personal Diary of Lieutenant Colonel J. Birch*, pp. 6–8
122. IWM, Captain J. Ogden, 67/267/1, *Memoirs*, p. 168
123. TNA, WO 167/707, *4th Royal Berkshire Regiment War Diary, (May)* pp. 4–5, *(June)* p. 1; TNA, WO 167/832, *1st Suffolk Regiment War Diary September 1939–June 1940, (June)* pp. 1–2; Brigadier Gordon Blight, *The History of the Royal Berkshire Regiment 1920–1947*, (London, 1953, Staples Press Ltd), p. 184
124. IWM, Lieutenant Colonel J. Birch MISC 105 ITEM 1667, *Personal Diary of Lieutenant Colonel J. Birch*, p. 12
125. TNA, WO 167/571, *1st Survey Regiment RA War Diary, (May)*, p. 3; IWM, Captain J. Ogden, 67/267/1, *Memoirs*, p. 68
126. TNA, WO 167/832, *1st Suffolk Regiment War Diary, (May)*, p. 5; Anon, *Infantry Officer*, p. 70
127. Brian Bond, 'The British Field Force in France and Belgium 1939–1940' in P. Addison & A. Calder (eds), *Time to Kill*, p. 45
128. IWM, A. Towle, 84/33/1, *Memoirs*, pp. 8–9
129. IWM, Signaller L. Cannon, 79/27/1, *Memoirs*, pp. 26–9
130. P. Hadley, *Third Class to Dunkirk*, p. 137
131. NAM, No. 1994-03-136, *War Diary of Captain T. Marks, A Company, 1/8th Middlesex Regiment, May 1940*, p. 4
132. *Right or Wrong? Elements of Training and Leadership Illustrated 1937*, (London, 1937, HMSO), p. 7
133. W. Saunders, *Dunkirk Diary*, pp. 78–9, 92; Brigadier G. Blight, *The History of the Royal Berkshire Regiment 1920–1947*, p. 208; TNA, WO 167/707, *4th Royal Berkshire Regiment War Diary, (May)*, p. 5; IWM, Captain J. Ogden, 67/267/1, *Memoirs*, p. 175; P. Hadley, *Third Class to Dunkirk*, p. 142
134. NAM, No. 1994-05-188, *D Company, 2nd Middlesex Regiment War Diary, (May 1940)*, p. 11
135. IWM, Major J. Finch, 90/6/1, *Memoirs*, p. 9
136. TNA, WO 167/832, *1st Suffolk Regiment War Diary, (June)* p. 1
137. D. French, *Raising Churchill's Army*, p. 147
138. P. Hadley, *Third Class to Dunkirk*, p. 140
139. Max Arthur, *Forgotten Voices of The Second World War*, (Haydock, 2004, The Book People Ltd), p. 65
140. L. Ellis, *The War in France and Flanders*, p. 247

141. Mark Connelly & Walter Miller, (2004), 'The BEF and the Issue of Surrender on the Western Front in 1940', *War in History*, Vol. 11, No. 4, p. 436
142. L. Ellis, *The War in France and Flanders*, p. 302
143. TNA, WO 163/415, *Report of the Committee on the Evacuation of the BEF from the French Ports, November 1940*, pp. 4–7
144. TNA, WO 163/415, *Report of the Committee on the Evacuation of the BEF from the French Ports, November 1940*, pp. 12–13, 20–1
145. TNA, WO 277/16, *Morale 1939–1945, (Official History of Morale, Compiled by Lieutenant Colonel J. Sparrow, 1949)*, p. 1
146. TNA, WO 277/7, *Discipline 1939–1945, (McPherson)*, p. 22
147. T. Thomas, *Signal Success*, p. 115
148. IWM, Major R. Cowan, 07/25/1, *Reminiscences*, p. 11
149. TNA, WO 167/260, *12th Division Provost Company War Diary, April – May 1940, (May)*, p. 2

7 Headquarters and Staff

1. TNA, WO 277/36, *Official History of Training 1939–1945, (compiled by Lieutenant Colonel J.W. Gibb)*, p. 6; TNA 355.3.WOM, *Army List September 1939*, pp. 1–1860; *Army List December 1939*, pp. 91–5; *Army List April 1940*, pp. 1–3582
2. Lieutenant Colonel F.W. Young, *The Story of the Staff College 1858–1958*, (Camberley, 1958, Gale & Polden Ltd), p. 7
3. LHCMA, BRIDGEMAN 1/1, *Lord Gort's Despatches of the Operations of the BEF*, p. 90
4. Brian Bond (ed.), *Chief of Staff: The Diaries of Lieutenant General Sir Henry Pownall – Volume One 1933–1940*, (London, 1972, Leo Cooper Ltd), pp. 359, 366–7
5. Major L.F. Ellis, *The War in France and Flanders 1939–1940*, (London, 1953, HMSO), pp. xiii, xv
6. Andy Simpson, *Directing Operations: British Corps Command On The Western Front 1914–18*, (Strood, 2006, Spellmount), pp. xiii, xv
7. TNA, WO 106/1775, *Bartholomew Committee Report On The Operations in Flanders 1940, (July 1940)*, p. 4
8. David French, *Raising Churchill's Army: The British Army and the War against Germany 1919–1945*, (Oxford, 2001, Oxford University Press), pp. 215–20, 226–30
9. Timothy Harrison Place, *Military Training in the British Army 1940–1944: From Dunkirk to D-Day*, (London, 2000, Frank Cass Publishers), pp. 157–9
10. A. Simpson, *Directing Operations*, pp. 224–5
11. TNA, 355.6.REG, *Field Service Regulations Vol. II (1935): Operations – General*, p. ix
12. IWM, *Field Service Regulations Vol. III (December 1935): Operations – Higher Formations*, pp. 12, 17–19, 27
13. Victoria Schofield, *Wavell: Soldier and Statesman*, (London, 2006, John Murray Publishers), pp. 103–5
14. John Connell, *Wavell: Scholar and Soldier – To June 1941*, (London, 1964, Collins) pp. 160–1

15. A. Simpson, Directing Operations, p. xvi
16. IWM, *FSR Vol. III (December 1935): Operations – H. Formations,* pp. 27–8, 30, 50–1, 54
17. Keith Jeffery, *Field Marshal Sir Henry Wilson: A Political Soldier,* (Oxford, 2008, Oxford University Press), pp. 80–1
18. IWM, Brigadier A. Walch, 01/11/2, *Memoirs,* p. 28
19. TNA, 355.6.FIE, *Field Service Pocket Book 1939–1940 (Pamphlets 1–13): FSPB Pamphlet No. 11 (1939) – Discipline, Office Work and Burial Parties,* p. 12
20. IWM, Brigadier A. Walch, 01/11/2, *Memoirs,* p. 28; IWM, Lieutenant Colonel E. Brush, 85/8/1, *Memoirs,* p. 58
21. IWM, Lieutenant Colonel T. Durrant, 05/44/1, *Memoirs,* p. 19
22. IWM, S. Beard, 06/99/1, *Memoirs,* p. 4
23. D. French, *Raising Churchill's Army,* p. 164
24. Tommy Thomas, *Signal Success,* (Lewes, 1995, The Book Guild Ltd), pp. 95, 108
25. IWM, Lieutenant Colonel E. Thornhill, 99/36/1, *Memoirs,* pp. 63–4
26. IWM, Brigadier J. Faviell, 82/24/1, *Memoirs – (Chapter 6) War Office & War Again,* p. 2
27. IWM, Major General L. Hawes, 87/4/1, *Memoirs,* p. W1
28. Andrew Cunningham, *A Sailor's Odyssey: The Autobiography of Admiral of the Fleet Viscount Cunningham of Hyndhope,* (London, 1952, Hutchinson & Co Ltd), p. 89
29. IWM, Major General G. Richards, 07/21/1, *Memoirs,* p. 31
30. IWM, Brigadier A. Walch, 01/11/2, *Memoirs,* p. 37
31. IWM, Colonel K. Chavasse, 98/23/1, *Memoirs,* p. 57
32. IWM, Brigadier J. Whitehead, 97/10/1, *Memoirs,* p. 36
33. D. French, *Raising Churchill's Army,* p. 164
34. BL, *Training Regulations 1934 (With Amendments) – With Special Reference to Manoeuvres,* pp. 113–116
35. IWM, Major General J. Haydon, 93/28/1, JCH 3/1, *Student Exercise No. 3 – Inter-Brigade Exercise with Troops (20/03/36),* pp. 1–3
36. 'Four Generations Of Staff College Students', *Army Quarterly,* October 1952, pp. 19–30, in Lieutenant Colonel F.W. Young, *The Story of the Staff College 1858–1958,* p. 26
37. IWM, Major J. Finch, 90/6/1, *Memoirs,* p. 1
38. P. Gribble, *The Diary of a Staff Officer,* (London, 1941, Methuen & Co Ltd), p. 3
39. B. Bond (ed.), *Chief of Staff,* pp. 366–7
40. Brigadier Gordon Blight, *The History of the Royal Berkshire Regiment (Princess Charlotte of Wales's) 1920–1947,* (London, 1953, Staples Press Ltd), pp. 131, 133; Colonel C.R.B. Knight, *Historical Records of the Buffs 1919–1948,* (London, 1951, The Medici Society Ltd) pp. 22–4, 27–9
41. *Official History of Operations on the N.W. Frontier of India 1936–1937,* (New Delhi, 1943, Manager of Publications, Delhi), pp. 26, 235
42. *Official History of Operations on the N.W. Frontier of India 1936–37,* pp. iv, 3; Brigadier C.N. Barclay, *The History of the Duke of Wellington's Regiment 1919–1952,* (London, 1953, William Clowes & Sons Ltd), pp. 12, 17; BL, *Nowshera Brigade: Standing Orders for War 1938,* p. 33
43. BL, *Battalion Standing Orders for War for Rifle Battalions,* (Aldershot, 1939, Gale & Polden Ltd), p. 5

44. BL, *Training Regulations 1934*, p. 19
45. TNA, 355.6.FIE, *FSPB 1939–40, Pamphlet No. 11, 1939*, p. 12
46. TNA, WO 191/70, *Military Lessons of the 1936 Arab Rebellion in Palestine, Written by General Staff Headquarters, British Forces Palestine and Trans-Jordan, February 1938*, p. 169
47. Peter Hadley, *Third Class to Dunkirk: A Worm's Eye View of the BEF 1940*, (London, 1944, Hollis & Carter Ltd), p. 34
48. F. Young, *The Story of the Staff College 1858–1958*, pp. 1, 7; Brian Bond, *The Victorian Army and the Staff College 1854–1914*, (London, 1972, Eyre & Methuen Ltd), pp. 76–7, 176–7, 202–3
49. B. Bond, *The Victorian Army and the Staff College 1854–1914*, pp. 3, 175, 326; Karl Demeter, *The German Officer-Corps in Society and State 1650–1945*, (London, 1965, Weidenfeld & Nicholson), pp. 104–5
50. B. Bond, *The Victorian Army and the Staff College 1854–1914*, p. 328
51. F. Young, *The Story of the Staff College 1858–1958*, p. 7; David French, *Military Identities: The Regimental System, the British Army and the British People c. 1870–2000*, (Oxford, 2008, Oxford University Press), p. 163
52. D. French, *Military Identities*, pp. 160–1
53. F. Young, *The Story of the Staff College 1858–1958*, p. 22; D. French, *Raising Churchill's Army*, p. 62
54. IWM, Lieutenant Colonel E. Brush, 85/8/1, *Memoirs*, p. 56
55. IWM, Lieutenant Colonel E. Thornhill, 99/36/1, *Memoirs*, p. 53; IWM, Brigadier J. Faviell, 82/24/1, *Memoirs*, ch. 4, pp. 10, 12
56. 'Four Generations of Staff College Students', *Army Quarterly*, October 1952, pp. 19–30, in F. Young, *The Story of the Staff College 1858–1958*, p. 25
57. IWM, Lieutenant Colonel E. Brush, 85/8/1, *Memoirs*, pp. 56–8
58. F. Young, *The Story of the Staff College 1858–1958*, p. 4
59. TNA, WO 32/3091, *Staff College Allotment of Vacancies by Competition 1927, Letter from Staff College to DSD (15/06/1927)*, pp. 1–2, *Letter from DSD to CIGS (15/07/1927)*, pp. 1–2, *Conclusions of Report on Competitive Vacancies (15/08/1927)*, pp. 1–3
60. TNA, WO 32/3103, *Entrance and Selection of Officers for Staff College (28/04/1927) – Meeting No. 529 of Army Council Military Members*, pp. 1–5
61. I.F.W. Beckett, *The Amateur Military Tradition 1558–1945*, (Manchester, 1991, Manchester University Press), p. 255; D. French, *Raising Churchill's Army*, p. 64
62. F. Young, *The Story of the Staff College 1858–1958*, p. 4
63. D. French, *Raising Churchill's Army*, p. 63
64. IWM, Major General J. Haydon, 93/28/1, JCH 3/1, *Paper V (20/03/35), Paper Z (02/06/35), Winchester Appreciation (05/07/35), Paper 1 (23/01/36), Student Exercise No. 3: Inter-Brigade Exercise With Troops (20/03/36)*, p. 1
65. IWM, Colonel K. Chavasse, 98/23/1, *Memoirs*, pp. 51–3
66. F. Young, *The Story of the Staff College 1858–1958*. p. i
67. Bernard Montgomery, *The Memoirs of Field Marshal The Viscount Montgomery of Alamein*, (London, 1968, Collins), p. 40; IWM, Major General G. Richards, 02/21/1, *Memoirs*, p. 28
68. Nikolas Gardner, *Trial by Fire: Command and the British Expeditionary Force in 1914*, (Westport, USA, 2003, Praeger Publisher), p. 23–4

69. Colonel R. Macleod & Denis Kelly (eds), *The Ironside Diaries 1937–1940*, (London, 1963, Constable & Company Ltd), p. 352
70. IWM, Brigadier J. Faviell, 82/24/1, *Memoirs*, ch. 4, p. 12
71. IWM, Lieutenant Colonel E. Thornhill, 99/36/1, *Memoirs*, p. 54; 'Four Generations of Staff College Students', *Army Quarterly*, October 1952, pp. 19–30, in F. Young, *The Story of the Staff College 1858–1958*, p. 28
72. IWM, Brigadier J. Faviell, 82/24/1, *Memoirs*, ch. 4, p. 12
73. IWM, Major General J. Haydon, 93/28/1, JCH 3/1, *Paper V (20/03/35)* pp. 1–3, *Student Exercise No. 3 (20/03/36)*, *Strategy Discussion (07/02/36)*, *Paper No. 3 – British Strategy (10/04/36)*, p. 1
74. 'Four Generations of Staff College Students', *Army Quarterly*, October 1952, pp. 19–30, in F.W. Young, *The Story of the Staff College 1858–1958*, p. 27
75. IWM, Colonel K. Chavasse, 98/23/1, *Memoirs*, p. 52
76. TNA, WO 190/585, *Notes on German Staff College (13/12/1937)*, pp. 1–2
77. D. French, *Military Identities*, p. 162
78. IWM, Major General J. Haydon, 93/28/1, JCH 3/1 *Paper No. 3 British Strategy (10/04/36)*, *Strategy Discussion (07/02/36)*, pp. 1–3
79. 'Four Generations of Staff College Student', *Army Quarterly*, October 1952, pp. 19–30, in F. Young, *The Story of the Staff College 1858–1958*, p. 26
80. N. Gardner, *Trial by Fire*, p. 37
81. LHCMA, KIRKE 4/4, *May 1932 Notes by Major General A. McNamara (DMT) on Training in Peacetime and War*, p. 1
82. IWM, Brigadier J. Faviell, 82/24/1, *Memoirs*, ch. 4, p. 12
83. IWM, Major General J. Haydon, 93/28/1, JCH 3/1, *Paper Z (02/06/35)*, pp. 1, 15
84. IWM, Major General J. Haydon, 93/28/1, JCH 3/1, *Strategy Discussion (07/02/36)*, pp. 1, 4
85. B. Montgomery, *Memoirs*, p. 61
86. IWM, Major General J. Haydon, 93/28/1, JCH 3/1, *Winchester Appreciation (05/07/35)*, p. 1; TNA, WO 33/1474, *Continental War Exercise For German and French Syndicates 1937*, p. 1
87. F. Young, *The Story of the Staff College 1858–1958*, pp. 10, 13, 17
88. V. Schofield, *Wavell: Soldier & Statesman*, pp. 104–5
89. J. Connell, *Wavell: Scholar and Soldier*, pp. 171–2
90. Martin Alexander, *The Republic in Danger: General Maurice Gamelin and the Politics of French Defence 1933–1940*, (Cambridge, 2002, Cambridge University Press), pp. 45–6, 242
91. M. Alexander, *The Republic in Danger*, pp. 31–2, 34–6, 381–3
92. IWM, Major General J. Haydon, 93/28/1 JCH 3/1, *Winchester Appreciation (05/07/35) – Role of Air Cooperation Appendix*, p. 1; *Official History of the N.W. Frontier of India 1936–37*, pp. 15, 18, 25–7
93. F. Young, *The Story of the Staff College 1858–1958*, pp. 10, 13, 28–9
94. J.P. Harris, 'The British General Staff and the Coming of War 1933–1939' in David French & Brian Holden Reid (eds), *The British General Staff: Reform and Innovation c. 1890–1939*, (London, 2002, Frank Cass), p. 176
95. IWM, Lieutenant Colonel E. Thornhill, 99/36/1, *Memoirs*, pp. 57–9, 62
96. IWM, Brigadier J. Faviell, 82/24/1, *Memoirs*, ch. 6, p. 3
97. Brigadier T. Gray, *The Imperial Defence College and the Royal College of Defence Studies 1927–1977*, (Edinburgh, 1977, HMSO), pp. 3, 6–11

98. A. Cunningham, *A Sailor's Odyssey*, pp. 138–9
99. J. Connell, *Wavell: Scholar and Soldier*, pp. 170–1; T. Gray, *The Imperial Defence College*, p. 5
100. T. Gray, *The Imperial Defence College*, pp. 8–14
101. F. Young, *The Story of the Staff College 1858–1958*, p. 4
102. TNA, WO 167/21, *GHQ Staff Duties and Training War Diary September 1939– May 1940 (January)*, p. 1; TNA, WO 167/215, *2nd Division Provost Company War Diary September 1939–June 1940 (December)*, p. 4
103. TNA, WO 167/148, *II Corps War Diary September 1939–June 1940 (January)*, pp. 2–4; Alex Danchev & Daniel Todman (eds), *War Diaries 1939–1945: Field Marshal Lord Alanbrooke*, (London, 2002, Phoenix Press), pp. 28–9
104. TNA, WO 167/357, *6th Infantry Brigade War Diary September 1939–June 1940 (December)*, p. 3
105. TNA, WO 167/21, *GHQ SD & T War Diary (November)* p. 8; TNA, 355.6.WOM, *Army List (April 1940)*, p. 1300
106. IWM, Brigadier A. Walch, 01/11/2, *Memoirs*, p. 39
107. TNA, WO 167/148, *II Corps War Diary: 2 Corps Training Instruction (26/11/39), Appendix TT*, p. 2
108. TNA, WO 277/36, *Training 1939–45 (Gibb)*, p. 6
109. IWM, A. Walch, 01/11/2, *Memoirs*, p. 40
110. N. Gardner, *Trial by Fire*, pp. 22–3
111. David French, (November 1996), 'Colonel Blimp and the British Army: British Divisional Commanders in the War against Germany 1939–1945', *English Historical Review*, Vol. 111, No. 444, p. 1187; D. French, *Military Identities*, p. 169
112. D. French, (November 1996), 'Colonel Blimp and the British Army: British Divisional Commanders in the War against Germany 1939–1945', *English Historical Review*, Vol. 111, No. 444, p. 1192
113. TNA, 355.3.WOM, *Army List December 1939*, pp. 91–5; *Army List April 1940*, pp. 1–3582; A. Danchev & D. Todman (eds), *War Diaries 1939–1945*, p. 141
114. Heinz Guderian, *Panzer Leader*, (London, 2000, Penguin Books Ltd), p. 98
115. TNA, 355.3.WOM, *Army List September 1939*, pp. 1–1860; *Army List April 1940*, pp. 1–3582
116. D. French, (November 1996), 'Colonel Blimp and the British Army: British Divisional Commanders in the War against Germany 1939–1945', *English Historical Review*, Vol. 111, No. 444, p. 1185
117. TNA, 355.3.WOM, *Army List September 1939*, pp. 1–1860; *Army List April 1940*, pp. 1–3582
118. TNA, WO 167/402, *150th Infantry Brigade War Diary January – June 1940 (April)*, p. 1; IWM, Colonel K. Chavasse, 98/23/1, *Memoirs*, pp. 53–4
119. A. Danchev & D. Todman (eds), *War Diaries 1939–1945*, p. 52; TNA, 355.6.WOM, *Army List April 1940*, pp. 1–3582
120. TNA, WO 167/11, *BEF GHQ Adjutant General War Diary September 1939– May 1940 (October)*, p. 1; B. Bond (ed.), *Chief of Staff*, pp. 232, 235, 242; A. Danchev & D. Todman (eds), *War Diaries 1939–1945*, pp. 4, 6; Colonel R. Macleod & D. Kelly (eds), *The Ironside Diaries*, p. 242
121. B. Bond (ed.), *Chief of Staff*, p. 242; B. Montgomery, *Memoirs*, p. 52

122. Brian Bond, *Britain, France and Belgium 1939–1940*, (London, 1990, Brassey's Ltd), p. 47

123. TNA, WO 167/24, *RASC GHQ War Diary September 1939–May 1940, (CRASC, GHQ Routine Order No. 3, 22/10/39)*, p. 1

124. TNA, WO 167/11, *BEF GHQ Adjutant General War Diary (December)*, p. 11; TNA, WO 167/1, *GHQ 2nd Echelon War Diary September 1939–June 1940 (December)*, p. 1

125. TNA, WO 167/1076, *GHQ Supply Directorate Transport (Petrol) RASC War Diary September 1939–May 1940 (January)*, p. 4

126. TNA, WO 167/33, *GHQ Paymaster-in-Chief War Diary September 1939–July 1940 (October)*, p. 1; TNA, WO 167/34, *GHQ Command Pay Office September 1939–May 1940, (September)* p. 3, *(November)* p. 1

127. TNA, WO 197/11, *Visits to BEF by War Office and other Staff Officers: Reports and Questionnaires – Questions Arising from Captain Dyke's Visit to GHQ from 01/11/39 to 04/11/39 (With Answers Obtained)*, p. 4

128. N. Gardner, *Trial by Fire*, pp. 37, 40

129. B. Bond (ed.), *Chief of Staff*, pp. 232, 241

130. TNA, WO 167/1076, *GHQ SDT (Petrol) War Diary (January)* p. 1

131. B. Bond (ed.), *Chief of Staff*, p. 289

132. P. Gribble, *The Diary of a Staff Officer*, p. 55

133. IWM, Lieutenant Colonel M. Reid, 83/37/1 & Con Shelf, *Report by Captain M. Reid, Liaison Officer, 1st (French) Army, Written 06/06/40*, p. 3

134. TNA, WO 197/23, *Demi-Official Correspondence between GHQ 1st Echelon BEF & British Military Mission in France October 1939–January 1940: Letter of Apology from Anglo-French Liaison Section at General Jamet's HQ to GHQ SD & T, dated 13/10/39*, p. 1

135. TNA, WO 167/203, *2nd Division War Diary September 1939–June 1940 (December)*, p. 2

136. TNA, WO 167/1076, *GHQ SDT (Petrol) War Diary (January)*, pp. 1–2

137. TNA, WO 167/224, *RASC GHQ War Diary (October)*, p. 3

138. TNA, WO 167/11, *BEF Adjutant General War Diary, (February)* p. 6, *APPENDIX UU, 10/02/40, War Office Concern at Expansion of Staffs*, pp. 1–2

139. TNA, WO 167/1, *GHQ 2nd Echelon War Diary, (September)* p. 2, *Field Returns for Other Ranks and Officers 02/12/39, 04/05/40, 06/05/40*, p. 1

140. TNA, WO 167/54, *No. 1 L of C HQ September 1939–June 1940, Field Returns for Other Ranks and Officers 04/05/40, 19/05/40, 30/05/40*, p. 1

141. TNA, WO 167/124, *I Corps War Diary September 1939–June 1940, I Corps Field Returns for Other Ranks and Officers 20/01/40, 05/05/40*, p. 1; TNA, WO 167/148, *II Corps War Diary, Field Returns for Other Ranks and Officers 20/01/40, 21/01/40, 13/04/40, 16/04/40, 30/04/40, 04/05/40, 06/05/40, 14/05/40*, p. 1

142. IWM, Lieutenant Colonel E. Thornhill, 99/36/1, *Memoirs*, pp. 64–7

143. TNA, WO 167/230, *4th Division War Diary September 1939–May 1940, Field Returns for Officers 23/03/40*, p. 1; TNA, WO 167/300, *50th Division War Diary January–May 1940, Field Returns for Officers 09/03/40 & 04/05/40*, p. 1

144. TNA, WO 167/21, *GHQ Staff Duties & Training War Diary, APPENDIX O – Notes on talk by Commander 4th Division on Division Exercise held 18–22*

March 1940, pp. 1–4, APPENDIX Y – *Report on talk by 5th Division GOC on Divisional Exercise 24–28 March 1940*, pp. 2–3

145. D. French, *Raising Churchill's Army*, pp. 182–3

146. TNA, WO 167/148, *II Corps War Diary*, (November) pp. 1–3, (January) pp. 1–10, (March Summary) p. 1, (March) pp. 1–9, (April) pp. 1–6, (May) pp. 5, 14

147. A. Simpson, *Directing Operations*, pp. 229–30, 237–8

148. TNA, WO 167/124, *I Corps War Diary* (January) pp. 1–13, (March) pp. 1–9

149. A. Danchev & D. Todman (eds), *War Diaries 1939–1945*, p. 58

150. TNA, WO 167/169, *III Corps War Diary April–May 1940*, (April) pp. 1–3; TNA, WO 167/275, *44th Division War Diary April – May 1940*, (April) pp. 7–8, (May) p. 1; NAM, No. 2001-02-444, *Reports by Various Officers & NCOs on the Buffs 1939–1945: Personal Diary of Captain E. Edlmann, 2nd Buffs Regiment, May 1940*, p. 2

151. TNA, WO 167/148, *II Corps War Diary (April)* pp. 1–3

152. TNA, WO 167/124, *I Corps War Diary (January)* pp. 1–13

153. D. French, *Raising Churchill's Army*, pp. 164–5

154. B. Bond (ed.), *Chief of Staff*, p. 315

155. IWM, Colonel K. Chavasse, 98/23/1, *Memoirs*, pp. 54–5

156. H. Guderian, *Panzer Leader*, pp. 100, 106

157. LHCMA, BRIDGEMAN 2/8, *BEF Report on the Organization of GHQ and HQ of Services with Recommendations*, pp. 1–3

158. B. Bond (ed.), *Chief of Staff*, p. 319

159. LHCMA, BRIDGEMAN 2/8, *BEF Report on the Organization of GHQ*, pp. 1–3; TNA, WO 167/124, *I Corps War Diary (Standing Orders)*, p. 3; B. Bond (ed.), *Chief of Staff*, p. 335

160. TNA, WO 106/1775, *Bartholomew Committee Report on the Operations in Flanders 1940*, (Evidence from 12/06/40), p. 6

161. A. Simpson, *Directing Operations*, p. xii

162. TNA, WO 106/1775, *Bartholomew Committee Report*, (Evidence from 12/06/40), pp. 7, 17–18; LHCMA, BRIDGEMAN 7/1, *Letter on BEF dated 10/10/75*, p. 3

163. IWM, Lieutenant General E. Osborne, 785 Con Shelf, *Personal Diary of Major General E. Osborne, 44th Division, May 1940*, pp. 4, 7; TNA, WO 167/169, *III Corps War Diary (May)*, p. 4

164. B. Montgomery, *Memoirs*, p. 59

165. IWM, Captain J. Ogden, 67/267/1, *Memoirs*, p. 1; TNA, WO 106/1775, *Bartholomew Committee Report*, (Evidence from 14/06/40), p. 4

166. TNA, WO 106/1775, *Bartholomew Committee Report*, pp. 1, 4–5, (Evidence from 12/06/40), pp. 1, 17–18, (Evidence from 14/06/40), pp. 1–4

167. LHCMA, BRIDGEMAN 2/3, *Notes on the Campaign of the BEF May 1940*, p. 8; LHCMA, BRIDGEMAN 1/1, *Lord Gort's Despatches*, pp. 48–9; L. Ellis, *The War in France and Flanders*, p. 64

168. IWM, *FSR Vol. III (December 1935): Operations – H. Formations*, p. 23

169. TNA, WO 106/1775, *Bartholomew Committee Report*, pp. 2, 12–13

170. B. Bond, *Britain, France and Belgium*, pp. 63, 75

171. D. French, *Raising Churchill's Army*, p. 175

172. L. Ellis, *The War in France and Flanders*, pp. 64–5, 123–4

173. B. Bond (ed.), *Chief of Staff*, pp. 332–3; TNA, WO 106/1775, *Bartholomew Committee Report – Evidence of 12/06/40*, p. 4

174. TNA, WO 167/1403, *Perowne's Rifles (Vickforce) War Diary May-June 1940*, p. 3
175. B. Bond (ed.), *Chief of Staff*, p. 337; TNA, WO 106/1775, *Bartholomew Committee Report – Evidence of 12/06/40*, p. 5
176. LHCMA, BRIDGEMAN 1/1, *Lord Gort's Despatches*, p. 54; LHCMA, LINDSELL 1/2, *War Diary of Quartermaster General W. Lindsell*, pp. 13, 17
177. IWM, *FSR Vol. III (December 1935): Operations – H. Formations*, p. 23; TNA, WO 167/1403, *Perowne's Rifles War Diary*, pp. 4–5

Bibliography

London, British Library

Battalion Standing Orders for War for Rifle Battalions, (Aldershot, 1939, Gale & Polden)

Field Service Manual: British Infantry Battalion in India 1926

Historical Record – Egypt Mobile Divisional Signals, 1 January 1939 – 31 March 1939

India's Army, (London, 1940, Sampson Low, Marston & Co Ltd)

Infantry Section Leading 1934

Infantry Section Leading 1938

Military Report and Gazetteer on the Peshawar District 1939, (Calcutta, 1940, Indian Army General Staff Branch)

Nowshera Brigade: Standing Orders for War 1938

Official History of Operations on the N.W. Frontier of India 1936–1937, (New Delhi, 1943, Manager of Publications)

Our Indian Empire: A Short Review and Some Hints for the Soldiers Proceeding to India, (Delhi, 1937, A. Stuart)

Right or Wrong? Elements of Training and Leadership Illustrated 1937, (London, 1937, HMSO)

Training Regulations 1934 (with Amendments) – with special reference to Manoeuvres

London, Imperial War Museum, Department of Documents

Atkins, H. 92/28/1; Barker, Brigadier C.N. 96/12/1; Beard, S.G.T. 06/99/1; Birch, Lieutenant Colonel J. MISC 105 Item 1667; Blaxland, Major W.G. 83/46/1; Boxshall, Brigadier R.A. 84/41/1; Brush, Lieutenant Colonel E.J.A.H. 85/8/1; Cannon, Signaller L.W. 79/27/1; Chavasse, Colonel K.G.F. 98/23/1; Cowan, Major R.T.B. 07/25/1; Durrant, Lieutenant Colonel T. 05/44/1; Faviell, Brigadier J.V. 82/24/1; Finch, Major J.H. 90/6/1; Gaskin, A.R. 87/44/1; Hawes, Major General L.A. 87/4/1; Haydon, Major General J.C. 93/28/1; Martin, Major General P.L. 07/7/1; Ogden, Captain J.N. 67/267/1; Osborne, Lieutenant General E.A. 785 Con Shelf; Page, Lieutenant Colonel R.K. 67/373/1; Reid, Lieutenant Colonel M. 83/37/1 & Con Shelf; Richards, Major General G.W. 02/21/1; Richards, Major General W.W. 84/32/2(P); Southall, F. 84/36/1; Thornhill, Lieutenant Colonel E.B. 99/36/1; Tong, Lieutenant Colonel R.P. 83/32/1; Towle, A. 84/33/1; Vinden, Brigadier F.H. 96/36/1; Walch, Brigadier A.G. 01/11/2; Whitehead, Brigadier J. 97/10/1; Wilkinson, Brigadier J.S. 88/56/1

Imperial War Museum, Department of Printed Books

Field Service Regulations, Volume III, 1935: Operations – Higher Formations (December 1935, Amended 1937)

256

London, Liddell Hart Centre for Military Archives

Alanbrooke Papers; Bridgeman Papers; Kirke Papers; Lindsell Papers

London, The National Archive

Air Ministry Papers: Air 2/1924; War Office Papers: WO 32, WO 33, WO 71, WO 82, WO 86, WO 90, WO 93, WO 106, WO 163, WO 166, WO 167, WO 191, WO 197, WO 213, WO 216, WO 231, WO 277, WO 282, WO 287

The National Archive, Reference Section

Army List (TNA 355.3.WOM)
Field Service Pocket Book (Pamphlets 1–13) 1939–1940 (TNA 355.6.FIE)
Field Service Regulations, Volume II, 1935: Operations – General (TNA 355.6.REG)

London, The National Army Museum

Anderson Papers; Arlington Papers; Barrell Papers; Brown Papers; Fane de Salis Papers; Notley papers; Porritt Papers; Prosser Papers; Willoghby Papers;
Reports by Various Officers & NCOs on Buffs Regiment (Various Battalions) 1939–1945 – No. 2001-02-444

Online Published Documents

[Cmd. 5686], *The General Annual Report On The British Army for the Year ending 30th September 1937*, Parliamentary Papers, March, 1938
[Cmd. 5950], *The General Annual Report On The British Army for the Year ending 31st December 1938*, Parliamentary Papers, February, 1939
HANSARD, Parliamentary Papers, 1939–1940
'Exchange Rates in 1937' Times [London, England] 8 February 1938: 33. *The Times Digital Archive*. Web 16 July 2012
'Exchange Rates in 1939' Times [London, England], 3 January 1940: 12. *The Times Digital Archive*. Web 16 July 2012
'Men Sentenced For Desertion' Times [London, England] 29 November 1945: 4. *The Times Digital Archive*. Web 16 July 2012
OUR OWN CORRESPONDENT 'New Prospect for French Finance' Times [London, England] 3 December 1938: 19. *The Times Digital Archive*. Web 16 July 2012
OUR OWN CORRESPONDENT 'French Exchange Control' Times [London, England] 18 September 1939: 13. *The Times Digital Archive*. Web 16 July 2012

Published Primary Sources

Anon, *Infantry Officer*, (London, 1943, B.T. Batsford)
Arthur, Max, *Forgotten Voices of The Second World War*, (Haydock, 2004, The Books People Ltd)

Bance, Alan (Translated by), *Blitzkrieg in Their Own Words*, (Barnsley, 2005, Pen & Sword Ltd)

Bond, Brian (ed.), *Chief of Staff: The Diaries of Lieutenant General Sir Henry Pownall, Volume 1, 1933–1940*, (London, 1972, Leo Cooper Ltd)

Campbell, Richard & Liddle, Peter, *For Five Shillings A Day: Personal Histories of World War II*, (London, 2000, Harper Collins Publishers)

Carton de Wiart, Lieutenant General Sir Adrian, *Happy Odyssey*, (London, 1950, Jonathan Cape Ltd)

Churchill, Winston, *Never Give In!: The Best of Winston Churchill's Speeches*, (London, 2003, Pimlico)

Cunningham, A., *A Sailor's Odyssey: The Autobiography of Admiral of the Fleet Viscount Cunningham of Hyndhope*, (London, 1952, Hutchinson & Co Ltd)

Danchev, Alex & Todman, Dan (eds), *War Diaries 1939–1945: Field Marshal Lord Alanbrooke*, (London, 2002, Phoenix Press)

De Gaulle, Charles, *War Memoirs Volume 1: The Call To Honour 1940–1942*, (London, 1955, Collins)

Gribble, P., *The Diary of a Staff Officer*, (London, 1941, Methuen & Co Ltd)

Guderian, Heinz, *Panzer Leader*, (London, 2000, Penguin Books Ltd)

Hadley, Peter, *Third Class To Dunkirk: A Worm's Eye View of the BEF 1940*, (London, 1944, Hollis & Carter Ltd)

Inter-Parliamentary Union, *What Would Be The Character Of A New War?*, (London, 1933, Victor Gollancz Ltd)

Macleod, Colonel R. & Kelly, Dennis (eds), *The Ironside Diaries 1937–1940*, (London, 1963, Constable & Company Ltd)

Marley, David (ed.), *The Daily Telegraph: Story of the War 1939–1941*, (London, 1942, Hodder & Stoughton Ltd)

Masefield, John, *The Twenty Five Days*, (Barnsley, 2004, Pen & Sword Ltd)

Montgomery, Field Marshal Bernard, *The Memoirs of Field Marshal The Viscount Montgomery of Alamein*, (London, 1968, Collins)

Niven, David, The Moon's A Balloon, (London, 1974, Coronet Books)

Poppell, Martin, *Heaven & Hell: The War Diary of a German Paratrooper*, (Staplehurst, 2000, Spellmount)

Reed, Douglas, *All Our To-Morrows*, (London, 1942, Jonathan Cape Ltd)

Saunders, W., *Dunkirk Diary of a Very Young Soldier*, (Studley, 2010, Brewin Books)

Slessor, John, *Air Power and Armies*, (London, 1936, Oxford University Press)

Slessor, John, *The Central Blue*, (London, 1956, Cassell & Co Ltd)

Smyth, Sir John, *Before The Dawn*, (London, 1957, Cassell & Co Ltd)

Spears, Sir Edward, *Assignment to Catastrophe: Volume 1: Prelude to Dunkirk July 1939 – May 1940*, (London, 1954, William Heinemann Ltd)

Spears, Sir Edward, *Assignment to Catastrophe: Volume 2: The Fall of France June 1940*, (London, 1954, William Heinemann Ltd)

The Belgian Ministry of Foreign Affairs, *Belgium: The Official Account of What Happened 1939–1940*, (London, 1941, Evans Brothers Ltd)

Thomas, Tommy, *Signal Success*, (Lewes, 1995, The Book Guild Ltd)

Secondary Sources: Books

Addison, P. & Calder, A. (eds), *Time to Kill: The Soldier's Experience of War in the West*, (London, 1997, Pimlico)

Alexander, Martin, *The Republic in Danger: General Maurice Gamelin and the Politics of French Defence*, (Cambridge, 2002, Cambridge University Press)

Barclay, Brigadier C.N, *The History of the Duke of Wellington's Regiment 1919–1952*, (London, 1953, William Clowes & Sons Ltd)

Bartov, Omer, *Hitler's Army: Soldiers, Nazis and War in the Third Reich*, (Oxford, 1991, Oxford University Press)

Baynes, John, *Far From A Donkey: The Life of General Sir Ivor Maxse*, (London, 1995, Brassey's Ltd)

Beckett, I.F.W., *The Amateur Military Tradition 1558–1945*, (Manchester, 1991, Manchester University Press)

Bidwell, Shelford & Graham, Dominick, *Firepower: The British Army Weapons & Theories of War 1904–1945*, (Barnsley, 2004, Pen & Sword Books Ltd)

Bielecki, Christine, *British Military Morale during the Italian Campaign 1943–1945*, (University of London, 2006, Unpublished PhD)

Birdwood, Lieutenant Colonel Lord, *The Worcestershire Regiment 1922–1950*, (Aldershot, 1952, Gale & Polden Ltd)

Blacker, General Sir Cecil & Woods, Major General H.G., *Change and Challenge: The Story of the 5th Royal Inniskilling Dragoon Guards 1928–1978*, (London, 1978, William Clowes & Sons Ltd)

Blaxland, Gregory, *The Buffs*, (London, 1972, Leo Cooper Ltd)

Blight, Brigadier Gordon, *The History of The Royal Berkshire Regiment (Princess Charlotte of Wales's) 1920–1947*, (London, 1953, Staples Press Ltd)

Bond, Brian, *Britain, France and Belgium 1939–1940*, (London, 1990, Brassey's Ltd)

Bond, Brian, *British Military Policy between the Two World Wars*, (Oxford, 1980, Oxford University Press)

Bond, Brian, *The Victorian Army and the Staff College 1854–1914*, (London, 1972, Eyre & Methuen Ltd)

Bond, Brian, *War and Society in Europe 1870–1970*, (London, 2005, Sutton Publishing Ltd)

Bowman, Timothy, *Irish Regiments in the Great War: Discipline and Morale*, (Manchester, 2003, Manchester University Press)

Boyes, Robert, *In Glass Houses: A history of the Military Provost Staff Corps*, (Colchester, 1988, Military Provost Staff Corps Association)

Calder, Angus, *The People's War*, (London, 1971, Granada Publishing Ltd)

Chaplin, Lieutenant Colonel H.D., *The Queen's Own Royal West Kent Regiment 1920–1950*, (London, 1954, Michael Joseph Ltd)

Collier, Richard, *The Sands of Dunkirk*, (London, 1961, Collins)

Colville, J.R., *Man of Valour: The Life of Field Marshal The Viscount Gort*, (London, 1972, Collins)

Connell, John, *Wavell: Scholar and Soldier – To June 1941*, (London, 1964, Collins)

Connelly, Mark, *We Can Take It: Britain and the Memory of the Second World War*, (Harlow, 2004, Pearson Education Ltd)

Connelly, Mark and Welch, David (eds), *War and the Media: Reportage and Propaganda, 1900–2003*, (London, 2005, I.B. Tauris and Co Ltd)

Corns, Cathryn and Hughes-Wilson, John, *Blindfold and Alone: British Military Executions in the Great War*, (London, 2001, Cassell & Co)

Crang, Jeremy, *The British Army and the People's War 1939–1945*, (Manchester, 2000, Manchester University Press)

David, Saul, *Churchill's Sacrifice of the Highland Division*, (London, 2004, Brassey's Ltd)

Demeter, Karl, *The German Officer-Corps in Society and State 1650–1945*, (London, 1965, Weidenfeld & Nicholson)

Ellis, John, *The Sharp End: The Fighting Man in World War II*, (London, 1993, Pimlico)

Ellis, Major L.F., *The War in France and Flanders 1939–1940*, (London, 1953, HMSO)

Farndale, General Sir Martin, *History of the Royal Regiment of Artillery: The Years of Defeat 1939–1941*, (London, 1996, Brassey's Ltd)

Fennell, Jonathan, *Combat and Morale in the North African Campaign: The Eighth Army and the Path to El Alamein*, (Cambridge, 2011, Cambridge University Press)

Forty, George, *The British Army Handbook 1939–1945*, (Strood, 1998, Sutton Publishing Ltd)

French, David, *Military Identities: The Regimental System, the British Army & the British People c.1870–2000*, (Oxford, 2008, Oxford University Press)

French, David, *Raising Churchill's Army: The British Army and the War against Germany 1939–1945*, (Oxford, 2001, Oxford University Press)

French, David & Holden Reid, Brian (eds), *The British General Staff: Reform and Innovation c.1890–1939*, (London, 2002, Frank Cass Publishers)

Gardner, Nikolas, *Trial by Fire: Command and the British Expeditionary Force in 1914*, (Westport (USA), 2003, Praeger Publishers)

Gat, Azar, *A History of Military Thought: From the Enlightenment to the Cold War*, (Oxford, 2001, Oxford University Press)

Godfrey, Simon, *British Army Communications in the Second World War: Lifting the Fog of Battle*, (London, 2013, Bloomsbury Academic)

Gray, Brigadier, T., *The Imperial Defence College and the Royal College of Defence Studies 1927–1977*, (Edinburgh, 1977, HMSO)

Harman, Nicholas, *Dunkirk: The Necessary Myth*, (London, 1980, Hodder & Stoughton)

Harrison-Place, Timothy, *Military Training in the British Army, 1940–1944: From Dunkirk to D-Day*, (London, 2000, Frank Cass Publishers)

Henning, Peter, *Doomed Battalion: Mateship and Leadership in War and Captivity – The Australian 2/40 Battalion 1940–1945*, (Australia, 1995, Allen & Unwin Pty Ltd)

Hinrich Jr, Ernest (ed.), *Listening In – Intercepting German Trench Communication in World War I*, (Shippenburg (USA), 1996, White Mane Books)

Holden Reid, Brian, *War Studies at the Staff College 1890–1930*, (London, 1992, HMSO)

Jackson, Julian, *The Fall of France: The Nazi Invasion of 1940*, (Oxford, 2003, Oxford University Press)

Jackson, Robert, *Dunkirk*, (London, 2002, Cassell)

James, Brigadier E.A., *The History of the 48th (South Midland) Divisional Signals Territorial Army, Volume II, 1933 to 1939*, (Birmingham, 1950, Unknown Publisher)

Jeffery, Keith, *Field Marshal Sir Henry Wilson: A Political Soldier*, (Oxford, 2008, Oxford University Press)

Jefferys, Alan & Rose, Patrick (eds), *The Indian Army 1939–1947: Experience and Development*, (Farnham, 2012, Ashgate Publishing Ltd)

Keegan, John (ed.), *Churchill's Generals*, (London, 2001, Abacus)

Kemp, P.K., *The Middlesex Regiment (Duke of Cambridge's Own) 1919–1952*, (Aldershot, 1956, Gale & Polden Ltd)

Knight, Colonel C.R.B., *Historical Records of the Buffs*, (London, 1951, The Medici Society)

Longden, Sean, *Dunkirk: The Men They Left Behind*, (London, 2008, Constable & Robinson)

Mackenzie, S.P., *Politics and Military Morale: Current-Affairs and Citizenship Education in the British Army 1914–1950*, (Oxford, 1992, Oxford University Press)

Marshall, S.L.A, *Men against Fire: The Problem of Battle Command*, (Oklahoma (USA), 2000, University of Oklahoma Press)

Moore, William, *Panzer Bait: With the 3rd Royal Tank Regiment 1940–1944*, (London, 1991, Leo Cooper Ltd)

Moreman, T.R., *The Jungle, The Japanese and the British Commonwealth Armies at War 1941–1945: Fighting Methods, Doctrine and Training for Jungle Warfare*, (London, 2005, Frank Cass Publishers)

Nalder, Major General R., *The Royal Corps of Signals: A History of its Antecedents and Developments c.1800–1955*, (London, 1958, Royal Signal Institution)

Orr, David & Truesdale, David, *The Rifles Are There: 1st & 2nd Battalions The Royal Ulster Rifles in the Second World War*, (Barnsley, 2005, Pen & Sword Books Ltd)

Peden, G.C., *British Rearmament and the Treasury 1932–1939*, (Edinburgh, 1979, Scottish Academic Press Ltd)

Rissik, David, *The D.L.I. At War: The History of the Durham Light Infantry 1939–1945*, (London, 1953, Charles Birchall & Sons Ltd)

Rubin, Gerry, *Murder, Mutiny and the Military: British Court Martial Cases, 1940–1966*, (London, 2005, Francis Boutle Publishers)

Schofield, Victoria, *Wavell – Soldier & Statesman*, (London, 2006, John Murray Publishers)

Sebag-Montefiore, Hugh, *Dunkirk: Fight to the Last Man*, (London, 2006, Viking)

Sheffield, Gary, *The Redcaps: A History of the Royal Military Police and its Antecedents from the Middle Ages to the Gulf War*, (London, 1994, Brassey's)

Simpson, Andy, *Directing Operations: British Corps Command On The Western Front 1914–18*, (Strood, 2006, Spellmount)

Sixsmith, Major General E.K.G., *British Generalship in the Twentieth Century*, (London, 1970, Arms and Armour Press)

Smart, Nick, *British Strategy and Politics during the Phony War: Before The Balloon Went Up*, (Westport (USA), 2003, Praeger Publishers)

Steppler, Glenn, *BRITONS, To Arms!: The Story of the British Volunteer Soldier and the Volunteer Tradition in Leicestershire and Rutland*, (Strood, 1997, Sutton Publishing Ltd)

Taylor, Eric, *Front-Line Nurse: British Nurses in World War II*, (London, 1997, Robert Hale Ltd)

Thompson, Julian, *Dunkirk: Retreat to Victory*, (London, 2009, Pan Macmillan Ltd)

Vansina, Jan, *Oral Tradition: A Study in Historical Methodology*, (London, 1965, Routledge and Kegan Paul Ltd)

Verney, Major General G.L., *The Desert Rats: The 7th Armoured Division in World War II*, (London, 1990, Greenhill Books)

Ward, John, *Hitler's Stuka Squadrons: The Ju 87 1936–1945*, (Strood, 2004, Spellmount)

Warner, Philip, *The Battle of France 1940*, (London, 2002, Cassell & Co)

Wickham-Legg, L.G. & Williams, E.T. (eds), *The Dictionary of National Biography 1941–1950*, (Oxford, 1959, Oxford University Press)

Williams, E.T. & Palmer, H.M. (eds), *The Dictionary of National Biography 1951–1960*, (Oxford, 1971, Oxford University Press)

Young, Lieutenant Colonel F.W., *The Story of the Staff College 1858–1958*, (Camberley, 1958, Gale & Polden Ltd)

Secondary Sources: Journals

Cherry, Brigadier R.G., (1939), 'Territorial Army Staffs and Training', *RUSI Journal*, Vol. 84, pp. 548–52

Clarke, Ken, (Spring 2007), 'Every Day A Bonus', (Account of his Service with the 1st Queen's Own Royal West Kent Regiment), *The Journal: The Regimental Association of The Queen's Own Buffs (PWRR)*, Number 14, pp. 38–50

Clarke, Ken, (Autumn 2007), 'Every Day A Bonus', (Account of his Service with the 1st Queen's Own Royal West Kent Regiment), *The Journal: The Regimental Association of The Queen's Own Buffs (PWRR)*, Number 15, pp. 19–27

Connelly, Mark & Miller, Walter, (November 2004), 'The BEF and the Issue of Surrender on the Western Front in 1940', *War in History*, Vol. 11, No. 4, pp. 424–41

French, David, (November 1996), 'Colonel Blimp and the British Army: British Divisional Commanders in the War against Germany 1939–1945', *The English Historical Review*, Vol. 111, No. 444, pp. 1182–1201

French, David, (October 1998), 'Discipline and the Death Penalty in the British Army in the War against Germany during the Second World War', *Journal of Contemporary History*, Vol. 33, No. 4, pp. 531–45

Hall, Brian, (2012), 'The British Army and Wireless Communication 1896–1918', *War in History*, Vol. 19, No. 3, pp. 290–321

Jacobs, W., (December 1982), 'Air Support for the British Army 1939–1943', *Military Affairs*, Vol. 46, No. 4, pp. 174–82

Sixsmith, Major General E.K.G., (1982), 'The British Army in May 1940 – A Comparison with the BEF 1914', *RUSI Journal*, Vol. 127, pp. 8–10

Index